P9-CQK-542

The Most Important Phrases in Any Language

English	Italian	Pronunciation
Greetings.	Salve.	sal-veh
Yes.	Sì.	see
No.	No.	no
Please.	Per favore.	per fah-**voh**-reh
	Per piacere.	per pee-ah-**cheh**-reh
Thank you.	Grazie.	**grah**-tsee-yeh
Excuse me.	Mi scusi.	mee skoo-zee
You're welcome.	Prego.	pray-goh
I'm sorry.	Mi dispiace.	me dees-pee-**ah**-cheh
Help!	Aiuto!	ah-**yoo**-toh
Where is …?	Dov'è …?	doh-veh
How much?	Quanto?	kwahn-toh
Pardon me.	Permesso.	per-**mes**-soh

Greetings and Helpful Expressions

English	Italian	Pronunciation
Good morning.	Buon giorno.	bwon jor-noh
Good evening.	Buona sera.	bwoh-nah seh-rah
Good night.	Buona notte.	bwoh-nah noh-teh
Mr.	Signore	see-**nyoh**-reh
Mrs./Ms.	Signora	see-**nyoh**-rah
Miss	Signorina	see-nyoh-**ree**-nah
Good-bye.	Ciao.	chow
See you later.	Arrivederci.	ah-ree-veh-**der**-chee
Keep in touch.	Ci vediamo.	chee veh-dee-**ah**-moh
What is your name?	Come si chiama?	koh-meh see kee-**yah**-mah
My name is …	Mi chiamo …	mee kee-**yah**-moh
How are you?	Come sta?	koh-meh stah
I am well, and you?	Sto bene, e Lei?	stoh beh-neh eh leh
When?	Quando?	kwahn-doh
How?	Come?	koh-meh
Where?	Dove?	doh-veh
I need …	Ho bisogno di …	oh bee-**zoh**-nyoh dee

ALPHA

Communications

English	Italian	Pronunciation
I understand.	Capisco.	kah-**pee**-skoh
I don't understand.	Non capisco.	non kah-**pee**-skoh
I don't speak Italian.	Non parlo italiano.	non par-loh ee-tah-lee-**ah**-noh
I am studying Italian.	Studio italiano.	stoo-dee-oh ee-tah-lee-**ah**-noh
Do you speak English?	Parla inglese?	par-lah een-**gleh**-zeh
Do you understand?	Capisce?	kah-pee-sheh
What does it mean?	Che cosa significa?	keh koh-zah see-**nyee**-fee-kah
What?	Che?	keh
How?	Come?	koh-meh
Please repeat that.	Lo ripeta per favore.	loh ree-**peh**-tah per fah-**voh**-reh
Please speak slowly.	Parli lentamente per piacere.	par-lee len-tah-**men**-teh per pee-ah-**cheh**-reh

The Weather and Time

English	Italian	Pronunciation
What's the weather like?	Che tempo fa?	keh tem-poh fah
It's beautiful out.	Fa bello.	fah bel-loh
It's ugly out.	Fa brutto.	fah broo-toh
What time is it?	Che ore sono?	keh oh-reh soh-noh
It is …	Sono le …	soh-noh leh

Your Health

English	Italian	Pronunciation
I feel bad.	Mi sento male.	mee sen-toh mah-leh
I have a stomachache.	Ho mal di stomaco.	oh mahl dee **stoh**-mah-koh
I have a headache.	Ho mal di testa.	oh mahl dee teh-stah
Is there a doctor?	C'è un dottore?	cheh oon doh-**toh**-reh

Places to Go and How to Get There

English	Italian	Pronunciation
We are going …	Andiamo …	ahn-dee-**ah**-moh
… to center/downtown.	… in centro.	een chen-troh
… to the airport.	… all'aeroporto.	ah-lay-eh-roh-**por**-toh
… to the bank.	… in banca.	een bahn-kah
… to the police.	… alla polizia.	ah-lah poh-lee-**tsee**-yah
… to the hospital.	… in ospedale.	een oh-speh-**dah**-leh
… to the hotel.	… in albergo.	een ahl-ber-goh

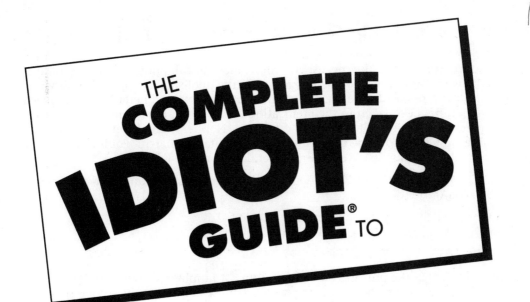

THE COMPLETE IDIOT'S GUIDE® TO

Learning Italian

Second Edition

by Gabrielle Euvino

ALPHA

A member of Penguin Group (USA) Inc.

International Standard Book Number: 0-02-864147-7
Library of Congress Catalog Card Number: 2001089688

05   04   03   9   8   7   6

Interpretation of the printing code: The rightmost number of the first series of numbers is the year of the book's printing; the rightmost number of the second series of numbers is the number of the book's printing. For example, a printing code of 01-1 shows that the first printing occurred in 2001.

Printed in the United States of America

Publisher
Marie Butler-Knight

Product Manager
Phil Kitchel

Managing Editor
Jennifer Chisholm

Acquisitions Editor
Brandon Hopkins

Development Editor
Amy E. Zavatto

Production Editor
Katherin Bidwell

Copy Editor
Krista Hansing

Illustrator
Jody Schaeffer

Cover Designers
Mike Freeland
Kevin Spear

Book Designers
Scott Cook and Amy Adams of DesignLab

Indexer
Angie Bess

Layout/Proofreading
Angela Calvert
Svetlana Dominguez
Natashia Rardin

Contents at a Glance

Part 1   The Basics   **1**

  1 Why You Should Study Italian   3
Imagine the reality of speaking Italian and see all the reasons.

  2 Immerse Yourself   11
Learn about dialect, the history of Italian, and using your dictionary. In addition, there's a quick grammar refresher to get your language studies started on the right foot.

  3 Sound Like an Italian   25
Learn the basic rules of Italian pronunciation.

  4 You Know More Than You Think   39
Tie English and Italian together using cognates.

  5 Expressively Yours   53
In this chapter you'll learn the fundamentals: how to say hello and good-bye, your days of the week, and idiomatic expressions.

  6 Almost Everything You Wanted to Know About Sex   69
In Italian all nouns are assigned a gender—learn what to do about it.

  7 What's the Subject?   85
Study the different ways of expressing "you" in Italian. Learn how to determine the subject in a sentence.

Part 2   You're Off and Running   **91**

  8 An Action-Packed Adventure   93
Learn about the different verb families and regular rules of conjugation.

  9 Being There   111
See all the different ways of using "to be" with the verbs essere *and* stare, *and learn how to construct several idiomatic expressions using the verb* avere *(to have).*

 10 Tell Me About Your Childhood   129
Learn how to express possession using adjectives and the preposition di, *as well as how to describe things with adverbs.*

 11 Finally, You're at the Airport   149
Now that you've landed, you'll be given helpful vocabulary to enable you to get around. Learn about prepositions and the imperative verb tense.

 12 Moving Around   165
Drive away with the terms you need to make your journey safe. Study your numbers to log those kilometers and talk about time. Also find out how to use the verb fare *(to do/to make).*

 13 Hallelujah, You've Made It to l'Hotel   187
Get comfortable inside your room using the practical vocabulary lists. Express your desires with volere *(to want), your potential with* potere *(to be able to), and what you've got to do with* dovere *(to have to).*

14 Rain or Shine 205
Talk about the weather, make a date, and discuss your horoscope.

Part 3 Fun and Games **221**

15 I Can't Believe My Eyes! 223
See the sights and study the verbs you need to get around and make suggestions, as well as how to use the present progressive tense.

16 Shop 'Til You Drop 241
Learn everything you wanted to know about objects and object pronouns while perusing Italy's wonderful shops.

17 Bread, Wine, and Chocolate 261
Visit the market and sample the many culinary delights while improving your linguistic abilities. Express your pleasure with the verb piacere.

18 Shall We Dine? 281
Chew on the terms and learn how to read an Italian menu and order special meals. See how reflexive verbs work.

19 Having Fun Italian Style 303
You can sing, dance, and paint the town red with these terms. Learn how to talk about what you had been doing using the passato prossimo.

Part 4 Getting Down to Business **323**

20 You're Not Having *Un Buon Giorno* 325
Cope with life's little nuisances, get your hair done, and learn how to make comparisons.

21 Is There a Doctor in the House? 341
Tell the doctor where it hurts with these terms. Learn how to talk about what used to be with the imperfect tense.

22 Can You Read Me? 355
Make a telephone call, send a package, and write a letter. See how to use the future tense to talk about what will be.

23 Home Sweet Home 369
In the market to own a home? Want to rent a villa? Talk about the conditional and learn how to express what you would like.

24 Money Matters 381
Learn the international language of money with these helpful banking terms. Also learn the subjunctive and past absolute.

Appendixes

A Answer Key 395

B Glossary 411

C Map of Italy 441

D An Idiot's Guide to Additional Resources 443

Index 445

Contents

Part 1: The Basics   **1**

1   Why You Should Study Italian   **3**

You Love Life 4
Get Real 5
Getting Wet 6
   Immerse Yourself—Literally! 6
   Become a Class Act 6
   Hang Out with Sophia 7
   Get the Right Tools 7
   Tune In! 7
   Read the Fine Print 7
   Find Birds of a Feather 7
   Play It Again, Salvatore 8
There's Nothing to Stop You 8

2   Immerse Yourself   **11**

Latin Lovers 12
   How Do You Say ...? Dialect 13
   Tuscan Italian 14
So What's Your Story? 15
How Much Italian Is Enough? 16
Your Dictionary Is Your Best Friend 16
Speak Easy 17
   Person, Place, or Pasta 17
   Descriptively Speaking 18
   Who's He? 18
   It's All Relative 18
   Where the Action Is 18
It All Depends on How You Look at It 19
   Practice Makes Perfetto 19
What's the Object; Who's the Subject? 21
Drawing from Esperienza 21
Read It, Write It, Say It 22

3   Sound Like an Italian   **25**

Italian Pronunciation 25
Your ABCs 26
   Getting the Accent 26
Don't Get Stressed Out 27
Rolling Your *R*'s 28
The Long and the Short of It: Vowels 28
The Hard and Soft of It: Consonants 29
   Practice Those Vowels 31
Give Me the Combo 31
   C *Is for* Casa 32
   G *Is for* Gamba 32
   S *Is for* Scandolo 33
Dipthongs 34
Double Consonants 35

A Is for *Ancona* 36
Get Help! 37
Patience and Practice Pay Off 38

4 You Know More Than You Think   **39**

Cognates: A Bridge Between Languages 39
  A Little Fantasia 40
If It Looks Like a Duck ... .41
  Where in the World: Places 42
  It's About Time 43
  How Intelligente *You Are!* 43
  Adjectives: How Grande! 44
Nouns 45
  Masculine Nouns 45
  Feminine Nouns 45
  English Words Used in Italian 46
Trojan Horses—False Friends 47
  How Much Do You Understand Already? 47
  Your Turn 47
Verb Cognates 48
  A Piece of Cake 49
Put It All Together 51
  Translation Please 51
  What's Your Take? 51
  Are You Well Read? 52

5 Expressively Yours   **53**

How Do You Do? 53
  You Say Hello and I Say Good-Bye 53
  Stranger in a Strange Land 54
  The Most Important Phrases in Any Language 55
  Informal Greetings and Salutations 56
Communications 57
I Giorni: Days 58
I Mesi: Months 58
Expressing Your Honest Opinion 60
Idiomatically Speaking 61
  Happy as a Lark 61
  What Is Slang? 62
Idiomatic Expressions in Italian 62
It's All in the Details 63
  Practice Makes Perfetto 64
  A Good Hour 64
  Going Mad 65
What's Your Opinion? 66
Seventh Heaven 67

6 Almost Everything You Wanted to Know About Sex   **69**

Determining Gender: He Versus She 69
  Masculine or Feminine 69
  Everyone Must Agree 70
An Article Is Not What You Read in a Newspaper 70
  The Definite Article (The) 70
  An Indefinite Article (A, An) 71

Singular Nouns 72
   Hermaphrodites 73
   Nouns Ending in –e 74
Rules Are Made to Be Broken 75
   Disconcerting Genders 75
   Misbehaving Males 76
   Rebellious Females 77
   Sex Changers 77
   The Apple Doesn't Fall Far 78
   Practice Makes Perfetto 78
More Is Better: Making Plurals 78
   Do We Agree? Plural Noun Markers 79
   The Rules 80
   Plural Spelling 81
   La Pratica 81
   What Does It Mean? 82
   Irregular Plural Nouns 82
   Always Plural 83
   Practice Those Plurals 83
   What Have You Learned About Gender? 83

7 What's the Subject?   **85**

Your Loyal Subject 85
Subject Pronouns 86
   When to Use Subject Pronouns 87
   Name That Subject 87
   Subject to Interpretation 88
You and You and You 88
   Hey You! 89

Part 2: You're Off and Running   **91**

8 An Action-Packed Adventure   **93**

All in the Family 94
   The Anatomy of a Verb 94
   The Present-Tense Conjugations 95
The –are Family 96
   C Is for Celebrare 96
   Regular –are Verbs 97
   Exceptions 100
   Practice Makes Perfetto 101
The –ere Verbs 102
   S Is for Scrivere 102
   Regular –ere Verbs 103
Practice Makes *Perfetto* II 105
The –ire Family 106
   D Is for Dormire 106
The –ire Verbs (Group I) 106
More –ire Verbs (Group II) 107
   C Is for Capire 107
   The –ire Verbs (Group II) 107
Asking Questions 109
   The Tags Vero? No? *and Giusto?* 109

And the Risposta *Is ...* *109*
A Whole Lot of Niente *110*

9   Being There   **111**

The Birds and the Be's 112
The Verb *Essere* 112
The Verb *Stare* 113
Essere vs. *Stare:* What's the Difference? 114
  When to Use Essere *114*
  Come Sei Intelligente! *114*
  When to Use Stare *115*
  Chitchat *115*
C'è and *Ci sono* (There Is, There Are) 116
  Asking Questions *116*
  Say It Isn't So *116*
  Fill in the Blanks *116*
It's Time to Have Some Fun: *Avere* 117
  When to Use Avere *118*
  An Idiot's Guide to Idioms with Avere *118*
  Express Yourself *119*
Professionally Speaking 120
In My Professional Opinion 120
So, What's Your Story? 122
We, the People 123
  Nationalities *124*
  Do You Believe? *125*
  Back to Your Roots *126*
Ecco! 126
  Eureka! *127*

10   Tell Me About Your Childhood   **129**

One of the *Famiglia* 129
Are You Possessed? 131
Using *Di* to Show Possession 131
  Forming Contractions with Di *131*
Possessive Adjectives 132
A Sense of Belonging 134
It's Good to Know 134
  Sapere: *To Know Something* *134*
  Conoscere: *To Know Someone/To Be Acquainted* *135*
Making Introductions 135
  This Is My *135*
  This Is My Brother *136*
Who Is Who 136
Tall, Dark, and Handsome 136
  Modifying Adjectives *136*
  Modifying Those Adjective Endings *137*
  Character Analysis *138*
  A Real Wise Guy *138*
  Take the Good with the Bad *140*
  I Colori *140*
  One Yellow Banana, Please *141*
  It's a Colorful World *142*
  Everyone's a Poet *142*

Bello and *Quello* 143
  Make the Connection *143*
Buono 144
How Do You Do: Adverbs 144
  Forming Adverbs from Adjectives *144*
  Take Your Place *145*
  A Lot of Adverbs *146*
  Adverbs of Time *146*
  Adverbs of Place *147*
  The More Things Change *147*

11 Finally, You're at the Airport   149

On the Plane 149
  In the Comfort Zone *150*
On the Inside 151
Going Crazy: The Verb *Andare* 152
  Going, Going, Gone *154*
  All Verbed Up and Everywhere to Go *154*
Prepositions: Sticky Stuff 154
  A Few Points on Prepositions *156*
Contractions 157
  Switcharoo *159*
The Imperative: Giving Directions 159
  The Regular Imperative Endings *159*
  The Imperative Using Tu *and* Lei *160*
  Tell Me What to Do *161*
Dazed and Confused 161
Passively Yours: *Si* 162
La Dogana (Customs) 162

12 Moving Around   165

Hoofing and Spinning 165
Which One? 166
On the Road 167
  Behind the Wheel *168*
  Automobile Parts *169*
  The Road Less Traveled *171*
  Tell Me Your Worries *172*
Baby, I Got Your Number 172
  Cardinal Numbers *172*
  Number Crunching *174*
  Time Is of the Essence *175*
  Time Will Tell *177*
It's Not What You Do, but with Whom You Do It 177
Questions, Questions 178
Ask Away 178
  All Aboard *179*
  Verbiage *181*
  Practice Those Conjugations *182*
Getting On with *Salire* 182
Things to Do: The Verb *Fare* (to Do; to Make) 182
  Idiomatic Expressions Using Fare *183*
  What Are You Doing? *184*
  What to Do, What to Do *184*

13 Hallelujah, You've Made It to *l'Hotel*   187

A Cave Will Do 187
A Room with a View 188
Simply Said 189
Get Cozy 189
Room Service, Please 191
Is There Room at the Inn? 191
Let's Make a Deal 192
Practice Makes Perfetto 192
Your Firma Here, Please 192
La Mancia *(Tipping)* 193
Who's on First? 194
The Ordinal Numbers 194
Feeling Moody: The Modal Verbs 195
I Want What I Want! (Volere) 195
I Think I Can, I Think I Can! (Potere) 196
I Have to ... (Dovere) 197
I'm in the Mood for ... .198
Infinitive Verbs and Prepositions 198
Alone at Last 199
Oddballs 199
The Preposition A 200
Learning by Example 201
A Review of the Irregular Verbs 201
Practice Makes Perfetto II 202

14 Rain or Shine   205

Talking About the Weather: *Che Tempo Fa?* 205
Il Clima: The Climate 207
Dipinto di Blu 208
La Temperatura: What's Hot and What's Not 209
The Four Seasons 210
Buon Viaggio! 210
Give Your Mind a Trip 211
It's a Date! 212
Talking About Months 212
What Century? 212
A.D. 212
1,000 Years Later 213
B.C. 214
Do You Have *un Appuntamento?* 214
About Last Night 214
The Dating Game 215
How Often? 215
Dating Dilemmas 216
Quando Quando Quando? 216
Quale Festa? 217
From What Realm Are You? 217
What's Your Sign? 218
Like a Fish to Water 219

Part 3: Fun and Games — 221

15 I Can't Believe My Eyes! — 223

Seeing Is Believing 223
Let's Go Visit, Find, See, Look At ... .225
Critters 225
More Irregular Verbs 226
   Uscire *(to Go Out/Exit)* 227
   Venire *(to Come)* 227
   Rimanere *(to Remain)* 228
   Your Turn 229
   Practice Makes Perfetto 230
   Dire *(to Say/Tell)* 231
The Power of Suggestion 231
   Perché non? 232
   Let's ... .232
How About ...? 232
   Using Non *to Make Suggestions* 233
   Yes or No 233
   Using Volere *to Make Suggestions* 233
The Big, Blue Marble 234
   Name That Nation 234
   I Continenti 235
Once Upon a Time 235
   A Refresher 236
Present Progressive Tense *(–ing)* 237
Making Progress 238
   That's the Fact, Giacomo 238

16 Shop 'Til You Drop — 241

Stores Galore 241
The Stationery Store: *La Cartoleria* 243
   Diamonds Are a Girl's Best Friend 244
   It's in the Jeans 245
   Accessories 246
   How Do I Look? 247
   One Size Does Not Fit All 248
The Florist 250
   Smooth as Seta 250
   Sock It to Me! 251
Objection! 253
   A Little Review 253
Objectify Me, Baby 253
   Follow the Rules 254
   When to Use the Direct Object Pronoun 255
   When to Use Indirect Object Pronouns 255
   Verbs That May Use an Indirect Object 256
   Who's in Command? 257
   Who's Who 257
   Who's Who II 258
   Who's Who—Final Round 259

17 Bread, Wine, and Chocolate **261**

To Market, to Market 261
Dal Negozio *(at the Store)* 261
I Love Olives 262
An Apple a Day 264
In Macelleria *(at the Butcher)* 265
Got Milk? La Latteria 267
Di Bocca Buona 268
Fruit of the Sea: La Pescheria 268
What's in a Name? 269
This Drink's on Me 270
Dolcezza! 271
Expressing Quantity 271
It's the Quantity That Counts 271
You Asked for It; You Got It! 273
Give Me Some! 273
Some or Any: The Partitive Ne 273
Some Practice 274
Facciamo La Spesa 274
What's Your Pleasure? The Verb *Piacere* 275
Using Piacere 275
Using the Verb Piacere 277
Using the Verb Piacere *II* 277
A Special Treat 278

18 Shall We Dine? **281**

So Many Restaurants 281
Two for Dinner, Please 282
What's the House Special? 282
A Table Setting 283
In the Kitchen 284
Il Bar 285
Il Caffè 286
Etiquette for Idiots 286
The Courses 287
What's on the Menu? 287
Ho Una Fame Da Lupo *(I'm as Hungry as a Wolf)* 289
La Pizza e Il Formaggio 289
That's the Way I Like It 291
Spice Up Your Life 291
Special People Have Special Needs 292
You Call This Food? 293
Fine Wine 294
A Bellini *Please* 295
What's Your Fancy? 295
La Dolce 295
Double Object Pronouns 296
You've Got Good Reflexes 297
I Call Myself 298
Flexing Those Muscles 299
A Little Reflection 300
Mirror, Mirror 300
Test Your Reflexes 301
Reciprocity 302

xiii

19 Having Fun Italian Style **303**

Name Your Game 303
You're Playing with My Head 305
Out in Left Field 305
Make a Date 306
The Arts 307
Il Cinema 307
La Musica 309
Life Imitates Art 312
Il Passato Prossimo (the Present Perfect) 313
Constructing the Past Participle 314
Forming the Past with Avere 315
Irregular Past Participles 315
Forming the Past with Essere 316
Verbs Taking Essere 317
Adverbs in Compound Tenses 319
Direct Object Pronouns in Compound Tenses 319
Indirect Object Pronouns and the Passato Prossimo 320
The Passato Prossimo *and Double Object Pronouns* 321

Part 4: Trouble in Paradise **323**

20 You're Not Having *Un Buon Giorno* **325**

Get Down to the Basics 325
Mirror Mirror on the Wall ... .327
Do Blondes Really Have More Fun? 328
In Tintoria (at the Dry Cleaner's) 329
Dal Calzolaio (at the Shoemaker's) 330
Dall'Ottica (at the Optician's) 330
Dal Negozio di Fotografia (at the Camera Shop) 331
In Gioielleria (at the Jeweler's) 331
Nel Negozio Elettronico (at the Electronics Store) 332
Help, I Lost My Passport! 332
Stressed Out 333
Stressful Exercise 334
Comparatives and Superlatives 335
Better Than the Best 336
Irregular Comparisons 337
Comparisons of Equality 338
Absolutely, Totally Superlative 339
Ci and Vi 339
Go On and Brag a Little 340

21 Is There a Doctor in the House? **341**

What a Bod! 341
Farsi 342
Express Yourself 343
What Ails You? 344
Tell Me Where It Hurts 345
This Isn't Funny Anymore 345
Feeling Funny 346
This Is What You Have 347

Alla Farmacia *(at the Pharmacy)* 348
Questions 349
La Profumeria (The Cosmetics Store) 349
I Was What I Was: The Imperfect 350
Formation of the Imperfect 351
Fill in the Spazio 352
La Pratica 352
What's Done Is Done 353
A Review 353

22 Can You Read Me?   355

Il Telefono 355
Types of Phone Calls 356
Reach Out 356
Call Me Sometime! 357
Say What? 358
Making Una Telefonata 358
Hello, Operator? 358
Just the Fax 359
Rain or Shine: The Post Office 360
Rain or Shine 361
Getting Service 361
Dear Gianni 362
Che Sarà Sarà: The Future 363
What Will Be Will Be 364
What Will You Have? 364
Look for the Pattern 365
Irregular Stems 365
Back to the Future 366
The Future Perfect 367

23 Home Sweet Home   369

Your Home Away from Home 369
Inside Your Home 370
Buying or Renting 371
Useful Verbs 372
Bright, Spacious, and Cheap 373
How's Your Italian? 373
That Would Be Nice: The Conditional Tense 374
Forming the Conditional Tense 374
What Would You Have? 375
Look for the Pattern II 376
Stem Changing Verbs 377
Coulda, Shoulda, Woulda 377
Practice Makes Perfetto 378

24 Money Matters   381

Bank on It 381
Transactions 384
The Wheel of Life 385

Everyone Has Needs: *Il Congiuntivo* (The Subjunctive) 386
  Using the Subjunctive 386
  Oh, So Moody 388
  Dependent Clauses and the Subjunctive 388
Practice Makes *Perfetto* 390
  The Past (Present Perfect) Subjunctive 391
  Purely Speculation: The Imperfect Subjunctive 392
  The Past Was Perfect 392
  Once Upon a Time: Il Passato Remoto 392
  Ci Fu Una Volta (Once Upon a Time) 393
  Cose Da Vedere 394
  What Am I? 394

Appendixes

A Answer Key   **395**

B Glossary   **411**

C Map of Italy   **441**

D An Idiot's Guide to Additional Resources   **443**

Index   **445**

Foreword

Learn Italian, and you can walk on water. Well, not quite, but I can tell you from personal experience that if you take up *la bella lingua,* miraculous things may happen to you. My own epiphany took place during my initial visit to Venice, when I wanted to practice my first-year Italian. Every year during the third weekend of July, the magical city called *La Serenissima* celebrates the *Festa del Redentore,* which commemorates the end of a particularly devastating plague in the sixteenth century. The festivities are marked with a colorful regatta and a spectacular fireworks display. During the event, a pontoon bridge of boats leads from *Piazza San Marco* to *Il Redentore,* a church across the Giudecca Canal designed and built by Andrea Palladio after the plague, which the faithful cross to attend a thanksgiving mass.

It was while bobbing and weaving across this makeshift bridge, surrounded by thousands of excited Italians with the bright sun sparkling off the water and the melodious church bells ringing, that I was literally swept off my feet. The last half of the trek was effortless, as the throngs of people transported me over the water and into the Church of the Redeemer. Once inside the red velvet-swathed interior, a swell of rapturous emotions overwhelmed me so completely that it wasn't until much later that evening, when darkness enveloped the city and the boats dispersed, that I was finally able to set foot on solid ground again.

If you, too, want to be transported to a timeless place, mesmerized and enchanted with the Italian language as your guide, I suggest starting with *The Complete Idiot's Guide to Learning Italian, Second Edition,* by Gabrielle Euvino. There are many ways to describe the book—New and improved! Idiot-proof! Better than ever!—but one thing is certain: What was already a comprehensive approach to learning *la bella lingua* has now become an even more exhaustive resource with new and exciting features that will enrich your Italian language learning experience and motivate you in unimaginable ways.

The new *Complete Idiot's Guide to Learning Italian* is a heavily rewritten version—"updated" is too mild a term—of the author's 1998 volume. Many chapters have been overhauled to reflect thoughtful suggestions and considerable input from a variety of students, educators, and professionals. In this edition, key concepts are introduced earlier, and new sidebars and images have been added that either expand on critical grammatical points or provide additional cultural context.

Because learning about the culture, history, and traditions of Italy is an integral part of learning the language, there are thematic sections that focus on work, food, family, and travel. No topic is left untouched. And because many of you, after whetting your appetite with *The Complete Idiot's Guide to Learning Italian* will want to travel to *il Bel Paese* to experience firsthand the passion and vitality that is Italy, there are chapters devoted to art, music, the weather, shopping, eating, and entertainment.

Lest you think that this book is all play and no work, the entire book is based on a solid foundation that includes the basics in language instruction: grammar, usage, parts of speech (remember nouns, pronouns, adjectives, and articles?), verbs and all their many flavors of tenses, and pronunciation—and it has several types of exercises to reinforce what you've learned. Each chapter is structured with an overview of concepts followed by straightforward, uncomplicated lessons, practice exercises, and a review of the key principles. Interspersed throughout the material are sidebars—boxes highlighting definitions of terms, historical facts about Italy, and notes on idiomatic usage.

You *can* learn Italian. But first, forget everything you've ever learned in high school language class. Second, ignore anyone who says you're too old, too young, too stupid, or too busy to learn Italian. Third, start turning the pages of *The Complete Idiot's Guide to Learning Italian* and *fare la practica con la bocca* (practice with your mouth). In other words, start talking, because isn't that what communicating is all about? This book has simple pronunciation guides, phonetic spellings, accent and dialect pointers, vocabulary lists, and two glossaries, all designed to encourage you to speak Italian.

When I'm retired and living in a Tuscan villa surrounded by vineyards and cypresses, sipping Montepulciano and biting into a big piece of *Pecorino stagionato*, I'll reminisce about the thrill of being able to communicate in another language and the empowerment of being able to exchange *cultura* and *amicizia* with friends and family in another land—and I'll remember the first time I walked on water in Italy.

Looking for an exhilarating romance? Grab yourself a full-bodied Tuscan red wine, a loaf of *pane toscano,* and *The Complete Idiot's Guide to Learning Italian!*

Tante belle cose!

Michael P. San Filippo

Guide
Italian Language at About.com
http://italian.about.com
italian.guide@about.com

Michael P. San Filippo earned a Master of Arts degree in Italian Studies at the Middlebury College Italian School Abroad program in Florence, Italy. He conducts private tutoring in Italian for students of all levels and was an editor for the lifestyle/e-commerce Web site Virtual Italy. In 1999, Michael founded Vespucci Ventures, a company that leads walking tours of Florence and Tuscany, and is the guide for the About.com Italian Language Web site, one of the leading destinations for exploring the topic on the Internet. Michael makes his home in New York City, where he nourishes his enthusiasm for all things Italian by participating in The Italian Table, a club for people passionate about Italian food and culture, and the Istituto di Cultura, a social organization promoting Italian art, history, and language.

Introduction

Whether you are too busy to take a class or merely want to supplement your language learning experience with additional materials, *The Complete Idiot's Guide to Learning Italian, Second Edition,* was written specifically for the independent study of Italian.

Any idiot can speak Italian, and lots of them do. The word "idiot" comes from the Greek root *idios* and means "of a particular person, private, own." In Latin, an *idiota* simply refers to a private person. You see this root in the words "idiom" and "idiosyncrasy."

Beware of the idiots! Lame and suffering from a speech impediment, Claudius (10 B.C.–54 A.D.) is remembered as a scholar and a competent administrator during the time he reigned. Against all odds, this "idiot" rose up to become Roman Emperor, making a fool of everyone.

The fact is, you're not an idiot, or you wouldn't be reading this book.

It's in the Program

Speaking a language seems to be the one thing we can almost all do with some degree of proficiency; it's in our programming. Amazingly, you learned how to speak long before you understood what a noun was. This book will show you how to speak Italian using what you already know.

The average English speaker knows about 50,000 words. Your brain is a living computer, and whenever it hears a foreign word, it goes to the foreign language section and pulls out whatever "comes to mind." Don't be surprised if the first thing that comes out of your mouth is French or Spanish (or whatever the last language you studied might have been).

Grammar Isn't Fun, but It Helps

This book outlines the most important aspects of grammar and idiomatic expressions. Using real-life situations, it guides you through the various elements of the Italian language, comparing and contrasting English and Italian with clear, idiot-proof explanations.

Live It Up!

Alas, one cannot live on grammar alone. You need to hear Italian every chance you get. Eat, breathe, drink, sleep, laugh, love, listen, sing, scream, and dance Italian. You'll learn a lot faster if you're enjoying yourself.

As your studies progress, why not reward yourself with a monthly (or weekly) night out in an authentic Italian restaurant? If you're plugged in, try doing an online search and subscribe to an Italian language bulletin. Visit a music library and listen to *Rigoletto* sung by five different artists. Start a collection of children's books. Read the Italian fashion magazines—whatever you do, make it fun, and you'll find that you can't get enough.

How to Use This Book

The best way to use *The Complete Idiot's Guide to Learning Italian* is by adopting it. Tuck it into your backpack, briefcase, or bag, and bring it with you everywhere you go. Contrary to what you were taught, this author encourages you to write in the margins, dog-ear the pages, and scribble on the cover. Read it from front to back and back to front.

Exposure and repetition are essential to learning the language. By the time you have thoroughly gone through this book (utilizing the helpful suggestions offered), you will be able to speak Italian. It's that simple.

What You'll Find in These Pages

Part 1, "The Basics," lays the foundation of your Italian-language learning experience, bringing you in-depth definitions and explanations of key grammatical forms, verbs, and parts of speech. You'll learn about cognates (a foreign word that retains the same sound and meaning) and how to connect the dots between Latin, Italian, and English. You'll get examples of the spoken poetry of slang and a few idiomatic expressions. You'll learn your manners—*per favore, grazie, mi scusi*—and how to properly address strangers in Italian.

Part 2, "You're Off and Running," should be sipped slowly and savored as though it were a glass of red wine. Here you'll learn about the marvels of conjugating verbs, the parts of speech that get you moving. You'll also get a lot of how-tos: how to introduce yourself and your family, how to catch a taxi or bus, and how to make your way from the airport to the hotel. Skip through the chapters that don't grip you, but continue to come back to the material until you have mastered it.

In Part 3, "Fun and Games," you'll be given keys to the Fiat and handed a map. If you love to hunt for treasure or want to pick up a pair of beautifully tailored trousers, you'll find all the terms you need. You'll learn how to order in a *ristorante*, choose a wine, and pick a super movie for your Italian *serata*. You'll also hear about the artists and composers that move you.

Part 4, "Getting Down to Business," prepares you for the inevitable challenges that are a part of the human experience. You'll learn how to describe the different aches and pains in your body to a *dottore*, where to go to get your glasses fixed, and how to find a good dry cleaner. You'll also learn how to make a phone call and deal with the post office—two things that can bring the most sane person to the edge. Included in this part are practical money and banking terms.

Appendix A, "Answer Key," gives you the answers to the exercises offered throughout the book. Find out how *intelligente* you really are.

Appendix B, "Glossary," has been updated and improved, with the addition of hundreds of helpful vocabulary words. Nouns have been marked with the appropriate definite articles. To aid you, irregular plurals and participles are given. In addition, you'll find cultural references and exclamations used by the Italians. This glossary should not substitute for a good Italian/English dictionary, but it can help you develop a working vocabulary.

Use Appendix C, "Map of Italy," to kick around ideas (like taking a trip).

Appendix D, "An Idiot's Guide to Additional Resources," gives further reading to enhance your study of Italian.

Extras

As an extra perk, featured throughout the book are interesting sidebars highlighting relevant aspects of the Italian language and culture. You'll see the following sidebars:

As a Rule

These sidebars highlight or expand on aspects of Italian grammar.

What's What

Here you'll find definitions of terms.

Attenzione!

These boxes highlight particularly ambiguous or irregular elements of the Italian language.

Did You Know?

These boxes provide cultural and historical facts about Italy.

La Bella Lingua

These are notes on dialect, idioms, and helpful vocabulary, which may or may not pertain directly to the lesson.

Acknowledgments

This book is dedicated to my great aunt Clara Kaye, who at the time of printing is 87 years old and remembers *everything*.

To the team that made this book happen: my development editor, Amy Zavatto, for keeping the boat on course during the storm—thank you; Brandon Hopkins for his steady availability;

Kathy Bidwell, for her artistic expertise; Krista Hansing, the copy editor, for her queries and edits; Angela Calvert, Svetlana Dominguez, and Jody Schaeffer for their skill in producing a book that exceeded my expectations.

A big *grazie* to my friend and technical editor Stefano Spadoni, my Jiminy Cricket.

A special welcome aboard to Michael San Filippo, who kindly shared his enthusiasm and knowledge of everything Italian.

Grazie to John and Marie Cataneo at ciaonewyork.com for reaching out through cyberspace with their fabulous Web site.

Warm thanks to Cristina Melotti for her eyes and contributions to the book, my life, and my spirit.

To my *famiglia* Herby, Sandy, and TL, the clowns; Rob and Frank; Andrea, David, and Rose; Shelly, Virgil, and Sharon; Barbara, Steve, and Miriam; and Anne, my adopted mom, for your encouragement and artistry.

A special thanks to Dr. Glenn Chiarello for taking such good care of my smile.

Thanks to all the people, my students and friends, both old and new, past and present, that have given their love and support so freely over the years:

Amy; Anna; Anne; Anne Mary; Anthony; Arthur; Beth; Bill; Bob; Carl; Carla; Carol; Catherine; Cathy; Chris; Cole; Colin; David H.; David S.; Debbie, Joe, and Joanna; the Ellison family; Deborah; Dipesh; Donna; Elaine; Ellen, Tom, and John; Flo; Frannie; Gina; Giovanni; Glenn; Gloria; Hege; Jeff; Jen; Jessica; Joanne; John; Kilian; Kimmie; Laurie; Leslie; Lisa; Lyn; Maggie, Marc, and Tony; Marissa; Michelle; Monica; Peter; Ralph; Ricardo; Rich; Rob; Sandy; Sasha; Scott; Soheil; Susan; Teal; Tom; Trish; Wendy; and Wen Wen

The author gratefully acknowledges the friendship and support received from the law offices of Seyfarth, Shaw, especially from Michael J. Album, Ray Anderson, Mara Anzalone, Margot Boyd, Edward Cerasia, and Devorah Serafini.

There can be no greater privilege than to be able to put words to print. I thank the heavens and the stars for listening.

Special Thanks to the Technical Reviewer

The Complete Idiot's Guide to Learning Italian, Second Edition, was reviewed by an expert who double-checked the accuracy of what you'll learn here, to help us ensure that this book gives you everything you need to know about learning the Italian language. Special thanks are extended to Stefano Spadoni for his expertise on this subject.

Trademarks

Part 1

The Basics

You're ready to go. You've purchased this book and have taken the first step to learning Italian. There's no better time than the present to begin your study, and whether it takes you five months or five years, remember: It's the journey that counts.

To accompany you on this trip, Part 1 gives you the fundamentals of Italian, focusing on important elements of grammar, verbs, and pronunciation.

Chapter 1, "Why You Should Study Italian," warms you up with a few reasons to learn Italian. In Chapter 2, "Immerse Yourself," you'll be given a mini grammar review to help prime your brain for the upcoming lessons. You'll also be offered suggestions on how you can begin practicing your new skills immediately.

Chapter 3, "Sound Like an Italian," gets you rolling your R's with an easy-to-read pronunciation guide to assist you. In Chapter 4, "You Know More Than You Think," you'll be shown cognates (similar-sounding words) and how you can use these to tie the Italian language to English. Chapter 5, "Expressively Yours," offers you a few basic greetings and salutations along with a sampling of idioms and idiomatic expressions used in Italian.

In Chapter 6, "Almost Everything You Wanted to Know About Sex," you'll learn about Italian nouns and the notion of gender. You'll discover several different ways to express the incredible, amazing individual that is you in Chapter 7, "What's the Subject?"

For now, skim through the materials and familiarize yourself with the different aspects of Italian. Interact with the pages; let your mind visit the places mentioned. Do the exercises. Later, come back and read through the book with more attention to detail.

When you undertake learning a new language, you are like a child again—so much to learn! Get your ego out of the way and play! Buon viaggio!

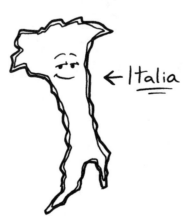
← Italia

Why You Should Study Italian

In This Chapter

➤ The many virtues of the Italian language

➤ Where you can use Italian

➤ Developing a learning strategy

➤ There's no reason to be afraid!

It's recognizable immediately: the gentle cadence of words as melodic as *musica,* the sexy rolling of *R*'s, the soothing, sensual lilt of voices that move you as does an *opera, una poesia,* or a beautiful work of *arte.* It's the *la bella lingua* of Italian, and there's nothing quite like it.

You've always wanted to learn *Italiano,* but until now, it's been something you wished you could do but never dared. Maybe you took a high school Italian class and remember the word *spaghetti* but not much else. Perhaps you come from an Italian *famiglia* and feel a desire to satisfy a primordial urge. You get weak-kneed when you hear an opera. You're an incurable romantic and want to murmur sweet nothings to your *amante* in Italian. You love traveling and want to follow in the *tradizione* of the great writers, from Shakespeare to Henry James to Goethe. Could it be that you want to learn *la lingua* because it will connect you to something wonderfully *misterioso,* ancient, and rich? Whatever your reason, that small peninsula in the center of the *Mediterraneo* has been affecting the lives of people, both great and ordinary, for as long as our *calendario* has existed and then some, and you want to be a part of it.

If you still need to ask "Why learn Italian?" read on for a few more reasons.

You Love Life

The Complete Idiot's Guide to Learning Italian, Second Edition, is *un libro* written for you. You sense this as soon as you pull it off the shelf. You can feel it almost vibrate with potential. *Sì,* this time you're going to stick to your *promessa* to learn Italian. You're not going to procrastinate any longer; you've been wanting this for a very long time and *la vita* is too short to spend wishing you had done something fully within your powers to do. The time is right, the *momento* is now, and with this *libro,* you will be one large step closer to making a dream come true.

Remember, every great accomplishment starts as an *idea. Immagina* the *realtà* of speaking Italian. You'll be able to …

➤ Order your favorite *piatto* in the local Italian *ristorante,* the one with the *pane fresco, buon vino,* and great *ospitalità.*

➤ Watch Fellini films without reading the subtitles.

➤ Have an accent! Didn't you always want one?

➤ Understand what your in-laws are saying about you while they smile and wipe the tomato sauce off their chins.

➤ Go beyond feeling the *passione* of one of Puccini's operas, and genuinely understand Mimì's tortured heart in *La Bohème.*

➤ Read the soccer scores from the Italian newspapers.

➤ Understand the labels on those incredible designer clothes that make otherwise even-keeled adults weep.

➤ Feel sexy.

➤ Sound *intelligente.*

Did You Know?

Italy's population has grown to almost 58 million. According to one myth, a vestal virgin gave birth to twin boys, Remus and Romulus. Saved from drowning by a she-wolf who suckled the children until they were old enough to go out on their own, Romulus later killed his brother and, sometime around 753 B.C., founded Rome. Another myth involves the Trojan Aeneas, who came to Italy after escaping Troy. The great Latin poet Virgil used this as the basis for the *Aeneid,* unquestionably the single greatest epic poem of classical literature.

Get Real

Now let's get down to some real reasons to speak Italian:

➤ Leonardo da Vinci, Michelangelo, Giotto, Galileo, San Francesco d'Assisi, and Dante (to name just a few) did.

➤ You're studying *storia d'arte*. So far, the closest you've actually been to the masterpieces is the slide projector in the back of the auditorium. You're thinking of spending a *semestre* in *Firenze* to study the works of the great Renaissance *artisti*—including Botticelli, Raffaello, Caravaggio, Pisano, Masaccio, and Ghirlandaio—and you want to follow the lectures offered in the local *università*.

➤ Think Verdi and Puccini.

➤ You love Italian food and want to go beyond *al dente*. You've found an adorable cooking school tucked away in the Tuscan countryside among the silvery leaves of the olive trees. You're ready to take the next step and learn the terms.

➤ You are an amateur wine connoisseur and plan to spend your next vacation visiting all the major Italian vineyards. You can sample a different *vino* every day while discussing the variables that contribute to the fine art of juicing a grape.

➤ Gardens! Visit the formal Renaissance *giardino* of the *Villa Lante di Bagnaia* (near Viterbo) and learn how the pros have been doing it for centuries.

➤ You're fascinated by ancient burial rituals and want to visit the *catacombe*. If you're not afraid of dark, moldy tunnels and love the sound of bats, Italy has an assortment of bones, skulls, and preserved body parts that can be viewed at a church near you. Just don't get lost in the *labirinto* of secret passages and chambers that once held the remains of early Christian martyrs.

➤ You love driving. Imagine motoring along the Amalfi coast in a cherry-red Ferrari. Sunlight sparkles off the emerald waters, and the legendary Franco Corelli is sitting beside you singing a private performance of Puccini's exotic *Turandot*. (Okay, so it's only the stereo.) You understand that life is as much about the journey as it is the destination. Enjoy your ride.

➤ You love walking. You want to amble through the winding *vie* of Siena, stroll past the limpid waters of Venice's canals, hike along the Appian way, and meander the ruins of Pompeii, where, in 79 A.D., Mt. Vesuvius buried 2,000 people under a layer of dust, lava, and stone. You'll walk so much you won't feel a twinge of guilt when the delicious food starts coming, and you'll say *sì* to dessert every time.

➤ You want to learn the secret that Italians have known for centuries—the healing elements of mud and mineral baths. You won't believe how something so stinky (the hot springs often smell like sulfur) could make your body feel so *vivo*, so *fresco*, so *puro!*

➤ You just bought your first digital camera and have decided to take a course in *fotografia*. What better place to take pictures than Italy?

➤ You've got to see for yourself the juicy Battle of the Oranges held every year in the town of Ivrea during the *carnevale* season.

➤ You're getting married. Where else than Italy should you spend your honeymoon?

Getting Wet

Whatever your reason is for wanting to learn *la bella lingua* of Italian, you need to begin somewhere. You'll never learn to swim if you don't get wet; the same principle applies to learning a language. Before you even get to Italy, your *viaggio* begins with your intent. You've already made a great start by picking up this *libro*. However, you also might want to consider some of the following tips.

Immerse Yourself—Literally!

The key is to familiarize yourself with the language by reading it. When you buy books of Italian *poesia* or a copy of Pirandello's plays, for example, buy the versions where the Italian *traduzione* is given alongside the English so that your eyes can move back and forth between the two. This saves you the effort of looking up every *parola* you don't understand and gives you a general *idea* of what is being communicated. Context is key: Absorb the significance of a *parola* by looking at the words surrounding it.

Speaking of the power of words, inspiration often comes from the unexpected. Go to your bookstore and leaf through several books in the Italian language section. See what interests you. Barrons has a terrific book that concentrates exclusively on verbs, aptly called *501 Italian Verbs*. Children's books are another fun way of building *vocabolario*. If you're in Italy, visit the *libreria* (bookstore) and pick up a few.

Italian publications, especially magazines, are usually quite entertaining, full of glossy, color ads and interesting facts. The elegant world of *la moda* (fashion), *il viaggio* (travel), and *la cucina* (food) are three popular topics. Pick up a copy and figure out the contents by studying the titles. *La Cucina, L'Espresso, Oggi, Panorama*, and *Vogue Italia* are but a few. Italian newspapers include *La Repubblica, Il Corriere della Sera*, and *La Stampa*. Also, the next time a friend takes a trip to Italy, ask him or her to bring back the in-flight magazine if it has both Italian and English. Alitalia produces a wonderful publication that has the Italian and the English side by side. You'll be surprised at how much you can pick up.

Become a Class Act

Call your local *università* and investigate whether it has an Italian department. Find out if it has a mailing list for events, and make a point of meeting other "Italophiles."

Hang Out with Sophia

Rent Italian movies! Every week, make it a ritual to sit in front of your *televisione* (for educational purposes, naturally). Needless to say, you want the subtitled versions (stay away from anything dubbed—a character is his voice). Listen to the actors and mimic them, or simply read the translations and enjoy. You will absorb far more if you are relaxed and having fun. Try to make out the different words within each *frase*. Isolate words that are repeated. Make it a challenge and see how many words you understand.

Get the Right Tools

Invest in a good bilingual dictionary, preferably one printed in *Italia* that offers various features, such as stress accentuation (many dictionaries will indicate irregularly stressed syllables) and parts of speech. Bigger is not necessarily better—choose a *dizionario* that isn't too cumbersome so you'll be more likely to bring it with you. Don't skimp on price here—a good dictionary is something you'll keep for a long time.

Flash cards are also a good resource. You can pick up a box of flash cards at any bookstore, or you can make your own. That unused box of business cards from your old job, or unused pages from your last address book are *perfetto*. Punch holes in them and put 10 or 20 on a key ring so you can put them in your pocket or bag for "study quickies." Five minutes stolen here and there, waiting in line at the *ufficio postale*, at the *banca*, or when stuck in *traffica* can add up to more than you imagine.

Tune In!

Find out what station has Italian news. RAI, the Italian television and radio network, airs programs every day. Even though it will sound as though they are speaking a million miles a *minuto*, exposing your ears to the *lingua* will evolve into understanding it.

Read the Fine Print

Keep the owner's manual to any appliances, electronics, or cameras that include multilingual instructions. This is a great way to learn technical terms—and, once more, you don't need to pick up a dictionary; the English translation is probably already there.

Find Birds of a Feather

Study the *lingua* with a friend. There's nothing like having a partner to keep you motivated and on your toes. Practice together, and maybe invest in a private tutor to meet with you every couple of weeks. The *costo* is usually reasonable considering the kind of *attenzione* you will receive, and it will be good incentive to keep up with your studies.

While you're at it, make some Italian friends—or, better yet, an Italian lover (assuming you don't already have one, that is). There's nothing like a good *conversazione* (or quarrel) to hone your skills.

Play It Again, Salvatore

Make tapes of yourself speaking Italian, and then play these tapes to a native Italian speaker (your new friends, the waiter in the local *ristorante,* your *nonna,* or anyone who will listen). Ask them to evaluate your linguistic strengths and weaknesses.

There's Nothing to Stop You

Learning *la bella lingua* will not occur overnight. Many people find that, as with all new projects, they are hard-working and organized for the first few lessons, but then life gets in the way … and you know the rest. Even if it's for only five minutes a day, be committed.

You can learn Italian; I've taught hundreds of people and know from *esperienza* it does not have to remain a dream. There is nothing to stop you from obtaining this goal. At times, your *progresso* will be obvious; other times, you will wonder what, if anything, is being accomplished. Remember, it's the *viaggio* that counts, not just the *destinazione.* The following *lista* outlines a few things to keep in mind that will make your journey a little easier:

➤ **Set realistic goals.** Whether you devote 10 *minuti* a day every *giorno,* or two hours a week on Sundays, stick to your *programma.* If you can't do it one week, no guilt trips. Make it up the next week.

➤ **Grammar isn't for geeks.** Grammar is simply a tool for learning a language. You figured out how to communicate your needs and understand what your *mamma* was telling you long before you could identify an adjective, noun, or verb. It probably started with a simple word, such as "cookie," which you mispronounced as *coo-coo.* As you matured, you began expressing your likes and dislikes with words such as "No!" or "Me!" Your mother did not follow you around saying, "That's a noun!" or "What a great verb you used!" She responded to your needs as best she could, based on your *abilità* to communicate. Grammar is simply the *vocabolario,* as any trade will have, used in language learning. Fear not.

➤ **Make mistakes.** Lots of them. You never know what mistake might end up being a discovery. Did the great Renaissance man Leonardo da Vinci draw the *Mona Lisa* (also titled *La Gioconda* in Italian) the first time he picked up a piece of charcoal? Would we recognize Christopher Columbus if he had made it to India? As the result of a major wrong turn, he stumbled upon the Americas.

➤ **Don't be intimidated.** The Italians are among the most warm, hospitable, easygoing, open-minded people you will ever meet. Your attempt to speak Italian, even in the most basic of ways, will elicit nothing less than enthusiasm and delight. Say *buon giorno* (good day) every time you walk into an establishment, and watch the response. They are listening to what you are trying to express, not what mistakes you may have made. Put yourself in their *scarpe* and remember the last time someone speaking English as a second language impressed you with her command of the language, the whole time murmuring, "I don't speak so good." "Are you kidding?" you wanted to ask. "You speak very well!"

Italian is an easy language to learn. It's another story to master this rich, complicated tongue, but you can cross that *ponte* when you come to it. You start at the beginning. One foot in front of the other, an entire *continente* can be traversed, step by step.

Now, as a fun exercise, go back through this chapter and count how many new Italian words you learned just for showing up here—and without even trying! *Bravi!*

The Least You Need to Know

➤ There's no time like the present to learn *la bella lingua* of Italian.

➤ Italian is an accessible language that anyone can learn.

➤ You can communicate even if your pronunciation and grammar are less than *perfetto*. Remember that *la lingua* is simply a means to communicate your thoughts to another *persona*. If you can learn to speak one language, you can learn to speak another.

➤ You have nothing to fear but fear itself. Whether it takes you three months or three years, one step in front of the other is the way you will achieve your goals. Find your pace. Stick with it.

Chapter 2

Immerse Yourself

In This Chapter

➤ A history of the Italian language

➤ What's a dialect?

➤ Using your bilingual dictionary

➤ Why grammar is the key to *la bella lingua*

In an increasingly international *comunità*, it seems that Italian has permeated every aspect of our *cultura*. Italian *ristoranti* specializing in different regional tastes have cropped up in just about every *villaggio* and *città*. Italian films have made us laugh so hard our sides hurt, yet we can never escape the *teatro* without having dabbed at the corners of our eyes at least once.

Advertisers have hooked into the enormous appeal that *l'Italia* has for almost every *prodotto* imaginable, and there is more than one commercial using the Italian language to make its point. Italian lingo (*ciao, bravo, ancora!*) has crept into English—not surprising since so much of the English language has its origins in Latin, Italian's *madre lingua* (mother tongue).

This chapter offers you a different eye on the Italian language and compares it with English. It also gives a summary of different parts of *grammatica* and attempts to take away some of the intimidation factor that often accompanies learning a new *lingua*.

La Bella Lingua

Latin originally developed in Central Italy in the area known as Latium. Within the Italian peninsula lived the Estrucans (giving Tuscany its name), Faliscans, Oscans, Umbrians, and a slew of other tribes. These Italic languages all contributed to the eventual development of the language we now recognize as Italian. It is not clear when Italian became a distinct language from Latin, since no Italian text has been recorded before the tenth century; however, we do know that by the fourth century, St. Jerome had translated the Bible from Latin into the language spoken by the common people.

Latin Lovers

The history of the Italian language spans centuries and begins with classical Latin, the literary language of ancient *Roma* and the language used principally by the upper classes, the educated, and later the clergy—hence the term Romance languages (from which French, Spanish, Portuguese, and Rumanian are also derived). These languages were all offshoots, or dialects. Italian is the Romance language closest to Latin.

La Bella Lingua

Set aside a predetermined amount of study time that you can realistically commit toward your goal of learning Italian. Whether it's eight *minuti* a day or *un'ora* twice a week, stick to it.

Languages are like seeds that drift from one area into another, germinating wherever there is ripe soil. Latin made its way into English during the seventh century as England was converting to Christianity, and later during a revival in classical scholarship stemming from the Renaissance (*Rinascimento,* literally meaning "rebirth"). During the sixteenth and seventeenth centuries, hundreds of Latin words were incorporated into English, resulting in much of today's legal and medical *terminologia*.

As a result, many small words in modern English have their origins in Latin, a hop from Italian. Chapter 4, "You Know More Than You Think," presents you with a more thorough listing of those similar words, or *cognates.* Keep in mind that English is a much broader language than Italian in terms of the sheer number of words it possesses.

You will see that in Italian it is sometimes much easier to express certain *diminutives* and *superlatives* than in English. For example, English has the pair "cat/kitten." The word "kitten" is quite different from the word "cat." In Italian, it's much easier to express a small cat: By adding the ending *–ino* to the word *gatto*, we create the word *gattino*. You're already familiar with the word *zucchini*, which comes from the Italian word *zucca* (pumpkin/squash).

A commonly used superlative in English is *–est* which is attached to adjectives to describe the smallest, biggest, or best. In Italian, this would be expressed with the ending *–issimo*, as in the adjective *bellissimo* (very beautiful, gorgeous).

In spite of the fact that Italian has fewer words than English, Italians have no difficulty expressing themselves, as you will find out for yourself.

> **What's What**
>
> A **diminutive** is a suffix, or ending, that denotes smallness, youth, or familiarity, such as *caro* (dear) and *carino* (cute), *ragazzo* (boy) and *ragazzino* (small boy). A **superlative** expresses the extreme, or highest degree of something, such as *bello* (beautiful) and *bellissimo* (gorgeous).

How Do You Say ...? Dialect

A dialect is a variation of a language, usually particular to a region and often quite different from the standard spoken vernacular. Due to its shape and long history of outside influences, Italy has hundreds of different dialects, many of which are still used today. Some dialects are virtually identical to Italian, but with particular colloquialisms and idiomatic expressions understood only by those familiar with the dialect.

Other dialects are like different languages. For example, up north in Lombardia, you'll hear a specifically German accent and a softening of the R's, a result of the district's rule by Austria at one time. In the Piedmont region, you can hear the French influence. Down south near Napoli, you can hear Spanish and French, whereas in Calabria, certain expessions are quite clearly Greek (*kalimera* means literally "Good day" in modern Greek) or Albanian in nature. The islands of *Sardegna* and *Sicilia* also have their own languages.

Many Italian immigrants brought their dialects to the United States, where they were further influenced by factors such as culture, English, and other dialects. This partly explains why the Italian spoken by many immigrants often differs greatly from the Italian presented in this book—and why you may still have difficulty communicating with your grandmother after having mastered the basics. Many variations or dialects of Italian are spoken around the world today, in such places as Switzerland and many parts of South America.

La Bella Lingua

The poet **Dante Alighieri** (1265–1321) is to the Italian language what Shakespeare is to English. It was his poetry that legitimized the Italian language as we know it today, since all his predecessors wrote exclusively in Latin. His most famous work, *La Divina Commedia*, is an epic poem depicting an imaginary journey through Hell, Purgatory, and Paradise. That work was actually influenced by another of the world's greatest poets, *Virgilio* (Virgil), who served as Dante's guide both literally, as a writer, and figuratively, in the story itself.

Tuscan Italian

In modern Italy, the standard language taught in schools and spoken on television is Tuscan Italian, primarily because this was the regional dialect used by the great medieval writers Dante, Petrarca, and Boccaccio, all of whom used what was then only a spoken language. Modern Italian is often quite different from the Italian used during the Middle Ages, but, as when you compare modern English to Old English, there are also striking similarities.

Look at this excerpt from Dante's *Inferno:*

> *Nel mezzo del cammin di nostra vita*
> *mi ritrovai per una selva oscura,*
> *che la diritta via era smarrita.*

Note the translation:

> In the middle of our life's journey
> I found myself in a dark wood,
> out of which the straight way was lost.

The Italian has a wonderful rhyme quality—the word *vita* working with the word *smarrita*. Although the translation to English loses some of the flow and meaning of the poem, you can still get a sense of what is being communicated; and you certainly can gain an understanding of the musicality of the language. It's like looking at a photograph of a bright, sunny day where you can see the *colori* but you can't feel the warmth of the sun, experience the expanse of blue sky, or hear the *vento* rustle the leaves in the trees.

La Bella Lingua

The works of **Francesco Petrarca** (1304–1374) differed from those of Dante. As an early Humanist, Petrarca's ideas focused more on love and other earthly concerns, making him very popular during the Renaissance. His major works, *I Trionfi* and *Il Canzoniere*, were both written in the vernacular, or in everyday (as opposed to formal) speech.

Giovanni Boccaccio (1313–1375) has been rated one of the greatest literary figures of Italy. A contemporary of Petrarca, he is most known for *The Decameron*. Written around the time of the Black Death of 1348, *The Decameron* is a collection of 100 novellas, many comic, some bawdy, a few tragic—and all captivating and engaging.

So What's Your Story?

"Etymology" is a fancy term used to describe the study of words, but you don't need to be a linguist to appreciate the *origine* of a word. By using your powers of deduction, it's often *possibile* to figure out a word's *significato* simply by looking at its root. *Per esempio,* the word *pomodoro* means "tomato" in Italian. Coming from the Latin words *pomum* ("apple" or "fruit") and *oro* (signifying "gold"), the word derives from the Latin *aurum* (connected to the word *aurora,* meaning "dawn" or "redness"). Thus the word *pomodoro* breaks down to literally mean "golden apple."

The English words "Vermont" and "verdant" both share a common root: *vert* (coming from Latin *viridis* and meaning "green"). In Italian, the word for the season spring is *primavera,* virtually meaning "first green." The words *carnivore, carnal, charnel,* and *carnival* all derive from the Latin stem *carn,* meaning "flesh." Are you a verbose person? Think verb, or in Latin, *verbum,* meaning "word."

There's no need to rush out and take a course in *Latino.* Rather than memorizing a list of words, try creating associations with words you already know. Sometimes it's as *semplice* as adding a vowel here and there, or tacking on an Italian ending. Your cognitive *abilità* to make sense will do the rest. Once you have an understanding of how the endings change from English to Italian, you'll be able to switch from one *lingua* to the other in no time at all.

How Much Italian Is Enough?

Understanding what your motives are for learning Italian is key to accomplishing your goals. Having a destination will help you map out the journey. It will help you to gloss over certain *lezioni* (lessons) that may be less relevant to your purpose, while concentrating on those elements of the language more suited to fit your needs. Here are some examples:

➤ If you're learning Italian to pass your art history exam, you might not need to spend a lot of time on idiomatic expressions, cognates, and helpful expressions. Instead, you should focus on verbs and their tenses, nouns, and adjectives.

➤ If you're learning Italian to be able to converse with your Italian business associates, you should aim to develop an "ear" for the language. Here, pronunciation is essential, and a knowledge of some common idiomatic expressions is helpful to break the ice.

➤ If food and travel are your passions, a strong *vocabolario* is *importante*. Developing a sizable repertoire of words related to your interests will make your *viaggio* to Italy that much more interesting as you seek new *ristoranti* and hidden treasures. It's good to know a few verb infinitives just to get you pointed in the right direction, but it might not be *necessario* to spend too much time on the many tenses. The point is to be able to meet your needs and express your thoughts.

La Bella Lingua

Expand your horizons! Many Italian streets are named after historical and religious figures, such as *Corso Vittorio Emanuele II* and *Via Savonarola*. Use the street signs as opportunities to gain insight about Italy and its rich culture.

Your Dictionary Is Your Best Friend

Having a good bilingual *dizionario* is essential to learning a new language, whatever your purpose may be. Use your dictionary as an adventurer would use a map. Keep it handy, somewhere where you do most of your studying so that you don't have far to reach every time a new word pops up. You'll be amazed at how often you'll use it if you're not climbing a ladder to get to the top shelf of your bookcase whenever a need arises. Most good English/Italian dictionaries indicate what kind of word it is. You should understand the significance of the abbreviations used in the definitions. The following table lists a few of them.

Dictionary Abbreviations

English Abbreviation	Italian Abbreviation	Meaning
adj.	*agg.*	Adjective
adv.	*avv.*	Adverb
—	*f.*	Singular feminine noun
—	*m.*	Singular masculine noun
s.	—	Singular noun
prep.	*prep.*	Preposition
pron.	*pron.*	Pronoun
v.i.	*v.i.*	Intransitive verb
v.t.	*v.t.*	Transitive verb
—	*v.rifl.*	Reflexive verb
fam.	*fam.*	Familiar/colloquial

Also take advantage of any tables, charts, or specialized vocabulary offered in your dictionary. There is often a handy summary of the language tucked away somewhere in the front or back pages. Read the small print.

Speak Easy

Some of you may not remember seventh-grade grammar as well as you would like. After all, at the time, you could see no practical purpose; you never envisioned that you would actually choose to learn a language on your own, and you were much too busy writing notes to your best friend to pay attention to your teacher. You're older now, your hormones are in check, and you're a little wiser, so take a trip down memory lane and review some of those parts of speech.

Person, Place, or Pasta

Nouns are people, places, things, and ideas. *Poet, Pompei, pasta,* and *principle* are all nouns. In Italian, all nouns have a gender: They are either masculine (m.) or feminine (f.). In addition, all nouns in Italian indicate number: They are either singular (s.) or plural (p.).

La Bella Lingua

If an explanation given in this book still leaves you confused, refer to that same topic in a grammar book such as *Italian Verbs and Essentials of Grammar,* by Carlo Graziano (Passport Books). Sometimes it takes two different explanations to fully grasp a new concept.

Descriptively Speaking

Adjectives describe nouns. They are big, little, pretty, ugly, and all the colors of the rainbow. Unlike English, Italian adjectives agree in number and gender (sex) with the nouns they modify. For example, if the noun is singular and masculine, as in *il vino* (the wine), then the adjective must also be singular and masculine, as in *il vino rosso* (the red wine).

In Italian, the adjective is almost always placed after the noun it modifies, as in *la casa bianca* (the house white), but exceptions exist, as in *il bravo ragazzo* (the good boy). You'll get a much clearer idea of how adjectives work in a little while.

Adverbs describe verbs, adjectives, and other adverbs. They move us quickly and happily toward our goal of learning Italian. Most adverbs in English end in *–ly*. In Italian, many adverbs end in *–mente,* such as *rapidamente* and *allegramente.*

Who's He?

Pronouns substitute for nouns and refer to a person, place, thing, or idea. For example: *We* ate a lot of food in the restaurant, and *it* (the food) cost quite a penny. In Italian, pronouns are a little more complicated because they must, like nouns, reflect sex and number. There is no neuter *it* in Italian. There are several kinds of pronouns, of which the most important to remember are subject pronouns (*he, she,* and so on), direct object pronouns, and indirect object pronouns (*it*).

It's All Relative

Prepositions are words (such as above, along, beyond, before, through, in, on, at, to, for, and so on) that are placed before nouns to indicate a relationship to other words in a sentence. Prepositions are best learned in connection with the expressions in which they are used. For example, you may think *about* someone, but you can also think *of* going on vacation.

Where the Action Is

Verbs indicate action. An infinitive verb is a verb that has not been conjugated, as in *to be, to eat,* or *to travel.* A conjugated verb is simply a form of the verb that agrees with the subject. You conjugate verbs in English all the time when you say "I am," "you are," and "he is." Verb conjugations will be discussed in greater depth later.

Intransitive verbs can stand alone, without a direct object, as "sing" does in the sentence "I sing." You can sing a song or just sing.

Transitive verbs can be followed by a direct object or require a reflexive pronoun, as in "We kissed *one another,*" or "Robert is going to the party." You see, Robert can't just "go"—he must "go" somewhere.

It All Depends on How You Look at It

You don't have to be a rocket scientist to use a bilingual dictionary, but a little inside knowledge of grammar doesn't hurt. It's important to remember how versatile words can be, and you do that by looking at the entire sentence. This is essential to extrapolating the meaning of the text or even a word that you don't recognize. Look at the word *inside*. Watch how the meaning changes in the following sentences:

The plane should arrive *inside* of an hour. (adverb)

The *inside* walls of the church are covered with art. (adjective)

It is very dark *inside* the tunnel. (preposition)

The *inside* of the Coliseum was once quite beautiful. (noun)

Change *inside* to the plural, and its meaning changes:

She laughed until her *insides* hurt. (colloquial, noun)

The following is what a listing in a good Italian/English dictionary might look like:

inside (in'said) 1. *avv.* dentro, in casa, entro; 2. *agg.* interno, interiore; 3. *prep.* in, dentro; 4. *n.* interno, parte interna (*fam.*), stomaco; informazioni riservate.

Did You Know?

If there's more than one translation listed in your dictionary for a given word, it's important to take your time and skim through the list. After you have found your word, if you are still not sure of whether it is the appropriate translation, look up the word you just chose in its opposite language. For example, if you are looking up the word *mean*, ask yourself whether you want the adjective *mean* (as in nasty) or the verb *to mean* (as in "to signify").

Practice Makes **Perfetto**

Using the Italian definitions just given, figure out the part of speech for "inside" in each of the following sentences, and complete the translated sentences in Italian:

1. We live inside the walls of the city.

   Abitiamo _____ le mura della città.

2. The woman's insides hurt.

   Alla donna fa male lo _____.

3. We will arrive home inside an hour.

   Arriviamo a casa _____ un'ora.

4. He has inside information on the *Palio*.

   Lui ha _____ sul Palio.

5. The inside of the church is dark.

   L' _____ della chiesa è scuro.

La Bella Lingua

Keep an eye out for English movies that have an Italian theme. You can improve your Italian without having to read a thing. Some titles include these:

Avanti

Big Night

Down by Law

The Godfather

Good Morning Babylon

Indiscretion of an American Housewife

Moonstruck

Queen of Hearts

Stealing Beauty

Summertime

Chapter 19, "Having Fun Italian Style," offers you additional suggestions.

What's the Object; Who's the Subject?

Okay, let's go back to the seventh grade again. The sun is shining outside the school windows, and the teacher is droning on about objects and subjects. As she's speaking, you're on the verge of falling asleep. The room is too hot, you're bored, and you're thinking, "I'm never going to need this to do anything!"

Of course, in retrospect, you know better. But you still aren't quite sure what an object is, unless it's something unidentified and coming from parts unknown.

Use a sentence from your first-grade book to look at what an object is …

Jack throws Jane a ball.

First things first. Take a *minuto* to find the *verbo* in this sentence. Remember, verbs are where the action is.

Did you figure out it was the verb "to throw"? *Bravi!* You're on your way. Next question: Who threw the ball? Answer: Jack did, that's who—and he is your subject.

The million-*lire* question now is, what did Jack throw? Answer: The ball! That's the direct object. A direct object is the recipient of the verb's action.

In sentences with two nouns following the verb, the first is generally the indirect object, the word that tells to whom or for whom the action was done (Jane).

Let's continue with Jack and Jane. Jane, never one to say no to a challenge, decides to keep the ball rolling. Analyze the next sentence for its subject and object pronouns:

She throws it back to him.

Did you figure out that "she" is the subject pronoun (substituting for "Jane") and "it" (substituting for "ball") is the object pronoun? So you see, there's nothing to worry about. You know everything you need to get this ball rolling and learn the language you've always dreamed of knowing.

La Bella Lingua

Make a list of 10 topics you would like to be able to talk about in Italian. Put the list at the front of your notebook so that you're reminded of your goals.

Drawing from *Esperienza*

Have you ever studied another *lingua?* Perhaps you took *spagnolo* when you were in high school. At the urging of your parents, you might have studied *Latino,* and after three semesters of it, all you can remember are the words *veni, vedi, vici* (came, saw, conquered). Whatever the last language was that you studied, whether it was *francese, russo, ebreo* (Hebrew), or *cinese,* it will be the first *lingua* to come out of your mouth

La Bella Lingua

If you can't think of the Italian word, use the word you remember from the last *lingua* you studied. If your *frase* comes out one-third *italiano*, one-third *francese*, and one-third *inglese*, it's still better than nothing.

La Bella Lingua

Pull out your old notes from the last time you studied a foreign *lingua*. If you've been out of *scuola* for a while, they will be a good reminder. You may be surprised to see that you actually learned something back then, even if your heart wasn't in it. As you wallow in nostalgic longing for those years, remind yourself that there's no time like the *presente* to begin something new.

when you try mustering up some Italian. It's *naturale*—your brain retains everything, although some of the *informazione* ends up stored away until you decide to dust off the cobwebs and reopen the files.

Your pronunciation may initially reflect those first language classes, but you'll soon be rounding your R's and wooing your partner Italian-style in no time flat. If you have studied another Romance language, you'll already be familiar with the basic *struttura* of Italian. Let's take a look at some of those basic *regole* (rules):

➤ All Romance languages possess masculine and feminine nouns.

➤ The definite article (the) agrees in gender and number with the noun it modifies.

➤ All adjectives must agree in both gender and plurality with the nouns they modify. *Per esempio,* if a noun is feminine singular, its adjective must also be feminine singular, as in *la lingua italiana.*

➤ As a general rule, most adjectives come after the noun, as with *il vino buono* and *la casa bianca.*

➤ All Romance languages possess a polite as well as a familiar form of "you." The polite form, *Lei,* is capitalized to distinguish it from *lei,* meaning "she," and should be used with strangers, authority figures, and elders. The familiar form, *tu,* is used with friends and children.

Read It, Write It, Say It

Writing things down helps you to retain the things you have read or heard. Your body will remember in ways your mind will not. Studying aloud will get your mouth into the habit of helping you to *ricordare*. If you read the words, write them down, and read aloud, you'll be speaking in no time.

The Least You Need to Know

➤ Italian comes from Latin and is connected to a history steeped in *tradizione*.

➤ You have no reason to be intimidated by grammar. Understanding the different parts of speech takes away the mystery of learning a second language.

➤ A bilingual *dizionario* is essential to language learning and can help you identify different parts of speech and understand common Italian expressions.

➤ Dante, Boccaccio, and Petrarca are three of Italy's greatest writers.

Chapter 3

Sound Like an Italian

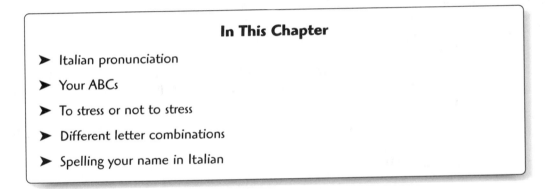

In This Chapter

➤ Italian pronunciation

➤ Your ABCs

➤ To stress or not to stress

➤ Different letter combinations

➤ Spelling your name in Italian

Learning a new language is like having a box filled with puzzle pieces that haven't been fit together. At first, it's all just a jumble of sounds and letters and words, but slowly, almost imperceptibly, your *confusione* is replaced with *comprensione* as a clear picture emerges.

Italian Pronunciation

Initially, it seems as though anyone speaking Italian is singing. There is a continuity and fluidity that reminds you of a beautifully sustained note. This has a great deal to do with the fact that almost all Italian words end in a vowel and are often pronounced as if joined together.

With few exceptions, Italian pronunciation is very easy to learn. As a phonetic language, what you see is what you say—at least most of the time. Once you learn how to read the music, you'll be able to play along with anyone.

The key is to understand the basic differences between the English and Italian rules of pronunciation. For example, in Italian, the word *cinema* is written exactly the same as

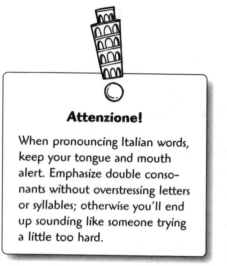

in English; however, in Italian it is pronounced *chee-nee-mah*. The same *ci* is used in the word *ciao*.

You'll find that certain Italian sounds may initially present a challenge to the English speaker, most notably the rolled *R* and the letter combination *gli* (pronounced *ylee*, like "million"). Nonetheless, after some time even these sounds will come easily to the attentive listener.

Italian requires clean diction with clearly pronounced vowels and *s*. Double consonants in words such as *anno* (year), *birra* (beer), and *gatto* (cat) should be emphasized. Avoid sounding overly nasal or guttural.

You will see less of the pronunciation in later chapters. Flip back to this chapter if you are not sure of how a word should be pronounced.

Your ABCs

The Italian language uses the Latin alphabet. Unlike English, however, the Italian alphabet contains only 21 letters, borrowing the letters *j, k, w, x,* and *y* for words of foreign origin.

As you read, you'll discover that the spelling of Italian words follows a logical pattern.

Getting the Accent

In this case, we're not talking about what Sofia Loren and Roberto Benigni have when speaking English. Italian uses the grave accent (`), pronounced *grav*, on words where the stress falls on the final syllable: *caffè, città, università.*

With Italians being who they are, and Italian being what it is, you may also see the acute accent used (especially in older text and phrasebooks), particularly with the words *benché* (although) and *perché* (because/why). Don't be surprised to find conflicting examples.

The written accent is also used to distinguish several Italian words from others that have the same spelling but a different meaning.

è	is	*e*	and
sì	yes	*si*	oneself
dà	gives	*da*	from
sè	himself	*se*	if
là	there	*la*	the
né	nor	*ne*	some

La Bella Lingua

In Italian, the apostrophe is generally used to indicate the dropping of the final vowel:

l'animale instead of *lo animale*

d'Italia instead of *di Italia*

dov'è instead of *dove è*

Don't Get Stressed Out

As a rule, most Italian words are stressed on the next-to-last syllable, such *signorina* (*see-nyoh-**ree**-nah*), and *minestrone* (*mee-neh-**stroh**-neh*).

Exceptions exist, making rules rather difficult to follow. Some words are stressed on the third-to-last syllable, such as *automobile* (*ow-toh-**moh**-bee-leh*) and *dialogo* (*dee-**ah**-loh-goh*).

Other words—mostly verb forms—are stressed on the fourth-to-last syllable, such as *studiano* (*stoo-dee-ah-noh*), and *telefonano* (*teh-**leh**-foh-nah-noh*).

Finally, stress should be placed on the last syllable when you see an accent mark at the end of a word, such as *città* (*chee-**tah***), *università* (*oo-nee-ver-see-**ta***), and *virtù* (*veer-**too***).

I've indicated in the early chapters where to put the stress in words of three syllables or more, and in words of two syllables with an accented (and thus stressed) syllable. In the future, consult a good dictionary when you are unclear about which syllable should be emphasized. Generally, you will see either an accent placed above, or a dot placed below the stressed vowel.

Attenzione!

Some Italian letter combinations are seldom found in English. These sounds include the *gl* combination in words such as *figlio* (son) (pronounced *fee-lyoh*); the word *gli* (the) (pronounced *ylee*, like the *ll* in the English word *million*); and the *gn* combination, seen in words such as *gnocchi* (potato dumplings) (pronounced *nyoh-kee*), and *bagno* (bathroom) (pronounced *bah-nyoh*, like the *ny* sound in *canyon* or the *ni* sound in *onion*).

As a Rule

For the purposes of clarity, the pronunciation used in this text is designed to be read phonetically.

Always remember to enunciate vowels clearly and not to slur your words. Say what you see.

Double *RR*'s should be held and emphasized when trilled.

Double consonants should always be emphasized—but never as separate sounds. They should be joined and slide into one another, as in the word *pizza* (*pee-tsah*).

Rolling Your *R's*

There are a few sounds in Italian that are not found in English, the most obvious being the rolled *R*. Some people can roll their *R*'s forever, but if you are not one of them, here's a mini-guide on rolling your *R:* place the tip of your tongue so that it's touching the roof of your mouth just behind your front teeth. Now curl the tip of your tongue and exhale. You should get the beginning trill of a rolled *R*. Once you get it, be subtle—a little trill will do.

La Bella Lingua

In linguistic parlance, the term "rhotacism" is defined, among other things, as the incorrect or overuse of *R*'s in pronunciation.

The Long and the Short of It: Vowels

The Italian word for "vowel"—*vocale*—is almost the same as the English word "vocal," a good reminder that Italian vowels should always be pronounced clearly. If you can master the vowels, you're already halfway to the point of sounding Italian. The following table shows how the vowels are pronounced. Read aloud to practice.

Pronouncing Vowels Properly

Vowel	Sound	Example	Pronunciation
a	*ah*	*artista*	ar-***tee***-stah
e	*eh*	*elefante*	eh-leh-***fahn***-teh
i	*ee*	*isola*	***ee***-zoh-lah
o	*oh*	*opera*	***oh***-peh-rah
u	*oo*	*uno*	*oo-noh*

The Hard and Soft of It: Consonants

The following table contains a list of consonants and includes letters recognized in foreign languages. Once you get the hang of it, Italian is so easy to pronounce that it would be just as simple to read the words without the pronunciation guide. Most Italian consonants are pronounced like the English ones. It's the different letter combinations that take a little study. Roll on.

Pronouncing Consonants Properly

Letter	Sound	Example	Pronunciation	Meaning
b	*bee*	*bambino*	bahm-***bee***-noh	child, m.
c + a, o, u	hard *c* (as in "cat")	*candela*	kahn-***deh***-lah	candle
c + e, i	*ch* (as in "chest")	*centro*	chen-troh	center/downtown
ch	hard *c* (as in "cat")	*Chianti*	kee-***ahn***-tee	Chianti (a red wine)
d	*dee*	*due*	doo-eh	two
f	*eff*	*frase*	frah-zeh	phrase
g + a, o, u	hard *g* (as in "go")	*gatto*	gah-toh	cat
g + e, i	*j* (as in "gem")	*gentile*	jen-***tee***-leh	kind
gli	*ylee* (as in "million")	*figlio*	fee-lyoh	son
gn	*nya* (as in "onion")	*gnocchi*	nyoh-kee	potato dumplings
h	silent	*hotel*	oh-tel	hotel
j*	*juh* (hard j)	*jazz*	jaz	jazz
k*	*kuh* (hard k)	*koala*	koh-***ah***-lah	koala
l	*ell*	*lingua*	leen-gwah	language
m	*em*	*madre*	mah-dreh	mother

continues

Pronouncing Consonants Properly (continued)

Letter	Sound	Example	Pronunciation	Meaning
n	*en*	*nido*	*nee-doh*	nest
p	*pee*	*padre*	*pah-dreh*	father
q	*kew*	*quanto*	*kwahn-toh*	how much
r	*er* (slightly rolled)	*Roberto*	*roh-**ber**-toh*	Robert
rr	*err* (really rolled)	*birra*	*bee-rah*	beer
s (at beginning of word)	*ess* (as in "see")	*serpente*	*ser-**pen**-teh*	snake
s	*s* (as in "rose")	*casa*	*kah-zah*	house
sc + a, o	*sk*	*scala*	*skah-lah*	stair
sc + e, i	*sh*	*scena*	*sheh-nah*	scene
t	*tee*	*tavola*	***tah**-voh-lah*	table
v	*v*	*vino*	*vee-noh*	wine
w*	*wuh*	*Washington*	***wash**-eeng-ton*	Washington
x*	*eeks*	*raggi-x*	*rah-jee eeks*	x-ray
y*	*yuh*	*yoga*	*yoh-gah*	yoga
z	*z*	*zebra*	*zeh-brah*	zebra
zz	*ts*	*pazzo*	*pah-tsoh*	crazy

*These letters are used in words of foreign origin.

La Bella Lingua

The best way to remember how a particular letter combination should be pronounced is to simply recall a word that you already know. *Per esempio,* the word *ciao* is pronounced with the soft *c,* as in "chow." Other words with the *c + i* combination include *cinema, bacio,* and *amici.*

The word *Chianti* is pronounced with a hard *c,* as in *kee-**ahn**-tee.* When you come across other words (such as *chi* and *perchè*) with this combination, you'll know just how they're pronounced.

Practice Those Vowels

Now try to pronounce these words, focusing just on the vowels.

A

Say *ah*, as in "father":

madre	fila	canto	casa	strada	mela
mah-dreh	*fee-lah*	*kahn-toh*	*kah-zah*	*strah-dah*	*meh-lah*
(mother)	(line)	(song)	(home)	(street)	(apple)

E

Say *eh*, as in "make" or "let":

padre	sera	festa	bene	età	pensione
pah-dreh	*seh-rah*	*fes-tah*	*beh-neh*	*eh-tah*	*pen-see-oh-neh*
(father)	(evening)	(party)	(well)	(age)	(motel)

I

Say *ee*, as in "feet":

idiota	piccolo	pulire	in	idea	turista
ee-dee-oh-tah	*pee-koh-loh*	*poo-lee-reh*	*een*	*ee-deh-ah*	*too-ree-stah*
(idiot)	(small)	(to clean)	(in)	(idea)	(tourist)

O

Say *oh*, as in "note" or "for":

donna	bello	cosa	albero	gatto	uomo
doh-nah	*beh-loh*	*koh-zah*	*ahl-beh-roh*	*gah-toh*	*woh-moh*
(woman)	(beautiful)	(thing)	(tree)	(cat)	(man)

U

Say *oo*, as in "crude":

luna	una	cubo	lupo	tuo
loo-nah	*oo-nah*	*koo-boh*	*loo-poh*	*too-oh*
(moon)	(a)	(cube)	(wolf)	(your)

Give Me the Combo

Italian pronunciation follows a pretty consistent, easy-to-remember format. The rules change depending on what vowel is connected to what consonant. By remembering even one word's pronunciation that follows a given rule, you can always fall back on that word as a way of checking yourself.

The following examples illustrate many letter combinations you'll find in Italian.

C *Is for* Casa

Look at all that you can do with the letter *c*.

Letter Combination		Sound	Pronunciation Guide
c + a, o, u		k	Say *c*, as in "camp"

casa	amico	caro	bocca
kah-zah	*ah-**mee**-koh*	*kah-roh*	*boh-kah*
(house)	(friend)	(expensive/dear)	(mouth)
colore	conto	cultura	giacca
*koh-**loh**-reh*	*kohn-toh*	*kool-**too**-rah*	*jah-kah*
(color)	(bill/check)	(culture)	(jacket)

Letter Combination		Sound	Pronunciation Guide
c + h		k	Say *c*, as in "camp"

chiamare	occhio	perché	Machiavelli
*kee-ah-**mah**-reh*	***oh**-kee-yoh*	*per-keh*	*mah-kee-ah-**veh**-lee*
(to call)	(eye)	(why)	(Machiavelli)
chiaro	chiuso	macchina	ricchi
*kee-**ah**-roh*	*kee-yoo-zoh*	***mah**-kee-nah*	*ree-kee*
(clear/light)	(closed)	(car)	(rich, m.p.)

Letter Combination		Sound	Pronunciation Guide
c + e, i		ch	Say *ch*, as in "cherry"

accento	cena	città	ceramica
*ah-**chen**-toh*	*che-nah*	*chee-**tah***	*cheh-**rah**-mee-kah*
(accent)	(dinner)	(city)	(ceramic)
ciao	bacio	Francia	cioccolata
chow	*bah-choh*	*frahn-chah*	*choh-koh-**lah**-tah*
(hi/bye)	(kiss)	(France)	(chocolate)

G *Is for* Gamba

Practice getting your *g*'s right.

Letter Combination		Sound	Pronunciation Guide
g + a, o, u		g	Say *g*, as in "great"

gamba	lago	gufo	prego
gahm-bah	*lah-goh*	*goo-foh*	*preh-goh*
(leg)	(lake)	(owl)	(you're welcome)

gambero	mago	strega	gusto
gahm-beh-roh	*mah-goh*	*streh-gah*	*goo-stoh*
(shrimp)	(wizard)	(witch)	(taste)

The letter combination *gh* is also pronounced like the *g* in *go*, as in *funghi* (mushrooms).

Letter Combination		Sound	Pronunciation Guide
g + e, i		j	Say *g* as in "gem"

gelato	giovane	giacca	viaggio
jeh-lah-toh	*joh-vah-neh*	*jah-kah*	*vee-ah-joh*
(ice cream)	(young)	(jacket)	(voyage)
formaggio	gente	giorno	maggio
for-mah-joh	*jen-teh*	*jor-noh*	*mah-joh*
(cheese)	(people)	(day)	(May)

Letter Combination		Sound	Pronunciation Guide
g + n		ny	Say "onion"

lavagna	signore	legno	gnocchi
lah-vah-nyah	*see-nyoh-reh*	*leh-nyoh*	*nyoh-kee*
(blackboard)	(sir, Mr.)	(wood)	(potato dumplings)
ragno	compagna	signora	guadagno
rah-nyoh	*kohm-pah-nyah*	*see-nyoh-rah*	*gwah-dah-nyoh*
(spider)	(countryside)	(Mrs., Ms.)	(earnings)

S Is for Scandolo

The letter *s* is quite slippery.

Letter Combination		Sound	Pronunciation Guide
sc + a, h, o, u		sk	Say *sk,* as in "skin"

sconto	scusa	scandalo	pesca
skohn-toh	*skoo-zah*	*skahn-dah-loh*	*pes-kah*
(discount)	(excuse)	(scandal)	(peach)
scuola	schifo	fiasco	schizzo
skwoh-lah	*skee-foh*	*fee-ah-skoh*	*skee-tsoh*
(school)	(disgust)	(fiasco)	(sketch)

Letter Combination		Sound	Pronunciation Guide
sc + e, i		sh	Say *sh,* as in "sheet"
sci	pesce	scena	lasciare
shee	*peh-sheh*	*sheh-nah*	*lah-**shah**-reh*
(skiing)	(fish)	(scene)	(to leave something)
sciroppo	sciocco	sciopero	scelto
*shee-**roh**-poh*	*shee-**oh**-koh*	***shoh**-peh-roh*	*shel-toh*
(syrup)	(fool)	(strike)	(choice)

As a Rule

Try using this expression the next time you want to ask someone how to say something in Italian:

Come si dice ...? (How do you say ...?)

Question: *Come si dice* ice cream *in italiano?*

Answer: *Si dice* gelato.

Did you notice any similarity between the words you just read and their English counterparts? You know more than you think! It's important to see how much Italian and English share. Remember that a lot of English derives from Latin. It helps to make associations with familiar words. Each time you do this, you are creating a bridge from one shore to another. For example, the word *luna* (moon) comes from Latin, as we see in the English word "lunatic." It was once believed that "lunacy" came from the full moon. All sorts of associations can be made to "illuminate" (in Italian, *illuminare*) these connections.

Attenzione!

Say "Ah!" The real key to success is to make sure you are pronouncing your vowels correctly: *a* (ah), *e* (eh), *i* (ee), *o* (oh), and *u* (oo).

Dipthongs

No, a dipthong is not a teeny-weeny bikini. The term "diphthong" refers to any pair of vowels that begins with one vowel sound and ends with a different vowel sound within the same syllable. The term literally means "two voices" (*di* = "two"; *thong* = "tongue/ voice") and originally comes from Greek.

Italian utilizes many diphthongs such as *olio* (pronounced *ohl-yoh*), *quanto* (*kwahn-toh*), and *pausa* (*pow-sah*). Keep in mind that not all pairs of vowels form dipthongs.

Double Consonants

Anytime you see a double consonant in a word, such as *birra* (beer) or *anno* (year), it is important to emphasize that consonant, or you may be misunderstood. Take a look at a few words whose meanings change when there is a double consonant. As you will see, in some cases you *definitely* want to emphasize those double consonants:

ano (ah-noh): anus	*anno (ahn-noh):* year
casa (kah-zah): house	*cassa (kahs-sah):* cash register
pena (peh-nah): pity	*penna (pehn-nah):* pen
pene (peh-neh): penis	*penne (pen-neh):* pens
sete (seh-teh): thirsty	*sette (set-teh):* seven
sono (so-noh): I am	*sonno (sohn-noh):* sleepy

As a Rule

Unless beginning a word, a single *s* is pronounced like *z*, as in the name *Gaza*, or *s*, as in "busy" and the Italian word *casa* (house).

A double *ss* is pronounced like the *s* in the English word "tassel" and the Italian word *passo* (pass).

A single *z* is pronounced like the *z* in the word "zebra."

A double *zz* is pronounced like the *ts* in the English word "cats" and the Italian word *piazza* (plaza).

Double consonants will not be highlighted in the pronunciation. It's up to you to emphasize them. Practice pronouncing the following words, remembering to slide the syllables together:

mamma	sorella	cappello	atto	pazzo	bocca	Anna
mah-mah	*soh-**reh**-lah*	*kah-**peh**-loh*	*ah-toh*	*pah-tsoh*	*boh-kah*	*ah-nah*
(mom)	(sister)	(hat)	(act)	(crazy)	(mouth)	(Ann)

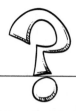

What's What

In Italian, two vowels do not necessarily produce a diphthong. The word *zia* (*zee–ah*) maintains two distinct, separate sounds and consequently does not produce a diphthong.

On the other hand, the word *Italia* (*ee–tahl–yah*) does produce a diphthong.

Keep in mind that diphthongs are always pronounced as one sound.

A Is for *Ancona*

When spelling out words, rather than using proper names like you do in English (*T* as in Tom), Italians often use the names of Italian cities. For example, *A come Ancona, I come Imola, T come Torino* (*A* as in *Ancona, I* as in *Imola, T* as in *Torino*), and so on. A practical way of remembering the alphabet is to learn how to spell your name in Italian. The name of the Italian letter is given beside the letter. The stressed syllable is in bold. Examples of foreign letters are given with commonly used nouns.

Letter	Italian Name of Letter	Example	Pronunciation
A	*a*	*Ancona*	*ahn-**koh**-nah*
B	*bi*	*Bologna*	*boh-**loh**-nyah*
C	*ci*	*Cagliari*	***kahl**-yah-ree*
D	*di*	*Domodossola*	*doh-moh-**doh**-soh-lah*
E	*e*	*Empoli*	***em**-poh-lee*
F	*effe*	*Firenze*	*fee-**ren**-zeh*
G	*gi*	*Genova*	***jeh**-noh-vah*
H	*acca*	*hotel*	*oh-tel*
I	*i*	*Imola*	*ee-moh-lah*
J*	*i lunga*	*jolly*	*jah-lee*
K*	*cappa*	*kaiser*	*ky-zer*
L	*elle*	*Livorno*	*lee-**vor**-noh*
M	*emme*	*Milano*	*mee-**lah**-noh*
N	*enne*	*Napoli*	***nah**-poh-lee*
O	*o*	*Otranto*	*oh-**tran**-toh*
P	*pi*	*Palermo*	*pah-**ler**-moh*

Letter	Italian Name of Letter	Example	Pronunciation
Q	*cu*	*quaderno* (notebook)	kwah-**der**-noh
R	*erre*	*Roma*	roh-mah
S	*esse*	*Sassari*	**sah**-sah-ree
T	*ti*	*Torino*	toh-**ree**-noh
U	*u*	*Udine*	**oo**-dee-neh
V	*vu*	*Venezia*	veh-**neh**-zee-ah
W*	*doppia vu*	*Washington*	**wash**-eeng-ton
X*	*Ics̀*	raggi-x	rah-jee eek-seh
Y*	*ipsilon*	York	*york*
Z	*zeta*	Zara	*zah-rah*

These letters have been borrowed from other languages.

Get Help!

The best way to learn how to speak another language is to spend time listening to it. If you don't have live entertainment, some suggestions include these:

➤ **Audiocassettes.** Visit your local *biblioteca* (library) or *libreria* (bookstore) to see what they have on hand. Audio cassettes are excellent for developing listening skills. You may want to see if your local *università* has a language lab you can use.

La Bella Lingua

Expand your vocabulary. Play the Italian name game with friends interested in learning Italian. Using the letters of a famous Italian name, see how many Italian words you can come up with. Keep your Italian dictionary close by.

For example: Leonardo Di Caprio

leone (lion)	*capra* (goat)
lepra (hare)	*rana* (frog)
principe (prince)	*cena* (dinner)
onore (honor)	*delirio* (delirium)

➤ **Language CDs for the computer.** If you're computer-savvy, invest in an Italian/English *dizionario* or educational translation program appropriate for your computer and purposes. Some even have "talking" programs that will pronounce the words for you.

➤ **Internet.** There are many wonderful sites now offering audio samples.

➤ **Music.** Listen to the Italian radio station or invest in some music you've never heard before. Aside from opera, you'll find Italian hip-hop, rock and roll, and traditional folk songs, often with lyrics. Listen to the different dialects.

Patience and Practice Pay Off

Anyone who has ever studied—or even heard someone studying—a new musical instrument knows that the first time you pick up a violin, you're not going to sound like a *virtuoso* (yet another Italian word). Fortunately, learning Italian is much easier than playing a *violino*. With a dash of *pazienza*, a dollop of dedication, and a pinch of *pratica*, you'll be rolling your *R*'s and sounding like a true Italian speaker in no time. Keep renting films, listening to *musica*, and getting out there. Practice makes *perfetto*.

The Least You Need to Know

➤ Let your tongue do the talking. Tickle a single *R*, but rrrrrrroll your double *RR*'s. Rev them like an engine, purr like a cat, or growl like a bear.

➤ Don't slur—enunciate vowels, yet keep your Italian from sounding forced and unnatural.

➤ Fluidity is key. Slide those syllables together!

➤ Look for interesting Italian Web sites and language cassettes to support your language studies.

➤ Practice, practice, practice!

Chapter 4

You Know More Than You Think

In This Chapter

➤ Bridging the gap between languages by using cognates

➤ You know a lot more Italian than you think

➤ Breaking it down: the nouns, verbs, and adjectives you already know

➤ Why you should beware of false friends (in the Italian language, that is!)

What if you were told that you were already halfway to speaking Italian? The fact is, you are. Remember that English, although a Germanic language, contains many words of Latin origin. The list of Italian words you already know is longer than you can imagine. Some are virtually the same, whereas most are easily identified by their similarity to English. *Telefono, attenzione, università, automobile, studente*—the list goes on and on.

Cognates: A Bridge Between Languages

Cognates show how seemingly different languages are connected. Any words that are similar to and look the same as other words in a foreign language are called *cognates*, or, in Italian, *parole simili* (literally, "similar words"). By the end of this chapter, you will be in the know for one of the mysteries of language learning—and with this key, many doors will be opened. *Andiamo!* (Let's go!)

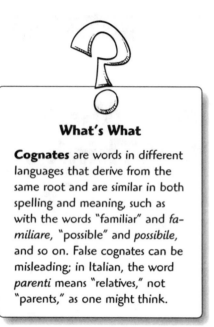

What's What

Cognates are words in different languages that derive from the same root and are similar in both spelling and meaning, such as with the words "familiar" and *familiare*, "possible" and *possibile*, and so on. False cognates can be misleading; in Italian, the word *parenti* means "relatives," not "parents," as one might think.

A Little Fantasia

You get off the *aeroplano* in Roma and push your way through *la dogana*—no, you're not declaring anything. You hail a *tassì* and tell the driver you want to go to *centro,* where an adorable *pensione* that a friend recommended awaits your *arrivo*. As you race away from the chaos of the *aeroporto* and onto the *autostrada,* you are amazed by how *veloce* the *automobili* travel; everyone seems to be in such a hurry!

The driver of the *tassì* asks *È la Sua prima volta in Italia?* You smile and nod your head: *Sì*. You saw the word *primo* from the last time you ordered a plate of pasta in your local Italian *ristorante* and remember that it means "first," like the word "primary." You guess that the driver is asking you if this is your first time in Italy, and you are amazed at how this *comunicazione* seems so *naturale*. It's a strange *sensazione,* but you feel as though you've been here before. How could that be?

As a Rule

Many English words can be made into Italian simply by changing the endings. Look what happens with the following examples:

English to Italian Endings	English to Italian Examples
–ty → –tà	identity → *identità*
–ble → –ibile	possible → *possibile*
–tion → –zione	action → *azione*
–ous → –oso	famous → *famoso*
–ent → –ente	president → *presidente*
–ence → –enza	essence → *essenza*
–ism → –ismo	socialism → *socialismo*

As a Rule

English has only one definite article: the. Italian has several definite articles, all of which indicate gender (masculine or feminine) and number (singular or plural). When you look at the following list of cognates, you'll notice that all Italian nouns are marked by a definite article. Although the gender of nouns is easily identifiable in Italian, it is best to learn the noun with its appropriate definite article. It might seem confusing at first. For now, keep in mind the following:

➤ *Il* is for masculine singular nouns.

➤ *Lo* is for masculine singular nouns beginning with *s* + consonant, or *z*.

➤ *L'* is for any singular noun that begins with a vowel.

➤ *La* is for feminine singular nouns.

If It Looks Like a Duck ...

The Italian language has only a few perfect cognates—such as the words "banana," "opera," "panorama," "pizza," "via," and "zebra." Although the endings and pronunciation may be slightly differente, near cognates are essentially the same.

La Bella Lingua

Collect menus from your favorite Italian *ristorante* and study the *ingredienti* for each *piatto*. Often, what sounds exotic is simply a description of the food. Angel hair pasta, called *capellini*, literally means "thin hairs." The ear-shaped pasta called *orecchiette* refers to "little ears." *Calzone* comes from the word *calza*, due to its resemblance to a cheese-filled "sock."

Let's start out with cognates of place and time. Study the places and the time and dates in the following two tables to get *un'idea* of how many *parole simili* exist between Italian and English. Nine out of ten times, your initial gut response will be correct—trust it!

Where in the World: Places

Where to begin? Wherever you are. Look at the cognates in the following table. Each noun is given with the appropriate definite article to get you started understanding gender.

La Bella Lingua

Why memorize a hundred words when you can study a handful of endings? The *possibilità* are endless!

Although exceptions exist, it's amazing how many English words can be easily converted into Italian by substituting a little letter:

English		Italian	Examples
al	→	o	practical → *pratico*
c	→	z	force → *forza*
k, ck	→	c, cc	sack → *sacco*
ph	→	f	telephone → *telefono*
th	→	t	theater→ *teatro*
x	→	s, ss	external → *esterno*
xt	→	st	extreme → *estremo*
y	→	i	style → *stile*

Places

Italian	English	Italian	English
l'aeroporto	the airport	*l'appartamento*	the apartment
l'agenzia	the agency	*la banca*	the bank

Italian	English	Italian	English
il bar	the bar	*l'oceano*	the ocean
il caffè	the café	*l'ospedale*	the hospital
il castello	the castle	*il paradiso*	the paradise
la cattedrale	the cathedral	*la piazza*	the plaza
il centro	center/downtown	*il ristorante*	the restaurant
il cinema	the cinema	*lo stadio*	the stadium
il circo	the circus	*la stazione*	the station
la città	the city	*lo studio*	the studio/office
la corsa	the course/track	*il supermercato*	the supermarket
la discoteca	the discoteque	*il teatro*	the theatre
la farmacia	the pharmacy	*la terrazza*	the terrace
il giardino	the garden	*l'ufficio*	the office
il mercato	the market	*l'ufficio postale*	the post office
la montagna	the mountain	*il villaggio*	the village
il museo	the museum		

It's About Time

You don't know what time it is? Sure you do—the following table lists some cognates related to time.

Time and Dates

Italian	English	Italian	English
l'anniversario	the anniversary	*il minuto*	the minute
annuale	annual	*la notte*	the night
biennale	biannual	*l'ora*	the hour
la data	the date	*il secondo*	the second
la festa	the holiday (as in "festive")	*il tempo*	the time (also, weather)
il millennio	the millennium		

How Intelligente You Are!

Convert the following words into Italian by changing the endings accordingly.

1. position   *posizione*
2. incredible   _____
3. nation   _____
4. presence   _____
5. identity   _____

6. pessimism   _____
7. prudent   _____
8. continent   _____
9. religious   _____
10. difference   _____

Adjectives: How Grande!

Thinking about everything you've learned so far in this chapter on cognates, cover the English translation in the following table with a piece of paper, and try to guess the meanings of these adjective cognates.

Cognate Adjectives

Italian	English	Italian	English
alto	tall	*moderno*	modern
ambizioso	ambitious	*naturale*	natural
biondo	blond	*necessario*	necessary
bruno	brunette	*nervoso*	nervous
calmo	calm	*normale*	normal
cortese	courteous	*numeroso*	numerous
curioso	curious	*onesto*	honest
delizioso	delicious	*organizzato*	organized
differente	different	*popolare*	popular
divorziato	divorced	*possibile*	possible
eccellente	excellent	*povero*	poor
elegante	elegant	*pratico*	practical
energico	energetic	*rapido*	rapid
falso	false	*ricco*	rich
famoso	famous	*romantico*	romantic
forte	strong (as in "fortitude")	*saggio*	wise (as in "sage")
fortunato	fortunate	*serio*	serious
frequente	frequent	*sicuro*	secure, sure
geloso	jealous	*sincero*	sincere
generoso	generous	*splendido*	splendid
gentile	kind, gentle	*sposato*	married (think "spouse")
grande	big, grand	*strano*	strange
ignorante	ignorant	*stupendo*	stupendous
importante	important	*stupido*	stupid
impossibile	impossible	*terribile*	terrible
incredibile	incredible	*tropicale*	tropical
intelligente	intelligent	*ultimo*	last, ultimate
interessante	interesting	*violento*	violent
lungo	long	*virtuoso*	virtuous
magnifico	magnificent		

Nouns

While I'm listing cognates, I thought I'd save you the trouble and throw in some nouns as a bonus. Additionally, they are listed according to their gender. Your job is to simply write down what they mean in English.

Masculine Nouns

Study the different articles used in front of these masculine nouns. Do you see a pattern beginning to emerge?

As a Rule

The letter *e* is actually a word, meaning "and." The accented letter *è* is also a word, meaning "is."

Masculine Cognates

Italian Masculine Nouns	English Translation	Italian Masculine Nouns	English Translation
l'aeroplano	_____	*il motore*	_____
l'anniversario	_____	*il museo*	_____
l'arco	_____	*il naso*	_____
l'attore	_____	*l'odore*	_____
l'autobus	_____	*il paradiso*	_____
il caffè	_____	*il presidente*	_____
il colore	_____	*il profumo*	_____
il comunismo	_____	*il programma*	_____
il continente	_____	*il rispetto*	_____
il cotone	_____	*il salario*	_____
il direttore	_____	*il servizio*	_____
il dizionario	_____	*il socialismo*	_____
il dottore	_____	*lo spirito*	_____
l'elefante	_____	*lo studente*	_____
il fatto	_____	*il tassì*	_____
il gruppo	_____	*il tè*	_____
l'idiota	_____	*il telefono*	_____
il limone	_____	*il treno*	_____
il meccanico	_____		

Feminine Nouns

Try the same thing with these feminine nouns in the following table.

Feminine Nouns

Italian Feminine Nouns	English Translation	Italian Feminine Nouns	English Translation
l'arte	_____	l'identità	_____
la bicicletta	_____	l'inflazione	_____
la carota	_____	l'insalata	_____
la chitarra	_____	la lampada	_____
la classe	_____	la lettera	_____
la condizione	_____	la lista	_____
la conversazione	_____	la medicina	_____
la cultura	_____	la musica	_____
la curiosità	_____	la nazione	_____
la depressione	_____	la persona	_____
la dieta	_____	la possibilità	_____
la differenza	_____	la probabilità	_____
la discussione	_____	la professione	_____
l'emozione	_____	la regione	_____
l'esperienza	_____	la religione	_____
l'espressione	_____	la rosa	_____
la festa	_____	la scultura	_____
la figura	_____	la temperatura	_____
la fontana	_____	la turista	_____
la forma	_____	l'università	_____
la fortuna	_____	la violenza	_____
l'idea	_____		

Now you're using that *cervello* of yours! Go ahead, tell the world you're studying Italian. My, aren't you proud?

English Words Used in Italian

Many English nouns have been incorporated into Italian. In Italian, these words are given a gender and, with a few exceptions, are pronounced similarly. Each word is shown with the appropriate Italian definite article.

l'antenna	il cinema	l'hotel	o shock
l'area	il cocktail	il jazz	lo shopping
l'autobus	il computer	i jeans	lo snob
il bar	l'idea	la radio	lo sport
il blues	il film	il rock and roll	il weekend
il camping	l'hamburger	lo shampoo	lo zoo

Trojan Horses—False Friends

A false cognate is a word in Italian that sounds like an English word but means something different. Fortunately, in Italian there aren't many false cognates, or *falsi amici*. The following table shows you a few false cognates of which you should be aware.

False Friends

Italian Word	Meaning	Italian Word	Meaning
ape	bee	*lunatico*	moody
argomento	issue	*magazzino*	department store
camera	room	*marrone*	brown
come	how	*morbido*	soft
con	with	*pesante*	heavy
commozione	emotion	*rumore*	noise
fabbrica	factory	*sano*	healthy
fattoria	farm	*sensibile*	sensitive (not "sensible")
firma	signature	*stampa*	press (not "stamp")
grosso	large	*testa*	head
libreria	bookstore		

How Much Do You Understand Already?

You've unpacked your bags and are ready to hit the town. Read the following sentences and try to determine their meaning. Check your pronunciation guide (especially with those *c*'s and *g*'s) to make sure you sound like a native:

1. *La città è bella.*
2. *Il ristorante è terribile.*
3. *La giacca è grande.*
4. *Il museo è interessante.*
5. *Il servizio è buono.*
6. *La montagna è alta.*

Your Turn

Now write and say the following sentences in Italian. Look back at your cognate list to make sure you are using the appropriate article. The equivalent of is in Italian is *è*.

1. The doctor is elegant.
2. The president is famous.
3. The bank is rich.
4. The violence is terrible.
5. The discussion is important.
6. The idiot is intelligent.

As a Rule

In Italian, adjectives must agree in number and gender with the nouns they modify or describe. In general, masculine nouns use adjectives ending in –o, and feminine nouns use adjectives ending in –a. Everything has to agree, as in *la lingua italiana* or *il dizionario italiano.*

Verb Cognates

Many Italian verbs are so simile to their English counterparts that you will recognize their *significato* almost immediately. *Per fortuna,* it is easy to identify an infinitive *verbo* in Italian because of the endings. Take a look at the following table and see if you can *determinare* the meanings of the verb cognates listed.

Verb Cognates

Verb Cognates	Pronunciation	English
accompagnare	*ah-kom-pah-**nyah**-reh*	to accompany
adorare	*ah-doh-**rah**-reh*	to adore
anticipare	*ahn-tee-chee-**pah**-reh*	to anticipate
arrivare	*ah-ree-**vah**-reh*	to arrive
assistere	*ah-**see**-steh-reh*	to assist
celebrare	*cheh-leh-**brah**-reh*	to celebrate
contare	*kohn-**tah**-reh*	to count
controllare	*kohn-troh-**lah**-reh*	to control
conversare	*kohn-ver-**sah**-reh*	to converse
cooperare	*koo-oh-peh-**rah**-reh*	to cooperate
costare	*koh-**stah**-reh*	to cost
creare	*kreh-**yah**-reh*	to create
danzare	*dan-**zah**-reh*	to dance
decidere	*deh-**chee**-deh-reh*	to decide
descrivere	*deh-**skree**-veh-reh*	to describe
desiderare	*deh-zee-deh-**rah**-reh*	to desire
diminuire	*dee-mee-noo-**ee**-reh*	to diminish

Verb Cognates	Pronunciation	English
disignare	dee-zee-**nyah**-reh	to design/draw
dividere	dee-vee-deh-reh	to divide
donare	doh-**nah**-reh	to donate/give
elevare	eh-leh-**vah**-reh	to elevate
eliminare	eh-lee-mee-**nah**-reh	to eliminate
entrare	ehn-**trah**-reh	to enter
finire	fee-**nee**-reh	to finish
ignorare	ee-nyoh-**rah**-reh	to ignore
immaginare	ee-mah-jee-**nah**-reh	to imagine
invitare	een-vee-**tah**-reh	to invite
istruire	ee-stroo-**ee**-reh	to instruct
modificare	moh-dee-fee-**kah**-reh	to modify
negare	neh-**gah**-reh	to negate
obbedire	oh-beh-**dee**-reh	to obey
osservare	oh-ser-**vah**-reh	to observe
passare	pah-**sah**-reh	to pass
perdonare	per-doh-**nah**-reh	to forgive/pardon
praticare	prah-tee-**kah**-reh	to practice
preferire	preh-feh-**ree**-reh	to prefer
preparare	preh-pah-**rah**-reh	to prepare
presentare	preh-zen-**tah**-reh	to present
prevenire	preh-veh-**nee**-reh	to prevent
riparare	ree-pah-**rah**-reh	to repair/fix
riservare	ree-zer-**vah**-reh	to reserve
rispettare	ree-speh-**tah**-reh	to respect
scrivere	**skree**-veh-reh	to write
studiare	stoo-dee-**ah**-reh	to study
telefonare	tel-eh-foh-**nah**-reh	to telephone
usare	oo-**zah**-reh	to use
vendere	**ven**-deh-reh	to sell (as in "vend")
verificare	veh-ree-fee-**kah**-reh	to verify
visitare	vee-zee-**tah**-reh	to visit

A Piece of Cake

Try to determine the meaning of the following verb cognates. If you can't figure out a particular verb's significance, refer to the verb chart in Chapter 8, "An Action-Packed Adventure."

What's What

The infinitive of a verb is simply a verb in its unconjugated form, as in "to eat," "to study," or "to travel." With few exceptions, there are three kinds of verb endings (also known as verb families) in Italian: *–are, –ere,* and *–ire.*

When you look up a verb in a dictionary, it is important to look it up under its infinitive form. Verbs are perhaps the trickiest aspect of learning any language because they have so many forms, or tenses, such as the present, simple past, future, conditional, and so on. Many Italian verbs change significantly after they are conjugated. As in English, if you do not know that the infinitive form of the word *ate* is "to eat," you cannot find it in the dictionary.

A Piece of Cake

Verb Cognates	English Translation	Verb Cognates	English Translation
alludere	_____	*glorificare*	_____
attribuire	_____	*implicare*	_____
cascare	_____	*indicare*	_____
consistere	_____	*intendere*	_____
convertire	_____	*navigare*	_____
corrispondere	_____	*occupare*	_____
deliberare	_____	*offendere*	_____
detestare	_____	*offrire*	_____
difendere	_____	*operare*	_____
discendere	_____	*pronunziare*	_____
discutere	_____	*raccomandare*	_____
disgustare	_____	*rappresentare*	_____
dissolvere	_____	*resistere*	_____
esaminare	_____	*ricevere*	_____
formare	_____	*rispondere*	_____
funzionare	_____		

Put It All Together

It's time for you to test yourself and see where you stand. How much have you learned so far? Test the waters with the following exercises.

Translation Please

You shouldn't have too much of a problem deciphering the meaning of these cognate-rich sentences:

1. *L'Italia fa parte del continente europeo.* _____
2. *Lo studente studia la matematica e storia.* _____
3. *L'attore è molto famoso nel cinema.* _____
4. *Il meccanico ripara l'automobile.* _____
5. *Il cuoco prepara un'insalata e un antipasto.* _____
6. *Il dottore conversa con il paziente.* _____
7. *La famiglia desidera un appartamento moderno e grande.* _____
8. *La turista giapponese visita il museo e la cattedrale.* _____
9. *Il presidente presenta il programma.* _____
10. *Roberto preferisce la musica classica.* _____

What's Your Take?

Imagine that you have just arrived in Italy, and you want to express your opinions to a fellow traveler. Use what you have learned in this chapter and try to express the following:

1. The chocolate is delicious. _____
2. The restaurant is excellent. _____
3. The city is splendid and magnificent. _____
4. The perfume is elegant. _____
5. The conversation is interesting. _____
6. The doctor is sincere. _____
7. The student is intelligent. _____
8. The museum is important. _____
9. The cathedral is high. _____
10. The train is fast. _____

Attenzione!

Italian adjectives ending in –e are used for both masculine and feminine singular nouns:

La grammatica è interessante.   Grammar is interesting.

Leggo un libro importante.   I'm reading an important book.

Are You Well Read?

The following literary titles here all contain cognates. Give their English equivalents:

Dante—*La Divina Commedia* _____

Di Lampedusa—*Il Gattopardo* _____

Eco—*Il Nome della Rosa* _____

Machiavelli—*Il Principe* _____

Morante—*La Storia* _____

Pirandello—*6 Personaggi in Cerca d'Autore* _____

The Least You Need to Know

➤ Italian and English share many common roots.

➤ Come up with other words that can express your meaning, and you may find a cognate more often than you think. For example, *guardare* is "to look at." Think of a "guard" standing at his post looking over the landscape.

➤ Beware of false friends. You may think you are saying one thing when you actually are saying another.

Chapter 5

Expressively Yours

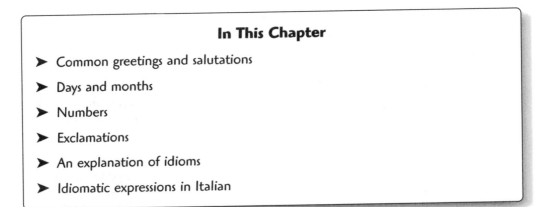

In This Chapter

➤ Common greetings and salutations

➤ Days and months

➤ Numbers

➤ Exclamations

➤ An explanation of idioms

➤ Idiomatic expressions in Italian

The only way to learn a foreign language is to fumble and mumble your way through it. In Chapter 4, "You Know More Than You Think," you saw how many cognates exist in Italian. That should give you a lift—it's time to go to the next level.

How Do You Do?

You should be looking for ways to practice your new salutations whenever there's an opportunity. Maybe it's when you speak to the elegant *signora* who greets you every Friday night at your local Italian *ristorante*. Perhaps it's with your *nonna*, if you can get her to speak in Italian. But if you have no friends or family to practice with, then it'll have to be the television screen as you watch Fellini's *Amarcord* for the fifth time.

You Say Hello and I Say Good-Bye

To start, it helps to know the basics. These are the first things (after the swear words) anyone learns in a foreign language. You want to know how to introduce yourself and be able to say, "Hello, I come in peace."

La Bella Lingua

Try using these expressions the next time you're in Italian-speaking company:

Cosa vuole dire?	What do you mean?
Che cosa significa?	What does it mean?
Come si dice ...?	How do you say ...?
Non capisco.	I don't understand.

Stranger in a Strange Land

You almost always want to begin a *conversazione* with a stranger in the polite form of address. It gives you a chance to warm up to someone and then switch into the *tu* once a relationship has been established. You'll learn more about the different ways of expressing that incredible being that is *you* in Chapter 7, "What's the Subject?"

The following table offers you some helpful greetings and salutations you can use with anyone. As you read aloud, try to sound *naturale*. To help you with the pronunciation, the stress has been indicated in words of three syllables and more. If it has not been indicated, each syllable should be pronounced equally. Emphasize those doubled consonants when you see them.

Formal and Generic Salutations and Expressions

Italian	Pronunciation	English
Buon giorno.	*bwon jor-noh*	Good morning/Good day/Good afternoon/ Hello (use until early afternoon).
Buona sera.	*bwoh-nah seh-rah*	Good evening (begin using after 3:00 P.M.).
Buona notte.	*bwoh-nah noh-teh*	Good night/Good-bye.
Signore	*see-**nyoh**-reh*	Mr./Sir
Signora	*see-**nyoh**-rah*	Mrs./Ms.
Signorina	*see-nyoh-**ree**-nah*	Miss
Come sta?	*koh-meh stah*	How are you?
Sto bene, e Lei?	*stoh beh-neh, eh leh?*	I am well, and you?
Molto bene.	*mol-toh beh-neh*	Very well.
Non c'è male.	*nohn cheh mah-leh*	Not bad.

Italian	Pronunciation	English
Abbastanza bene.	*ah-bah-**stahn**-zah beh-neh*	Pretty well.
Come si chiama?	*koh-meh see kee-**ah**-mah*	What is your name?
Mi chiamo …	*mee kee-**ah**-moh*	My name is (literally, "I call myself") …
Piacere.	*pee-ah-**cheh**-reh*	It's a pleasure.
ArrivederLa.	*ah-ree-veh-**der**-lah*	Until next time.

What's What

Arrivederci literally means "to re-see one another"; the word is commonly used to say good-bye to friends or colleagues. ***ArrivederLa*** is used under more formal circumstances. ***Ci vediamo*** is also used often to express "see you later."

Ciao is similar to saying "hi" and "bye." The term ***salve*** is used in a similar fashion.

The Most Important Phrases in Any Language

The following table summarizes the most important phrases you should learn in any language.

Pleasantries

English	Italian	Pronunciation
Greetings.	*Salve.*	*sal-veh*
Yes.	*Sì.*	*see*
No.	*No.*	*no*
Please.	*Per favore.*	*per fah-**voh**-reh*
	Per piacere.	*per pee-ah-**cheh**-reh*
Thank you.	*Grazie.*	***grah**-tsee-yeh*
Excuse me.	*Mi scusi.*	*mee skoo-zee*
You're welcome.	*Prego.*	*pray-goh*
I'm sorry.	*Mi dispiace.*	*me dees-pee-**ah**-cheh*

continues

Pleasantries (continued)

English	Italian	Pronunciation
Help!	*Aiuto!*	*ah-**yoo**-toh*
Where is ...?	*Dov'è ...?*	*doh-**veh***
How much?	*Quanto?*	*kwahn-toh*

La Bella Lingua

All the ways to say "Thank you" ...

Grazie.	Thank you.
Mille grazie.	Thanks a million.
Tante grazie.	Thanks so much.

... and to say "You're welcome":

Prego.	You're welcome.
Niente.	It's nothing.

Informal Greetings and Salutations

Some useful informal greetings and phrases you can use in more casual, friendly situations are given in the following table. Mix and match.

Informal Salutations

Italian	Pronunciation	English
Ciao!	*chow*	Hi/Bye-bye!
Saluti!	*sah-**loo**-tee*	Greetings!
Salve!	*sahl-veh*	Hello!
Come stai?	*koh-meh stah-ee*	How are you?
Come va?	*koh-meh vah*	How's it going?
Va bene.	*vah beh-neh*	Things are good.
Va benissimo.	*vah beh-**nee**-see-moh*	Things are great.

Italian	Pronunciation	English
Non c'è male.	*nohn cheh mah-leh*	Not bad.
Okay.	*oh-kay*	Okay.
Così così.	*koh-zee koh-zee*	So-so.
Arrivederci.	*ah-ree-veh-der-chee*	See you later.
A più tardi.	*ah pyoo tar-dee*	Until later.
A domani.	*ah doh-mah-nee*	See you tomorrow.
A presto.	*ah pres-toh*	See you soon.

La Bella Lingua

Here are a few exclamations you might hear:

Ahi!	Ouch!
Caspita!	Wow!
Zitto!	Shut up!
Via!	Go away!
Ladro!	Thief!

Communications

You'll want to explain that you're studying Italian. The following expressions will tell you how to tell them what you're doing.

Communications

Italian	Pronunciation	English
Capisco.	*kah-pee-skoh*	I understand.
Non capisco.	*non kah-pee-skoh*	I don't understand.
Non parlo italiano.	*non par-loh ee-tah-lee-ah-noh*	I don't speak Italian.

continues

Communications (continued)

Italian	Pronunciation	English
Studio italiano.	*stoo-dee-oh ee-tah-lee-ah-noh*	I am studying Italian.
Parla inglese?	*par-lah een-gleh-zeh*	Do you speak English?
Capisce?	*kah-pee-sheh*	Do you understand?
Che cosa significa?	*keh koh-zah seeg-nee-fee-kah*	What does it mean?
Che?	*keh*	What?
Come?	*koh-meh*	How?
Dov'è ...?	*doh-veh*	Where is ...?
Lo ripeta per favore.	*loh ree-peh-tah per fah-voh-reh*	Please repeat that.
Non lo so.	*non loh soh*	I don't know.
Parli lentamente per piacere.	*par-lee len-tah-men-teh per pee-ah-cheh-reh*	Please speak slowly.

I Giorni: Days

When pronouncing days of the week, the accent tells you to emphasize the last sylla-ble. Italians have adopted the English way of expressing the end of the week by using our word "weekend," but you will also hear *il fine della settimana*.

Days of the Week

Day of the Week	Italian	Pronunciation
Monday	*lunedì*	*loo-neh-dee*
Tuesday	*martedì*	*mar-teh-dee*
Wednesday	*mercoledì*	*mer-koh-leh-dee*
Thursday	*giovedì*	*joh-veh-dee*
Friday	*venerdì*	*ven-er-dee*
Saturday	*sabato*	*sah-bah-toh*
Sunday	*domenica*	*doh-meh-nee-kah*
the weekend	*il fine settimana*	*eel fee-neh seh-tee-mah-nah*

I Mesi: Months

If you're planning your next trip or want to talk astrology, knowing the month is im-portant. Like the days of the week, the months are not capitalized in Italian. Find that special date in the following table.

Attenzione!

Unlike English, Italian days of the week and months are not capitalized unless beginning a sentence. Proper names, cities, and titles are capitalized.

La Bella Lingua

April showers bring May flowers. Italians have a similar saying, *Aprile, ogni goccia un bacile.* (April, every drop a kiss.)

I Mesi (The Months)

Month	*Mese*	Pronunciation
January	*gennaio*	jeh-**nah**-yoh
February	*febbraio*	feb-**rah**-yoh
March	*marzo*	mar-zoh
April	*aprile*	ah-**pree**-leh
May	*maggio*	mah-joh
June	*giugno*	joo-nyoh
July	*luglio*	loo-lyoh
August	*agosto*	ah-**goh**-stoh
September	*settembre*	seh-**tem**-breh
October	*ottobre*	oh-**toh**-breh
November	*novembre*	noh-**vem**-breh
December	*dicembre*	dee-**chem**-breh

Did You Know?

Here's a little trivial pursuit for you: The original calendar used by the Romans was based on a 10-month year. What two months were added to the calendar?

La Bella Lingua

The days of the week correspond to these planets.

lunedì: la luna (the Moon)

martedì: Marte (Mars)

mercoledì: Mercurio (Mercury)

giovedì: Giove (Jupiter)

venerdì: Venere (Venus)

sabato: Saturno (Saturn)

domenica: (Sunday; refers to "God's day")

Expressing Your Honest Opinion

You can sound like a veritable Italian with just a few exclamations. Start with *Che bello!*

Exclamations

Expression	Pronunciation	Meaning
Che bello!	*keh beh-loh*	How beautiful!
Che brutto!	*keh broo-toh*	How ugly!
Che chiasso!	*keh kee-**ah**-soh*	What a ruckus!

Expression	Pronunciation	Meaning
Che disastro!	keh dee-**sas**-troh	What a disaster!
Eccellente!	eh-cheh-**len**-teh	Excellent!
Fantastico!	fan-**tas**-tee-koh	Fantastic!
Favoloso!	fah-voh-**loh**-zoh	Fabulous!
Magnifico!	mag-**nee**-fee-koh	Magnificent!
Meraviglioso!	meh-rah-vee-**lyoh**-zoh	Marvelous!
Orribile!	oh-**ree**-bee-leh	Horrible!
Ridicolo!	ree-**dee**-koh-loh	Ridiculous!
Stupendo!	stoo-**pen**-doh	Stupendous!
Terribile!	teh-**ree**-bee-leh	Terrible!

Idiomatically Speaking

Okay, now that you've learned the hellos and the good-byes, it's time to move on to the big-people stuff: idioms.

Idioms are important for a complete and correct understanding of a language. They are the spice that makes language interesting. If verbs and grammar are the brain of a language, then idioms are the personality. They express the various idiosyncrasies of the speaker's customs, values, and social mores.

Happy as a Lark

Idiomatic expressions are speech forms that cannot be understood through literal translation; they must be learned and memorized along with their meaning. Many idiomatic expressions find their roots in the truth. For example, common sense dictates that you really shouldn't put all your eggs in one basket.

Often, but not necessarily, there is an allusion to something else, as with the expression "Happy as a lark." If you were a foreigner studying English, would you understand how happy that actually was?

It's the same with Italian. Most idioms cannot be translated without losing their meaning, although occasionally, the same idiom can exist in two or more languages. In Italian, you can ask, *Posso dare una mano?* (literally translating to "Can I give you a hand?") However, in Italian you would not be able to say that it's raining dogs and cats without raising an eyebrow. Do you get the picture?

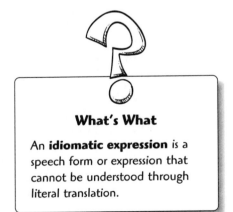

What's What

An **idiomatic expression** is a speech form or expression that cannot be understood through literal translation.

Our speech is peppered with idiomatic expressions or colloquialisms, such as these:

He was caught red-handed.	It's raining cats and dogs.
No strings attached.	Naked as a jay bird.
Don't hold your breath.	Once in a blue moon.
It runs in the family.	Practice makes perfect.
I'm in seventh heaven.	It's up in the air.

Did You Know?

You probably already know a handful of dirty words, aptly called "vulgarities" in grammatical parlance, but did you know that the word "vulgar" comes from Latin and translates to mean "of the people"?

What Is Slang?

Slang is generally regional and refers to unconventional, popular words or phrases that are used in everyday speech. In many respects, slang develops to express what is new and undefined. It sticks a word to a meaning that hadn't necessarily been there before. Of course, obscenities and vulgarities are considered slang. Being in the know, however, is another element of slang. If you speak the same language with someone, there's a natural bond. You can think of slang as a very specialized vocabulary spoken by a small segment of a population. Teenagers use slang. Truckers use slang. Computer geeks use slang. Mothers use slang.

What's up?	Awesome!
Give it up.	You're playing with my head.
What a scene.	Hang out.

Idiomatic Expressions in Italian

The Italian language is packed with idioms—so many, in fact, that it is impossible for even an Italian to know all of them. An innocent word in one region might have a completely different idiomatic usage in another part of the country (often accompanied by a great deal of snickering and laughing).

Although every Italian child is schooled in the standard language spoken on television and used in writing, that child has also been exposed to the idioms, nuances, dialects, and slang particular to the region in which he or she lives. As a result, standard grammar is taught from early on. And make no mistake—the Italians love their language! Not only do they love to talk *in* Italian, but they love to talk *about* Italian. Ask anyone from any walk of life, young or old, about parts of speech, idioms, conjugations, and they'll tick off a dozen examples for you, offering involved explanations and elaborate elucidation.

Lucky for you, many of those idioms are presented in this book. You can start using them immediately, or you can come back to them after you have studied the upcoming chapters.

Did You Know?

March 8 is celebrated internationally as *Il Giorno della Donna* (Woman's Day) to commemorate the Triangle Shirtwaist Fire. On March 25, 1911, this tragic event in New York City took the lives of 146 factory workers, mostly young Italian and Jewish immigrant women. The tragedy led to the creation of many labor laws governing the welfare and safety of workers.

It's All in the Details

Sometimes it's all in the details. For instance, a simple preposition can completely change the significance of an expression.

Study the following idiomatic expressions that describe various modes of transportation and travel. Whereas English speakers use the preposition "by" to describe how they are going somewhere, in Italian, the preposition changes. You'll learn more about how these are used in Chapter 11, "Finally, You're at the Airport."

Idioms for Travel and Transportation

English	Italian	Pronunciation
by bicycle	*in bicicletta*	*een bee-chee-**kleh**-tah*
by boat	*in barca*	*een bar-kah*
by bus	*in autobus*	*een **ow**-toh-boos*
by car	*in macchina*	*een **mah**-kee-nah*
by foot	*a piedi*	*ah pee-**eh**-dee*
by plane	*in aereo*	*een eh-**reh**-roh*
by scooter	*in moto*	*een moh-toh*
by subway	*in metro*	*een met-roh*
by taxi	*in tassì*	*een tah-**see***
by train	*in treno*	*een treh-noh*
on horseback	*a cavallo*	*ah kah-**vah**-loh*

Attenzione!

Although they often impart bits of allegorical wisdom, idioms are not necessarily politically correct. Aside from making everyday speech more interesting, some idioms—such as jokes—can be downright rude, sexist, racist, or elitist.

La Bella Lingua

Why not get out your Italian–English dictionary and pick an interesting word to see how many idiomatic expressions are associated with it? You'll be amused to find all sorts of treats hidden within those pages.

Practice Makes Perfetto

A little repetition and practice can go a long way. Familiarize yourself with idioms by telling how you would get to the following places from your home.

Example: *al museo* (to the museum)

If you lived only five blocks away from the Metropolitan Museum, your answer would probably be *Vado a piedi.*

If you had to drive across the George Washington Bridge into Manhattan, you would say *Vado in macchina.*

If you took the subway from Brooklyn, you would say *Vado in metro.*

1. *a scuola* (to school)
2. *al cinema* (to the movies)
3. *dal dottore* (to your doctor)
4. *in ospedale* (to the hospital)
5. *in Europa* (to Europe)
6. *al parco* (to the park)
7. *in un'isola tropicale* (to a tropical island)
8. *a pescare* (to go fishing)
9. *in farmacia* (to the pharmacy)
10. *in biblioteca* (to the library)

A Good Hour

The following idioms all deal with an hour. Simply shifting the placement of an adjective can affect the significance of an idiom.

Timely Expressions

Expression	Pronunciation	Meaning
di buon ora	*dee bwon oh-rah*	early
un'ora buona	*oh-rah bwoh-nah*	a full hour
un'oretta	*oon oh-**reh**-tah*	about an hour
a tutte le ore	*ah too-teh leh oh-reh*	at any time

Expression	Pronunciation	Meaning
essere in orario	*eh*-seh-reh een oh-***rah***-ree-yoh	to be on time
nelle prime ore	*neh-leh pree-meh oh-reh*	in the early afternoon
le ore piccole	*leh oh-reh **pee**-koh-leh*	the wee hours
l'ora di punta	*loh-rah dee poon-tah*	rush hour
ora legale	*oh-rah leh-**gah**-leh*	daylight savings time

Going Mad

The following table shows you all the things you can do with the verb *andare* (to go). You'll see this verb in Chapter 11.

Idioms with *Andare*

Idiom	Pronunciation	Meaning
andare bene	*ahn-**dah**-reh beh-neh*	to go well
andare male	*ahn-**dah**-rah mah-leh*	to go poorly
andare in giro	*ahn-**dah**-reh een jee-roh*	to go around
andare in pezzi	*ahn-**dah**-reh een peh-tsee*	to go to pieces
lasciare andare	*lah-**shah**-reh ahn-**dah**-reh*	to let something go

As a Rule

In Italian, you use the verb *fare* (to do/make) most often when you would use the English verb "to take." You take a shower in English, but you "do a shower" (*fare la doccia*) in Italian. This also applies to taking a photo, a nap, and so on. The reverse is true for the expression "make a decision." In Italian, you would use the verb *prendere* (to take) *una decisione.*

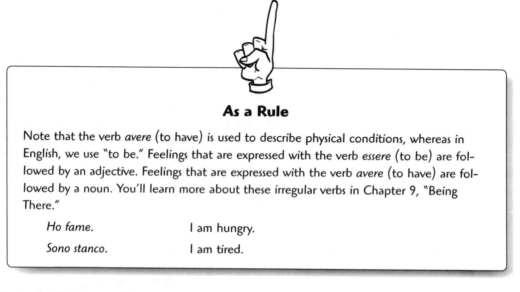

As a Rule

Note that the verb *avere* (to have) is used to describe physical conditions, whereas in English, we use "to be." Feelings that are expressed with the verb *essere* (to be) are followed by an adjective. Feelings that are expressed with the verb *avere* (to have) are followed by a noun. You'll learn more about these irregular verbs in Chapter 9, "Being There."

Ho fame.	I am hungry.
Sono stanco.	I am tired.

What's Your Opinion?

Everyone has an opinion, whether they admit it or not. It may be some time before you feel confident enough to use the idioms in the next table, but if you listen carefully, you'll hear them used a great deal. The first four examples all utilize an important verb you'll be learning in Chapter 9: the irregular verb *avere* (to have). Later, as your Italian skills increase, flip back to this chapter and see how much more you understand. You'll be pleasantly surprised.

If You Ask Me

Italian	Pronunciation	English
Ho capito.	*oh kah-__pee__-toh*	I understand.
Ha capito?	*ah kah-__pee__-toh*	Do you understand?
Hai ragione.	*ay rah-__joh__-neh*	You are right. (fam.)
Hai torto.	*ay tor-toh*	You are wrong. (fam.)
Che peccato!	*keh peh-__kah__-toh*	What a shame!
Credo di sì/no.	*kreh-doh dee see/no*	I believe so/not.
Penso di sì/no.	*pen-soh dee see/no*	I think so/not.
Non importa.	*non eem-__por__-tah*	It doesn't matter.
Per carità!	*per kah-ree-tah*	No way!
al contrario	*al kon-__trah__-ree-oh*	on the contrary
allora	*ah-loh-rah*	now then, well
comunque	*koh-__moon__-kweh*	anyhow
d'accordo	*dah-__kor__-doh*	agreed
dunque	*doon-kweh*	now then/so

Italian	Pronunciation	English
naturalmente	*nah-too-rahl-mehn-teh*	naturally
per dire la verità	*per dee-reh lah veh-ree-**tah***	to tell the truth
secondo me	*seh-**kohn**-doh meh*	in my opinion
senza dubbio	*sen-zah doo-bee-oh*	without a doubt

Seventh Heaven

In Italian, to wish someone luck, we say *in bocca al lupo* (in the mouth of the wolf). Anyone familiar with the expression would respond *Crepi!* (That he dies!) This idiomatic sampler is just the tip of the iceberg. The English translation is offered with its idiomatic equivalent as well.

Idiomatic Expressions and Colloquialisms

Italian Expression	Literal Translation	Equivalent English
al settimo cielo	In seventh heaven	*
andare all'altro mondo	To go to the other world	To go to the other side
andare in giro	To go around	To take a spin
avere una fame da lupo	To be hungry as a wolf	To be hungry as a bear
Basta!	That's enough!	*
Che cavolata!	What cabbage!	What bull!
Che cretino!	What a cretin!	*
Chi dorme non piglia pesci.	Those that sleep won't catch fish.	The early bird gets the worm.
come mamma l'ha fatto	Like mamma made him	Naked as a jay bird
costare un occhio della testa	To cost an eye from your head	To cost an arm and a leg
dare una mano	To give a hand	*
Di mamma c'è n'è una sola.	Of mothers, there is only one.	*
due gocce d'acqua	Two drops of water	Two peas in a pod
essere nei guai	To be in trouble	*
essere nelle nuvole	To be in the clouds	To have your head in the clouds
essere solo come un cane	To be alone as a dog	To be without a soul in the world
essere un pesce fuor d'acqua	To be a fish out of water	*
Fa un freddo cane.	It's dog cold.	It's freezing out.
fare alla Romana	To go Roman	To go Dutch
fare finta	To pretend	To fake
fare il furbo	To be clever	*
fare le ore piccole	To do the wee hours	To burn the midnight oil

continues

Idiomatic Expressions and Colloquialisms (continued)

Italian Expression	Literal Translation	Equivalent English
fare lo spiritoso	To be spirited	To be a wise-guy
fare una vita da cani	To live like a dog	*
fumare come un turco	To smoke like a Turk	To smoke like a chimney
fuori moda	Out of fashion	Out of style
girare la testa	To spin one's head	*
Le bugie hanno le gambe corte.	Lies have short legs.	Lies always catch up to you.
mancino	Little hand	South paw
mangiare come una bestia	To eat like a beast	To eat like a pig
non sapere nulla di nulla	To know nothing about nothing	*
nudo e crudo	Nude and crude	The plain truth
prendere in giro	To take around	To tease/joke with
Santo cielo!	Holy heaven!	Good heavens!
sfumare nel nulla	To fade into nothing	To go up in smoke
Sogni d'oro	Dreams of gold	Sweet dreams
stanco da morire	Dead tired	*
stringere la cinghia	To tighten the belt	*
toccare ferro	To touch iron	To knock on wood
volere la botte piena e la moglie ubriaca	To want the bottle full and the wife drunk	To have your cake and eat it, too

*The literal translation of the idiom is the same in Italian and English.

Whether lonely dogs, hungry wolves or depressed potatoes, Italian possesses thousands of idiomatic expressions and colloquialisms.

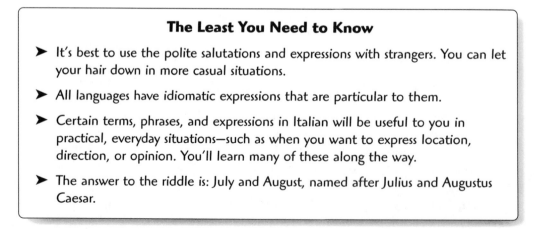

The Least You Need to Know

➤ It's best to use the polite salutations and expressions with strangers. You can let your hair down in more casual situations.

➤ All languages have idiomatic expressions that are particular to them.

➤ Certain terms, phrases, and expressions in Italian will be useful to you in practical, everyday situations—such as when you want to express location, direction, or opinion. You'll learn many of these along the way.

➤ The answer to the riddle is: July and August, named after Julius and Augustus Caesar.

Chapter 6

Almost Everything You Wanted to Know About Sex

In This Chapter

➤ How to determine gender

➤ Definite and indefinite articles

➤ Producing plurals

Once upon a time, the masculine energy of *il sole* (the Sun) ruled the Earth during the day, and the feminine energy of *la luna* (the Moon) ruled the night. When politically correct English speakers came across the land, they called this sexism and made everything neuter. Not so in Italian. In this chapter, you might not learn everything you wanted to know about sex, but you *will* learn about gender.

Determining Gender: He Versus She

Unlike English, where women are women and men are men, and everything else is a nongender, in Italian, every single noun (person, place, thing, or idea) is designated as masculine or feminine. The sun, the stars, and the moon all have a specific gender. How is this determination made? Sometimes it's obvious, sometimes there are clues, and sometimes it's just downright tricky. A *dizionario* comes in handy during these times of confusion, and if you imagine yourself as a mystic unveiling the mysteries of the *mondo*, determining gender can be an adventure you never imagined.

Masculine or Feminine

All Italian nouns are either masculine or feminine. Whether you're talking about *il gatto* (the cat), *il cane* (the dog), or *la macchina* (the car), all nouns are one gender or the other.

The reason *why* a particular noun is masculine or feminine is not always obvious. Determining a noun's gender, however, is quite easy in Italian. The clue is in the endings. Whether a noun is masculine or feminine, the endings are almost always consistent. Remember this basic rule of thumb: Nouns ending in *–o* (*libro, ragazzo, gatto*) are generally masculine, while nouns ending in *–a* (*casa, scuola, pizza*) are feminine.

Occasionally, you will come across a word that does not conform to this rule (*animale, cane, computer*), making memorization necessary, but even then, the article preceding the noun will often indicate its gender.

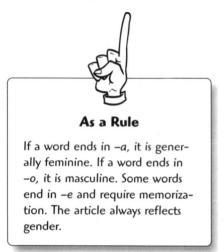

As a Rule

If a word ends in *–a*, it is generally feminine. If a word ends in *–o*, it is masculine. Some words end in *–e* and require memorization. The article always reflects gender.

Everyone Must Agree

The gender of a noun affects its relationship with other words in a *frase*, including adjectives (a word that describes a noun). If you learn the definite articles along with the nouns, it is easier for you to form sentences correctly later.

The key word here is "agreement." Everyone and everything has to get along. Nouns and adjectives must always agree. For example, if we want to say "the small cat" (*il gatto piccolo*), the adjective "small" (*piccolo*) must agree in gender with the word "cat" (*il gatto*). We'll get to adjectives later; just keep in mind that they follow the same rules.

An Article Is Not What You Read in a Newspaper

Before you get into Italian nouns, there's one little challenge you must face: the noun marker that precedes the noun. The term *noun marker* refers to an article or adjective that tells us whether a noun is masculine (m.) or feminine (f.), singular (s.) or plural (p.). The noun markers shown in the following table are singular, definite articles expressing "the" and indefinite articles expressing "a," "an," or "one."

Singular Noun Markers

English	Masculine	Feminine
the	*il, lo, l'*	*la, l'*
a, an, one	*un, uno*	*una, un'*

The Definite Article (The)

What?! Five different singular definite articles? You're probably thinking this is a little too much grammar for you. Rest assured; it's not as confusing as you think. Here's how these definite articles work in the singular:

➤ *Il* is used in front of singular, masculine nouns beginning with a consonant (other than *z* or *s* + a consonant), such as *il ragazzo* (the boy), *il sole* (the sun), and *il vino* (the wine).

➤ *Lo* is used in front of all singular, masculine nouns that begin with a *z* or an *s* followed by a consonant, such as *lo zio* (the uncle), *lo studio* (the study), and *lo sci* (the ski/skiing).

➤ *L'* is used in front of all singular nouns, both masculine and feminine, that begin with a vowel, such as *l'uomo* (the man), *l'opera* (the opera), and *l'atleta* (the female athlete).

➤ *La* is used in front of all other singular, feminine nouns, such as *la ragazza* (the girl, the girlfriend), *la musica* (the music), and *la luna* (the moon).

What's What

Definite articles are the singular masculine (*il, lo, l'*) and feminine (*la, l'*) articles that precede Italian nouns and correspond with "the" in English. Unlike the English "the," these articles show the gender of a noun. The plural masculine (*i, gli*) and plural feminine (*le*) articles reflect gender and plurality.

A **noun marker** can be any of a variety of articles, such as *il, lo, l', la, i, gli, le* (the equivalent of "the" in English) and *uno, una, un'* (the equivalent of "a" in English).

An Indefinite Article (A, An)

Indefinite articles are simple to use. Remember that they are used only before *singular* nouns.

Masculine:

➤ *Un* is used before singular masculine nouns beginning with either a consonant or a vowel, such as *un palazzo* (a building), *un signore* (a gentleman), and *un animale* (animal). This does not include those nouns beginning with a *z* or an *s* followed by a consonant.

➤ *Uno* is used just like the definite article *lo* before singular masculine nouns beginning with a *z* or an *s* followed by a consonant, such as *uno zio* (an uncle) and *uno stadio* (a stadium).

Feminine:

> ➤ *Una* is used before any feminine noun beginning with a consonant, such as *una farfalla* (a butterfly), *una storia* (a story), and *una strada* (a street).

> ➤ *Un'* is the equivalent of *an* in English and is used before all feminine nouns beginning with a vowel, such as *un'italiana* (an Italian woman), *un'amica* (a friend), and *un'opera* (an opera).

Singular Nouns

Some nouns in Italian are easy to mark because they obviously refer to masculine or feminine people. Pay special attention to their endings.

La Bella Lingua

You use the definite article in front of a day to describe something you always do:

*Andiamo in chiesa **la domenica**.*   We go to church **on Sundays.**

*Faccio yoga **il mercoledì**.*   I do yoga **on Wednesdays.**

Gender-Obvious Nouns

Masculine Noun	Feminine Noun	Pronunciation	English
il padre		*eel pah-dreh*	the father
	la madre	*lah mah-dreh*	the mother
il marito		*eel mah-**ree**-toh*	the husband
	la moglie	*lah mol-yeh*	the wife
il nonno		*eel noh-noh*	the grandfather
	la nonna	*lah noh-nah*	the grandmother
il fratello		*eel frah-**teh**-loh*	the brother
	la sorella	*lah soh-**reh**-lah*	the sister
il cugino		*eel koo-**jee**-noh*	the cousin (m.)
	la cugina	*lah koo-**jee**-nah*	the cousin (f.)
il ragazzo		*eel rah-**gah**-tsoh*	the boy
	la ragazza	*lah rah-**gah**-tsah*	the girl

Masculine Noun	Feminine Noun	Pronunciation	English
lo zio		*loh zee-oh*	the uncle
	la zia	*lah zee-ah*	the aunt
l'uomo		*lwoh-moh*	the man
	la donna	*lah doh-nah*	the woman
l'amico		*lah-**mee**-koh*	the friend (m.)
	l'amica	*lah-**mee**-kah*	the friend (f.)

Pretty soon you'll be watching Fellini films and won't have to read *i sottotitoli* (subtitles) anymore. Let's add a few more words to your *vocabolario*.

Hermaphrodites

A few nouns can be either masculine or feminine. All you have to do is change the identifier—without altering the spelling—to refer to either gender. Nouns beginning with a vowel, such as *artista*, make determining their gender difficult to determine (except in context), since the noun marker *l'* is used. Study the following sentences to see how this works:

> *Il dentista mangia la cioccolata.*
>
> *La dentista mangia la frutta.*
>
> *L'artista è molto brava.*

The following table shows several examples of either-gender nouns.

La Bella Lingua

The word *ragazzo* can mean "boy" or "boyfriend." The word *ragazza* can mean "girl" or "girl-friend."

Attenzione!

All nouns, with the exception of one's immediate family members, require an article in front of them.

Either-Gender Nouns

Italian	English
l'artista	the artist
l'atleta	the athlete
il/la cantante	the singer
il/la dentista	the dentist
il/la dirigente	the director/executive
l'erede	the heir
il/la giovane	the youth
il/la nomade	the nomad
il/la parente	the relative
il/la turista	the tourist

La Bella Lingua

You might want to create tricks to help you remember the gender of a noun; for example, *la notte* (the night) belongs to the feminine, as does *la luna* (the Moon). Be creative—maybe you'll remember the metaphor given at the beginning of this chapter, where the day is ruled by the masculine energy of *il sole* (the Sun). When we say *la macchina* or *l'automobile* (a car) runs well, we say *she* runs smoothly. Again, any association you can make to help you remember a word is acceptable, no matter how strange. It's your brain. Work it. Even if you make a gender bender, it's really not that serious—as long as you've chosen the correct noun, you'll be understood.

Nouns Ending in –e

Some nouns ending in *–e* may be masculine or feminine. You must memorize the gender of these nouns. See the following table for common nouns ending in *–e* and their genders.

Nouns Ending in –e

Masculine	English	Feminine	English
il cane	the dog	*l'automobile*	the car
il sole	the sun	*la nave*	the ship
il nome	the name/noun	*la notte*	the night
il mare	the ocean	*la stazione*	the station

Rules Are Made to Be Broken

Just to drive you *pazzo*, there are a few exceptions to these rules. Remember that rules are man-made, designed by linguists to make sense of an otherwise chaotic *universo*. All languages, including Italian, are dynamic. They evolve, expand, and contract with time, in accordance with trends, other cultural influences, and values.

Disconcerting Genders

Sometimes the ending of a word completely changes that word's significance. The only way to remember these oddities is to memorize them. In any event, fear not: Even if you get the gender wrong, 99 percent of the time, the person to whom you are speaking will know what you're saying. The following table provides a list of words whose meanings change according to the ending.

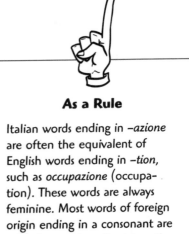

As a Rule

Italian words ending in *–azione* are often the equivalent of English words ending in *–tion*, such as *occupazione* (occupation). These words are always feminine. Most words of foreign origin ending in a consonant are masculine, such as *l'autobus, il bar, il computer, il film,* and *lo sport.*

Disconcerting Genders

Masculine	Feminine
il ballo (dance)	*la balla* (bundle, bale)
il collo (neck)	*la colla* (glue)
il colpo (blow)	*la colpa* (fault, guilt)
il costo (cost)	*la costa* (coast)
il filo (thread)	*la fila* (line)
il foglio (sheet of paper)	*la foglia* (leaf)
il legno (wood)	*la legna* (firewood)
il manico (handle)	*la manica* (sleeve)
il mento (chin)	*la menta* (mint)

continues

Disconcerting Genders   (continued)

Masculine	Feminine
il partito (political party)	*la partita* (sports match)
il porto (port)	*la porta* (door)
il posto (place)	*la posta* (mail)
il punto (detail, dot)	*la punta* (tip)
il torto (mistake)	*la torta* (cake)
il velo (veil)	*la vela* (sail, sailing)

Words are like the colors on a painter's palette, allowing us to express our thoughts to others. The more colors you have to paint with, the more you can say. Just as there are many more colors than there are words for them, there are many nouns that just won't conform to the rules but exist anyway.

Did You Know?

Although Ms. is a common feminine form of address in the United States, an Italian woman can be addressed only as either *signorina* (Miss) or *signora* (Mrs.). However, the Italian women, progressively minded as they are, have decided to use *signora* in lieu of Ms. In any case, it is still a compliment for a woman to be referred to as *signorina*.

Misbehaving Males

Look at the following table for a few of these misbehaving masculine nouns.

Masculine Nouns That End in *–a*

Noun	Pronunciation	English
il clima	*eel klee-mah*	the climate
il cruciverba	*eel kroo-chee-ver-bah*	the crossword (puzzle)
il dramma	*eel drah-mah*	the drama
il pianeta	*eel pee-ah-neh-tah*	the planet
il problema	*eel proh-bleh-mah*	the problem
il programma	*eel proh-grah-mah*	the program

Rebellious Females

Feminine nouns can be troublemakers, too. The following table mentions some of them.

Feminine Nouns That End in –o

Noun	Pronunciation	English
la foto (short for *fotografia*)	*lah foh-toh*	the photo
la mano	*lah mah-noh*	the hand
la moto (short for *motocicletta*)	*lah moh-toh*	the motorcycle
la radio	*lah **rah**-dee-yoh*	the radio

Sex Changers

Certain words can be made feminine by changing the ending to *–a*, *–essa*, or *–ice*, depending on the gender of the person performing the action. You'll learn more about professions in Chapter 9, "Being There."

Noun Endings

Masculine	Feminine	English
l'attore	*l'attrice*	actor/actress
l'avvocato	*l'avvocatessa*	lawyer
il cameriere	*la cameriera*	waiter/waitress
il direttore	*la direttrice*	director
il dottore	*la dottoressa*	doctor
il maestro	*la maestra*	teacher
il padrone	*la padrona*	boss
il pittore	*la pittrice*	painter
il poeta	*la poetessa*	poet
il professore	*la professoressa*	professor
lo studente	*la studentessa*	student

In modern usage, the feminine endings of professionals such as actors, doctors, professors, and lawyers are used with less frequency than they used to be. It is appropriate, for example, to refer to a male or female lawyer as *l'avvocato*.

The Apple Doesn't Fall Far

Fruit is almost always referred to in the feminine as *la frutta*, but a piece of fruit is referred to as *un frutto*. When a specific fruit is made masculine, it becomes the fruit tree.

> *l'arancia* (the orange) → *l'arancio* (the orange tree)
>
> *la ciliegia* (the cherry) → *il ciliegio* (the cherry tree)
>
> *la mela* (the apple) → *il melo* (the apple tree)
>
> *la pera* (the pear) → *il pero* (the pear tree)

Practice Makes Perfetto

Determine the gender by placing the appropriate definite article in front of the following nouns. You might have to consult a dictionary for a couple of them. Don't forget to look at the endings!

1. ___ *casa* (house)
2. ___ *cane* (dog)
3. ___ *albero* (tree)
4. ___ *piatto* (plate)
5. ___ *lezione* (lesson)
6. ___ *estate* (summer)
7. ___ *chiesa* (church)
8. ___ *straniero* (foreigner)
9. ___ *cattedrale* (cathedral)
10. ___ *pianeta* (planet)

More Is Better: Making Plurals

In English, it's relatively easy to talk about more than one thing; usually, you just add an –*s* to the word, although there are many plurals that confuse people learning English as a second language. How many "childs" do you have, or rather, "children"? Fortunately, forming plural nouns in Italian is as easy as floating in a gondola. Yes, you do have to memorize the endings, and again, the ending must always reflect gender. But you don't have to memorize a hundred different words just to say more than one. The following table illustrates how the ending should change in the plural.

Plural Endings

Singular		Plural	Singular		Plural
–*o*	→	–*i*	*ragazzo*	→	*ragazzi*
–*a*	→	–*e*	*donna*	→	*donne*
–*ca*	→	–*che*	*amica*	→	*amiche*
–*e*	→	–*i*	*cane*	→	*cani*

Attenzione!

In certain cases, the plural of certain nouns and adjectives follows different rules:

1. Singular feminine nouns and adjectives ending in *–ca* or *–ga* form the plural by changing the endings to *–che* or *–ghe*.

   amica → *amiche*

   bianca → *bianche*

2. Singular feminine nouns ending in *–cia* and *–gia* form the plural with ...

   ... *cie/gie* (if a vowel precedes the singular ending)

   camicia → *camicie*

   valigia → *valigie*

   ... *ce/ge* (if a consonant precedes the singular ending)

   arancia → *arance*

   pioggia → *piogge*

3. Singular masculine nouns and adjectives ending in *–co* and *–go* generally form the plural by replacing the singular endings with *–chi* and *–ghi*.

   pacco → *pacchi*

   bianco → *bianchi*

   lago → *laghi*

   largo → *larghi*

Do We Agree? Plural Noun Markers

When an Italian noun refers to more than one thing, you must change the noun marker.

The following table outlines the definite articles and demonstrates how singular noun markers change in the plural. Remember that funny rule about the definite article *lo*, which is used only in front of words beginning with *s* (or *z*) + a consonant. The same applies to *gli*.

The Definite Article (The)

Gender	Singular		Plural	When It's Used	Examples
Masculine	*lo*	→	*gli*	In front of all masculine nouns beginning with a *z* or *s* + consonant	*lo zio → gli zii* *lo studente → gli studenti*
	l'	→	*gli*	In front of all masculine nouns beginning with a vowel	*l'amico → gli amici*
	Il	→	*i*	In front of all other masculine nouns	*il nonno → i nonni*
Feminine	*l'*	→	*le*	In front of all feminine nouns beginning with a vowel	*l'amica → le amiche*
	la	→	*le*	In front of all other feminine nouns	*la sorella → le sorelle*

As a Rule

Family names do not change endings in the plural. Use the article to indicate plurality. For example, if you were talking about the Leonardo family, you would say *i Leonardo* (the Leonardos).

Nouns ending in a consonant (such as many words of foreign origin) or accented on the last vowel do not change form in the plural. Only the article changes. For example:

l'autobus	→	*gli autobus*
il caffè	→	*i caffè*
la città	→	*le città*
l'università	→	*le università*

The Rules

The following summarizes everything you could ever want to know about making plurals:

➤ *Gli* is used in front of all plural, masculine nouns beginning with a *z* or an *s* followed by a consonant, and plural, masculine nouns beginning with a vowel, such as *gli studenti* (the students), *gli zii* (the uncles), *gli animali* (the animals), and *gli amici* (the friends).

➤ *I* is used in front of all plural, masculine nouns beginning with all other consonants, such as *i ragazzi* (the boys) and *i vini* (the wines).

➤ *Le* is used in front of all plural, feminine nouns, such as *le ragazze* (the girls), *le donne* (the women), and *le automobili* (the cars).

Plural Spelling

Look at what happens to the nouns in the following table when made plural.

Singular and Plural Nouns

Singular Noun	English	Plural Noun	English
la monaca	the nun	*le monache*	the nuns
l'amica	the friend (f.)	*le amiche*	the friends (f.)
l'amico	the friend (m.)	*gli amici*	the friends (m.)
il nemico	the enemy (m.)	*i nemici*	the enemies (m.)
l'ago	the needle	*gli aghi*	the needles
il luogo	the place	*i luoghi*	the places

You already know one plural—*spaghetti*! Because you could never eat one *spaghetto*—which isn't a real word—you must always use it in the plural. Let's try a sentence: *In Italia, i turisti mangiano gli spaghetti al pomodoro.*

La Pratica

Try making the following nouns plural using the rules you just learned. I've done the first one for you:

1. *il libro* (the book) → <u>*i libri*</u> (the books)

2. *il gatto* (the cat) → _____ (the cats)

3. *la ragazza* (the girl) → _____ (the girls)

4. *la stazione* (the station) → _____ (the stations)

5. *l'amico* (the friend, m.) → _____ (the friends)

6. *l'amica* (the friend, f.) → _____ (the friends)

La Bella Lingua

Both gods and men are irregular in the plural.

il dio (the god)   *gli dei* (the gods)

l'uomo (the man)   *gli uomini* (the men)

What Does It Mean?

Without knowing the significance of a word, it is still easy to determine whether it is singular or plural. Look at the following words and determine their gender and plurality. Place the appropriate noun marker in front of the word and guess at their meanings. Remember that some nouns end in *–e* in the singular.

1. _____ *aeroplani*
2. _____ *bambini*
3. _____ *birra*
4. _____ *dollari*
5. _____ *invenzione*
6. _____ *libro*
7. _____ *nome*
8. _____ *notte*
9. _____ *odore*
10. _____ *ragazze*
11. _____ *scuole*
12. _____ *stranieri*
13. _____ *supermercati*
14. _____ *tavole*
15. _____ *vacanza*
16. _____ *viaggi*

Irregular Plural Nouns

Some masculine nouns become plural in the feminine. As you can see, many parts of the body are included.

Irregular Plural Nouns

Singular	Plural
il braccio (the arm)	*le braccia* (the arms)
il dito (the finger)	*le dita* (the fingers)
il ginocchio (the knee)	*le ginocchia* (the knees)

Singular	Plural
il labbro (the lip)	*le labbra* (the lips)
la mano (the hand)	*le mani* (the hands)
il miglio (the mile)	*le miglia* (the miles)
il paio (the pair)	*le paia* (the pairs)
l'uovo (the egg)	*le uova* (the eggs)

Always Plural

Some nouns are only used in the plural. For instance, when you look for your glasses, it is assumed that you are referring to the ones you see with.

Always Plural Nouns

Italian	English
le forbici	scissors
le pinzette	tweezers
le redini	reins
i pantaloni	pants
le mutande	underwear
gli occhiali	eyeglasses

Practice Those Plurals

You've just arrived in Rome, and you need to pick up a few odds and ends. You're in a *negozio* (store) and want to buy more than one of the following items. Start by saying *Cerco …* (I am looking for …) and the plural of the item. Don't forget to use the appropriate article.

Example: *il regalo* (gift)

Cerco i regali. (I am looking for the gifts.)

1. *la cartolina* (postcard)
2. *la rivista* (magazine)
3. *la collana* (necklace)
4. *il profumo* (perfume)
5. *la cravatta* (tie)
6. *la penna* (pen)

What Have You Learned About Gender?

You've always wanted to be in a movie. You remember watching all those spaghetti westerns where tall men wore big hats and the women always looked pretty, even

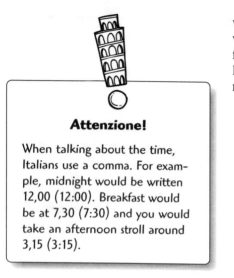

Attenzione!

When talking about the time, Italians use a comma. For example, midnight would be written 12,00 (12:00). Breakfast would be at 7,30 (7:30) and you would take an afternoon stroll around 3,15 (3:15).

with dirt smudged across their cheeks. You're in Rome visiting the famous movie studio *Cinecittà* where those films were made, and you see a listing for auditions. Determine whether the part requires a male or female role.

Attrice matura (40–50 anni), cercasi con la capacità di parlare l'inglese e il francese per interpretare il ruolo di una contessa. Aspetto distinto. Inviare curriculum con foto a Via Garibaldi 36, Roma.

Attore forte, atletico, giovane, cercasi con i capelli chiari per interpretare il ruolo di Cesare. Presentarsi il 25 giugno ore 9,00 alla palestra Superforte, secondo piano.

Uomini e donne veramente sexy, cercasi per apparire nudi in una scena sulla spiaggia: Varie età. Esperienza non necessaria. Telefonare al 06/040357.

The Least You Need to Know

➤ Certain endings are almost always masculine (*o, i,* consonants) or feminine (*a, e*).

➤ Some nouns can be changed from masculine to feminine by adding an appropriate ending.

➤ Always look at the article to determine the gender and plurality of a noun.

➤ Plural nouns end in either *–i* or *–e.*

Chapter 7

What's the Subject?

In This Chapter

➤ Subject pronouns: the key to smooth communication in *la bella lingua*

➤ Friendly or polite? Formal and informal pronouns in Italian

➤ You or all of you? How Italians directly address one person or lots of people

In the previous chapter, you learned about nouns—how to determine their gender and make them plural. You can take *mela* (apple) and make it *mele* (apples), and you enjoy not just one *libro* (book), but many *libri* (books). (And you thought there could be no greater thrill.) To add to your plate, this chapter discusses the titillating world of subject pronouns. Beware: The next two chapters are power chapters—meat and potatoes chapters (or if you're a vegetarian, rice and beans chapters). Come back to them as often as you need until you are using verbs without pause.

Your Loyal Subject

As you learned in Chapter 4, "You Know More Than You Think," an infinitive verb is a verb in its unconjugated form, as in *cucinare* (to cook), *mangiare* (to eat), *dormire* (to sleep), and *viaggiare* (to travel). Determining the subject of a verb is essential to conjugation. To determine the subject, you need to ask the simple question, "What or who is doing the action?" The subject may be a person, a thing (such as the car), or a pronoun replacing the noun (such as he or it).

Look at the following sentences to better understand what is the subject of the verb.

What's What

The pronouns *egli* (he) and *ella* (she) often replace the pronouns *lui* and *lei* in writing. Instead of using the pronouns *lui, lei,* and *loro,* you may also hear—depending on gender and number—the pronouns *esso, essi, essa,* and *esse* used in reference to people, animals, and inanimate objects.

Determining the Subject

Sentence	Subject
I want to visit Venice.	I
You want to learn Italian.	You
The bus is leaving at 4:30.	The bus *or* it
Eat, drink, and be merry!	You
Robert and I are brother and sister.	Robert and I *or* we
You are all very intelligent.	You (plural)
The Italians love life.	The Italians *or* they

What's What

There are two kinds of objects: direct and indirect. The **direct object** of a sentence is the recipient of a verb's action. The **indirect object** of a sentence tells *to whom* or *for whom* the action was done.

Subject Pronouns

There are six ways to describe persons (or, in the third person, things) as pronouns: I, you, he or she, we, you (plural), and they. There are no other options. The linguists decided to call these *persons.* Look at the subject pronouns in the following table.

Subject Pronouns

Person	Singular	Plural
First	*io* (I)	*noi* (we)
Second	*tu* (you, informal)	*voi* (you)
Third	*lui/lei/Lei* (he/she/You)	*loro* (they)

The pronoun Lei (with a capital "L") signifies "You" (polite or formal); the pronoun lei signifies "she." Both, however, are third person.

La Bella Lingua

In Italian, subject pronouns are used much less frequently than in English and other languages because the verb endings usually indicate the subject quite clearly. It is not necessary to use a subject pronoun to say the sentence *Mangio la pasta* (I eat the pasta) because the ending *–o* already tells us it's the first person.

When to Use Subject Pronouns

Subject pronouns are useful for:

➤ **Clarity:** To differentiate who the subject is in cases where verb forms are the same and when there is more than one subject:

> *Lui parla l'italiano ma lei parla il francese.*
> (**He** speaks Italian but **she** speaks French.)

➤ **Emphasis:** To clearly underline the fact that the subject will be performing the action:

> *Tu viaggi in Italia; io sto qui.* (**You** travel to Italy; **I'm** staying here.)

➤ **Politeness:** To show respect and maintain a formality with another person.

> *Lei è molto gentile.* (**You** are very kind.)

What's What

An **object pronoun** replaces the object in a sentence. In English, this is equivalent to *it*.

In Italian, all object pronouns must reflect *gender* and *plurality*.

Name That Subject

Just to make sure you're on track, determine the subject of the verb in the following sentences; then ascertain the appropriate subject pronoun for each sentence:

1. The stars twinkled brightly.
2. Jessica knows how to have fun.
3. Leslie travels a lot.
4. My mother was a painter.
5. Louis was an engineer.
6. The food is delicious.
7. Italian is easy to learn.
8. Anna flies a plane.

Subject to Interpretation

Now that you're cooking with gas, let's take this one step further: Determine the subject in the following Italian sentences. If you're feeling brave, try translating them:

1. *Davide prende l'autobus.*

2. *Io mangio il pesce.*

3. *Patrizia e Raffaella studiano arte.*

4. *L'insalata è fresca.*

5. *La farmacia è aperta.*

6. *Lo studente conversa con il professore.*

7. *Io e Gianni andiamo in Italia.*

8. *La ragazza va a casa.*

Attenzione!

In English, the subject pronoun "I" is always capitalized, regardless of its position in the sentence. In Italian, *io* is capitalized only at the beginning of a sentence.

The Italian polite "you" subject pronoun *Lei* is always capitalized to distinguish it from *lei*, meaning "she." At the beginning of a sentence, there is no distinction between the two pronouns, requiring the reader to determine the significance through the context of the sentence.

You and You and You

Have you ever addressed a group of people and not known quite how to acknowledge all of them? In the southern United States, you might say, "Y'all." In the North, you might say, "All of you."

Italian solves this problem by having a separate, plural form of "you" (the second-person plural). It also has an informal "you" (second-person singular) used specifically with friends and family members and a separate form of "you" used in formal situations, which we call the *polite* form (third-person singular). You've already seen these pronouns in an earlier table. Take a look at them again in the following table, just to make sure you understand.

Forms of "You"

English	Italian	When to Use	Person
you (informal)	*tu*	Informal, used with family, friends, and children	Second singular
You (polite)	*Lei*	Polite, used to show respect to strangers, authority figures, and elders; always capitalized	Third singular
you (plural)	*voi*	Plural, used when addressing more than one person	Second plural
You (plural polite)	*Loro**	Plural, polite; used in extreme cases (as when addressing the pope)	Third plural

*This form, although plural, would be used to address the pope as the polite form of voi. *It probably stems from the notion that when speaking to the pope, one is also addressing God. Although Pope John Paul II often uses the first-person singular form when giving his own personal opinion, he may also use the plural* noi *(we) form of the verb, as in* pensiamo *(we think), which is the traditional form used by popes.*

Hey You!

What subject pronouns would you use when speaking to the following people?

1. Your best friend
2. Mr. and Mrs. Carini
3. Giorgio and Filippo
4. Your in-laws
5. Pope John Paul II
6. Your baby brother
7. Your boss

La Bella Lingua

Pope John Paul II, formerly Karol Wojtyla, will go down in history as being the first pope to launch his own comic book series. The Vatican-approved *Il Giornalino* (The Little Paper) is available on newsstands and depicts the pontiff's life and times.

Did You Know?

Each region has its own particularities. In Rome, it is not uncommon to use the *tu* form of a verb when addressing a stranger in an informal setting, such as a small shop or while waiting for a bus.

In Italian, using the *Lei* form is equal to our using a last name to address someone, as in "Mr. Rossi."

In parts of the south and in older movies, the *voi* form of a verb may be commonly used in lieu of *Lei*.

The Least You Need to Know

➤ Determining the subject of a verb is essential to conjugation—and, therefore, speaking.

➤ Subject pronouns are used much less frequently in Italian than in English because the verb endings usually indicate the subject; however, you will sometimes hear subject pronouns used for clarity, emphasis, or courtesy.

➤ There are four forms of "you" in Italian: the second-person plural, the second-person singular, the third-person singular, and the third-person plural.

Part 2

You're Off and Running

Every house needs a foundation, and Part 1, "The Basics," focused on giving you the fundamentals. You've learned about parts of speech, cognates, and idiomatic expressions. You studied the notion of gender, and learned some common introductory phrases used by Italian speakers.

Part 2 is loaded with useful information that can't be absorbed in one sitting; you'll probably want to have a little bite, savor the flavor, and let your mind digest the material before going too far ahead. Take your time and really absorb the lessons.

You're going to learn your verbs in this part. Chapter 8, "An Action-Packed Adventure," outlines the regular rules of conjugation, offering you hundreds of verbs that you will read or hear spoken. Use it as a convenient reference section that you can come back to as necessary. In Chapter 9, "Being There," you'll learn the most important verbs of all: essere *and* stare, *both of which mean "to be." You'll also be served the verb* avere *(to have), with a few idiomatic expressions on the side.*

Chapter 10, "Tell Me About Your Childhood," shows you how to modify adjectives, use adverbs, and tie it all together with prepositions and prepositional phrases.

In Chapter 11, "Finally, You're at the Airport," you'll look at the imperative, the tense used for giving directions and making requests. You'll be given practical vocabulary to help you go from the airport to the hotel. In Chapter 12, "Moving Around," you'll master telling time and learn about an important verb used in myriad situations: fare *(to do; to make). In Chapter 13, "Hallelujah, You've Made It to l'Hotel," you'll study the modal verbs* volere *(to want),* potere *(to be able to), and* dovere *(to have to). Chapter 14, "Rain or Shine," talks about that universal conversation topic:* il tempo *(the weather).*

As you study the next few chapters, remember that there's nothing like exposure to help you learn Italian. Use the book as a map, but don't hesitate to support your study with other tools such as language cassettes and films.

Chapter 8

An Action-Packed Adventure

In This Chapter

➤ Verb families and conjugation

➤ Common regular Italian verbs

➤ Taking conjugation a step further: asking questions

➤ Forming negative statements

Verbs are where the action is, so study them closely. *I verbi* are the skeleton of a *lingua*. Without *i verbi*, nothing would get done; nothing could happen. Verbs are what move us, shape us, and allow us to convey messages.

You've already studied some verbs in Chapter 4, "You Know More Than You Think." As you know, it is important to be able to recognize verb infinitives in order to look them up in your *dizionario* (verb conjugations are generally not included). The infinitive form of a verb is simply the unconjugated verb, as in to love, to dance, and to dream, or loving, dancing, and dreaming.

An infinitive, however, doesn't tell us who is doing the action. This is where conjugation comes in. Every time you speak, you conjugate verbs to reflect the subject of the verb. In the previous chapter, you studied the subject pronouns. It's time to put it all together.

Included in this chapter are many regular verbs you may want to use as your Italian language skills progress. The list is long—rather than trying to learn all the verbs at once, use this chapter as a reference section you can come back to as *necessario*.

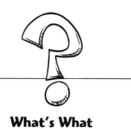

What's What

Infinitive form refers to a verb in its unconjugated form. In Italian, the infinitive form can also be used as a subject, object, or predicate, as in **Mangiare** *la pasta è buono.* (To eat [Eating] pasta is good.) All verbs are listed in the dictionary in the infinitive form.

All in the Family

Most of the time, Italian verbs follow certain rules. We call these regular verbs. We'll get to irregular verbs later.

All verbs in Italian belong to one of three families, easily identified by their endings. The rules are the same for each family, so after you've learned the pattern for one verb, you know how to conjugate all the verbs in that family.

Also called the first conjugation, the *–are* family is the largest and most regular. The *–ere* family—known as the second conjugation—has its own set of rules. The *–ire* family has two methods of conjugation and is called the third conjugation. These verb families include infinitive verbs such as *parlare* (to speak), *rispondere* (to respond), *partire* (to depart), and *capire* (to understand).

The Anatomy of a Verb

Understanding the anatomy of a verb will help you conjugate. Keep in mind that every infinitive verb has a *stem* that can be distinguished from its *infinitive ending.* Most infinitive verbs end in *–are*, *–ere*, or *–ire*.

To conjugate any regular verb in the present tense, keep the stem, drop the infinitive ending, and replace it with the appropriate conjugation. Following this formula, you should be able to conjugate any regular verb (whether you understand its meaning or not).

La Bella Lingua

In English, the present tense can be expressed in three different ways:

The simple present: "I study."

The present progressive: "I am studying."

The emphatic present: "I do study."

The Italian present tense expresses all three of these meanings, as in *Studio.*

The Anatomy of a Verb

Conjugation	Infinitive Verb	Stem	Infinitive Ending
First	*parlare* (to speak)	*parl–*	*–are*
Second	*rispondere* (to respond)	*rispond–*	*–ere*
Third	*partire* (to depart)	*part–*	*–ire*
Third	*capire* (to understand)	*cap–*	*–ire*

The Present-Tense Conjugations

For a general overview, the following table outlines the correct endings for all three verb families, as represented by the verbs *parlare* (to speak), *rispondere* (respond), *partire* (to depart), and *capire* (to understand). (Note the two different conjugations for *–ire* verbs.)

Regular Verb Endings

Subject Pronoun	*Parl<u>are</u>*	*Rispond<u>ere</u>*	*Part<u>ire</u>*	*Cap<u>ire</u>*
io	*parlo*	*rispondo*	*parto*	*capisco*
tu	*parli*	*rispondi*	*parti*	*capisci*
lui/lei/Lei	*parla*	*risponde*	*parte*	*capisce*
noi	*parliamo*	*rispondiamo*	*partiamo*	*capiamo*
voi	*parlate*	*rispondete*	*partite*	*capite*
loro	*parlano*	*rispondono*	*partono*	*capiscono*

What's What

The **stem** of a word or verb is the base from which other words are formed. In regular verbs, the stem remains the same when conjugated. In **irregular verbs,** the stem may change form once it has been conjugated. This is called a **stem-changing verb,** as with the verb *bere* (to drink), whose stem changes to *bev–* when conjugated.

The *-are* Family

The largest family in the batch, the *-are* verbs, are also the most regular.

C *Is for* Celebrare

Take a look at the verb *celebrare* (to celebrate) and see how it conjugates. (And you're going to celebrate when you finish this chapter!) Break down the verb to its infinitive stem by detaching the *-are* ending, and attach the endings you just saw.

Celebrare (to Celebrate)

Italian	English
io celebro	I celebrate
tu celebri	you celebrate
lui/lei/Lei celebra	he/she celebrates; You celebrate
noi celebriamo	we celebrate
voi celebrate	you celebrate
loro celebrano	they celebrate

La Bella Lingua

As you know, pronouncing Italian is easy; the challenge is knowing where to place the stress. When pronouncing all forms of the verbs, note that—except for *noi* and *voi*—stress should be placed on the stem of the verb, *not* the ending. Although there are exceptions, this is particularly helpful to recall when you're pronouncing the third-person plural (*loro*) conjugations:

mangiano	**mahn**-jah-noh	they eat
parlano	**par**-lah-noh	they speak
vedono	**veh**-doh-noh	they see

Remember that double consonants should be emphasized but not separated, and all syllables should slide together in a flow of melodic *musica!*

Regular –are Verbs

The following table is a fairly comprehensive list of the –are verbs. Don't be intimidated by the sheer number of verbs there are—think of them as *colori* for your palette. The more you know, the better you will express yourself. For now, carefully study the verbs listed. Later, cover the translations with a piece of paper and see if you can ascertain their meaning by associating them with English words you already know. Look for cognates.

Regular –are Verbs

Verb	Pronunciation	Meaning
abbronzare	ah-brohn-**zah**-reh	to tan
abitare	ah-bee-**tah**-reh	to live
abusare	ah-boo-**zah**-reh	to abuse
accompagnare	ah-kohm-pah-**nyah**-reh	to accompany
adorare	ah-doh-**rah**-reh	to adore
affermare	ah-fer-**mah**-reh	to affirm
affittare	ah-fee-**tah**-reh	to rent
aiutare	ah-yoo-**tah**-reh	to help
alzare	ahl-**tsah**-reh	to raise/lift up
amare	ah-**mah**-reh	to love
ammirare	ah-mee-**rah**-reh	to admire
anticipare	ahn-tee-chee-**pah**-reh	to anticipate/wait
arrestare	ah-reh-**stah**-reh	to stop/arrest
arrivare	ah-ree-**vah**-reh	to arrive
aspettare	ah-speh-**tah**-reh	to wait/expect
avvisare	ah-vee-**sah**-reh	to inform/advise
ballare	bah-**lah**-reh	to dance
bloccare	bloh-**kah**-reh	to block
bussare	boo-**sah**-reh	to knock
buttare	boo-**tah**-reh	to throw
calcolare	kal-koh-**lah**-reh	to calculate
camminare	kah-mee-**nah**-reh	to walk
cancellare	kahn-cheh-**lah**-reh	to cancel
cantare	kahn-**tah**-reh	to sing
causare	kow-**zah**-reh	to cause
celebrare	cheh-leb-**rah**-reh	to celebrate
cenare	cheh-**nah**-reh	to dine
chiamare	kee-ah-**mah**-reh	to call
comprare	kohm-**prah**-reh	to buy

continues

Regular *–are* Verbs (continued)

Verb	Pronunciation	Meaning
consumare	kohn-soo-**mah**-reh	to consume
contare	kohn-**tah**-reh	to count
controllare	kohn-troh-**lah**-reh	to control/to check
conversare	kohn-ver-**sah**-reh	to converse
costare	koh-**stah**-reh	to cost
cucinare	koo-chee-**nah**-reh	to cook
deliberare	deh-lee-beh-**rah**-reh	to deliberate/to resolve
depositare	deh-poh-zee-**tah**-reh	to deposit
desiderare	deh-zee-deh-**rah**-reh	to desire
determinare	deh-ter-mee-**nah**-reh	to determine
detestare	deh-teh-**stah**-reh	to detest
dimostrare	dee-moh-**strah**-reh	to demonstrate
disegnare	dee-zen-**yah**-reh	to draw/design
disgustare	dee-sgoo-**stah**-reh	to disgust
disperare	dee-speh-**rah**-reh	to despair
diventare	dee-ven-**tah**-reh	to become
domandare	doh-mahn-**dah**-reh	to question
donare	doh-**nah**-reh	to donate/give
elevare	eh-leh-**vah**-reh	to elevate
eliminare	eh-lee-mee-**nah**-reh	to eliminate
entrare	ehn-**trah**-reh	to enter
esaminare	eh-zah-mee-**nah**-reh	to examine
evitare	eh-vee-**tah**-reh	to avoid
firmare	feer-**mah**-reh	to sign
formare	for-**mah**-reh	to form/create
fumare	foo-**mah**-reh	to smoke
funzionare	foon-zee-oh-**nah**-reh	to function
gettare	jeh-**tah**-reh	to throw
gridare	gree-**dah**-reh	to yell/scream
guardare	gwar-**dah**-reh	to look at something
guidare	gwee-**dah**-reh	to drive
immaginare	ee-mah-jee-**nah**-reh	to imagine
imparare	eem-pah-**rah**-reh	to learn
informare	een-for-**mah**-reh	to inform
invitare	een-vee-**tah**-reh	to invite
lavare	lah-**vah**-reh	to wash
lavorare	lah-voh-**rah**-reh	to work

Verb	Pronunciation	Meaning
liberare	lee-beh-**rah**-reh	to liberate/to set free
limitare	lee-mee-**tah**-reh	to limit
lottare	loh-**tah**-reh	to struggle, to fight
mandare	mahn-**dah**-reh	to send
meritare	meh-ree-**tah**-reh	to deserve
misurare	mee-zoo-**rah**-reh	to measure
modificare	moh-dee-fee-**kah**-reh	to modify
nuotare	nwoh-**tah**-reh	to swim
occupare	oh-koo-**pah**-reh	to occupy
odiare	oh-dee-**ah**-reh	to hate
operare	oh-peh-**rah**-reh	to operate
ordinare	or-dee-**nah**-reh	to order
organizzare	or-gah-nee-**zah**-reh	to organize
osservare	oh-ser-**vah**-reh	to observe
parlare	par-**lah**-reh	to speak
partecipare	par-teh-chee-**pah**-reh	to participate
passare	pah-**sah**-reh	to pass
pensare	pen-**sah**-reh	to think
perdonare	per-doh-**nah**-reh	to forgive, to pardon
pesare	peh-**zah**-reh	to weigh
pettinare	peh-tee-**nah**-reh	to comb
portare	por-**tah**-reh	to bring, to carry, to wear
pranzare	prahn-**zah**-reh	to eat lunch, to dine
pregare	preh-**gah**-reh	to pray, to request
prenotare	preh-noh-**tah**-reh	to reserve
preparare	preh-pah-**rah**-reh	to prepare
presentare	preh-zen-**tah**-reh	to present
prestare	preh-**stah**-reh	to lend
provare	proh-**vah**-reh	to try
raccomandare	rah-koh-mahn-**dah**-reh	to recommend, to register
raccontare	rah-kohn-**tah**-reh	to tell, to recount
rappresentare	rah-preh-zehn-**tah**-reh	to represent
respirare	reh-spee-**rah**-reh	to breathe
rifiutare	ree-fyoo-**tah**-reh	to refuse, to reject
rilassare	ree-lah-**sah**-reh	to relax
riparare	ree-pah-**rah**-reh	to repair, to fix
riservare	ree-zer-**vah**-reh	to reserve, to put aside
rispettare	ree-speh-**tah**-reh	to respect

continues

Regular –*are* Verbs   (continued)

Verb	Pronunciation	Meaning
ritornare	ree-tor-**nah**-reh	to return
saltare	sahl-**tah**-reh	to jump
salvare	sahl-**vah**-reh	to save
scusare	skoo-**zah**-reh	to excuse
soddisfare	soh-dee-**sfah**-reh	to satisfy
sognare	sohn-**yah**-reh	to dream
sposare	spoh-**zah**-reh	to marry
suonare	swoh-**nah**-reh	to play an instrument, to sound
telefonare	teh-leh-foh-**nah**-reh	to telephone
terminare	ter-mee-**nah**-reh	to terminate
trovare	troh-**vah**-reh	to find
usare	oo-**zah**-reh	to use
vietare	vee-eh-**tah**-reh	to forbid/prohibit
visitare	vee-zee-**tah**-reh	to visit
volare	voh-**lah**-reh	to fly
votare	voh-**tah**-reh	to vote

Exceptions

Here are a few exceptions to keep in mind:

➤ Most verbs ending in -*iare,* such as *cominciare* (to begin) and *studiare* (to study), drop the extra –*i* when conjugating to the *tu* and *noi* forms of the endings.

Subject	*Cominciare*	*Studiare*
io	*comincio*	*studio*
tu	*cominci*	*studi*
lui/lei/Lei	*comincia*	*studia*
noi	*cominciamo*	*studiamo*
voi	*cominciate*	*studiate*
loro	*cominciano*	*studiano*

Other verbs falling under this category include:

   abbracciare (to hug)

   assaggiare (to taste)

   baciare (to kiss)

cambiare (to change)

cominciare (to begin)

lasciare (to leave something)

mangiare (to eat)

tagliare (to cut)

viaggiare (to travel)

➤ Many verbs ending in *–care* and *–gare* add an *–h* to the stem in front of the vowels *i* and *e* to maintain the hard *c* and *g* sounds. Look at the verbs *cercare* (to search for) and *spiegare* (to explain) to see how this works.

Subject	Cercare	Spiegare
io	*cerco*	*spiego*
tu	**cerchi**	**spieghi**
lui/lei/Lei	*cerca*	*spiega*
noi	**cerchiamo**	**spieghiamo**
voi	*cercate*	*spiegate*
loro	*cercano*	*spiegano*

Other verbs falling under this category include:

comunicare (to communicate)

giocare (to play)

indicare (to indicate)

navigare (to navigate)

notificare (to notify)

pagare (to pay)

toccare (to touch)

verificare (to verify)

Practice Makes **Perfetto**

Use the correct form of the verb in the following sentences. If the subject is not identified in the sentence, it is given in parenthesis. Don't forget to determine what your subject is and whether the verb should be conjugated in its singular or plural form:

1. *Paolo* _____ *(lavorare) in ufficio.*

2. *Luca ed io* _____ *(aspettare) il treno.*

3. _____ *(abitare) in una casa splendida. (tu)*

4. _____ *(parlare) la lingua italiana. (io)*

5. _____ *(passare) la notte in una bella pensione. (voi)*

6. *Antonella e Dina* _____ *(preparare) la cena.*

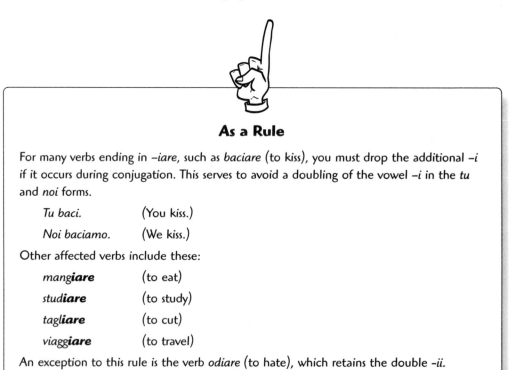

As a Rule

For many verbs ending in *–iare*, such as *baciare* (to kiss), you must drop the additional *–i* if it occurs during conjugation. This serves to avoid a doubling of the vowel *–i* in the *tu* and *noi* forms.

Tu baci.	(You kiss.)
Noi baciamo.	(We kiss.)

Other affected verbs include these:

mang**iare**	(to eat)
stud**iare**	(to study)
tagl**iare**	(to cut)
viagg**iare**	(to travel)

An exception to this rule is the verb *odiare* (to hate), which retains the double *-ii.*

The *–ere* Verbs

In most cases, *–ere* verbs are conjugated similarly to the *–are* verbs. Drop the infinitive ending from your stem and add the endings from the "Regular *–ere* Verbs" table.

S Is for Scrivere

Notice how this works with the verb *scrivere* (to write).

Scriver (to Write)

Italian	English
io **scrivo**	I write
tu **scrivi**	you write
lui/lei/Lei **scrive**	he/she writes; You write

Italian	English
*noi scriv**iamo***	we write
*voi scriv**ete***	you write
*loro scriv**ono***	they write

Regular –ere Verbs

As you can see from the list in the following table, there are fewer regular verbs in the *–ere* family. Study the verbs in the table.

Regular –ere Verbs

Verb	Pronunciation	Meaning
accendere	*ah-**chen**-deh-reh*	to light/turn on
affliggere	*ah-flee-**jeh**-reh*	to afflict
aggiungere	*ah-**joon**-jeh-reh*	to add
alludere	*ah-**loo**-deh-reh*	to allude/refer
ammettere	*ah-**meh**-teh-reh*	to admit/let in
apprendere	*ah-**pren**-deh-reh*	to learn
assistere	*ah-**see**-steh-reh*	to assist
assumere	*ah-**soo**-meh-reh*	to hire
attendere	*ah-**ten**-deh-reh*	to attend/to wait for
cadere	*kah-**deh**-reh*	to fall
chiedere	*kee-**yeh**-deh-reh*	to ask
chiudere	*kee-**yoo**-deh-reh*	to close
commettere	*koh-**meh**-teh-reh*	to commit/join
commuovere	*kohm-**woh**-veh-reh*	to move/touch/affect
comprendere	*kohm-**pren**-deh-reh*	to understand
concedere	*kohn-**cheh**-deh-reh*	to concede/grant/award
concludere	*kohn-**kloo**-deh-reh*	to conclude
confondere	*kohn-**fon**-deh-reh*	to confuse
conoscere	*koh-**noh**-sheh-reh*	to know someone
consistere	*kohn-**see**-steh-reh*	to consist
convincere	*kohn-**veen**-cheh-reh*	to convince
correggere	*koh-**reh**-jeh-reh*	to correct
correre	***koh**-reh-reh*	to run
corrispondere	*koh-ree-**spohn**-deh-reh*	to correspond
credere	***kreh**-deh-reh*	to believe
crescere	***kreh**-sheh-reh*	to grow

continues

Regular –ere Verbs   (continued)

Verb	Pronunciation	Meaning
decidere	*deh-**chee**-deh-reh*	to decide
descrivere	*deh-**skree**-veh-reh*	to describe
difendere	*dee-**fen**-deh-reh*	to defend
dipendere	*dee-**pen**-deh-reh*	to depend
dipingere	*dee-**peen**-jeh-reh*	to paint
discutere	*dee-**skoo**-teh-reh*	to discuss
dissolvere	*dee-**sohl**-veh-reh*	to dissolve
distinguere	*dee-**steen**-gweh-reh*	to distinguish
distruggere	*dee-**stroo**-jeh-reh*	to destroy
dividere	*dee-**vee**-deh-reh*	to divide
emergere	*eh-**mer**-jeh-reh*	to emerge
esistere	*eh-**zee**-steh-reh*	to exist
esprimere	*es-**pree**-meh-reh*	to express
fingere	***feen**-geh-reh*	to pretend
godere	*goh-**deh**-reh*	to enjoy
includere	*een-**kloo**-deh-reh*	to include
insistere	*een-**see**-steh-reh*	to insist
intendere	*een-**ten**-deh-reh*	to intend
interrompere	*een-teh-**rom**-peh-reh*	to interrupt
invadere	*een-**vah**-deh-reh*	to invade
leggere	***leh**-jeh-reh*	to read
mettere	***meh**-teh-reh*	to put/place/set
muovere	***mwoh**-veh-reh*	to move
nascondere	*nah-**skon**-deh-reh*	to hide
offendere	*oh-**fen**-deh-reh*	to offend
perdere	***per**-deh-reh*	to lose
permettere	*per-**meh**-teh-reh*	to permit
piangere	*pee-**yahn**-jeh-reh*	to cry
prendere	***pren**-deh-reh*	to take
proteggere	*proh-**teh**-jeh-reh*	to protect
rendere	***ren**-deh-reh*	to render/give back
resistere	*reh-**zee**-steh-reh*	to resist
ricevere	*ree-**cheh**-veh-reh*	to receive
ridere	***ree**-deh-reh*	to laugh
riflettere	*ree-**fleh**-teh-reh*	to reflect
ripetere	*ree-**peh**-teh-reh*	to repeat
risolvere	*ree-**zol**-veh-reh*	to resolve

Verb	Pronunciation	Meaning
rispondere	ree-**spon**-deh-reh	to respond
rompere	**rom**-peh-reh	to break
scendere	**shen**-deh-reh	to descend
scrivere	**skree**-veh-reh	to write
sorridere	soh-**ree**-deh-reh	to smile
sospendere	soh-**spen**-deh-reh	to suspend
spendere	**spen**-deh-reh	to spend
succedere	soo-**cheh**-deh-reh	to happen/occur
uccidere	oo-**chee**-deh-reh	to kill
vedere	veh-**deh**-reh	to see
vendere	**ven**-deh-reh	to sell
vincere	**veen**-cheh-reh	to win
vivere	**vee**-veh-reh	to live

Practice Makes *Perfetto* II

Your plate is full and your eyes are bloodshot from the feast of verbs. Refer to the previous table and provide the correct verb form that best completes the sentences:

prendere	*accendere*	*risolvere*
vedere	*spendere*	*scrivere*

1. *(Loro)* _____ *molti soldi.*
2. *(Io)* _____ *una lettera.*
3. *(Tu)* _____ *la luce.*
4. *(Noi)* _____ *il film,* Cinema Paradiso.
5. *(Lei)* _____ *il problema.*
6. *(Voi)* _____ *il treno.*

As a Rule

Some verbs are only used in the third person: *piovere* (to rain), *nevicare* (to snow).

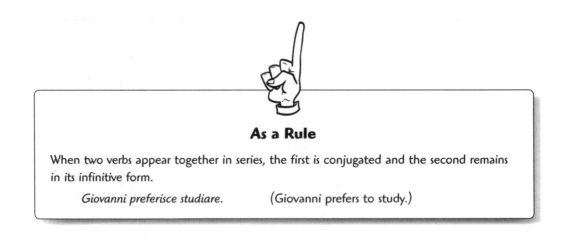

As a Rule

When two verbs appear together in series, the first is conjugated and the second remains in its infinitive form.

> *Giovanni preferisce studiare.*   (Giovanni prefers to study.)

The *–ire* Family

There are two groups of *–ire* verbs. The first group follows conjugation rules that are similar to those for the *–ere* verbs. As a matter of fact, they are the same except for the second-person plural (*voi*), as shown in the following table.

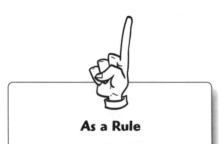

As a Rule

Two kinds of infinitive verbs end in *–ire*, both of which follow separate rules of conjugation. The first group includes verbs such as *aprire, dormire,* and *partire*. The second group includes the verbs *capire, finire,* and *pulire*. How do you determine which rules of conjugation to follow? The old-fashioned way: Practice and memorize the rules!

D *Is for* Dormire

As an example of the first group, see how this works with the verb *dormire* (to sleep).

Dormire (to Sleep)

Italian	English
io dormo	I sleep
tu dormi	you sleep
lui/lei/Lei dorme	he/she sleeps; You sleep
noi dormiamo	we sleep
voi dormite	you sleep
loro dormono	they sleep

The *–ire* Verbs (Group I)

A handful of verbs fall under this category. The following table shows you some of them.

Group I: Regular –*ire* Verbs

Verb	Pronunciation	Meaning
aprire	*ah-**pree**-reh*	to open
bollire	*boh-**lee**-reh*	to boil
convertire	*kohn-ver-**tee**-reh*	to convert
coprire	*koh-**pree**-reh*	to cover
dormire	*dor-**mee**-reh*	to sleep
fuggire	*foo-**jee**-reh*	to escape
mentire	*men-**tee**-reh*	to lie
offrire	*oh-**free**-reh*	to offer
partire	*par-**tee**-reh*	to depart
seguire	*seh-**gwee**-reh*	to follow
servire	*ser-**vee**-reh*	to serve

More –*ire* Verbs (Group II)

The second group of –*ire* verbs is still considered regular but must be conjugated differently from other –*ire* verbs. Once you learn the endings, you'll have no problem conjugating them.

C Is for Capire

A commonly used verb from this family is the verb *capire* (to understand). Look at how this verb conjugates. If you can remember this verb, the others follow quite easily:

Capire (to Understand)

Italian	English
io capisco	I understand
tu capisci	you understand
lui/lei/Lei capisce	he/she understands; You understand
noi capiamo	we understand
voi capite	you understand
loro capiscono	they understand

The –ire Verbs (Group II)

The second group of –*ire* verbs includes interesting verbs such as *capire* (to understand), *impazzire* (to go crazy), and *tradire* (to betray)—all the verbs you'll need for a good juicy opera like *La Traviata*.

As a Rule

To make a negative statement, as in "I don't understand," add the word *non* in front of the verb.

Non capisco *la lezione.*	I don't understand the lesson.
Antonio **non mangia** *la carne.*	Antonio doesn't eat meat.
Non partiamo *per l'America.*	We're not leaving for America.

Double negatives are acceptable in Italian, as in *No, non desidero niente,* which literally translates to "No, I don't want *nothing.*" (Of course, in English you would say, "No, I don't want *anything.*")

Group II: *–ire* Verbs

Verb	Pronunciation	Meaning
aderire	*ah-deh-**ree**-reh*	to adhere
attribuire	*ah-tree-boo-**ee**-reh*	to attribute
capire	*kah-**pee**-reh*	to understand
colpire	*kol-**pee**-reh*	to hit/strike
costruire	*kohs-troo-**wee**-reh*	to construct
definire	*deh-fee-**nee**-reh*	to define
digerire	*dee-jeh-**ree**-reh*	to digest
diminuire	*dee-mee-noo-**wee**-reh*	to diminish
esaurire	*eh-zow-**ree**-reh*	to exhaust
fallire	*fah-**lee**-reh*	to fail/go bankrupt
finire	*fee-nee-reh*	to finish
garantire	*gah-rahn-tee-reh*	to guarantee
gestire	*jeh-**stee**-reh*	to manage/administrate
guarire	*gwah-**ree**-reh*	to heal/recover
impazzire	*eem-pah-**tsee**-reh*	to go crazy
istruire	*ee-stroo-**wee**-reh*	to instruct/teach
obbedire	*oh-beh-**dee**-reh*	to obey
preferire	*preh-feh-**ree**-reh*	to prefer
proibire	*pro-ee-**bee**-reh*	to prohibit/forbid

Verb	Pronunciation	Meaning
pulire	*poo-**lee**-reh*	to clean
punire	*poo-**nee**-reh*	to punish
riunire	*ree-yoo-**nee**-reh*	to reunite
spedire	*speh-**dee**-reh*	to send
stabilire	*sta-bee-**lee**-reh*	to establish
suggerire	*soo-jeh-**ree**-reh*	to suggest
tradire	*trah-**dee**-reh*	to betray/deceive
trasferire	*tras-feh-**ree**-reh*	to transfer
unire	*oo-**nee**-reh*	to unite

Asking Questions

No one knows everything. The curious mind wants to understand, so it needs to ask questions. In Italian, it is very easy to ask a question. This section shows you how to ask basic questions.

The Tags Vero? No? and Giusto?

Another way to ask a simple yes/no *domanda* (question) is to add the tags *vero?* ("true?" or "right?"), *no?* and *giusto?* ("is that so?" or "is that correct?") to the end of a sentence:

Partiamo alle otto, no?	We're leaving at 8:00, no?
Capisci la lezione, vero?	You understand the lesson, right?

Attenzione!

Be careful of sounding like a robot when you read aloud. Say it like you mean it! When asking questions, be sure to change your intonation. Your voice should start out lower and gradually rise until the end of a sentence, as you do in English: *Parla l'italiano?* (Do you speak Italian?)

And the Risposta Is ...

To answer a question affirmatively (yes), use *sì* and give your *risposta* (response).

To answer a question negatively (no), use *no* attached to *non* before the conjugated verb form. This is equivalent to our "don't," as in, "No, I don't smoke."

Question	Affirmative Answer	Negative Answer
Lei fuma le sigarette?	*Sì, fumo le sigarette.*	*No, **non** fumo le sigarette.*
Do you smoke cigarettes?	Yes, I smoke cigarettes.	No, I don't smoke cigarettes.
Capisci la lezione?	*Sì, capisco la lezione.*	*No, **non** capisco la lezione.*
Do you understand the lesson?	Yes, I understand the lesson.	No, I don't understand the lesson.

A Whole Lot of Niente

If you are answering a question and starting your sentence with "No," these negative expressions generally come directly after the conjugated verb. Try to determine the meaning of these examples. If you have difficulty determining the significance of the verbs, find the stem of the verb and use the charts to find the infinitive form.

Italian	English	Example
mai	never	*Non fumo **mai**.*
niente	nothing	*Non desidero **niente**.**
nulla	nothing	*Non compra **nulla**.**
nessuno	no one	*Nessuno **arriva**.*

* Unlike English, Italian allows for double negatives.

Take a deep breath and let it out. Crack your spine, stretch your arms, and roll your head around a couple of times.

If you're finding the lessons increasingly challenging, it's because you're in the thick of the woods right now. Even if you went no further than this chapter, you would have enough Italian to get by. However, you might want to browse your bookstore for a good verb book, such as Barron's *501 Italian Verbs,* to deepen your understanding of them.

After you've had time to digest this rather heavy meal, come back to this chapter as you progress in your studies. It will serve you well.

The Least You Need to Know

➤ Any verb that follows a subject noun or pronoun must be properly conjugated.

➤ There are three verb families: *–are, –ere,* and *–ire.* Each has its own set of conjugation rules.

➤ The verbs are the most essential aspect of learning a foreign language. Take your time and learn the verbs that you'll use the most.

Chapter 9

Being There

In This Chapter

➤ To be or not to be: the verbs *essere* and *stare*

➤ What you have: the verb *avere*

➤ Idiomatic expressions using *essere* and *avere*

➤ Professions

➤ Nationalities and religions

➤ *Ecco*

➤ *C'è* and *ci sono*

Your commitment and discipline are beginning to pay off. In Chapter 5, "Expressively Yours," you learned how to say hello and good-bye. In Chapter 6, "Almost Everything You Wanted to Know About Sex," you learned everything you ever wanted to know about gender issues. In Chapter 7, "What's the Subject?" you became clear on how to address strangers and what to call your friends and family. In the last chapter, you learned all about regular verbs. You may have noticed an essential verb missing from the list, the *most* essential verb: *to be*. This chapter is going to tell you everything you ever wanted to know—and maybe a little more—about the different ways to be.

You'll also learn about another important verb: *to have*. You'll find out that there's a lot to be had with this versatile verb.

In short, it's time to learn your first irregular verbs.

What's What

A **helping verb** is used to form other tenses, including compound tenses such as the *present perfect* tense. In English, we usually use the **auxiliary verb** *to have*, as in "I have eaten." In Italian, there are three helping verbs: *essere* (to be), *avere* (to have), and *stare* (to be), the latter being principally to create the *present progressive* tense (as in "I am leaving").

The Birds and the Be's

Two different *verbi* are used to express "to be" in Italian: *essere* and *stare*.

When you ask someone, *Come stai?* (How are you?), you're using the verb *stare*. When you say, *L'Italia è bella* (Italy is beautiful), you're using the verb *essere*. Because the two verbs mean the same thing, the difference between the two concerns usage. Both verbs can stand on their own, but they can also be used as *helping* or *auxiliary* verbs. You'll need helping verbs when you want to talk about the past and when you want to form compound tenses.

Attenzione!

Don't be confused between *è* (is) and *e* (and)—the accent tells you when it's the verb.

The Verb *Essere*

Look at how the highly irregular verb *essere* conjugates in the following table. It might be a good idea to refer back to Chapter 7 to review the many ways of expressing "you" in Italian. You'll get a lot of mileage out of this one verb—learn it like the back of your hand.

The Verb Essere

Italian	English	Italian	English
io sono	I am	*noi siamo*	we are
tu sei	you are	*voi siete*	you are
lui/lei/Lei è	he/she (it)* is; You are	*loro sono*	they are

*Italian has no neuter "it"—it uses the verb form alone to refer to things or animals.

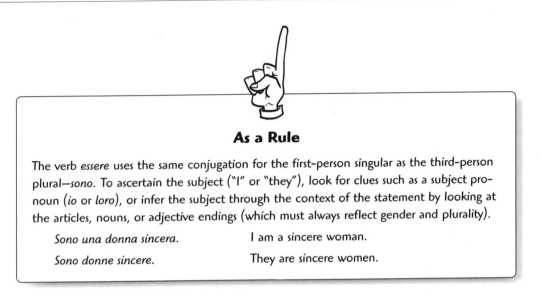

As a Rule

The verb *essere* uses the same conjugation for the first-person singular as the third-person plural—*sono*. To ascertain the subject ("I" or "they"), look for clues such as a subject pronoun (*io* or *loro*), or infer the subject through the context of the statement by looking at the articles, nouns, or adjective endings (which must always reflect gender and plurality).

Sono una donna sincera. I am a sincere woman.

Sono donne sincere. They are sincere women.

The Verb *Stare*

The verb *stare* is easy to learn. Study the following table to see how it is conjugated.

The Verb *Stare*

Italian	English	Italian	English
io **sto**	I am	*noi* **stiamo**	we are
tu **stai**	you are	*voi* **state**	you are
lui/lei/Lei **sta**	he/she (it) is; You are	*loro* **stanno**	they are

Attenzione!

You should always address a man as *Signore* (Mr./Sir) and a woman as *Signora* (Mrs./Ms.); young girls can be addressed as *Signorina* (Miss). When asking someone how they are, you should err on the side of formality and use the polite form of the verb *stare*, as in:

Come sta? How are you?

The response will generally be:

Sto bene, grazie, e Lei? I am well, thanks, and you?

Essere vs. Stare: What's the Difference?

Although the verbs *essere* and *stare* both mean "to be," each verb follows specific rules of usage.

When to Use Essere

The verb *essere* is used in several different ways:

➤ To describe nationalities, origins, and inherent unchanging qualities:

Maurizio è di Verona.	Maurizio is from Verona.
I Gambini sono italiani.	The Gambinis are Italian.
La banana è gialla.	The banana is yellow.

➤ To identify the subject or describe the subject's character traits:

Maria è bionda.	Maria is blond.
Sono io.	It's me.

➤ To talk about the time:

Che ore sono?	What time is it?
Sono le tre e mezzo.	It is 3:30.

➤ To talk about the date:

Natale è il 25 dicembre.	Christmas is December 25.
Che giorno è?	What day is it?
Oggi è lunedì.	Today is Monday.

➤ To indicate possession:

Questo è lo zio di Anna.	This is Anna's uncle.
Quella è la mia casa.	That is my house.

➤ For certain impersonal expressions:

È una bella giornata.	It is a beautiful day.
È molto importante studiare.	It is very important to study.

Come Sei Intelligente!

Now, prove how smart you are. Use the correct form of *essere* in the following phrases:

1. *Luisa _____ una bella persona.*
2. *Grazie per i fiori! Tu _____ romantico.*
3. *Abelardo e Antonella _____ di Firenze.*
4. *Gli occhi _____ le finestre dell'anima.*
5. *Voi _____ generosi.*

When to Use Stare

You're already familiar with the most commonly used expression in Italian, *Come sta?* With few exceptions, the verb *stare* is also used in the following ways:

➤ To describe a temporary state or condition of the subject:

Come **sta?**	How are you?
Sto *bene, grazie.*	I am well, thanks.

➤ To express a location:

Stiamo *in albergo.*	We are staying in a hotel.
Patrizia **sta** *a casa.*	Patricia is at home.

➤ In many idiomatic expressions:

Sta *attento!*	Pay attention!
Sta *zitto!*	Be quiet!

➤ To form the progressive tenses (see Chapter 15, "I Can't Believe My Eyes!"):

Stiamo andando *al cinema.*	We are going to the movies.
Sto studiando *il mio libro.*	I am studying my book.

As a Rule

The preposition *di* (of, from) is often used to show origin or possession, or to describe what something is made of. If the noun preceding *di* begins with a vowel, the *i* is dropped and a contraction is formed.

Di is always preceded by the verb *essere:*

Siamo **di** *Napoli.*	We are from Naples.
Questa macchina è **di** *Beppino.*	This car is Beppino's.
L'anello è **d'***argento.*	The ring is (made of) silver.

Chitchat

You're having a *conversazione* with the person sitting next to you on the plane. Should you use the verb *essere* or *stare?* Complete the following *frasi* with the correct form of the necessary *verbo:*

1. *Noi* _____ *nella pensione Paradiso per due giorni.*
2. *Come* _____ *Lei?*
3. *Io* _____ *bene, grazie.*
4. *Loro* _____ *turisti.*
5. *Il ristorante Caffè Greco* _____ *famoso.*
6. *Villa Borghese* _____ *molto bella.*

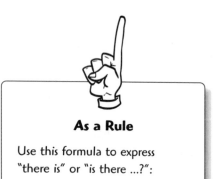

As a Rule

Use this formula to express "there is" or "is there ...?":
ci + è = c'è.

C'è and Ci sono (There Is, There Are)

The word *ci* used with the third person of *essere* indicates "there is" and "there are." This important little adverb states the existence or presence of something or someone. When *ci* is used with the third-person singular *è*, the contraction *c'è* is created:

C'è tempo; non c'è fretta.	There is time; there is no hurry.
Ci sono molti turisti a Roma.	There are many tourists in Rome.

Asking Questions

When asking a question, intonation is everything. When using *c'è* in a question, the word order stays the same. Like in English, you should raise your voice at the end of the sentence:

C'è una banca?	Is there a bank?
Ci sono letti?	Are there beds?

Say It Isn't So

To make negative statements, simply add the word *non* in front of the sentence:

Non c'è problema.	There is no problem.
Non ci sono letti.	There are no beds.

Fill in the Blanks

Study the following phrases and fill in the blanks with either *c'è* or *ci sono*. Translate the sentences. Don't forget to look at the endings to determine whether the subject is singular or plural. If you're unsure about the meaning of a word, consult the glossary in the back of the book.

Example: _____ *un supermercato?*

Answer: __*C'è*__ *un supermercato?*

1. _____ *un museo?*
2. _____ *58.000.000 abitanti in Italia.*
3. _____ *due piazze.*
4. _____ *un bagno privato in camera?*
5. _____ *molti ristoranti a Roma.*
6. _____ *quattro stagioni.*
7. _____ *molti treni?*
8. *Non* _____ *benzina.*

It's Time to Have Some Fun: *Avere*

The irregular verb *avere* (to have) is used in myriad situations and idiomatic *espressioni* and is virtually unrecognizable from its infinitive when it has been conjugated. The following table outlines this useful verb.

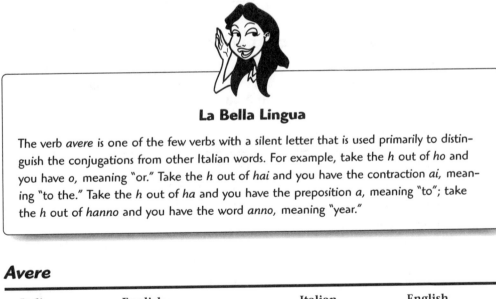

La Bella Lingua

The verb *avere* is one of the few verbs with a silent letter that is used primarily to distinguish the conjugations from other Italian words. For example, take the *h* out of *ho* and you have *o*, meaning "or." Take the *h* out of *hai* and you have the contraction *ai*, meaning "to the." Take the *h* out of *ha* and you have the preposition *a*, meaning "to"; take the *h* out of *hanno* and you have the word *anno*, meaning "year."

Avere

Italian	English	Italian	English
io **ho**	I have	*noi* **abbiamo**	we have
tu **hai**	you have	*voi* **avete**	you have
lui/lei/Lei **ha**	he/she has; You have	*loro* **hanno**	they have

If you're interested in understanding just how many more ways you can communicate with *avere,* check out that friendly companion, your *dizionario,* or better yet, invest in a book such as *2001 Italian and English Idioms,* published by Barron's Educational Series.

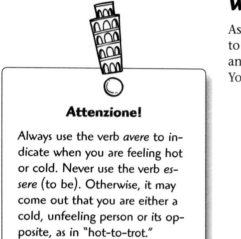

Attenzione!

Always use the verb *avere* to indicate when you are feeling hot or cold. Never use the verb *essere* (to be). Otherwise, it may come out that you are either a cold, unfeeling person or its opposite, as in "hot-to-trot."

When to Use Avere

Aside from meaning "to have," the verb *avere* is used to express when you are hungry, when you feel cold, and when you want to talk about how old you are. You use *avere* in these situations:

➤ To ask someone his or her age.

➤ With idiomatic expressions. Many Italian expressions are metaphors. For example, if you're really hungry, you can say, *Ho una fame da lupo!* (I am hungry as a wolf!)

➤ As an auxiliary—or helping—verb. Use this verb to form the present perfect tense, as in *Ho mangiato* (I have eaten). You'll learn more about this tense in Chapter 19, "Having Fun Italian Style."

An Idiot's Guide to Idioms with Avere

Translations are not always literal. The idiomatic expressions in the following table will help you express your needs and feelings. The infinitive form of the verb is given in parenthesis; it is up to you to conjugate it.

Needs and Feelings

Italian	English
(avere) l'abitudine di	to have the habit of
(avere) ____ anni	to be ____ years old
(avere) bisogno di	to need
(avere) caldo	to be hot (literally, to feel hot)
(avere) colpa	to be at fault, to be guilty
(avere) fame	to be hungry
(avere) la fortuna di	to have the fortune to/of
(avere) freddo	to be cold (literally, to feel cold)
(avere) l'intenzione di	to have the intention of
(avere) mal di	to have pain/to be sick
(avere) l'occasione di	to have the chance to

Italian	English
(avere) l'opportunità di	to have the opportunity to
(avere) paura	to be afraid
(avere) la possibilità di	to have the possibility to
(avere) ragione	to be right
(avere) sete	to be thirsty
(avere) sonno	to be sleepy
(avere) torto	to be wrong
(avere) vergogna	to be ashamed
(avere) voglia di	to be in the mood, to feel like

La Bella Lingua

In Italian, you would never ask how *old* someone is. *Old* never enters the equation. Instead, ask how many years a person has:

Quanti anni hai?   How many years do you have?

Express Yourself

Express your needs. Start by using either *ho* (I have) or *sono* (I am), and add the appropriate Italian word to say the following:

Example: When you are afraid, you say … *Ho paura.*

1. When you are hungry, you say … _____.
2. When the temperature drops below freezing and you don't have a coat, you say … _____.
3. When your legs feel like lead weights and you can't keep your eyes open, you say … _____.
4. When you want to indicate your age, you say … _____.
5. When you are embarrassed, you might say … _____.

Professionally Speaking

As you learned back in Chapter 6, in English, most professional *titoli* (titles) are neuter (doctor, lawyer, teacher), with a few exceptions such as waiter/waitress and actor/actress. Italian professions must reflect the gender of the subject. Exceptions include professions ending in *–a*, such as *dentista* (dentist) and *artista* (artist). In these cases, you will have to pay attention to the article preceding the *professione* to know whether the subject is *maschile* or *femminile*.

➤ Many professions ending in *–o* or *–e* often change to *–a* to reflect gender:

> *l'archeologo* becomes *l'archeologa* (archeologist)
>
> *lo scienziato* becomes *la scienziata* (scientist)

➤ Certain Italian professions have gender-specific endings such as *–ice:*

> *l'attore* becomes *l'attrice* (actor/actress)
>
> *lo scrittore* becomes *la scrittrice* (writer)

➤ Other professions end in *–essa:*

> *il dottore* becomes *la dottoressa* (doctor)
>
> *il poeta* becomes *la poetessa* (poet)
>
> *il professore* becomes *la professoressa* (professor)

In My Professional Opinion

The following table lists several common professions. If you have a *professione* that is atypical, such as a dog walker or floral designer, you may want to consult your *dizionario*. Note that some words such as *il* (or *la*) *contabile* and *il* (or *la*) *dentista* can be used for either gender. I have also indicated when there are separate words such as *attore* and *attrice* (actor and actress) for the same *professione*.

Professions

Profession	*Professione*	Pronunciation
accountant	*il/la contabile*	*eel/lah kon-tah-bee-leh*
actor	*l'attore*	*lah-toh-reh*
actress	*l'attrice*	*lah-tree-cheh*
archeologist	*l'archeologo*	*lar-keh-oh-loh-goh*
	l'archeologa	*lar-keh-oh-loh-gah*

Profession	*Professione*	Pronunciation
architect	*l'architetto*	*lar-kee-teh-toh*
	l'architetta	*lar-kee-teh-tah*
artist	*l'artista*	*lar-tees-tah*
banker	*il bancario*	*eel bahn-kah-ree-yoh*
	la bancaria	*lah bahn-kah-ree-yah*
barber	*il barbiere*	*eel bar-bee-yeh-reh*
cashier	*il cassiere*	*eel kah-see-eh-reh/*
	la cassiera	*lah kah-see-eh-rah*
consultant	*il/la consulente*	*eel/lah kon-soo-len-teh*
dentist	*il/la dentista*	*eel/lah den-tees-tah*
doctor	*il dottore*	*eel doh-toh-reh*
	la dottoressa	*lah doh-toh-reh-sah*
editor	*l'editore*	*leh-dee-toh-reh*
	l'editrice	*leh-dee-tree-cheh*
electrician	*l'elettricista*	*eh-leh-tree-chee-stah*
environmentalist	*l'ecologo*	*eh-koh-loh-goh*
	l'ecologa	*eh-koh-loh-goh*
firefighter	*il pompiere*	*eel pom-pee-yeh-reh*
	il/la vigile del fuoco	*eel/lah vee-jeh-leh del fwoh-koh*
hair dresser	*il parrucchiere*	*eel pah-roo-kee-eh-reh*
	la parrucchiera	*lah pah-roo-kee-eh-rah*
housewife	*la casalinga*	*lah kah-zah-leen-gah*
jeweler	*il/la gioielliere*	*eel joh-yeh-lee-eh-reh*
lawyer	*l'avvocato*	*lah-voh-kah-toh*
manager	*il/la dirigente*	*eel/lah dee-ree-jen-teh*
mechanic	*il meccanico*	*eel meh-kah-nee-koh*
musician	*il/la musicista*	*eel/lah moo-zee-chee-stah*
nurse	*l'infermiere*	*leen-fer-mee-eh-reh*
	l'infermiera	*leen-fer-mee-eh-rah*
plumber	*l'idraulico*	*lee-drow-lee-koh*
police officer	*il vigile*	*eel vee-jee-leh*
	la vigilessa	*lah vee-jee-leh-sah*
professor	*il professore*	*eel proh-feh-soh-reh*
	la professoressa	*lah proh-feh-soh-reh-sah*
scientist	*lo scienziato*	*loh shee-en-zee-ah-toh*
	la scienziata	*lah shee-en-zee-ah-tah*
secretary	*il segretario*	*eel seh-greh-tah-ree-oh*
	la segretaria	*lah seh-greh-tah-ree-ah*

continues

Professions   (continued)

Profession	Professione	Pronunciation
stock broker	*l'agente di borsa*	*lah-jen-teh dee bor-sah*
student	*lo studente*	*loh stoo-den-teh*
	la studentessa	*lah stoo-den-teh-sah*
teacher	*l'insegnante*	*leen-sen-ahn-teh*
waiter	*il cameriere*	*eel kah-meh-ree-eh-reh*
waitress/maid	*la cameriera*	*lah kah-meh-ree-eh-rah*
worker	*l'operaio*	*loh-per-ay-oh*
	l'operaia	*loh-per-ay-ah*
writer	*lo scrittore*	*loh skree-toh-reh*
	la scrittrice	*lah skree-tree-cheh*

What's What

In Italian, one way to show possession is with the use of **possessive adjectives** (my, your, his, her, its, our, and their). They're considered adjectives (unlike in English, where they're considered pronouns) because they must agree in gender and number with the noun possessed, *not* with the possessor. The definite article must usually precede the possessive adjective. For example:

la mia casa	my house
il suo libro	his book

You're most certainly familiar with this common Italian expression that utilizes a possessive adjective:

Mamma mia!	Mother of mine!

You'll see more of these in Chapter 10, "Tell Me About Your Childhood."

So, What's Your Story?

You can only go so far with the niceties; it's time to get into the nitty-gritty. You want to ask about someone else, and the first thing that comes to mind is profession. This is where the verb *essere* comes in handy. You'll learn more about asking questions in Chapter 12, "Moving Around," but for now, give it a shot. Begin your response with *sono* (I am), as in *"Sono dentista.*

*Qual è la **Sua** professione?*	What is your profession?

If the other person is a peer and you feel comfortable enough to use the *tu* form, note how the possessive changes:

*Qual è la **tua** professione?*	What is your profession?

La Bella Lingua

If you're lucky enough to be self-employed, you can say, *Lavoro in proprio.*

We, the People

It's *impossibile* not to meet people from different nationalities and backgrounds when you are traveling. Aside from the guidebook you carry in your right hand and the camera hanging from your neck, it's obvious that you are a *straniero* (foreigner), and the Italians are going to be curious about why you have come to Italy. Don't be surprised if you are asked your origins when you visit Italy.

Lei è d'origine italiana? (polite)	*Sì, sono d'origine italiana.*
Are you of Italian origin?	Yes, I am of Italian origin.
Sei d'origine italiana? (familiar)	*No, sono d'origine russa.*
Are you of Italian origin?	No, I am of Russian origin.

Nationalities

The following table provides a general listing of nationalities. With only a few exceptions, most of these should be easy to remember because they're similar to their English counterparts. Nationalities are adjectives; gender must be reflected in the ending. You'll learn everything you need to know about adjectives in Chapter 10.

Nationalities

English	Italian	Pronunciation
African	*africano(a)*	*ah-free-kah-noh(ah)*
American	*americano(a)*	*ah-meh-ree-kah-noh(ah)*
Belgian	*belga*	*bel-gah*
Canadian	*canadese*	*kah-nah-deh-zeh*
Chinese	*cinese*	*chee-neh-zeh*
Danish	*danese*	*dah-neh-zeh*
Dutch	*olandese*	*oh-lan-deh-zeh*

continues

Nationalities   (continued)

English	Italian	Pronunciation
Egyptian	*egiziano(a)*	*eh-jee-zee-ah-noh(ah)*
English	*inglese*	*een-gleh-zeh*
European	*europeo(a)*	*eh-oo-roh-peh-oh(ah)*
French	*francese*	*frahn-cheh-zeh*
German	*tedesco(a)*	*teh-des-koh(ah)*
Greek	*greco(a)*	*greh-koh(ah)*
Indian	*indiano(a)*	*een-dee-ah-noh(ah)*
Israeli	*israeliano(a)*	*ees-rah-eh-lee-ah-noh(ah)*
Irish	*irlandese*	*eer-lahn-deh-zeh*
Italian	*italiano(a)*	*ee-tah-lee-yah-noh(ah)*
Japanese	*giapponese*	*jah-poh-neh-zeh*
Korean	*coreano(a)*	*koh-ree-ah-noh(ah)*
Mexican	*messicano(a)*	*meh-see-kah-noh(ah)*
Norwegian	*norvegese*	*nor-veh-jeh-zeh*
Polish	*polacco(a)*	*poh-lah-koh(ah)*
Russian	*russo(a)*	*roo-soh(ah)*
Spanish	*spagnolo(a)*	*spahn-yoh-loh(ah)*
Swedish	*svedese*	*sveh-deh-zeh*
Swiss	*svizzero(a)*	*svee-tseh-roh(ah)*
Turkish	*turco(a)*	*toor-koh(ah)*

As a Rule

In Italian, nationalities are *not* capitalized. Countries, however, are always capitalized. Countries should always be preceded with the definite article.

italiano	Italian
l'Italia	Italy

Do You Believe?

You might be asked about your *religione;* some answers are provided in the following table.

Religions

English	Italian	Pronunciation
agnostic	*agnostico(a)*	*ah-nyoh-stee-koh(ah)*
atheist	*ateo(a)*	*ah-teh-oh(ah)*
Buddhist	*buddista*	*boo-dees-tah*
Catholic	*cattolico(a)*	*kah-toh-lee-koh(ah)*
Christian	*cristiano(a)*	*kree-stee-ah-noh(ah)*
Jewish	*ebreo(a)*	*eh-breh-oh(ah)*
Hindu	*indù*	*een-doo*
Muslim	*mussulmano(a)*	*moo-sool-mah-noh(ah)*
Protestant	*protestante*	*proh-tes-tahn-teh*

La Cupola di S. Pietro.

Back to Your Roots

Translate the following sentences into Italian. Determine what the subject is and modify your nationality accordingly.

Example: Wen Wen is Chinese.

Answer: *Wen Wen è cinese.*

1. Olivier is French and lives in Paris.
2. Patrizia is Catholic and has five sisters.
3. Primo Levi is Jewish.
4. Massimo is of Italian origin.
5. There are many Japanese tourists in Italy.

Did You Know?

Here's a Who's Who of mythological archetypes. The Romans and Greeks shared many of the same gods. The Greek equivalents are in parentheses.

The Gods	**The Goddesses**
Apollo (Apollo)	Ceres (Demeter)
Jupiter (Zeus)	Diana (Artemis)
Mars (Ares)	Juno (Hera)
Mercury (Hermes)	Minerva (Athena)
Neptune (Poseidon)	Venus (Aphrodite)
Vulcan (Hephaistos)	Vesta (Hestia)

Ecco!

The word *ecco* is not what you hear when you scream into a canyon. We're not talking about Nietzche's *Ecce Homo,* either. An adverb, *ecco* can mean "here" or "there."

Ecco la stazione!	Here's the station!
Ecco Gabriella!	Here's Gabriella!
Eccomi!	Here I am!

Ecco can also be used to express understanding or agreement, and it is very similar to the French word *voilà*, meaning, "Here it is! Got it!"

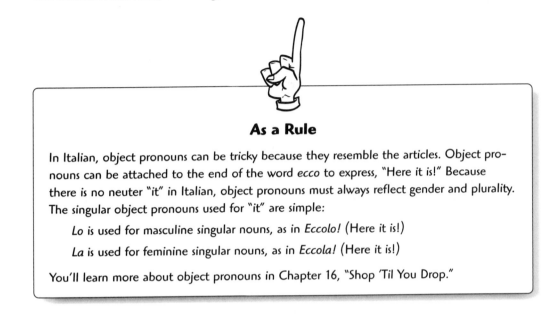

As a Rule

In Italian, object pronouns can be tricky because they resemble the articles. Object pronouns can be attached to the end of the word *ecco* to express, "Here it is!" Because there is no neuter "it" in Italian, object pronouns must always reflect gender and plurality. The singular object pronouns used for "it" are simple:

Lo is used for masculine singular nouns, as in *Eccolo!* (Here it is!)

La is used for feminine singular nouns, as in *Eccola!* (Here it is!)

You'll learn more about object pronouns in Chapter 16, "Shop 'Til You Drop."

Eureka!

Imagine that you're in Italy walking through the streets of *Roma*. Using *ecco,* try expressing the fact that you've found the following places:

1. *il museo*
2. *il ristorante*
3. *la banca*
4. *il negozio*
5. *la strada*
6. *la stazione*
7. *l'albergo*
8. *il bar*
9. *l'ospedale*
10. *l'autobus*
11. *lo stadio*
12. *il supermercato*

The Least You Need to Know

➤ Two verbs express the action "to be": *essere* (used to express various states of existence) and *stare* (used to describe a temporary condition).

➤ *Avere* (to have) is an important verb that can also be used to express expressions of luck, intention, and opportunity. It is also used as an auxiliary verb.

➤ Italian professions almost always reflect the gender of the subject.

Chapter 10

Tell Me About Your Childhood

In This Chapter

➤ Making introductions

➤ Expressing possession using *di*

➤ Using possessive adjectives

➤ Describing things: adjectives

➤ Forming and using adverbs

You've covered the nouns and their noun markers, learned about your verbs and are ready to add some color. In this chapter you'll learn all about adjectives, adverbs, and how to express possession

One of the *Famiglia*

In Italy, one of the first things people want to know about is your family. Do you have brothers or sisters? Are you of Italian descent or one of the many who have fallen in love with the *cultura*, the beautiful landscapes, and the *arte?* It's time to take the chitchat a step further. First, let's take a look at who's who in *la famiglia* in the following table.

Family Members

Female	Pronunciation	Meaning	Male	Pronunciation	Meaning
madre	mah-dreh	mother	padre	pah-dreh	father
moglie	moh-lyeh	wife	marito	mah-ree-toh	husband
nonna	noh-nah	grandmother	nonno	noh-noh	grandfather
figlia	fee-lyah	daughter	figlio	fee-lyoh	son
bambina	bahm-bee-nah	infant	bambino	bahm-bee-noh	infant
sorella	soh-reh-lah	sister	fratello	frah-teh-loh	brother
cugina	koo-jee-nah	cousin	cugino	koo-jee-noh	cousin
zia	zee-ah	aunt	zio	zee-oh	uncle
nipote	nee-poh-teh	granddaughter	nipote	nee-poh-teh	grandson
nipote	nee-poh-teh	niece	nipote	nee-poh-teh	nephew
suocera	swoh-cheh-rah	mother-in-law	suocero	swoh-cheh-roh	father-in-law
nuora	nwoh-rah	daughter-in-law	genero	jen-eh-roh	son-in-law
cognata	koh-nyah-tah	sister-in-law	cognato	koh-nyah-toh	brother-in-law
madrigna	mah-dree-nyah	stepmother	padrigno	pah-dree-nyoh	stepfather
sorellastra	soh-reh-lah- strah	stepsister	fratellastro	frah-teh-lah-stroh	stepbrother
madrina	mah-dree-nah	godmother	padrino	pah-dree-noh	godfather
ragazza	rah-gah-tsah	girlfriend	ragazzo	rah-gah-tsoh	boyfriend
fidanzata	fee-dahm-zah-tah	fiancée	fidanzato	fee-dahm-zah-toh	fiancé
vedova	veh-doh-vah	widow	vedovo	veh-doh-voh	widower

Are You Possessed?

You will always be somebody's somebody: your mother's child, your brother's sister, your dog's owner, your wife's husband. In English, we use 's or s' to show possession. In Italian there are two ways of showing possession.

You show possession by using *di*, as in:

> *Silvia è la figlia di Pepe.*
>
> Silvia is Pepe's daughter. (Silvia is the daughter of Pepe.)

You can show possession by using a possessive adjective, as in the familiar expressions:

> *Dio mio!*   My God!
>
> *Mamma mia!*   Mother of mine!

As a Rule

When discussing the collective "children," Italian reverts to the masculine plural: *i figli*. The same goes for friends: *gli amici*. One's *genitori* (parents) can be simply referred to as *i miei* (coming from the possessive adjective "my," as in "my parents"). The word used to describe a niece/nephew and a granddaughter/grandson is the same: *nipote*.

Using *Di* to Show Possession

The simplest way to express possession is to use *di*, meaning "of." Look at the following example to see how this works.

> *Questa è la casa di Mario.*
>
> This is Mario's house. (This is the house of Mario.)

Forming Contractions with Di

Notice how the endings of the contractions correspond to the articles, and pay attention to how *di* changes form when forming a contraction. Contractions are explained in more detail in Chapter 11, "Finally, You're at the Airport."

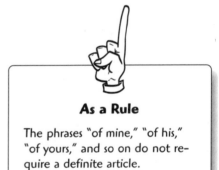

As a Rule

The phrases "of mine," "of his," "of yours," and so on do not require a definite article.

una mia speranza	a hope of mine
due suoi amici	two friends of his
una sua collega	a colleague of his

Contractions with *Di*

Singular	Plural
di + il = del	*di + i = dei*
di + lo = dello	*di + gli = degli*
di + l' = dell'	*di + le = delle*
di + la = della	

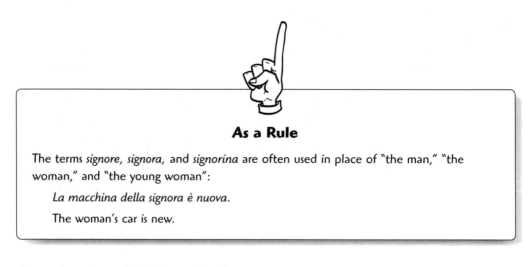

As a Rule

The terms *signore*, *signora*, and *signorina* are often used in place of "the man," "the woman," and "the young woman":

La macchina della signora è nuova.

The woman's car is new.

Examples using contractions with *di* are …

Ecco le chiavi della macchina.

Here are the car keys. (Here are the keys of the car.)

C'è il figlio del presidente.

There is the president's son. (There is the son of the president.)

Attenzione!

When it isn't clear who the possessor is, use *di* to indicate the subject:

Il libro di Rosetta.

Rosetta's book. (The book of Rosetta.)

La macchina di Antonio.

Antonio's car. (The car of Antonio.)

Possessive Adjectives

"A possessive what?" you ask. Don't panic. In English, we call them possessive pronouns, such as my, your, his, and our. In Italian, the possessive adjectives must be followed by the noun it is possessing or modifying ("my house," "your house," and so on). It will help to keep a few things in mind.

First, you have to ask what is being possessed. Second, you need to choose the possessive adjective that agrees with it. In Italian, what is important is the gender of the noun. For instance, if what is being possessed is masculine singular, then your possessive adjective must also be masculine singular. Compare the English possessives to their Italian counterparts in these examples. Contrary to English usage, Italian forms do not distinguish between "his" and "her"; pay special attention to how *suo* and *sua* are used.

*Gino ama **sua** madre e **suo** padre.*	Gino loves **his** mother and **his** father.
*Beatrice ama **sua** madre e **suo** padre.*	Beatrice loves **her** mother and **her** father.

As a Rule

When speaking of family members, there is no article required before the possessive adjective. Take a look at the following examples:

Mia madre è una donna forte.

My mother is a strong woman.

The following table summarizes the use of possessive adjectives. Keep in mind that in most cases, the possessive adjectives require the use of the definite article.

Possessive Adjectives

	Singular		Plural	
Possessive	Masculine	Feminine	Masculine	Feminine
my	*il mio*	*la mia*	*i miei*	*le mie*
your	*il tuo*	*la tua*	*i tuoi*	*le tue*
his/her (its)	*il suo*	*la sua*	*i suoi*	*le sue*
Your*	*il Suo*	*la Sua*	*i Suoi*	*le Sue*
our	*il nostro*	*la nostra*	*i nostri*	*le nostre*
your	*il vostro*	*la vostra*	*i vostri*	*le vostre*
their	*il loro*	*la loro*	*i loro*	*le loro*

As you may remember, Lei, the polite form of "You," is capitalized to distinguish it from lei *(she). The possessive adjectives are also capitalized to make this distinction.*

A Sense of Belonging

Determine the appropriate possessive adjective using the previous list for the following:

Example: her house

Answer: *la sua casa*

1. his house
2. my school
3. her books

4. his books
5. your (familiar) friend Mario

La Bella Lingua

If someone asks you a question you don't know the answer to, shrug your shoulders and say *Chi sa?* (Who knows?) or *Non lo so.* (I don't know.)

It's Good to Know

Two verbs are equivalent to the English verb "to know": *sapere* (to know something) and *conoscere* (to know someone).

Sapere: *To Know Something*

The verb *sapere* is what you use to talk about all the information you have stuck inside that head of yours.

Sapere

Italian	English
io so	I know
tu sai	you know
lui/lei/Lei sa	he/she knows; You know
noi sappiamo	we know
voi sapete	you know
loro sanno	they know

Conoscere: *To Know Someone/To Be Acquainted*

The verb *conoscere* is generally used to talk about someone with whom you are acquainted, but you can also use it when referring to a city or place, or even *una lingua*.

Conoscere

Italian	English	Italian	English
io conosco	I know	*noi conosciamo*	we know
tu conosci	you know	*voi conoscete*	you know
lui/lei/Lei conosce	he/she knows; You know	*loro conoscono*	they know

Making Introductions

If you are in mixed company, it's always considered polite to introduce your new friends and family to one another. If you are being introduced, a handshake and a nod are all that is required.

This Is My ...

You can express the demonstrative pronouns "this" and "these," shown in the following table, if you want to say, "*This* is my sister and *these* are my parents."

The Demonstrative Pronouns "This" and "These"

Gender	This	These
Masculine	*questo* libro	*questi* libri
	*quest'anno**	*questi* anni
Feminine	*questa* penna	*queste* penne
	*quest'idea**	*queste* idee

*All singular nouns beginning with a vowel take quest'.

This Is My Brother ...

When referring to singular nouns denoting family members (*madre, padre, sorella, fratello ...*, and not *mamma, babbo ...*) there's no need to put an article in front of the person being possessed. If you are introducing your *fratello* (brother), then you have to use the masculine singular demonstrative pronoun *questo*, as in:

Questo è mio *fratello.*   This is my brother.

If it's your mother you are introducing, you have to use a feminine singular demonstrative pronoun, such as:

> *Questa è **mia** madre.*   This is my mother.

In most other cases, you must include the article before the noun. Even if a friend may feel just like family, she should be introduced using the article. For example:

> *Questa è **la mia** amica Cristina.*   This is my friend Cristina.

Who Is Who

You'll need to know how to use the following expressions to make introductions.

Helpful Introductory Expressions

Italian	English
Vorrei presentare …	I'd like to present …
Conosce …?	Do you know …?
*È un piacere conoscerti.**	It's a pleasure to meet you. (informal)
*È un piacere conoscerLa.**	It's a pleasure to meet you. (polite)
Il piacere è mio.	The pleasure is mine.
Questo è mio fratello.	This is my brother.
Questa è mia sorella.	This is my sister.
Questi sono i miei amici.	These are my friends.
Queste sono le mie amiche.	These are my girlfriends.

*Both of these constructions use the direct object pronoun. You'll learn more about these in Chapter 16, "Shop 'Til You Drop."

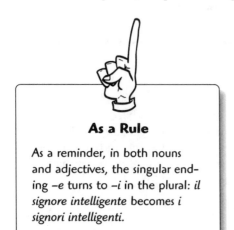

As a Rule

As a reminder, in both nouns and adjectives, the singular ending –e turns to –i in the plural: *il signore intelligente* becomes *i signori intelligenti*.

Tall, Dark, and Handsome

What a bland world it would be without descriptive adjectives. Everything would be all action and no illustration. If verbs are the skeleton of a language and nouns are the flesh, adjectives are the color. They're pretty, ugly, big, little, black, white, young, old, and all of what's in between.

Modifying Adjectives

Unlike English, Italian adjectives must reflect both the gender (masculine or feminine) and number (singular or plural) of the nouns and pronouns they describe.

Fortunately, the following endings used for adjectives are pretty much the same as the noun endings. Like in a *concerto*, everything has to work together. Keep in the mind the following:

➤ If describing a masculine noun, simply leave the adjective as is. (Adjectives default to the masculine—it goes way back before women's lib.)

> *Tuo fratello è un **ragazzo simpatico**.*
> Your brother is a nice boy.

➤ In most cases, when you change an adjective to the feminine, the ending will be *–a*.

> *Tua sorella è una **ragazza simpatica**.*
> Your sister is a nice girl.

➤ Many adjectives that end in *–e*, such as *intelligente, giovane, grande, verde, triste,* and *cortese,* can be used to describe both masculine and feminine nouns. The plural endings of these adjectives follow the same rules as nouns ending in *–e*.

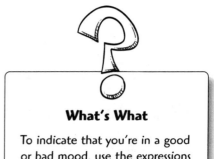

What's What

To indicate that you're in a good or bad mood, use the expressions *Sono di buon umore* (I am in a good mood) and *Sono di cattivo umore* (I am in a bad mood).

Modifying Those Adjective Endings

You've already seen how many Italian adjectives are cognates to English in Chapter 4, "You Know More Than You Think." Look at the following endings, and compare them to the noun endings you learned in Chapter 6, "Almost Everything You Wanted to Know About Sex."

La Bella Lingua

Although most adjectives come after the noun, the following adjectives often precede the nouns they modify, such as *Che bella casa!* (What a beautiful house!):

altro (other)	*cattivo* (evil)
bello (beautiful)	*grande* (big)
bravo (good, able)	*piccolo* (small)
brutto (ugly)	*stesso* (same)
buono (good)	*vecchio* (old)

Adjective Endings

Endings	Examples
o → i	*famoso→ famosi*
a → e	*curiosa → curiose*
ca → che	*magnifica → magnifiche*
e → i	*intelligente → intelligenti*

Character Analysis

Using the adjectives you just learned, try describing the people around you. For example:

> *Il mio fidanzato è generoso, intelligente, sincero, e ricco.*
>
> My fiancé is generous, intelligent, sincere, and rich.

1. Your significant other (or your fantasy)
2. Your mother
3. Your brother, sister, or cousin
4. Your cat, dog, or other domestic companion
5. Your best friend
6. Your boss

What's What

Some adjectives have different words for men and woman, such as *celibe* (a single man) and *nubile* (a single woman).

A Real Wise Guy

You want to describe your wonderful wife or husband, your children, your new boyfriend or girlfriend, your ex, your best friend, or your cat. Are they kind or cruel, good or bad, generous or stingy? The list of adjectives and their antonyms in the following table will add to your array of options.

Emotions and Characteristics

English	Italian	Pronunciation	English	Italian	Pronunciation
ambitious	ambizioso	ahm-bee-zee-oh-zoh	lazy	pigro	pee-groh
beautiful	bello	beh-loh	ugly	brutto	broo-toh
blond	biondo	bee-ohn-doh	brunette	bruno	broo-noh
calm	calmo	kahl-moh	nervous	nervoso	ner-voh-zoh
clever/sly	furbo	foor-boh	slow/dull	lento	len-toh
courageous	coraggioso	koh-rah-joh-zoh	cowardly	codardo	koh-dahr-doh
courteous	cortese	kor-teh-zeh	discourteous	scortese	skor-teh-zeh
cute/pretty	carino	kah-ree-noh	unattractive	bruttino	broo-tee-noh
fat	grasso	grah-soh	skinny	magro	mah-groh
funny	buffo	boo-foh	boring	noioso	noy-oh-zoh
generous	generoso	jeh-ner-oh-zoh	stingy	tirchio	teer-kee-yoh
good	bravo	brah-voh	evil	cattivo	kah-tee-voh
happy	allegro	ah-leh-groh	sad	triste	tree-steh
healthy	sano	sah-noh	sick	malato	mah-lah-toh
honest	onesto	oh-nes-toh	dishonest	disonesto	dee-soh-nes-toh
intelligent	intelligente	een-tel-ee-jen-teh	stupid	stupido	stoo-pee-doh
kind/polite	gentile	jen-tee-leh	impolite	scortese	skor-teh-zeh
loyal	fedele	feh-deh-leh	unfaithful	infedele	een-fed-eh-leh
lucky	fortunato	for-too-nah-toh	unlucky	sfortunato	sfor-too-nah-toh
married	sposato	spoh-zah-toh	divorced	divorziato	dee-vor-zee-ah-toh
nice	simpatico	seem-pah-tee-koh	mean	antipatico	ahm-tee-pah-tee-koh
organized	organizzato	or-gah-nee-zah-toh	unorganized	disorganizzato	dee-zor-gah-nee-zah-toh
perfect	perfetto	per-feh-toh	imperfect	imperfetto	eem-per-feh-toh
proud	fiero	fee-yeh-roh	ashamed	vergognoso	ver-goh-nyoh-zoh
romantic	romantico	roh-mahn-tee-koh	practical	pratico	prah-tee-koh
sensitive	sensibile	sen-see-bee-leh	insensitive	insensibile	een-sen-see-bee-leh
sincere	sincero	seen-cheh-roh	insincere	bugiardo	boo-jar-doh
strong	forte	for-teh	weak	debole	deh-boh-leh
tall	alto	ahl-toh	short	basso	bah-soh
young	giovane	joh-vah-neh	old	vecchio	veh-kee-yoh
wise	saggio	sah-joh	uncultured	incolto	een-kol-toh

Take the Good with the Bad

If you want to describe things, including the lamp you just bought, the food you just ate, and the cost of something, the following list of adjectives and their opposites will help you.

Adjectives and Their Antonyms

English	Italian	Pronunciation	English	Italian	Pronunciation
big	*grande*	*gran-deh*	small	*piccolo*	*pee-koh-loh*
clean	*pulito*	*poo-lee-toh*	dirty	*sporco*	*spor-koh*
complete	*completo*	*kom-pleh-toh*	incomplete	*incompleto*	*een-kohm-pleh-toh*
dear/ expensive	*caro*	*kah-roh*	inexpensive	*economico*	*eh-koh-noh- mee-koh*
first	*primo*	*pree-moh*	last	*ultimo*	*ool-tee-moh*
full	*pieno*	*pee-yeh-noh*	empty	*vuoto*	*vwoh-toh*
good	*buono*	*bwoh-noh*	bad	*male*	*mah-leh*
hard	*duro*	*doo-roh*	soft	*morbido*	*mor-bee-doh*
heavy	*pesante*	*peh-zahn-the*	light	*leggero*	*leh-jeh-roh*
hot	*caldo*	*kahl-doh*	cold	*freddo*	*freh-doh*
light	*leggero*	*leh-jeh-roh*	heavy	*pesante*	*peh-zahn-teh*
long	*lungo*	*loon-goh*	short	*basso*	*bah-soh*
new	*nuovo*	*nwoh-voh*	used	*usato*	*oo-zah-toh*
next	*prossimo*	*proh-see-moh*	last	*ultimo*	*ool-tee-moh*
normal	*normale*	*nor-mah-leh*	strange	*strano*	*strah-noh*
open	*aperto*	*ah-per-toh*	closed	*chiuso*	*kee-yoo-soh*
perfect	*perfetto*	*per-feh-toh*	imperfect	*imperfetto*	*eem-per-feh-toh*
pleasing	*piacevole*	*pee-ah-cheh-voh-leh*	displeasing	*spiacevole*	*spee-ah-cheh- voh-leh*
real	*vero*	*veh-roh*	fake	*finto*	*feen-toh*
safe/sure	*sicuro*	*see-koo-roh*	dangerous	*pericoloso*	*per-ee-koh-loh-zoh*
strong	*forte*	*for-teh*	weak	*debole*	*deh-boh-leh*
true	*vero*	*veh-roh*	false	*falso*	*fahl-zoh*

I Colori

Colors are adjectives and must agree with the nouns they are describing, whether masculine or feminine, singular or plural. Check out the rainbow in the following table.

La Bella Lingua

To describe any color as light, simply add the adjective *chiaro* to the color to form a compound adjective, as in *rosso chiaro* (light red).

To describe any color as dark, add the word *scuro*, as in *rosa scuro* (dark pink). (*Rosa* is masculine unless you are talking about *la rosa*, the flower.)

Colori

Color	*Colore*	Pronunciation
beige	*beige*	*behj*
black	*nero*	*neh-roh*
blue	*blu*	*bloo*
brown	*marrone*	*mah-roh-neh*
gold	*oro*	*or-oh*
gray	*grigio*	*gree-joh*
green	*verde*	*ver-deh*
orange	*arancione*	*ah-ran-choh-neh*
pink	*rosa*	*roh-zah*
purple	*viola*	*vee-oh-lah*
red	*rosso*	*roh-soh*
silver	*argento*	*ar-jen-toh*
white	*bianco*	*bee-ahn-koh*
yellow	*giallo*	*jah-loh*

One Yellow Banana, Please

Fill in the blank with the adjective modified by the subject and then translate the sentences:

Example: *La banana è* _____. (yellow)

Answer: *La banana è* ___*gialla*___.

1. *La casa* _____ (white) *è* _____ (clean).
2. *Il Colosseo è molto* _____ (old).
3. *Le montagne in Svizzera sono* _____ (high).

141

4. *Il negozio è* _____ (closed) *la domenica.*

5. *Quest'albergo è* _____ (inexpensive).

6. *Lo Scrooge è un uomo molto* _____ (cheap).

La Bella Lingua

The next time you're in a produce store, take your list of *colori*. Start with a color like *rosso* and note all the red fruits and vegetables you can find, making sure your adjective agrees with the noun such as *la mela rossa* (the red apple). Do the same with all of the *colori*.

It's a Colorful World

The colors are easy to learn in Italian—even easier if you connect them to things you know, such as "white as snow." The Italian language is riddled with fun *espressioni* having to do with *i colori*. Here are some of them with both the literal translation and the figurative one:

mettere nero su bianco	to put black to white (to put down in writing)
vedere rosa	to see pink (to see through rose-colored glasses)
vedere nero	to see black (to be angry or pessimistic)
rosso come un peperone	red as a pepper
essere nero	to be black (to be in a bad mood)
un numero verde	a green number (a toll-free number)

Everyone's a Poet

Try to come up with your own *espressione idiomatica* for the colors listed. If you get stumped, think of some fruits or vegetables that might help:

1. *Arancione come* _____ (orange as …)

2. *Azzurro come* _____ (azure as …)

3. *Bianco come* _____ (white as …)

4. *Blu come* _____ (blue as …)

5. *Beige come* _____ (beige as …)

6. *Giallo come* _____ (yellow as …)

7. *Grigio come* _____ (gray as …)

8. *Marrone come* _____ (brown as …)

9. *Nero come* _____ (black as …)

10. *Rosa come* _____ (pink as …)

11. *Rosso come* _____ (red as …)

12. *Viola come* _____ (purple as …)

Bello and *Quello*

The adjectives *bello* (beautiful, handsome, nice, good, fine) and *quello* (that/those) follow the same rules, as you can see in the following table. Both have forms similar to those of the definite article.

Bello and *Quello*

Gender	Singular	Plural	When It Is Used
Masculine	*bello/quello*	*begli/quegli*	Before *s* + consonant or *z*
	bell'/quell'	*begli/quegli*	Before vowels
	bel/quel	*bei/quei*	Before consonants
Feminine	*bella/quella*	*belle/quelle*	Before all consonants
	bell'/quell'	*belle/quelle*	Before vowels

Generally speaking, *bello* and *quello* come before the noun, like in English.

> *Che **bei** bambini!*
> What beautiful children!

> ***Quelle belle** donne sono anche simpatiche.*
> Those beautiful women are also nice.

When the adjective *bello* follows the verb *essere*, it retains its full form. (However, it must still reflect the gender and number of the noun it describes.)

> *Quell'albergo è **bello**.*
> That hotel is beautiful.

> *Quella ragazza è **bella**.*
> That girl is beautiful.

La Bella Lingua

Bello is used to describe anything wonderful: a good meal, a sunset, a beautiful person. If you want to sound like an Italian, use this *espressione* the next time you are moved by something you find extraordinary: *Che bello!* (literally meaning "How beautiful!").

Make the Connection

Fill in the appropriate forms of the definite article and its corresponding forms of *quello*, and translate.

Definite Article	Translation	Quello	Translation
1. _il_ *libro*	the book	_quel_ *libro*	that book
2. _____ *libri*	_____	_____ *libri*	_____
3. _____ *penna*	_____	_____ *penna*	_____
4. _____ *penne*	_____	_____ *penne*	_____
5. _____ *articolo*	_____	_____ *articolo*	_____

143

6. _____ *articoli*   _____   _____ *articoli*   _____
7. _____ *studente*   _____   _____ *studente*   _____
8. _____ *studenti*   _____   _____ *studenti*   _____

Buono

Similar to the rules followed by the indefinite articles, the adjective *buono* (good) changes form in the singular when preceding a noun. (However, when following the verb *essere* or the noun it modifies, it uses the regular forms *buono* and *buona* in the singular.) The plural form of this adjective is regular. Consult the following table for the different forms.

Buono

Gender	Singular	Plural	When It Is Used
Masculine	il **buono** studente	i **buoni** studenti	Before masculine nouns beginning with s + consonant or z
	il **buon** libro i **buoni** libri	il **buon** amico i **buoni** amici	Before all other masculine nouns (both consonants and vowels)
Feminine	la **buona** ragazza	le **buone** ragazze	Before feminine nouns beginning with a consonant
	la **buon'**amica	le **buone** amiche	Before feminine nouns beginning with a vowel

The following are a few examples of how to use this adjective:

Trovare un buon amico è difficile.   A good friend is hard to find.

Maria, tu sei una buon'amica.   Maria, you are a good friend.

How Do You Do? Adverbs

How are you doing? I hope that you're doing "well" and that everything is "fine." As you recall from Chapter 2, "Immerse Yourself," adverbs describe verbs or adjectives and indicate how you do something, such as, "She plays the piano *beautifully*," or "You are *sincerely* the *most* beautiful person I've ever met." In addition to irregular adverbs, which are covered next and need to be memorized, you can also create an adverb from an adjective.

Forming Adverbs from Adjectives

Many English adverbs end in *–ly*. In Italian, you can form several adverbs by adding *–mente* to the end of the feminine form of the adjective:

seria → *seriamente*   serious → serious**ly**

profonda → *profondamente*   profound → profound**ly**

chiara → *chiaramente*   clear → clear**ly**

Adjectives ending in *–le* or *–re* drop the final *–e* before adding *–mente*:

facile (easy) → **facilmente** (easily)

gentile (kind) → **gentilmente** (kindly)

Did You Know?

Every time you use the word *non* in a sentence, you are using an adverb. I'll bet you *never* (also an adverb) knew that the words *no* and *sì* (yes) are both adverbs. Other commonly used irregular adverbs include these:

better	*meglio*
by no means	*nemmeno*
certainly	*certamente*
exactly	*appunto*
maybe	*forse*
never	*mai*
not even	*neanche*
really	*davvero*
well	*bene*

Take Your Place

A couple of points about the placement of adverbs will help you easily incorporate them into your growing *vocabolario*.

➤ Adverbs are generally placed after the verb:

*Puoi imparare **facilmente** l'italiano.* You can **easily** learn Italian.

*Siete **gentilmente** pregati di lasciare un messaggio.* You are **kindly** asked to leave a message.

*Ti parlo **seriamente**.* I'm speaking to you **seriously**.

145

➤ Some adverbs may come *before* the verb or adjective:

Probabilmente vado domani.   I'm **probably** going tomorrow.

Firenze è sempre bella.   Florence is **always** beautiful.

A Lot of Adverbs

When talking about quantity, you might want less or more, depending on your mood. The following table gives you some of these.

Irregular Adverbs of Quantity

English	Italian	English	Italian
enough	*abbastanza*	quite a lot of	*parecchio*
hardly, scarcely	*appena*	rather, somewhat	*piuttosto*
less	*meno*	too	*troppo*
not very	*poco*	very, much, a lot	*molto*
not any more, no more	*non più*		

Adverbs of Time

Many adverbs relating to time—like those of place—aren't formed from an adjective. The following table offers you some of these timely words.

Adverbs of Time

English	Italian	English	Italian
after	*dopo, poi*	slowly	*piano, lentamente*
again	*ancora*	soon	*subito*
always	*sempre*	still	*ancora*
before	*prima*	then	*allora, poi*
early	*presto*	today	*oggi*
immediately	*subito*	tomorrow	*domani*
never	*mai*	usually	*di solito*
now	*adesso, ora*	in a hurry	*in fretta*
often	*spesso*	when	*quando*
quickly	*presto*	yesterday	*ieri*

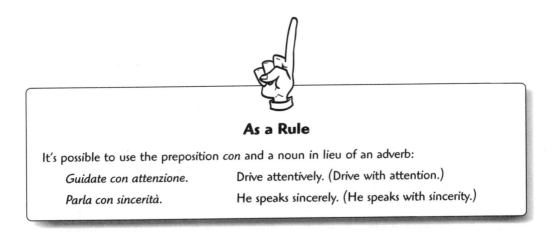

As a Rule

It's possible to use the preposition *con* and a noun in lieu of an adverb:

Guidate con attenzione.   Drive attentively. (Drive with attention.)

Parla con sincerità.   He speaks sincerely. (He speaks with sincerity.)

Adverbs of Place

In the last chapter, you learned about the adverb *ci* when it is used with the verb *essere*. It's good to know your place. The adverbs in the following table will help.

Adverbs of Place

English	Italian	English	Italian
above	*sopra*	in back of	*dietro*
anywhere	*dovunque*	in front of	*davanti*
behind	*indietro*	inside	*dentro*
beneath	*sotto*	near	*vicino*
down	*giù*	on	*sopra*
down there	*laggiù*	on top of	*su*
elsewhere	*altrove*	outside	*fuori*
everywhere	*dappertutto*	there	*ci, là, lì*
far	*lontano*	up	*su*
here	*qui, qua*		

The More Things Change

Make the following adjectives into adverbs. Many of these adjectives will require that you make them feminine before converting them to adverbs. You can also use the formula *con* (with) + the noun, such as *con attenzione* (with attention).

Example: *breve* (brief)

Answer: *brevemente* (briefly)

1. *dolce* (sweet)
2. *sincero* (sincere)
3. *intelligente* (intelligent)
4. *necessario* (necessary)
5. *veloce* (fast/quick)

6. *regolare* (regular)
7. *difficile* (difficult)
8. *probabile* (probable)
9. *solo* (only)
10. *gentile* (kind)

The Least You Need to Know

➤ To show possession in Italian, use the possessive adjectives or the preposition *di*.

➤ The adjective *buono* follows a pattern similar to the indefinite article.

➤ Italian adjectives must agree in gender and number with the nouns they modify.

➤ Adverbs are formed by adding *–mente* to many feminine adjectives. Many adverbs of time and place are irregular and must be memorized.

Chapter 11

Finally, You're at the Airport

In This Chapter

➤ All about planes and airports

➤ The verb *andare* (to go)

➤ Connections and asides: using prepositions and contractions

➤ Being direct: how to use the imperative

➤ Expressing confusion

➤ Passively yours: using *si* to construct the passive voice

The best way to communicate is often in the simplest manner. No need to start quoting Dante; just get your point across. Sometimes it takes pointing to something and saying, *questo* (this). Other times it may mean using a combination of vocabulary, mime, and facial expressions to make yourself understood.

On the Plane

Most international flights to and from Italy communicate with passengers in both English and Italian. This is a wonderful *opportunità* to develop your listening skills. Instead of relying on your native *lingua,* pay close attention to the *voce* coming over the loud speaker when Italian is used. Try to grasp the general meaning. The vocabulary in the following table contains many of the words you might hear.

Inside the Plane

English	Italian	Pronunciation
airline	*la linea aerea*	*lah lee-neh-ah ah-eh-reh-ah*
airline terminal	*il terminal*	*eel ter-mee-nahl*
airplane	*l'aereo*	*lah-eh-reh-roh*
airport	*l'aeroporto*	*lah-eh-roh-por-toh*
aisle	*il corridoio*	*eel koh-ree-doy-oh*
aisle seat	*un posto vicino al corridoio*	*oon pos-toh vee-chee-noh ahl koh-ree-doy-oh*
exit	*l'uscita*	*loo-shee-tah*
... emergency exit	*... l'uscita d'emergenza*	*loo-shee-tah deh-mer-jen-zah*
flight	*il volo*	*eel voh-loh*
... domestic	*... nazionale*	*nah-zee-oh-nah-leh*
... international	*... internazionale*	*een-ter-nah-zee-oh-nah-leh*
flight number	*il numero del volo*	*eel nooh-meh-roh dehl voh-loh*
gate	*il cancello*	*eel kahn-cheh-loh*
headphones	*le cuffie*	*leh koo-fee-ay*
landing	*l'atterraggio*	*lah-ter-ah-joh*
life vest	*il giubbotto di salvataggio*	*eel joo-boh-toh dee sahl-vah-tah-joh*
luggage	*i bagagli*	*ee bah-gahl-yee*
magazine	*la rivista*	*lah ree-vee-stah*
newspaper	*il quotidiano*	*eel kwoh-tee-dee-ah-noh*
nonsmoking seat	*un posto per non fumatori*	*oon pos-toh per nohn foo-mah-toh-ree*
on board	*a bordo*	*ah bor-doh*
row	*la fila*	*lah fee-lah*
seat	*il posto*	*eel poh-stoh*
seat belt	*la cintura di sicurezza*	*lah cheen-too-rah dee see-kor-eh-zah*
steward	*l'assistente di volo*	*lah-sees-ten-teh dee voh-loh*
stewardess	*l'hostess*	*l'hostess*
take-off	*il decollo*	*eel deh-koh-loh*
trip	*il viaggio*	*eel vee-ah-joh*
window seat	*un posto vicino al finestrino*	*oon poh-stoh vee-chee-noh ahl fee-nes-treh-noh*

In the Comfort Zone

Look at the following paragraph from an Italian in-flight magazine on the various services offered to passengers, and see how much you understand:

> *A bordo dell'aereo sono a disposizione dei passeggeri: riviste italiane e straniere, coperte e cuscini, medicine, carta da lettera, giochi per bambini, penne, cartoline, sigarette, spumanti italiani, vino, birra, e bibite varie.*

La Bella Lingua

You may find the following verbiage comes in handy when traveling. Several of these verbs can have more than one meaning.

essere in anticipo	to be early
essere in ritardo	to be delayed
fumare	to smoke
imbarcare	to board, to embark
perdere (un volo)	to miss (a flight), to lose
prenotare	to reserve
salire	to get on, to ascend
scendere	to get off, to descend

On the Inside

You've landed safely. You're ushered off the plane toward customs. After your *passaporto* is stamped, you grab your bags off the luggage carousel: You need to find a bathroom, change money, and find out when your connecting flight to Sicily (or Milan, or Pisa) is leaving. Did you lose something *importante* and now need to find the *Ufficio Oggetti Smarriti* (the lost and found)? How are you going to communicate all of these things? Look no further; the following table gives you virtually all the vocabulary you may need.

Inside the Airport

English	Italian	Pronunciation
arrival	*l'arrivo*	*lah-ree-voh*
arrival time	*l'ora d'arrivo*	*loh-rah dah-ree-voh*
baggage claim	*la riconsegna bagagli*	*lah ree-kohn-sehn-yah bah-gahl-yee*
bathroom	*la toilette*	*lah toy-leht*
	il bagno	*eel-bah-nyoh*
(bus) stop	*la fermata (dell'autobus)*	*lah fer-mah-tah*

continues

Inside the Airport (continued)

English	Italian	Pronunciation
car rental	*l'autonoleggio*	low-toh-noh-leh-joh
cart	*il carrello*	eel kah-reh-loh
connection	*la coincidenza*	lah koh-een-cheh-den-zah
customs	*la dogana*	lah doh-gah-nah
departure	*la partenza*	lah par-ten-zah
departure time	*l'ora di partenza*	loh-rah dee pahr-ten-zah
destination	*la destinazione*	lah des-tee-nah-zee-oh-neh
elevator	*l'ascensore*	lah-shen-soh-reh
entrance	*l'entrata*	len-trah-tah
information	*le informazioni*	leen-for-mah-zee-oh-nee
money exchange	*il cambio*	il kahm-bee-oh
porter	*il portiere*	eel por-tee-eh-reh
reservation	*la prenotazione*	lah preh-noh-tah-zee-oh-neh
stairs	*le scale*	leh skah-leh
taxi	*il tassì*	eel tah-see
telephone	*il telefono*	eel tel-eh-foh-noh
ticket	*il biglietto*	eel bee-lyeh-toh

In addition, the following helpful expressions will at the very least get you to Italy comfortably:

Dov'è la dogana?	Where is customs?
Vorrei un posto vicino al finestrino/corridoio.	I'd like a seat near the window/aisle.
Vorrei viaggiare in prima/seconda classe.	I'd like to travel in first/second class.
Vorrei fare il biglietto di andata e ritorno.	I'd like to order a round-trip ticket.
Vorrei prendere l'aereo.	I'd like to take a plane.
Vorrei consegnare i bagagli al deposito bagagli.	I'd like to consign bags in the baggage claim.
Vorrei prenotare un posto.	I'd like to reserve a place.
Dove si trova la biglietteria?	Where does one find the ticket office?

Going Crazy: The Verb *Andare*

The verb *andare* (to go) can come in handy as you make your way around. This is an irregular verb, so you will need to memorize the parts outlined in the following table. (You can cram on the seven-hour plane ride.)

The Verb *Andare*

Italian	English	Italian	English
io **vado**	I go	noi **andiamo**	we go
tu **vai**	you go	voi **andate**	you go
lui/lei/Lei **va**	he/she goes; You go	loro **vanno**	they go

As a Rule

You use the preposition *a* when you want to express going to or staying in a city:

> *Vado a Roma.* (I'm going to Rome.)

The preposition *in* is generally used when you are traveling to a country:

> *Andiamo in Italia.* (We are going to Italy.)

Andare is generally followed by the preposition *a* (to), as it usually is in English (I am going to …) when you want to say you're going somewhere or going to do something. Often, you must create a contraction when using the preposition *a* with a definite article (you'll learn about contractions later in this chapter).

Vado all'università.	I am going to the university.
Andiamo al ristorante.	We're going to the restaurant.
Andate a mangiare?	Are you going to eat?

Andare may also be followed by the preposition *in* (to) when describing means of transportation. Naturally, you'll still have to conjugate the infinitive verb:

andare in macchina	to go by car
andare in bicicletta	to go by bicycle
andare in treno	to go by train
andare in aeroplano	to go by plane

Did You Know?

The Italians often say *Andiamo!* much in the same way we say "Let's go!"

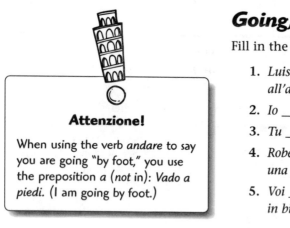

Going, Going, Gone

Fill in the appropriate form of *andare*:

1. *Luisa e Marta* _____ *in macchina all'aeroporto.*

2. *Io* _____ *a New York.*

3. *Tu* _____ *alla stazione.*

4. *Roberto ed io* _____ *a mangiare una pizza.*

5. *Voi* _____ *a piedi. Loro* _____ *in bicicletta.*

Attenzione!

When using the verb *andare* to say you are going "by foot," you use the preposition *a* (not *in*): *Vado a piedi.* (I am going by foot.)

All Verbed Up and Everywhere to Go

The regular verb *prendere* (to take) is used when traveling. If necessary, refer back to Chapter 8, "An Action-Packed Adventure," to remember how to conjugate regular *-ere* verbs. Together with the irregular verb *andare,* use the two verbs in the following sentences. Remember that the gerund form in English is equivalent to the simple present in Italian.

1. *(Io)* _____ *l'autobus per andare in centro. (prendere)*

   I am taking the bus to get downtown.

2. *(Noi)* _____ *in macchina in spiaggia. (andare)*

   We are going by car to the beach.

3. *(Loro)* _____ *il treno da Roma per arrivare a Milano. (prendere)*

   They are taking the train from Rome to get to Milan.

4. *(Tu)* _____ *a piedi al negozio. (andare)*

   You are going by foot to the store.

5. *(Voi)* _____ *la metro per arrivare alla piramide in Via Ostiense. (prendere)*

   You (plural) are taking the subway to get to the pyramid on Via Ostiense.

6. *(Lui)* _____ *in bicicletta a vedere la campagna. (andare)*

   He is going by bicycle to see the country.

Prepositions: Sticky Stuff

You've used these words thousands of times and probably never knew they were all prepositions. You've already seen a lot of prepositions because they are often the glue of a phrase, tying the words together. The following table provides a comprehensive list of Italian prepositions and their meanings.

What's What

The most commonly used prepositions follow:

a (to, at)	*Andiamo a Roma.*	We're going to Rome.
con (with)	*Vado con Roberto.*	I am going with Robert.
da (from, by)	*Vengo da lontano.*	I'm coming from far away.
di (of, from)	*Di dove sei?*	Where are you from?
in (in, to)	*Viaggiano in Italia.*	They are traveling to Italy.
per (for)	*Questo regalo è per te.*	This present is for you.
su (on)	*Il libro sta sulla scrivania.*	The book is on the table.

Prepositions

Italian	English
a	to, at, in
accanto a	beside
attorno a	around
avanti	in front of, before, ahead
circa	about, around (when making an estimation)
con	with
contro	against, opposite to
da	from, by
davanti a	before
dentro a	inside
di	of, from, about
dietro a	behind
dopo	after
eccetto	except, save
fino a	until, as far as
fra, tra	between, among, in, within
fuori di	outside
in	in, into, by, on

continues

Prepositions (continued)

Italian	English
lontano da	far from
oltre	besides, beyond
per	for, in order to
senza	without
sopra	above
sotto	under
su	on, upon
vicino a	near

A Few Points on Prepositions

Prepositions in Italian can be tricky. Does the Italian preposition *in* mean "to" or "by" or "in"? Does *a* mean "at" or "in"? Here are a few general rules about the most commonly used prepositions, all of which can be used to form contractions (we'll get to those next).

➤ The preposition *a* (at, to, in) is used with cities and towns. It is also used after many infinitive verbs, which will be outlined in Chapter 13, "Hallelujah, You've Made It to *l'Hotel*."

➤ The preposition *da* (from, at, by) is used to express when you've been *at* somewhere, whether an office, the doctor's, or far away.

➤ The preposition *di* (of, from, about) is also used to express possession and is used in many idiomatic expressions.

➤ The preposition *in* (at, in, to) is used before the names of countries, when talking about modes of transportation, and when talking about what street you live *on*.

La Bella Lingua

There is no equivalent to the preposition *on* before the names of days:

Arriviamo lunedì.	We are arriving (on) Monday.
Giuseppe arriva sabato.	Giuseppe is arriving (on) Saturday.

Contractions

No one is having a baby here. A *contraction,* in linguistic terms, is a single word made out of two words. The prepositions in the following table form contractions when followed by a definite article. Notice that the endings remain the same as the definite article. A contraction can be as simple as *alla* (to the) or *sul* (on the).

Contractions

Preposition	Masculine					Feminine		
	Singular			Plural		Singular		Plural
	il	*lo*	*l'*	*i*	*gli*	*la*	*l'*	*le*
a	al	allo	all'	ai	agli	alla	all'	alle
in	nel	nello	nell'	nei	negli	nella	nell'	nelle
di	del	dello	dell'	dei	degli	della	dell'	delle
su	sul	sullo	sull'	sui	sugli	sulla	sull'	sulle
da	dal	dallo	dall'	dai	dagli	dalla	dall'	dalle

As a Rule

To express *in* with months, the Italians use either the preposition *in* or *a:*

*Il mio compleanno è **a** giugno.*	My birthday is in June.
*Fa ancora freddo **in** marzo.*	It's still cold in March.

To express the notion of being *in* with seasons, the Italians use either the preposition *in* or *di:*

*Andiamo in Italia **d'**inverno.*	We are going to Italy in the winter.
***In** primavera fa bello.*	It's beautiful in the spring.

You can use prepositions in so many different ways that it's almost *impossibile* to outline every one of them here. The best way to learn prepositions is by studying the basic rules and listening for idiomatic usage. If you want a more comprehensive explanation of speech parts and their different uses, you might want to pick up a copy of a good Italian grammar book.

Switcharoo

Replace the bold words with the words in parentheses, changing the preposition or contraction as necessary. Accommodate any changes in gender or plurality.

1. *Silvia ed io andiamo **al cinema.** (festa)*

2. *Il tassì va **in centro.** (piazza)*

3. *Andate **a piedi?** (macchina)*

4. *La giacca sta **sulla tavola.** (armadio)*

5. *Mangiamo **del riso.** (spaghetti)*

As a Rule

The preposition *da* (from/by/of/since) can mean "since" or can describe an amount of time. For example, use the present tense of the verb *essere* + *da* to create the following:

Da quanto tempo sei in Italia?   Literally, "You are in Italy from how much time?"

Sono in Italia da ottobre.   Literally, "I am in Italy since October."

As a Rule

You can use the preposition *di* plus an article to express an unspecified quantity or "some" of a greater amount:

Mangio della pasta.   I am eating some pasta.

Bevo del vino.   I am drinking some wine.

Vuole della frutta?   Do you want some fruit?

The Imperative: Giving Directions

Getting lost while traveling can be half the fun, but sometimes you have a particular place in mind and don't want to spend your entire afternoon wandering around the streets. Being able to ask for directions is easy enough. You can point to your map and ask *Dov'è …?* or you can form a simple question using what you've learned in this book. Understanding the response you're given is another story. When someone directs you to a location, that person is using the imperative.

The imperative is used for giving suggestions, orders, and directions. You're already familiar with the imperative *Mangia!* a commonly uttered command heard across tables of millions of Italian families.

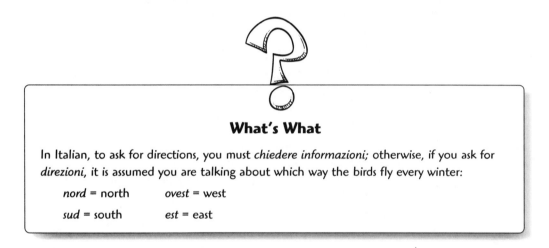

What's What

In Italian, to ask for directions, you must *chiedere informazioni;* otherwise, if you ask for *direzioni*, it is assumed you are talking about which way the birds fly every winter:

nord = north   *ovest* = west

sud = south   *est* = east

The Regular Imperative Endings

Look at the following endings to see how you can make any verb imperative. Notice how the imperative endings for *noi* and *voi* are exactly the same as they are in the present tense.

Imperative Endings

Subject	*–are*	*–ere*	*–ire*
tu	*–a*	*–i*	*–i*
lui/lei/Lei	*–i*	*–a*	*–a*
noi	*–iamo*	*–iamo*	*–iamo*
voi	*–ate*	*–ete*	*–ite*
loro	*–ino*	*–ano*	*–ano*

The Imperative Using Tu *and* Lei

The following table offers some of the most common commands you'll hear, using the polite *Lei* and familiar *tu*. The irregular forms have been indicated.

Imperative Forms

Verb	Tu	Lei	Meaning
*andare**	*Va!*	*Vada!*	Go!
attraversare	*Attraversa!*	*Attraversi!*	Cross!
*avere**	*Abbi!*	*Abbia!*	Have!
camminare	*Cammina!*	*Cammini!*	Walk!
continuare	*Continua!*	*Continui!*	Continue!
*dire**	*Di'!*	*Dica!*	Say/Tell!
*essere**	*Sii!*	*Sia!*	Be!
*fare**	*Fa'! or Fai!*	*Faccia!*	Do! Make! Take!
girare	*Gira!*	*Giri!*	Turn!
passare	*Passa!*	*Passi!*	Pass!
prendere	*Prendi!*	*Prenda!*	Take!
*salire**	*Sali!*	*Salga!*	Get on! Go up!
scendere	*Scendi!*	*Scenda!*	Go down!
seguire	*Segui!*	*Segua!*	Follow!
*stare**	*Stai!*	*Stia!*	Stay!
*venire**	*Vieni!*	*Venga!*	Come!

*These verbs have irregular imperatives.

As a Rule

To form a negative command, such as "Don't go!" in the *tu* form, you don't need to worry about endings. Just use the formula of *non* + infinitive:

Non andare!	Don't go!
Non girare!	Don't turn!

You may hear some of the following imperatives used while you're shopping or chatting.

Abbia pazienza!	Have patience! (polite)
Mi dica!	Tell me. (polite)
Dimmi tutto.	Tell me everything. (familiar)
Faccia quello che vuole.	Do what you want. (polite)

Tell Me What to Do

Use the imperative form with the following nondirectional verbs:

	Tu	*Lei*
aiutare (to help)	_____	_____
mangiare (to eat)	_____	_____
portare (to bring)	_____	_____
telefonare (to telephone)	_____	_____

Dazed and Confused

You've figured out how to ask for the help you need, and you've been given a response. What do you do if you don't understand? Rather than stand there looking like an idiot, just have them repeat themselves, but more slowly this time. The following table gives you a few phrases you can use to let people know you just don't get it. The verb is always used in the polite form.

Expressing That You Just Don't Get It

English	Italian
Excuse me.	*Mi scusi.*
Speak slowly please— I don't speak Italian well.	*Parli piano, per favore— non parlo bene l'italiano.*
Speak more slowly, please.	*Parli più lentamente, per favore.*
Repeat another time, please.	*Ripeti un'altra volta, per favore.*
I didn't understand.	*Non ho capito.*
I understood.	*Ho capito.*
How? (a much nicer way of saying "Huh?")	*Come?*

Passively Yours: *Si*

The *si* construction is used to express the passive voice or when *one* is (or *you* are) talking about an unspecified subject. Notice the distinction between the pronoun *si* (one/you) and the word *sì* (yes).

This form is used in Italian to make general statements such as:

Si mangia bene in Italia.	One eats well in Italy.

Often this tense is used to ask or give directions:

Con l'autobus si arriva subito.	With the bus, one arrives immediately.
Come si arriva in centro?	How does one get to the center?
Per andare in piazza si va diritto.	One goes straight to arrive in the piazza.

La Dogana (Customs)

Imagine that you're an Italian filling out a customs form. Notice the *si* construction used in the repeated expression *Si prega*. In writing, this is often used in lieu of "please" and is equivalent to "you are kindly asked."

MODULO I-94

IMMIGRAZIONE

Si prega di rispondere alle seguenti domande (cognome, nome, data di nascita, nazionalità, ecc.). Si prega di compilare solamente il davanti del formulario. Si prega anche di tenere questo modulo nel passaporto. È necessario un modulo per ogni membro della famiglia. Si prega di compilarlo in stampatello.

1. Cognome _____
2. Nome _____
3. Data di Nascita: Giorno/Mese/Anno _____
4. Cittadinanza _____
5. Sesso: Maschile/Femminile _____
6. Numero del passaporto _____
7. Linea aerea e numero di volo _____
8. Stato dove abitate _____
9. Città dove è stato ottenuto il visto_____
10. Data del visto: Giorno/Mese/Anno_____

The Least You Need to Know

➤ Prepositions are the glue that ties words together and are frequently used with an article, forming a contraction.

➤ The imperative is the command form of a verb; it is used to tell people what to do and where to go. The most commonly used forms of the imperative are the *tu* and the *Lei* forms.

➤ The *si* construction is used when *one* wants to talk in general terms.

Chapter 12

Moving Around

In This Chapter

➤ The modes of transportation you'll use in *Italia*

➤ Which bus? What train? The importance of *quale* (which)

➤ The language of Ferrari: learning the lingo of the road

➤ Numerically speaking: learning numbers and how to tell time

➤ Becoming curious: asking questions

➤ Take a trip with the verb *fare*

This chapter gives you all the vocabulary you need to be as independent as *possibile* and the means to *navigare* through just about any travel challenge.

Hoofing and Spinning

When traveling within a *città,* you have a few choices about how you're going to get around. It's best to take advantage of the *economico* and efficient modes of public transportation. However, walking or cycling is always a terrific way of getting to know the corners of a city that you won't see from inside a bus or taxi—as well as a splendid way to stay in shape. Or, if you dare, you can rent a car.

Before you decide how you're going to get around, however, you need to know what you're talking about (in Italian, that is). The Modes of Transportation Table covers all your bases (and wheels). You'll notice there are two words used for "car."

Did You Know?

In Italy, public transportation is quite efficient, with buses, trains, and *la metro* (subway) to take you just about anywhere you want to go. It's a good idea to purchase bus tickets at a *cartoleria* or *tabacchi* to keep in your wallet because buses do not accept cash or coins. You can also buy *biglietti* (tickets) at train stations and from automated machines. Once you get on *l'autobus*, you must *convalidare* your ticket by punching it into a small box located on the back of the bus. Hold on to your ticket in case of a surprise check by stern-faced inspectors eager to find transgressions. When using *la metro*, you must also buy a ticket from either one of the automated machines or from a ticket booth. It's possible to buy daily, weekly, and monthly tickets.

Modes of Transportation

English	Italian	Pronunciation
bus	*l'autobus*	*low-toh-boos*
car	*l'automobile*	*low-toh-moh-bee-leh*
	la macchina	*lah mah-kee-nah*
bicycle	*la bicicletta*	*lah bee-chee-kleh-tah*
railway	*la ferrovia*	*lah feh-roh-vee-yah*
subway	*la metro*	*lah meh-troh*
taxi	*il tassì*	*eel tah-see*
train	*il treno*	*eel treh-noh*

Which One?

The interrogative pronoun and adjective *quale* means "which" or "what" and is used to ask questions. There are two forms: *quale* (which one), and *quali* (which ones).

Ecco i libri; quale preferisce?	Here are the books; which do you prefer?
Quali sono gli autobus per il centro?	What are the buses (going) downtown?

Qual è ...? expresses the question "What is ...?"

Qual è il tuo numero di telefono?	What is your telephone number?

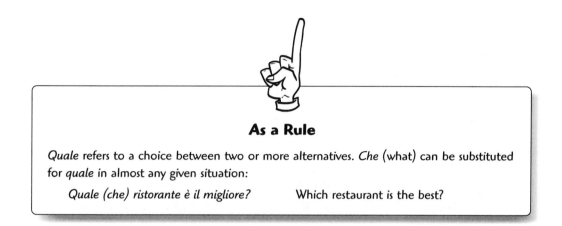

As a Rule

Quale refers to a choice between two or more alternatives. *Che* (what) can be substituted for *quale* in almost any given situation:

Quale (che) ristorante è il migliore?   Which restaurant is the best?

On the Road

Italy's *autostrade* are among the best in the world, but *le macchine* move pretty fast (often drivers do not abide by the speed limit), so keep in the right lane unless you're prepared to speed. Getting a handle on international driving laws is always a good idea, and your local AAA can probably give you a hand in learning more about the do's and don'ts. It also wouldn't hurt to be able to understand directions and signs. Although most signs are fairly obvious, some can be pretty tricky.

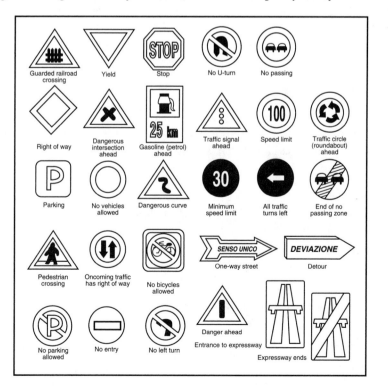

You should also familiarize yourself with the names of the amenities inside a car before you get in one. You can't keep your eyes on the road while searching for the button that means "air conditioner," now can you? Check out the following table for hints about car features.

Inside the Car

English	Italian	Pronunciation
accelerator	*l'acceleratore*	*lah-cheh-leh-rah-toh-reh*
air conditioning	*l'aria condizionata*	*lah-ree-yah kohn-dee-zee-oh-nah-tah*
brakes	*i freni*	*ee freh-nee*
dashboard	*il cruscotto*	*eel kroo-skoh-toh*
gear stick	*il cambio*	*eel kahm-bee-yoh*
glove compartment	*il vano portaoggetti*	*eel vah-noh por-tah-oh-jeh-tee*
handbrake	*il freno a mano*	*eel freh-noh ah mah-noh*
horn	*il clacson*	*eel klak-son*
ignition	*l'accensione*	*lah-chen-see-oh-neh*
keys	*le chiavi*	*leh kee-ah-vee*
radio	*la radio*	*lah rah-dee-oh*
rear-view mirror	*lo specchietto*	*loh speh-kee-yeh-toh*
speed limit	*il limite di velocità*	*eel lee-mee-teh dee veh-loh-chee-tah*
speedometer	*il tachimetro*	*eel tah-kee-met-roh*
steering wheel	*il volante*	*eel voh-lahn-teh*
turn signal	*la freccia*	*lah freh-chah*

Behind the Wheel

Renting a car is easiest from the airport because most of the competitors have booths with English-speaking staff. If you find yourself in a small, out-of-the-way town, however, the following phrases will help you get some wheels:

Vorrei noleggiare una macchina.
I would like to rent a car.

Preferisco una macchina con il cambio automatico.
I prefer a car with automatic transmission.

Quanto costa al giorno (alla settimana/al chilometro)?
How much does it cost per day (per week/per kilometer)?

Quanto costa l'assicurazione per l'auto?
How much does automobile insurance cost?

Quale tipo di pagamento preferite?
What form of payment do you prefer?

Accettate carte di credito?
Do you accept credit cards?

La Bella Lingua

There are several types of roads in Italy:

➤ *L'autostrada:* Just like the throughway, expect to pay high tolls on these fast-paced lanes.

➤ *La superstrada:* Like a local highway, these roads are well maintained and can be quite scenic.

➤ *La statale:* This state road is slower than a *superstrada* but faster than the *strada comunale.*

➤ *La strada comunale:* On these local roads, watch out for slow-moving tractors and the occasional flock of sheep.

Automobile Parts

If you've decided to rent *una macchina,* carefully inspect it inside and out. Make sure there is *un cricco* (a jack) and *una ruota di scorta* (a spare tire) in the trunk, in case you get a *gomma a terra* (flat tire)—and it doesn't hurt to check for any pre-existing damages you could later be charged for.

The following table gives you the Italian words for car parts and predicaments. You never know—that cherry-red Ferrari you rented could turn out to be a lemon.

Automobile Parts and Predicaments

English	Italian	Pronunciation
antenna	*l'antenna*	*lahn-teh-nah*
battery	*la batteria*	*lah bah-ter-ee-yah*
breakdown	*un guasto*	*oon gwah-stoh*
bumper	*il paraurti*	*eel pah-rah-oor-tee*
carburetor	*il carburatore*	*eel kar-boor-ah-toh-reh*
door	*la portiera*	*lah por-tee-eh-rah*
door handle	*la maniglia*	*lah mah-nee-lyah*
fan belt	*la cinghia del ventilatore*	*lah cheen-ghee-yah del ven-tee-lah-toh-reh*
fender	*il parafango*	*eel pah-rah-fahn-goh*

continues

Automobile Parts and Predicaments (continued)

English	Italian	Pronunciation
filter	*il filtro*	*eel feel-troh*
flat tire	*una gomma a terra*	*oo-nah goh-mah ah ter-rah*
	una ruota bucata	*oo-noh roo-woh-tah boo-kah-tah*
fuse	*un fusibile*	*oon foo-see-bee-leh*
gas tank	*il serbatoio*	*eel ser-bah-toy-oh*
headlights	*i fari*	*ee fah-ree*
hood	*il cofano*	*eel koh-fah-noh*
license	*la patente*	*lah pah-ten-teh*
license plate	*la targa*	*lah tar-gah*
motor	*il motore*	*eel moh-toh-reh*
muffler	*la marmitta*	*lah mar-mee-tah*
radiator	*il radiatore*	*eel rah-dee-yah-toh-reh*
sign	*il segnale*	*eel sen-yah-leh*
spark plug	*la candela d'accensione*	*lah kahn-deh-lah dah-chen-see-oh-neh*
tail light	*la luce di posizione*	*lah loo-cheh dee poh-zee-zee-oh-neh*
tire	*la ruota*	*lah rwoh-tah*
traffic officer	*il vigile*	*eel vee-jee-leh*
trunk	*il bagagliaio*	*eel bah-gah-lyah-yoh*
window	*il finestrino*	*eel fee-neh-stree-noh*
windshield	*il parabrezza*	*eel pah-rah-breh-zah*
windshield wiper	*il tergicristallo*	*eel ter-jee-kree-stah-loh*

La Bella Lingua

Tools are the last thing you think of when learning a second language, but if you're stranded, the following might be helpful:

pliers	*le pinze*
screwdriver	*il cacciavite*
hammer	*il martello*
monkey wrench	*la chiave inglese*

The Road Less Traveled

The following table contains more useful verbs and expressions related to the road.

More Words for the Road Warrior

English	Italian
to break down	*guastarsi*
to change a tire	*cambiare la ruota*
to check	*controllare*
... the water	*... l'acqua*
... the oil	*... l'olio*
... the tires	*... le ruote*
to drive	*guidare*
to fill it up	*fare il pieno*
to get gas	*fare benzina*
to get a ticket	*prendere una multa*
to give a ride	*dare un passaggio*
to obey traffic signs	*rispettare i segnali*
to park	*parcheggiare*
to run/function	*funzionare*
to run out of gas	*rimanere senza benzina*

La Bella Lingua

Follow the signs!

Deviazione	Detour
Divieto di Ingresso	No Entrance
Divieto di Sorpasso	No Passing
Divieto di Sosta	No Parking
Sosta Autorizzata	Parking Permitted
Doppio Senso	Two-Way Traffic
Senso Unico	One-Way Traffic

Tell Me Your Worries

You're driving along, minding your own business, when—pop! You blow a tire. A kind stranger pulls over and asks you what happened and whether you need help.

Did You Know?

In Italy, schedules are given in military time. If you are leaving at 2:00 P.M., for example, you are told 14,00 hours. This may be tricky at first, so confirm that you have understood correctly by asking if it is A.M. (*di mattino*) or P.M. (*di sera*).

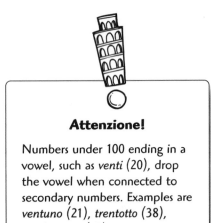

Attenzione!

Numbers under 100 ending in a vowel, such as *venti* (20), drop the vowel when connected to secondary numbers. Examples are *ventuno* (21), *trentotto* (38), *quarantuno* (41), and so on. *Mille* (1000) turns to *mila* in the plural, as with the number *due mila* (2000).

Replace the English with its Italian equivalent to describe to the good Samaritan what your problem is and how he can help:

> *Signore: C'è un problema?*
>
> *Turista: Si, c'è* (a flat tire).
>
> *Signore:* (The car) *è Sua?*
>
> *Turista: No,* (I am renting) *questa macchina per una settimana. Sono in vacanza.*
>
> *Signore: C'è* (a jack) *nel portabagagli?*
>
> *Turista: Credo di sì. Lei è molto* (kind).

Baby, I Got Your Number

Public transportation is a great way to get around, but how are you going to get on the right bus if you don't know which number it is, or take the right train if you don't know what time it leaves? Numerically speaking, you'd have a pretty hard time. Take *un momento* to learn how to count and tell time (and you won't be late for your date with that attractive stranger you met on the plane).

Cardinal Numbers

In Italy, you're going to need to be able to count to a million since the Italian currency (*lira*) requires you to be able to understand high numbers. For instance, a *cappuccino* on average is 2,000 *lire* (L2.000). (Don't panic; it's only about a buck and a half.) If you want to make a date, tell the time, or find out prices, you need to know your cardinal numbers (1, 2, 3, ...).

Fortunately, you don't need to use Roman numerals to do your math. Numbers that express amounts, known as cardinal numbers, are called *numeri cardinali* in Italian. Let the counting begin.

Numeri Cardinali

English	Italian	Pronunciation
0	*zero*	*zeh-roh*
1	*uno*	*oo-noh*
2	*due*	*doo-weh*
3	*tre*	*treh*
4	*quattro*	*kwah-troh*
5	*cinque*	*cheen-kweh*
6	*sei*	*sey*
7	*sette*	*seh-teh*
8	*otto*	*oh-toh*
9	*nove*	*noh-veh*
10	*dieci*	*dee-ay-chee*
11	*undici*	*oon-dee-chee*
12	*dodici*	*doh-dee-chee*
13	*tredici*	*treh-dee-chee*
14	*quattordici*	*kwah-tor-dee-chee*
15	*quindici*	*kween-dee-chee*
16	*sedici*	*sey-dee-chee*
17	*diciassette*	*dee-chah-seh-teh*
18	*diciotto*	*dee-choh-toh*
19	*diciannove*	*dee-chah-noh-veh*
20	*venti*	*ven-tee*
21	*ventuno*	*ven-too-noh*
22	*ventidue*	*ven-tee-doo-eh*
23	*ventitrè*	*ven-tee-treh*
24	*ventiquattro*	*ven-tee-kwah-troh*
25	*venticinque*	*ven-tee-cheen-kweh*
26	*ventisei*	*ven-tee-sey*
27	*ventisette*	*ven-tee-seh-teh*
28	*ventotto*	*ven-toh-toh*
29	*ventinove*	*ven-tee-noh-veh*
30	*trenta*	*tren-tah*
40	*quaranta*	*kwah-rahn-tah*
50	*cinquanta*	*cheen-kwahn-tah*
60	*sessanta*	*seh-sahn-tah*
70	*settanta*	*seh-tahn-tah*
80	*ottanta*	*oh-tahn-tah*
90	*novanta*	*noh-vahn-tah*

continues

Numeri Cardinali **(continued)**

English	Italian	Pronunciation
100	*cento*	*chen-toh*
101	*centouno*	*chen-toh-oo-noh*
200	*duecento*	*doo-ay-chen-toh*
300	*trecento*	*treh-chen-toh*
400	*quattrocento*	*kwah-troh-chen-toh*
500	*cinquecento*	*cheen-kweh-chen-toh*
1.000	*mille*	*mee-leh*
1.001	*milleuno*	*mee-leh-oo-noh*
1.200	*milleduecento*	*mee-leh-doo-eh-chen-toh*
2.000	*duemila*	*doo-eh-mee-lah*
3.000	*tremila*	*treh-mee-lah*
10.000	*diecimila*	*dee-ay-chee-mee-lah*
20.000	*ventimila*	*ven-tee-mee-lah*
100.000	*centomila*	*chen-toh-mee-lah*
200.000	*duecentomila*	*doo-eh-chen-toh-mee-lah*
1.000.000	*un milione*	*oon mee-lyoh-neh*
1.000.000.000	*un miliardo*	*oon mee-lyar-doh*

Number Crunching

Keep in mind these brief notes on writing numbers in Italian:

➤ Italian uses a period to indicate units of thousands.

English	Italian
2,000	*2.000*

➤ In Italian, you must use commas in decimal numbers. It is read as *e* (and):

English	Italian
1.25	*1,25*

➤ When writing down the time, Italian uses a comma (and not a colon) and is again read as *e* (and):

English	Italian
3:30 A.M.	*3,30 di mattino*
9:45 P.M.	*9,45 di sera*

Time Is of the Essence

Time is easy to learn. You need to remember the verb *essere* for asking what time it "is." You use the verb *sapere* to ask if someone "knows" the time.

You can ask the time in several ways:

Che ore sono?	What time is it?
Che ora è?	What time is it?
Sa l'ora?	Do you know what time it is?

Use the third person of *essere* to respond.

È l'una.	It is one o'clock.
È mezzogiorno.	It is noon.
Sono le due.	It is two o'clock.
Sono le nove.	It is nine o'clock.

If someone is already wearing a watch and asks you for the time, beware. Otherwise, the following expressions will help talk about the time.

> **Attenzione!**
>
> Be careful of the Italian word *tempo* because this word is primarily used when talking about the weather (as in *temperatura*), not time.

Time Expressions

English	Italian	English	Italian
What time is it?	*Che ore sono? Che ora è?*	early/late	*in anticipo/in ritardo*
The time is ...	*Sono le ...*	half past	*e mezzo*
At what time?	*A che ora?*	in	*fra*
an hour	*un'ora*	... a while	*... un po'*
a half hour	*un mezz'ora*	... an hour	*... un'ora*
a minute	*un minuto*	... a half hour	*... una mezz'ora*
a quarter past	*e un quarto*	in the afternoon	*di pomeriggio*
a quarter to	*meno un quarto*	in the evening	*di sera*
a second	*un secondo*	in the morning	*di mattino*
ago	*fa*	less than/before	*meno (le)*
and	*e*	on time	*in tempo*
before/after	*prima/dopo*	since	*da*

Use *è* when it is one o'clock. For all other times, because they are plural, use *sono*.

È l'una.	It is 1:00.
Sono le tre.	It is 3:00.

To express time after the hour, use *e* (without the accent, meaning "and") plus the number of minutes past the hour:

Sono le quattro e dieci.	It is 4:10.
Sono le sei e cinque.	It is 6:05.
È l'una e un quarto.	It is 1:15.

To express time before the next hour (in English, we say "ten to," "quarter to," and so on), use the next hour + *meno* (meaning less) + whatever time is remaining before the next hour:

Sono le otto meno un quarto.	It is a quarter to eight—literally, eight minus a quarter.
È l'una meno dieci.	It's ten to one—literally, one minus ten.

It is not unusual to hear the time expressed as follows:

Sono le sette e quarantacinque.	It is 7:45.

The following table spells out exactly how to tell the time minute by minute, hour by hour.

Telling Time

English	Italian
It is 1:00.	*È l'una.*
It is 2:00.	*Sono le due.*
It is 2:05.	*Sono le due e cinque.*
It is 3:10.	*Sono le tre e dieci.*
It is 4:15.	*Sono le quattro e un quarto.*
It is 5:20.	*Sono le cinque e venti.*
It is 6:25.	*Sono le sei e venticinque.*
It is 6:30.	*Sono le sei e trenta.*
It is 7:30.	*Sono le sette e mezzo.*
It is 8:40. (20 minutes to 9)	*Sono le nove meno venti.*
It is 9:45. (a quarter to 10)	*Sono le dieci meno un quarto.*
It is 10:50. (10 minutes to 11)	*Sono le undici meno dieci.*
It is 11:55. (5 minutes to noon)	*È mezzogiorno meno cinque.*
It is noon.	*È mezzogiorno.*
It is midnight.	*È mezzanotte.*

Time Will Tell

Answer the following questions as best you can using complete sentences. Remember that the answer is usually in the question.

      Example: *A che ora finisci di lavorare?* (What time do you finish working?)

      Answer: *Finisco di lavorare alle sei e mezzo.* (I finish working at 6:30.)

1. *A che ora andiamo al cinema?* (6:00 P.M.)
2. *A che ora parte il volo?* (8:25 A.M.)
3. *A che ora è la cena?* (7:00 P.M.)
4. *Quando c'è un autobus per Verona?* (noon)
5. *Che ore sono?* (4:44 P.M.)
6. *A che ora c'è il treno per Roma?* (2:33 P.M.)
7. *A che ora andiamo a fare colazione?* (7:30 A.M.)

It's Not What You Do, but with Whom You Do It

You want to find out the bus schedule, where the museum is, how much the tickets will cost you, and with whom you should speak to make reservations for the opera. Getting the information you need is an essential communication skill that will take you places. The following table contains a list of words and expressions that will help you get what you want, find out where you want to go, and meet the people you would like to know.

Information Questions

English	Italian	Pronunciation
how	*come*	*koh-meh*
how much	*quanto*	*kwahn-toh*
what	*che cosa* (can be broken up to *che* or *cosa*)	*kay koh-zah*
what time	*a che ora*	*ah kay oh-rah*
when	*quando*	*kwahn-doh*
where	*dove*	*doh-veh*
where is ...?	*dov'è ...?*	*doh-veh*
who	*chi*	*kee*
why	*perché*	*per-kay*

Questions, Questions

The best way to get to know someone is to ask questions. The easiest way to ask a question is to make your sentence sound like a question, as in *Questo treno va a Roma?* (Does this train go to Rome?)

In Italian, you can also put the question word before the conjugated verb. Don't forget to sound like you're asking a question by raising the intonation of your voice at the end of the phrase. You don't want to sound like you're reading from a phrase book.

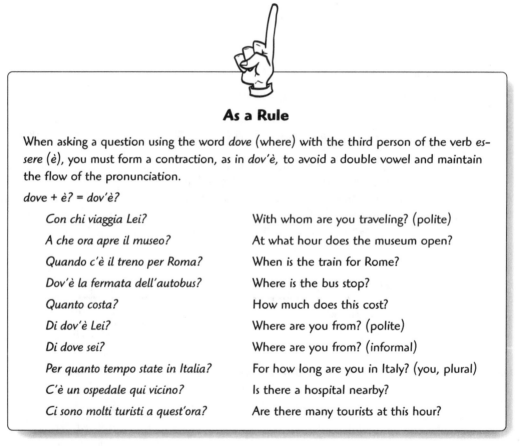

As a Rule

When asking a question using the word *dove* (where) with the third person of the verb *essere* (*è*), you must form a contraction, as in *dov'è*, to avoid a double vowel and maintain the flow of the pronunciation.

dove + è? = dov'è?

Con chi viaggia Lei?	With whom are you traveling? (polite)
A che ora apre il museo?	At what hour does the museum open?
Quando c'è il treno per Roma?	When is the train for Rome?
Dov'è la fermata dell'autobus?	Where is the bus stop?
Quanto costa?	How much does this cost?
Di dov'è Lei?	Where are you from? (polite)
Di dove sei?	Where are you from? (informal)
Per quanto tempo state in Italia?	For how long are you in Italy? (you, plural)
C'è un ospedale qui vicino?	Is there a hospital nearby?
Ci sono molti turisti a quest'ora?	Are there many tourists at this hour?

Ask Away

Each of the following paragraphs is an answer to a question. Figure out what the questions are based on the following information. In the first paragraph, use the *tu* form to ask Cinzia about herself based on her responses. In the second paragraph, ask *Signore Pesce* about himself using the *Lei* form of the verb.

Mi chiamo Cinzia Bell e abito negli Stati Uniti. Sono una studentessa. Studio storia dell'arte. Viaggio in macchina con la mia amica in Italia. Passiamo un mese in Italia. Andiamo a visitare tutte le città importanti. Ritorno all'università a settembre.

Mi chiamo Signore Mario Pesce e sono un bancario. Non parlo l'inglese molto bene. Abito a Milano con mia moglie. Abbiamo due figli, Giorgio e Isabella. A dicembre vado con mia moglie a New York.

All Aboard

I mezzi pubblici (public transportation) in Italy is quite efficient, with buses, taxis, trains, and subways to take you where you want to go. Now that you know when to get on board, you need to know what you're getting onto.

La Bella Lingua

In Italy, taxis are usually not hailed. You must go to a *posteggio* (taxi stand) or call to get a taxi, especially late at night. Most taxis have meters, but it's a wise idea to agree upon a *tariffa* for longer trips. You may pay extra for baggage and late-night rides, with a possible surcharge for the taxi driver's return trip. It's a wise idea to find out from your guidebook or hotel the *numero di telefono* for late-night taxis. Expect to pay—taxis in Italy aren't cheap! If you're satisfied with your ride, it is customary (although not necessary) to give the driver a 5 percent *mancia* (tip).

In the following table, you'll find the what, where, and how to complement the when.

Getting Around

English	Italian	Pronunciation
bus	*l'autobus*	*low-toh-bus*
bus stop	*la fermata dell'autobus*	*lah fer-mah-tah dow-toh-boos*
connection	*la coincidenza*	*lah koh-een-chee-den-zah*
information	*l'ufficio informazioni*	*loo-fee-choh een-for-mah-zee-oh-nee*
taxi	*il tassì*	*eel tah-see*
train	*il treno*	*eel treh-noh*
... by train (railway)	*... per ferrovia*	*per feh-roh-vee-yah*
... train station	*... la stazione ferroviaria*	*lah stah-zee-oh-neh feh-roh-vee-yah-ree-ah*

continues

Getting Around   (continued)

English	Italian	Pronunciation
ticket	*il biglietto*	*eel bee-lyeh-toh*
... round-trip ticket	*... il biglietto di andata e ritorno*	*dee ahn-dah-tah eh ree-tor-noh*
... one-way ticket	*... il biglietto di corsa semplice*	*dee kor-sah sem-plee-cheh*
... first/second class	*... di prima/seconda classe*	*dee pree-mah/sehk-ohn-dah klah-seh*
ticket counter	*la biglietteria*	*lah bee-lyeh-teh-ree-yah*
schedule	*l'orario, la tabella*	*lor-ah-ree-oh, lah tah-beh-lah*
track	*il binario*	*eel bee-nah-ree-oh*
waiting room	*la sala d'aspetto*	*lah sah-lah dah-speh-toh*
seat	*il sedile/il posto*	*eel sed-ee-leh/eel pohs-toh*
window	*il finestrino*	*eel fee-neh-stree-noh*

La Bella Lingua

There's nothing more *romantico* than riding along *la costa* by *ferrovia* ("railway," coming from *ferro*, meaning "iron," and *via*, meaning "way"). Italian trains are generally well maintained, inexpensive, and comfortable. They are by far one of the best ways to get around and meet Italians (and practice your Italian!). There are several kinds of trains used within Italy:

➤ *Diretto:* This train actually takes the longest route because it makes most local stops.

➤ *Espresso:* Having nothing to do with coffee, this train stops at all major *stazioni.*

➤ *Pendolino–ETR* (Pendulum): Named for the high number of commuters, this is the fastest way to get between major cities. Designed like a bullet, this train costs more and requires *una prenotazione,* but is well worth the extra money if time is an issue.

➤ *Rapido:* This city-to-city train is an economical way of getting from one end of the country to the other.

➤ *Regionale:* Like a *diretto,* this local train weaves its way into the smallest of villages.

Verbiage

The following table shows you some helpful travel-related verbs and expressions:

Travel Verbs

English	Italian
to be (running) late	*essere in ritardo*
to be (running) early	*essere in anticipo*
to be (running) on time	*essere in orario*
to change	*cambiare*
to commute	*fare il pendolare*
to get on	*salire su*
to get off	*scendere da*
to leave	*partire*
to miss, to lose	*perdere*
to stop	*fermare*
to take	*prendere*

La Bella Lingua

Bring a couple of empty folders with you when you travel to Italy. You can organize the many pieces of information, brochures, ticket stubs, and maps you collect along the way. When you get home, you can use them as "real-life" study aids for your growing note and scrapbook.

Here are some other handy phrases:

Vorrei un biglietto di andata e ritorno.	I would like a round-trip ticket.
Dov'è la fermata dell'autobus?	Where is the bus stop?
C'è la coincidenza?	Is there a connection?
A che ora parte il treno?	At what times does the train leave?
I voli sono in orario.	The planes (are running) on time.

Partiamo subito.	We're leaving immediately.
Su quale binario parte il treno?	On what track does the train leave?
Prenda quest'autobus.	Take this bus.
C'è un posto vicino al finestrino?	Is there a seat near the window?
Posso aprire il finestrino?	May I open the window?

Practice Those Conjugations

Try conjugating these travel-related regular verbs. You've been given the first person (*io*) to get your started:

chiedere (to ask)	*chiedo* ...
prendere (to take)	*prendo* ...
prenotare (to reserve)	*prenoto* ...
ritornare (to return)	*ritorno* ...
scendere (to get off)	*scendo* ...

Getting On with *Salire*

The irregular verb *salire* (to climb) is used to get on, mount, and go up. Use it to get on the bus or train.

The Verb *Salire:* to Climb

Italian	English
io *salgo*	I climb
tu *sali*	you climb
lui/lei/Lei *sale*	he/she climbs; You climb
noi *saliamo*	we climb
voi *salite*	you climb
loro salgono	they climb

Things to Do: The Verb *Fare* (to Do; to Make)

The verb *fare* expresses when you want to make or do something. In addition, it is often used like the English verb *to take* and appears in many idiomatic expressions. For example, in Italian, you don't "take a trip"—rather, you "make a trip" (*fare un viaggio*).

The verb *fare* is used to talk about the weather, or when you "take" that perfect picture (the one you always thought should be submitted to *National Geographic*). With this versatile verb, you can go shopping, pretend, or indicate where something hurts.

You'll use it when you take a shower, a walk, or a spin. You'll see this verb a lot—and use it often during your travels. Because *fare* is irregular, you must memorize the different parts in the following table.

The Verb *Fare:* to Do; to Make

Italian	English	Italian	English
io *faccio*	I do	noi *facciamo*	we do
tu *fai*	you do	voi *fate*	you do
lui/lei/Lei *fa*	he/she does; You do	loro *fanno*	they do

La Bella Lingua

Aside from its principal significance, **fare** is a verb used in many idiomatic *espressioni*, including when you talk about *il tempo* (the weather). Your Italian *dizionario* offers many of these idioms.

In English you "take" a shower, while in Italian you "make" a shower, as in: *fare una doccia.*

Conversely, while in English you "make" a decision, in Italian you "take" a decision, as in: *prendere una decisione.*

You may also see and hear the verb as *far*, as in *far le compere* (to go shopping).

Idiomatic Expressions Using Fare

The following table contains some idiomatic expressions using the verb *fare.* Remember that, like idiomatic expressions using the verb *avere*, you must conjugate the verb. To remind you, the verb is given in (parenthesis).

Expressions Using *Fare*

Italian	English	Italian	English
(fare) l'amore	to make love	*(fare) il bagno*	to take a bath
(fare) l'autostop	to hitchhike	*(fare) del bene*	to do good
(fare) baccano	to make a ruckus	*(fare) benzina*	to get gas

continues

Expressions Using *Fare*   (continued)

Italian	English	Italian	English
(fare) un controllo	to get a tune-up	*(fare) una passeggiata*	to take a walk
(fare) una bella figura	to make a good impression	*(fare) il pieno*	to fill it up
(fare) una brutta figura	to make a bad impression	*(fare) presto*	to be early
		(fare) un regalo	to give a gift
(fare) colazione	to have lunch	*(fare) le spese*	to go shopping
(fare) la doccia	to take a shower	*(fare) tardi*	to be late
(fare) una domanda	to ask a question	*(fare) le valigie*	to pack/prepare one's bags
(fare) finta	to pretend		
(fare) una fotografia	to take a picture	*(fare) vedere*	to show
(fare) un giro	to take a spin	*(fare) un viaggio*	to take a trip
(fare) male a qualcuno	to hurt someone		

What Are You Doing?

Look at the following sentences to get a better idea of what you can express with the verb *fare:*

*Perché non **fate** un giro?*	Why don't you take a spin?
***Faccio** le valigie per la mia vacanza in Italia.*	I am preparing my bags for my vacation to Italy.
*Noi **facciamo** un bel viaggio.*	We are taking a beautiful trip.
*Posso **fare** una domanda?*	May I ask a question?
*Ti voglio **fare** vedere qualcosa.*	I want to show you something.
***Fammi** vedere!*	Show me!
*Lui sta **facendo** una passeggiata.*	He is taking a walk.

What to Do, What to Do

Fill in the appropriate form of *fare* in the following sentences, and translate:

1. *Perché non _____ un giro? (noi)*
2. *Vado al supermercato per _____ le spese.*
3. *Il turista _____ una fotografia.*
4. *Lo studente _____ una domanda all'ufficio informazioni.*
5. *Il bambino _____ il letto.*

The Least You Need to Know

➤ Read the road signs!

➤ Telling time is easy; remember the key words *meno* (less than) and *e* (and).

➤ *Che* and *quale* are used to ask "what?" and "which?"

➤ Questions are a great way to start a conversation (and let others do the talking).

➤ *Fare* is an incredibly versatile verb used in many idiomatic expressions.

Chapter 13

Hallelujah, You've Made It to *l'Hotel*

In This Chapter

➤ The comfort zone: getting the most from your hotel

➤ First things first: ordinal numbers

➤ How to get what you want with *volere, potere,* and *dovere*

➤ Verbs and prepositions

Whether you're willing to live on a shoestring or you want the best of the best, this chapter will help you get what you need when you want it.

A Cave Will Do

For most people with limited vacation time, it's a good idea to make reservations in advance, especially during the busy season (called *alta stagione*), which lasts from May through August.

For others, the fun of travel is the unexpected, the sense of living in the *momento*. You don't mind not knowing where you'll be next week because you want to go with the flow. In that case, it's a good idea to shop around before settling on a hotel or *pensione* (inn); prices may vary, and with a smile and bit of wit, you might be able to get yourself a terrific deal.

Whether you decide to pick a place to lay your head early in the game or later on, you're going to need the following vocabulary to help you find the place that's right for you.

The Hotel and Nearby

Facilities	Italian	Pronunciation
bar	*il bar*	*eel bar*
barber	*il barbiere*	*eel bar-bee-eh-reh*
cashier	*la cassa*	*lah kah-sah*
doorman	*il portiere*	*eel por-tee-eh-reh*
dry cleaner	*la tintoria*	*lah teen-toh-ree-ah*
elevator	*l'ascensore*	*lah-shen-soh-reh*
gift shop	*il negozio di regali*	*eel neh-goh-zee-oh dee reh-gah-lee*
gym	*la palestra*	*lah pah-leh-strah*
hairdresser	*la parrucchiere*	*lah pah-roo-kee-eh-reh*
hotel	*l'albergo*	*lahl-ber-goh*
	l'hotel	*loh-tel*
	la pensione	*lah pen-see-yoh-neh*
laundry service	*la lavanderia*	*lah lah-vahn-deh-ree-yah*
maid	*la domestica*	*lah doh-mes-tee-kah*
parking lot	*il parcheggio*	*eel par-keh-joh*
pharmacy	*la farmacia*	*lah far-mah-chee-ah*
room service	*il servizio in camera*	*eel ser-vee-zee-oh een kah-meh-rah*
sauna	*la sauna*	*lah sah-oo-nah*
swimming pool	*la piscina*	*lah pee-shee-nah*
tailor	*la sartoria*	*lah sar-toh-ree-yah*

A Room with a View

You might think you want to stand at your window and look at the wonderful hub-bub that makes Rome such a lively place. Beware: Windows facing the street can be bothersome if you want to sleep in a little. After you unpack, maybe you want to take a nice bath to unwind. Don't assume there will be a tub in your room; you must ask. The following table will help you ask for the kind of room you want. Start with *Vorrei ...* (I would like ...).

Your Room

Amenity	Italian	Pronunciation
a room	*una camera*	*oo-nah kah-meh-rah*
a double room	*una doppia*	*oo-nah doh-pee-yah*
... with a double bed	*... con letto matrimoniale*	*kohn leh-toh mah-tree-moh-nee-ah-leh*

Amenity	Italian	Pronunciation
a single room	*una singola*	*oo-nah seen-goh-lah*
... on the garden	*... sul giardino*	*sool jar-dee-noh*
... on the sea	*... sul mare*	*sool mah-reh*
with ...	*con ...*	*kohn*
... air conditioning	*... l'aria condizionata*	*lah-ree-yah kohn-dee-zee-oh-nah-tah*
... (private) bathroom	*... bagno (privato)*	*kohn bah-nyoh pree-vah-toh*
... bathtub	*... la vasca da bagno*	*lah vah-skah dah bah-nyoh*
... refrigerator	*... il frigorifero*	*eel free-goh-ree-feh-roh*
... telephone	*... il telefono*	*eel teh-leh-foh-noh*
... television	*... la televisione*	*lah teh-leh-vee-zee-oh-neh*
... terrace	*... terrazza*	*kohn teh-rah-tsah*
... every comfort	*... ogni confort*	*kohn oh-nyee kohn-fort*
elevator	*l'ascensore*	*lah-shen-soh-reh*
fax	*il fax*	*eel fax*
heat	*il riscaldamento*	*eel ree-skahl-dah-men-toh*
key	*la chiave*	*lah kee-yah-veh*
safe deposit box	*la cassaforte*	*lah kah-sah-for-the*

Simply Said

It's nice to understand how a language works, but it can take a while for it all to sink in. In the meantime, the following simple phrases will help you ask for what you need without breaking out your list of conjugated verbs:

Vorrei ...	I would like ...
Ho bisogno di ...	I need ...
Mi serve ...	I need ...
Mi servono ...	

Get Cozy

The following table will help you find the word for whatever amenity you may be lacking.

Did You Know?

Italy has few laundromats. Traditionally, you must give your *biancheria sporca* (dirty laundry) to the hotel or bring it to a *lavanderia*, where it will be cleaned and pressed for you. Usually, you pay per piece and not by weight. If you want something dry-cleaned, you must bring it to *la tintoria*.

Inside Your Room

Necessities	Italian	Pronunciation
alarm clock	*la sveglia*	*lah sveh-lyah*
ashtray	*il portacenere*	*eel por-tah-cheh-neh-reh*
blanket	*la coperta*	*lah koh-per-tah*
blow-dryer	*l'asciugacapelli*	*lah-shoo-gah-kah-peh-lee*
	il fon	*eel fohn*
closet	*il guardaroba*	*eel gwar-dah-roh-bah*
cot	*il lettino*	*oon leh-tee-noh*
hanger	*la gruccia*	*lah groo-chah*
	la stampella	*lah stahm-peh-lah*
ice	*il ghiaccio*	*eel ghee-ah-choh*
matches	*i fiammiferi*	*ee fee-ah-mee-feh-reh*
mineral water	*l'acqua minerale*	*lah-kwah mee-ner-ah-leh*
pillow	*il cuscino*	*eel koo-shee-noh*
shampoo	*lo shampoo*	*loh sham-poo*
shower	*la doccia*	*lah doh-chah*
soap	*il sapone*	*eel sah-poh-neh*
stationery	*la carta da lettere*	*lah kar-tah dah leh-teh-reh*
tissues	*i fazzoletti di carta*	*ee fah-tsoh-leh-tee dee kar-tah*
toilet	*la toilette*	*lah toy-lett*
toilet paper	*la carta igienica*	*lah kar-tah ee-jen-ee-kah*
towel	*l'asciugamano*	*lah-shoo-gah-mah-noh*
transformer	*il trasformatore*	*eel trah-sfor-mah-toh-reh*

As a Rule

When using the reflexive verb *servirsi*, the number of things you need must agree with the verb. You'll learn more about reflexive verbs later.

Mi serve una coperta in più.	I need an extra blanket.
Mi servono due coperte in più.	I need two extra blankets.

Room Service Please

Ask the hotel for something from the previous list using one of the expressions you just learned. You might have to add the words *in più* after the item if you want an extra towel, blanket, and so on.

If you want to ask for "some" more, use the preposition *di* + the appropriate article, as in *del, della, dei,* and so on:

> Example: *un cuscino*
>
> Answer: *Vorrei un cuscino in più, per favore.*
>
> Example: *la carta igienica*
>
> Answer: *Mi serve della carta igienica.*

1. *carta da lettere*
2. *chiave*
3. *asciugamano*
4. *sveglia*
5. *saponetta*

Is There Room at the Inn?

In a pinch, you can use the following phrases to express yourself and get the information you need. The last thing you want to do is rifle through your *dizionario* while the concierge taps his foot.

Useful Expressions

English	Italian
Do you have any rooms?	*Avete delle camere?*
I'd like to make a reservation.	*Vorrei fare una prenotazione.*
... for one night.	*... per una notte*
... for one week.	*... per una settimana*
At what time is check-out?	*Qual è l'orario per lasciare la camera?*
Is breakfast included?	*Colazione compresa?*
I'll take it (the room).	*La prendo.*
I need ...	*Ho bisogno di ...*
Compliments!	*Complimenti!*
Did I receive any messages?	*Ho ricevuto dei messaggi?*
May I leave a message?	*Posso lasciare un messaggio?*
Thank you so much.	*Grazie tanto.*
This room is too ...	*Questa camera è troppo ...*
... small.	*... piccola.*
... dark.	*... buia.*
... noisy.	*... rumorosa.*

Let's Make a Deal

You may find yourself struggling to negotiate or pay for a room in Italian. The following phrases should help.

Let's Make a Deal

English	Italian
How much does it cost ...	*Quanto costa ...*
... per day?	*... al giorno?*
... per week?	*... alla settimana?*
It's too expensive.	*È troppo caro.*
Is there anything less expensive?	*Non c'è qualcosa di più economico?*
Can I pay ...	*Posso pagare ...*
... in cash?	*... in contanti?*
... by check?	*... con assegno?*
... by credit card?	*... con carta di credito?*
The check, please.	*Il conto per favore.*

Practice Makes Perfetto

Complete the following sentences with the appropriate Italian word. Don't forget to use the correct article when necessary; then translate the sentences.

1. *Mi servono _____ in più per favore. Fa freddo stasera!* (two blankets)

2. *Ho bisogno di un altro _____.* (pillow)

3. *Vorrei _____ per i miei capelli.* (a hair dryer)

4. *C'è un'altra _____ per la nostra camera?* (key)

5. *Ci sono dei buoni _____ qui vicino?* (restaurants)

6. *Vorrei _____ diversa. Questa non va bene.* (a room)

7. *Mi serve _____.* (a bottle of mineral water)

Your Firma Here, Please

You may be given a *fattura* (invoice), *conto* (bill), or *ricevuta* (receipt) that looks something like the following.

While reading this invoice, what can you tell? Did I have a single or a double room? How much did my room cost? Were there any extra costs? When was I there?

Villa Vallerosa **Via Vallerosa 27** **02040 Selci Sabino (Rieti)** **Telefono e fax (0765) 519179**	**RICEVUTA FISCALE** FATTURA N°: 243 DATA:25.09.00 PERS. N°: 01 CAMERA N°: 26

Signorina: Euvino, Gabrielle	Indirizzo: P.O. Box 602 New York, NY 10025

QUANTITÀ, NATURA E QUALITÀ DEI SERVIZI		IMPORTO
SOGGIORNO IN CAMERA TRIPLA	☐	
SOGGIORNO IN CAMERA DOPPIA	☐	
SOGGIORNO IN CAMERA SINGOLA	☑	
DAL: 21.09.00 AL: 25.09.00		
AL GIORNO: L. 100.000 x 4		400.000
EXTRA: Telefono L. 11.000		11.000
FIRMA: *Gabrielle Euvino*	TOTALE	411.000

La Mancia *(Tipping)*

While you were out catching the sights, some elves seem to have mysteriously neatened your room and made the bed.

Although tipping is optional, it's always nice to leave something extra to show your appreciation for good service. In restaurants, *il coperto e servizio* is included in the *conto*. At *il bar* it is customary to leave a small token of appreciation (100 *lire* will do). When staying for any length of time in a hotel, it's appropriate to leave a tip in an envelope or with the reception as you leave. The following tip suggestions came from a tourist pamphlet. See how well you understand them.

> *In Italia la mancia in genere viene inclusa nel conto. Una guida semplice di mance suggerisce segue:*

Tassista	5%
Cameriere	5–10%
Fattorino	L1.000–2.000
Portiere	L1.000–2.000
Domestica	L1.000–2.000 *al giorno*
Concierge	L5.000–10.000
Guardiano	L3.000–5.000

It is customary to tip *il guardiano* (custodian) for opening up churches or museums, especially if they've done so especially for you.

Who's on First?

When you *ordinare* your dinner in a *ristorante,* you start with your *primo piatto* (first course). Maybe you order *pasta primavera* (which means "springtime" and translates literally as "first green"). You move along to your *secondo piatto* (second course), and afterward, you might have *per ultimo* (for last)—a nice *tiramisù,* so sweet and light and lovely that you feel like you died and went to heaven.

What do all these things have in common (other than they are *delizioso*)? They all use ordinal numbers.

The Ordinal Numbers

Ordinal numbers specify the order of something in a series. The word *primo* is similar to the English word "primary," *secondo* is like "secondary," *terzo* is like "tertiary," *quarto* is like "quarter," *quinto* is like "quintuplets," and so on. (Remember cognates: You should always be thinking of like-sounding words in English to help you retain your Italian vocabulary.) The following table gives you a rundown of useful ordinal numbers you need and how to write them in abbreviated form.

Ordinal Numbers

English	Italian	Masc.	Fem.	Pronunciation
first	*primo*	1°	1ª	*pree-moh*
second	*secondo*	2°	2ª	*seh-kohn-doh*
third	*terzo*	3°	3ª	*ter-zoh*
fourth	*quarto*	4°	4ª	*kwahr-toh*
fifth	*quinto*	5°	5ª	*kween-toh*
sixth	*sesto*	6°	6ª	*sehs-toh*
seventh	*settimo*	7°	7ª	*seh-tee-moh*
eighth	*ottavo*	8°	8ª	*oh-tah-voh*
ninth	*nono*	9°	9ª	*noh-noh*
tenth	*decimo*	10°	10ª	*deh-chee-moh*
eleventh	*undicesimo*	11°	11ª	*oon-dee-cheh-zee-moh*
twelfth	*dodicesimo*	12°	12ª	*doh-dee-cheh-zee-moh*
twentieth	*ventesimo*	20°	20ª	*ven-teh-zee-moh*
twenty-first	*ventunesimo*	21°	21ª	*ven-too-neh-zee-moh*
twenty-third*	*ventitreesimo*	23°	23ª	*ven-tee-treh-eh-zee-moh*
sixty-sixth*	*sessantaseiesimo*	66°	66ª	*seh-sahn-tah-seh-eh-zee-moh*
seventy-seventh	*settantasettesimo*	77°	77ª	*seh-tahn-tah-seh-teh-zee-moh*
hundredth	*centesimo*	100°	100ª	*chen-teh-zee-moh*
thousandth	*millesimo*	1000°	1000ª	*mee-leh-zee-moh*

Note: The final vowel of the cardinal number is not dropped with numbers ending in 3 (–tre) and 6 (–sei).

There are some basic rules for using ordinal numbers in Italian:

➤ Like any adjective, ordinal numbers must agree in gender and number with the nouns they modify. As in English, they precede the nouns they modify. Notice how they are abbreviated, as in 1° (1st), 2° (2nd), and 3° (3rd)—much easier than the English. The feminine abbreviation reflects the ending –*a*, as in 1ª, 2ª, and 3ª.

la prima volta (1ª)	the first time
il primo piatto (1°)	the first course

➤ The first 10 ordinal numbers all have separate forms, but after the tenth ordinal number, they simply drop the final vowel of the cardinal number and add the ending –*esimo*.

tredici	*tredicesimo*	13th
venticinque	*venticinquesimo*	25th
ventisei	*ventiseiesimo*	26th

➤ You need to use ordinal numbers whenever you reference a Roman numeral, as in Enrico V (*quinto*) or Papa Giovanni Paolo II (*secondo*).

➤ Unlike in English, dates in Italian require cardinal numbers, unless you are talking about the first day of a month, as in *il primo ottobre*. June 8th is *l'otto (di) giugno* because the day always comes before the month. The use of the preposition *di* is optional. Therefore, it's important to remember that in Italian, 8/6/98 is actually June 8, 1998 (and not August 6, 1998). You'll learn more about dates in Chapter 14, "Rain or Shine."

Did You Know?

In Italian, the word for "floor" is *piano* (just like the instrument). The *primo piano* (first floor) is actually the floor above the *pianterreno* (ground floor) and equal to what is considered the second floor in the United States.

Feeling Moody: The Modal Verbs

Do you *want* to learn Italian? You *can*, but you *must* study. The modal verbs *potere* (to be able to), *dovere* (to have to), and *volere* (to want) express a mood, such as when you say, "I want! I can! I must!"

Before you plunge in, take stock of what you've already learned—and be patient with yourself. Learning a language is a *processo*. It takes time—time to sink in, time to kick in—and when it does, there's nothing like it.

I Want What I Want! (Volere)

An important verb you have already been using in its conditional form is the verb *volere*. When you say, *Vorrei*, you are saying, "I would like." Because you "would like" to express your wants as delicately as possible, you use the conditional. Sometimes, however, you just want what you want and there's no doubt about it. The following table shows you how to express want, pure and simple, in the present tense.

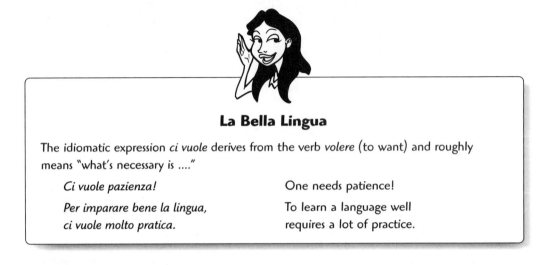

La Bella Lingua

The idiomatic expression *ci vuole* derives from the verb *volere* (to want) and roughly means "what's necessary is ...."

Ci vuole pazienza!	One needs patience!
Per imparare bene la lingua, ci vuole molto pratica.	To learn a language well requires a lot of practice.

The Verb *Volere:* to Want

Italian	English
io **voglio**	I want
tu **vuoi**	you want
lui/lei/Lei **vuole**	he/she wants; You want
noi **vogliamo**	we want
voi **volete**	you want
loro **vogliono**	they want

I bambini vogliono mangiare un gelato.	The children want to eat an ice cream.
Vuole una mano?	Do you want a hand?

I Think I Can, I Think I Can! (Potere)

You use the verb *potere* to say that you are able to do something. It's the same as what the little train said as it puffed up the hill—and it's what you use to express that you *can* speak Italian. Using it will help you to remember it. Your *potential* is unlimited, as long as you think you can. The verb *potere* is always used with an infinitive.

La Bella Lingua

Most modal verbs are followed by an infinitive:

Posso			I can		
Voglio	} *partire*		I want to	} leave	
Devo			I must		

The Verb *Potere:* to Be Able to/Can

Italian	English
io **posso**	I can
tu **puoi**	you can
lui/lei/Lei **può**	he/she/You can
noi **possiamo**	we can
voi **potete**	you can
loro **possono**	they can

Posso venire con te?	Can I come with you?
Possiamo imparare questa lingua.	We can learn this language.

I Have to ... (Dovere)

The verb *dovere,* outlined in the following table, is what you use to express "to have to" and "must," and is also used to express "to owe." Like the verb *potere, dovere* is almost always used in front of an infinitive, such as when you say, "I must study."

The Verb *Dovere:* to Have to/Must/to Owe

Italian	English
io **devo**	I must
tu **devi**	you must
lui/lei/Lei **deve**	he/she/You must
noi **dobbiamo**	we must
voi **dovete**	you must
loro **devono**	they must

Devo trovare una banca.	I must find a bank.
Dobbiamo partire subito.	We have to leave immediately.
Devo molti soldi.	I owe a lot of money.

I'm in the Mood for ...

Read through the *frasi* and determine which *verbo* is most appropriate to each *situazione*. There may be more than one correct *risposta*. Don't forget to conjugate the verb according to the subject. The Italian pronouns are given in parentheses to help you determine the subject. Read the entire *frase* before giving your *risposta*.

1. *(Io)* _____ *studiare italiano ogni giorno.*
2. *Cinzia, (tu)* _____ *venire alla festa domani sera?*
3. *Pino* _____ *fare una prenotazione.*
4. *(Io)* _____ *una camera singola per favore.*
5. *Tiziana e Maria* _____ *incontrare un'amica più tardi.*
6. *(Noi)* _____ *andare in macchina.*
7. *(Voi)* _____ *mangiare gli spaghetti al ristorante?*
8. *Giorgio* _____ *parlare il greco.*
9. *Leonardo non* _____ *mai studiare.*

Infinitive Verbs and Prepositions

The infinitive of a verb, as you know, is a verb before it has been conjugated, or the "to" form of a verb, as in "to study," "to laugh," and "to cry." Sometimes an infinitive takes a different form, as in the sentence "I plan on *studying* a lot this summer."

In Italian, when a verb does not have a subject, it is usually in its infinitive form, even if this form resembles the gerund (*–ing* form) of the verb.

Some Italian verbs are preceded by a preposition, others are followed by a preposition, and some take none at all. Knowing when to use a preposition is often a question of usage because the meaning of a verb can change when used with one. This applies in English as well; compare these two sentences and see how the meaning changes by changing the preposition:

I want to go **on** the plane.	I want to go **to** the plane.

Italian prepositions sometimes change while their English counterparts do not.

(pensare di)	*Penso **di** andare in italia.*	I am thinking **of** going to Italy.
(pensare a)	*Penso **a** te.*	I'm thinking **of** you.

Memorization might work for the few who have a photographic memory, but for the rest of us, practice and usage are the only way to remember which verb takes what. After you have repeated something three times, you generally remember it.

Alone at Last

For some verbs, you don't have to worry about the preposition at all. The following verbs can be followed by an infinitive without a preposition.

Verbs Without a Preposition

Italian	English
amare	to love
bastare	to suffice
desiderare	to desire
dovere	to have to
fare	to do/make
lasciare	to leave (something behind)
occorrere	to be necessary
parere	to seem
potere	to be able
preferire	to prefer
sapere	to know (something)
sembrare	to seem
sentire	to listen
vedere	to see
volere	to want

Anna preferisce bere la birra.	Anna prefers to drink beer.
Vogliamo vedere un film.	We want to see a film.

Oddballs

There are always going to be peculiarities that cannot be translated. The verbs and idiomatic expressions used in the following table require the preposition *di* when followed by an infinitive.

As a Rule

It is important to avoid literally translating from one language to another—context is key—because you might get caught up in details that cannot be completely "decoded." For example, in Italian you must use the preposition *in* when visiting a country and *a* for cities. In English, you simply use *to.* When translating from Italian to English, there is no distinction between the two.

Verbs and Idiomatic Expressions Taking *di* Before an Infinitive

English	Italian	English	Italian
to accept from	*accettare di …*	to hope to	*sperare di …*
to admit to	*ammettere di …*	to intend to	*avere intenzione di …*
to ask for	*chiedere di …*	to offer to	*offrire di …*
to be afraid of	*avere paura di …*	to order to	*ordinare di …*
to be in the mood for	*avere voglia di …*	to permit to	*permettere di …*
to be right about	*avere ragione di …*	to pray to	*pregare di …*
to believe in	*credere di …*	to remember to	*ricordare di …*
to decide to	*decidere di …*	to repeat to	*ripetere di …*
to dream of	*sognare di …*	to respond to	*rispondere di …*
to expect to	*aspettare di …*	to say to	*dire di …*
to finish to	*finire di …*	to speak of	*parlare di …*
to forget to	*dimenticare di …*	to think of	*pensare di …*
to have need of	*avere bisogno di …*	to search for	*cercare di …*

*Ho voglia **di** mangiare un gelato subito.*	I'm in the mood to eat an ice cream.
*Ho paura **di** essere in ritardo.*	I am afraid of being late.
*Cristina sogna **di** sposarsi.*	Christina dreams of getting married.
*Natalia ha bisogno **di** studiare.*	Natalia needs to study.

The Preposition A

Some verbs, as in the following table, take the preposition *a* before an infinitive. Pay attention to how the preposition in the English changes from one verb to the next.

While you "help *to* protect someone," you "succeed *at* your job." (This flexible nature of prepositions is what makes them as annoying as fruit flies.)

The Preposition *A* Before an Infinitive

English	Italian	English	Italian
to be at	*stare a …*	to help to	*aiutare a …*
to be careful to	*stare attento a …*	to invite to	*invitare a …*
to be ready to	*essere pronto a …*	to learn to	*imparare a …*
to begin to	*cominciare a …*	to pass to	*passare a …*
to bring to	*portare a …*	to prepare for/to	*preparare a …*
to come to	venire a …	to return to	*tornare a …*
to enter into	*entrare a …*	to run to	*correre a…*
to exit to	*uscire a …*	to succeed at	*riuscire a …*
to go to	*andare a …*	to teach to	*insegnare a …*

Watch how some of these verbs work in the following sentences:

*Comincio **a** capire.*   I am beginning to understand.

*Impariamo **a** parlare l'italiano.*   We are learning to speak Italian.

*Vengo **a** trovarti.*   I am coming to see you.

Learning by Example

Complete the sentences using the subjects provided. Translate the sentences.

Example: _____ *essere brava. (io/cercare di)*

Answer: *Cerco di essere brava.*

Translation: I try to be good.

1. _____ *studiare. (voi/avere bisogno di)*
2. _____ *parlare l'italiano. (tu/imparare a)*
3. _____ *lavorare mentre studia. (Cristoforo/ continuare a)*
4. _____ *dormire presto. (noi/andare a)*
5. _____ *fumare le sigarette. (io/smettere di)*
6. _____ *mangiare alle 8,00. (Loro/finire di)*

A Review of the Irregular Verbs

You've studied verbs until you thought you would go nuts trying to understand the different conjugations, stems, tenses, and persons. Don't try to rush through any of it. You'll learn Italian with perseverance and patience. At some point, it might be a good idea to review the first two parts of this book to reinforce what you have learned. In the meantime, the following table offers a quick review of some of the more important verbs you have learned.

Irregular Verbs

Italian	Conjugation (Present Indicative)
andare (to go)	*vado, vai, va, andiamo, andate, vanno*
avere (to have)	*ho, hai, ha, abbiamo, avete, hanno*
dare (to give)	*do, dai, dà, diamo, date, danno*
dovere (to must/have to)	*devo, devi, deve, dobbiamo, dovete, devono*
essere (to be)	*sono, sei, è, siamo, siete, sono*
fare (to do/make)	*faccio, fai, fa, facciamo, fate, fanno*
potere (to be able to/can)	*posso, puoi, può, possiamo, potete, possono*
sapere (to know)	*so, sai, sa, sappiamo, sapete, sanno*
stare (to be/to stay)	*sto, stai, sta, stiamo, state, stanno*
volere (to want)	*voglio, vuoi, vuole, vogliamo, volete, vogliono*

Practice with a friend and see if you have these verbs memorized. At first, you'll probably fumble a bit, but after a while, they'll come naturally. It's like doing scales on a musical instrument. Once you can play them three times in a row with no mistakes, you've pretty much got them down pat.

Practice Makes **Perfetto II**

Conjugate and insert the correct verb where appropriate in each of these sentences. Note that not all verbs will be used.

dovere	*finire di*
amare	*fare*
chiedere di	*volere*
aiutare a	*credere di*

1. *Io _____ mangiare la pasta.*

2. *Enrico _____ fare la valigia.*

3. *Sandra e Filippo _____ preparare la cena.*

4. *Voi _____ essere poveri, ma siete ricchi—avete l'amore.*

5. *_____ pulire la tua camera!*

6. *Posso _____ una domanda?*

The Least You Need to Know

➤ Ordinal numbers specify the order of things, as in first, second, and third.

➤ If you can't remember the Italian word for an ordinal number, think about how you'd say it in English; chances are, you'll remember the Italian word because the English is so similar.

➤ Some verbs require a preposition when followed by an infinitive.

Chapter 14

Rain or Shine

In This Chapter

➤ The weather and the verb *fare*

➤ *Il clima:* talking about the climate

➤ It's a date!

➤ What's your sign: the zodiac in Italian

You're ready to go. Forget jet lag; you took your melatonin on the plane, your body's clock is totally in synch with Italian time, and now you're raring to go out and see the sights. You walk downstairs and the *portiere* gives you a big smile and says *Fa bello oggi,* and you agree: The *temperatura* is a perfect 24° and the sky is blue. So, come on; let's talk about the weather. To do so, you'll have to use the irregular verb *fare* (to do; to make) that you learned in Chapter 12, "Moving Around."

Talking About the Weather: *Che Tempo Fa?*

Several verbs can be used to talk about *il tempo* (the weather). You'll need the verb *fare,* and you'll see the *ci + essere* combination here, too, as in *c'è il sole* (it's sunny). Some of the information in the following table might be review, and some is new.

La Bella Lingua

If you're interested in hearing *le previsioni del tempo* (the weather report) in Italian, consult your cable company to determine when you can listen to the radio and television transmissions by the Italian broadcasting company RAI.

Don't be intimidated by how fast the newscasters speak; listen for key words such as *freddo* (cold), *caldo* (hot), *piovoso* (rainy), and *sereno* (calm). The more you hear the Italian language spoken, the better you'll be able to speak it!

La Bella Lingua

The next time you want to express how nasty the weather is, try using one of the following idiomatic expressions to talk about that temperamental *tempo:*

Fa un tempo da cani.	It's dog's weather.
Fa un tempo da lupi.	It's wolf's weather.

Weather Expressions

Italian	English
Che tempo fa?	What's the weather?
Fa caldo.	It's hot.
Fa freddo.	It's cold.
Fa fresco.	It's cool.
Quanto fa oggi?	What is the temperature today?
Fa trenta gradi.	It's 30° (Celsius).
C'è il sole.	It's sunny.

Italian	English
C'è nebbia.	It's foggy.
C'è un temporale.	There is a storm.
C'è vento.	It's windy.
È nuvoloso.	It's cloudy.
È umido.	It's humid.
È bello.	It's beautiful.
È brutto.	It's bad.
Grandina.	It's hailing.

As a Rule

The verbs *piovere* (to rain), *nevicare* (to snow), and *tuonare* (to thunder) are used only in the third person singular.

Piove.	It's raining.
Nevica.	It's snowing.
Tuona.	It's thundering.

Il Clima: The Climate

There's a lot more out there than *la pioggia* (rain), *il sole* (sun), and *la neve* (snow). How about snowflakes? Rainbows? Sunsets and sunrises? Some of the following words and phrases will help you talk about the beautiful *clima d'Italia*. After you've read through the words, try reading the Italian without the English and see how well you understand. *Capito?*

Cats and Dogs

English	Italian	English	Italian
air	*l'aria*	Centigrade	*grado centigrado*
atmosphere	*l'atmosfera*	climate	*il clima* (m.)
breeze	*la brezza, il venticello*	cloud	*la nuvola*

continues

Cats and Dogs   (continued)

English	Italian	English	Italian
Fahrenheit	*grado Fahrenheit*	rainbow	*l'arcobaleno*
fog	*la nebbia*	sky	*il cielo*
frost	*la brina*	sleet	*la pioggia ghiacciata, il nevischio*
hail	*la grandine*	smog	*lo smog*
humidity	*l'umidità*	snow	*la neve*
ice	*il ghiaccio*	snowball	*la palla di neve*
lightning bolt	*il fulmine, il lampo*	snowflake	*il fiocco di neve*
mud	*il fango*	sun	*il sole*
nature	*la natura*	sunrise	*l'alba*
ozone	*l'ozono*	sunset	*il tramonto*
plain	*la pianura*	temperature	*la temperatura*
pollution	*l'inquinamento*	thermometer	*il termometro*
rain	*la pioggia*	wind	*il vento*

La Bella Lingua

The next time you're hanging around the fatalists and doomsdayers, impress them with your knowledge of natural disasters, in Italian.

avalanche	*la valanga*	fire	*il fuoco*
calamity	*la calamità*	flood	*l'alluvione*
disaster	*il disastro*	pestilence	*la pestilenza*
earthquake	*il terremoto*	plague	*la peste*
famine	*la carestia*	vulcano	*il vulcano*

Dipinto di Blu

In the song *Volare* written by Domenico Modugno, the expression *dipinto di blu* refers to the sky painted blue. Some helpful adjectives used to talk about *il tempo* can be found in the following table.

Describing the Weather

English	Italian	English	Italian
calm	*sereno*	nice	*bello*
cloudy	*nuvoloso*	overcast	*coperto*
cold	*freddo*	rainy	*piovoso*
cool	*fresco*	sky blue	*celeste, azzurro*
dry	*secco*	starry	*stellato*
hot	*caldo*	tropical	*tropicale*
humid	*umido*	ugly	*brutto*
mild	*mite*		

La Temperatura: **What's Hot and What's Not**

To refer to *la temperatura* (the temperature), you use the verb *fare* in the third person, as you do with the weather.

If someone asks, *Quanto fa oggi?* what they're really asking is, "How many degrees (*gradi*) are there today?" The word *gradi* is implied.

If it's 20° Centigrade, you simply reply, *Fa venti gradi.* (It's 20°.)

If it's 10 *below*, you say, *Fa dieci sotto zero.*

As a Rule

In Italy, as in all of Europe, the metric system is used to determine the temperature. To convert Centigrade to Fahrenheit, multiply the Centigrade temperature by 1.8 and add 32.

To convert Fahrenheit to Centigrade, subtract 32 from the Fahrenheit temperature and multiply the remaining number by .5.

Here are some basic temperature reference points:

Freezing: 32°F = 0°C

Room temperature: 68°F = 20°C

Body temperature: 98.6°F = 37°C

Boiling: 212°F = 100°C

La Bella Lingua

In Italy, *il ferragosto* refers to the August holidays many Italians take during the hot, humid month. If you're planning a trip during this time, don't be surprised to find many of the smaller businesses closed for the holidays. Along the major routes, it's hard to avoid the long lines of cars escaping the sultry cities as they snake their way toward the cool breezes of *il mare*.

The Four Seasons

Ah! What's nicer than springtime in *Toscana* or a beautiful summer day lounging on the beaches of *Sardegna?* Before you start daydreaming about the seasons in which you'd like to travel, first you need to learn how to say them in Italian.

The Seasons

Italian	English
la primavera	spring
l'estate (f.)	summer
l'autunno	autumn
l'inverno	winter
la stagione	season

When talking about *in* a particular season, Italian uses the prepositions *in* and *di*.

| *Fa freddo **d'**inverno?* | Is the winter cold? |
| *Piove **in** primavera.* | It rains in spring. |

Buon Viaggio!

The following table and the sample sentences that follow contain a few *espressioni* and some *vocabolario* related to trip-taking that will help you express some of the events of your fabulous Italian *vacanza*, regardless the weather. You can use several verbs such as *andare*, *essere*, and *fare*.

La Bella Lingua

In Italy, instead of making a big deal out of birthdays, many people celebrate their *onomastico* (Saint's Day), or one's name day. Pick up an Italian calendar and see if there's a day for you!

Expressions of Leisure

Italian	English
Andiamo …	Let's go …
… al mare.	… to the seashore.
… all'estero.	… abroad.
… in giro.	… around, on tour.
… in campagna.	… to the country.
… in montagna.	… to the mountains.
… in vacanza.	… on vacation.

Andiamo *al mare quest'estate.*	We are going to the seashore this summer.
Siamo *in vacanza il mese d'agosto.*	We are on vacation for the month of August.
Facciamo *il campeggio in montagna.*	We are camping in the mountains.

Give Your Mind a Trip

You're familiar with all these words but may not have seen them used in these idiomatic expressions related to *la vacanza*. Match up the Italian and English sentences.

1. *essere in ferie*
2. *essere in vacanza*
3. *fare il campeggio*
4. *fare un viaggio*
5. *fare una crociera*
6. *fare una vacanza*
7. *festeggiare*

a) to take a cruise
b) to take a trip
c) to be on holiday
d) to party, to celebrate
e) to be on vacation
f) to go camping
g) to take a vacation

It's a Date!

To talk about the date requires a particular order. (Consult Chapter 5, "Expressively Yours," for a review of the days of the week and months.) Often this simply means that, in Italian, you must place the day *before* the month—for example: *5 settembre* (September 5). In addition, you should know that when Italians talk about *il cinquecento* (literally, the five hundred), they are actually referring to the sixteenth century (and not the year 500).

Talking About Months

With the exception of the *first* day of the month, dates in Italian require cardinal numbers (1, 2, 3, …). As indicated previously, in Italian the day must come before the month. This is not difficult to realize when you're talking about *il 25 dicembre* (December 25), but with some dates it can get tricky. For instance, if you wrote the abbreviation 4/5, in Italian it would be read as the fourth of May. If you meant the fifth of April, you were off by almost a month! It's crucial that you remember to reverse the two numbers when dealing with any kinds of documents, such as a car lease or apartment contract. Or, avoid this problem altogether and always be sure to write out the month.

In Italian, you must always put the definite article in front of the day after which comes the month. Unless beginning a sentence, months are not capitalized.

il 25 (venticinque) giugno	June 25th
il tre ottobre	October 3rd

As a Rule

The definite article goes in front of the cardinal number when telling the date, as in *il sette luglio* (July 7th). The exception here is the first day of the month, which *is* indicated with the ordinal number *primo* (first), as in *il primo giugno* (June 1st).

What Century?

Talking about centuries can be confusing in both English and Italian. For example, in English when you talk about the *third century*, you're really talking about the century before (200–299). Additionally, you're using an *ordinal* number (first, second, third, …).

Italian, on the other hand, always uses cardinal numbers (1, 2, 3 …), unless referring to the *first* (day/month/year).

A.D.

The basis for today's calendar finds its roots in Christianity. As you probably know, the abbreviation A.D. comes from Latin and literally stands for *Anno Domini,* meaning, "in the year of the Lord." In writing, the Italian language uses both the Latin abbreviation A.D. and the Italian abbreviation d.C. (from *dopo Cristo*, meaning "after Christ") to express time *after* the birth of Christ. (When speaking, the tendency is to use the words *dopo Cristo*.)

In Italian, to talk about dates from 1 A.D. *until* the year 1000 A.D., you must use cardinal numbers plus the words *dopo Cristo* (in abbreviated form here).

79 d.C.	*Il Vesuvio distrusse Pompei.*
79 A.D.	Vesuvius destroyed Pompei.

You may also see *anno domini* or the abbreviation A.D. written on monuments and tombstones.

121–180 A.D.	*Marco Aurelio, Imperatore*
121–180 A.D.	Marcus Aurelius, Emperor

As a general rule, you don't need to use A.D. for dates after the year 1000.

1,000 Years Later

To express centuries *after* the year 1000, it gets a little tricky. To talk about the sixteenth century (1500–1599) like an Italian, you must omit the first thousand and say, "the five hundred," as in *il cinquecento*. There is no need to indicate that this occurred after the birth of Christ.

However, it is also possible to use an ordinal number (first, second, third, ...) when referring to centuries, as in *il quindicesimo secolo* (the fifteenth century).

In writing, the apostrophe before the number shows that it is after the year 1000.

'100—*La Crociata*
1100—the Crusades

'300–'600—*Il Rinascimento*
1300–1600—the Renaissance

Did You Know?

The word *calendar* originally comes from the Latin word *calends*, signifying the day of the new moon. During the Middle Ages, the *calender* was what money lenders called their account books, being that the monthly interest was due on the *calends*. The original "old style" Roman calendar, instituted by Julius Caesar in 46 B.C., was used until 1583 when Pope Gregory XIII made official the "new style" calendar—also referred to as the Gregorian calendar.

La Bella Lingua

Many *monumenti* (monuments) in Italy are written with the dates expressed in Roman numerals. Often, you will see A.D.—which stands for *Anno Domini*—written after a date, meaning "in the year of the Lord." This is used in English as well.

B.C.

To express time *before* the birth of Christ (B.C.), as in 400 B.C., Italian uses the abbreviation a.c. (from *avanti Cristo,* meaning "before Christ").

753 a.c.—*La fondazione di Roma*	753 B.C.—The foundation of Rome
106–43 a.c.—*Cicero, oratore*	106–43 B.C.—Cicero, orator

To talk about the year 1965, you would say it like any other number: *millenovecentosessantacinque* (one thousand nine hundred sixty-five).

Do You Have *un Appuntamento?*

In Italian, you make an *appuntamento* to meet people, whether it's social or business-related. The following table offers some helpful time-related words.

It's a Date

English	Italian	Pronunciation
afternoon	*il pomeriggio*	*eel poh-meh-ree-joh*
appointment	*l'appuntamento*	*lah-poon-tah-men-toh*
calendar	*il calendario*	*eel kah-len-dah-ree-yoh*
century	*il secolo*	*eel seh-koh-loh*
date	*la data*	*lah dah-tah*
day	*il giorno*	*eel jor-noh*
decade	*il decennio*	*eel deh-cheh-nee-yoh*
evening	*la sera*	*lah seh-rah*
holiday	*la festa*	*lah fes-tah*
millennium	*il millennio*	*eel mee-leh-nee-yoh*
month	*il mese*	*eel meh-zeh*
morning	*la mattina*	*lah mah-tee-nah*
week	*la settimana*	*lah seh-tee-mah-nah*
year	*l'anno*	*lah-noh*

About Last Night

This year, last year, the day before, the day after—all of these times have significance. Was it good for you, too? The following table offers you some helpful *vocabolario* you'll find useful when talking about the past. You'll learn how to talk about the past in Chapter 19, "Having Fun Italian Style."

About Last Night

English	Italian	Pronunciation
ago	*fa*	*fah*
every (day)	*ogni (giorno)*	*oh-nyee (jor-noh)*
in (two weeks)	*fra (due settimane)*	*frah (doo-yeh seh-tee-mah-neh)*
last night	*ieri notte*	*ee-eh-ree noh-teh*
last year	*l'anno scorso*	*lah-noh skor-soh*
next	*prossimo*	*proh-see-moh*
this evening	*stasera**	*stah-seh-rah*
this morning	*stamattina**	*stah-mah-tee-nah*
today	*oggi*	*oh-jee*
tomorrow	*domani*	*doh-mah-nee*
yesterday	*ieri*	*ee-eh-ree*
yesterday evening	*ieri sera*	*ee-eh-ree seh-rah*

*Note: The terms stamattina *and* stasera *are abbreviated from* questa mattina *and* questa sera.

The Dating Game

How do you express the following? Remember that adjectives must agree with the nouns they modify. Nouns must always reflect number.

Example: Last week   Answer: *La settimana scorsa*

Example: 3 years ago   Answer: *Tre anni fa*

1. Last month
2. Last year
3. Next year
4. In ten years
5. Last spring
6. Next winter
7. Seven years ago
8. Last night
9. Yesterday evening
10. This morning

How Often?

Some events occur once in a lifetime, whereas others reoccur, such as your birthday or getting your daily newspaper. The following terms may come in handy.

La Bella Lingua

When referring to the day after tomorrow, Italians use *dopodomani* (literally, "after tomorrow"). To talk about the day before yesterday, Italians use *l'altro ieri* (literally, "the other yesterday").

How Often?

English	Italian	Pronunciation
annual	*annuale*	*ah-noo-ah-leh*
biannual	*biennale*	*bee-eh-nah-leh*
bimonthly	*bimestrale*	*bee-meh-strah-leh*
biweekly	*bisettimanale*	*bee-seh-tee-mah-nah-leh*
centennial	*centenario*	*chen-teh-nah-ree-yoh*
daily	*quotidiano*	*kwoh-tee-dee-ah-noh*
monthly	*mensile*	*men-see-leh*
quarterly	*trimestrale*	*tree-me-strah-leh*
weekly	*settimanale*	*seh-tee-mah-nah-leh*

Dating Dilemmas

Determine how to say the following *feste* (holidays) or important dates in Italian:

1. *Natale*

2. *Capodanno*

3. *Il tuo compleanno*

4. *L'anniversario dei tuoi genitori*

La Bella Lingua

Many of the more important Christian holidays coincide with the major Roman celebrations of Bacchanalia and Saturnalia.

Quando Quando Quando?

See if you can answer the following questions. They are posed using the familiar form of the verb, but you should answer them using the first person:

1. *Quando è il tuo compleanno?*   When is your birthday?

2. *Quando vai in vacanza?*   When are you going on vacation?

3. *Quando è l'anniversario dei tuoi?*   When is your (parents') anniversary?

Quale Festa?

Make no mistake: In Italy, Christmas is a big deal. The holiday season is dotted with many opportunities to celebrate. Practice your comprehension skills and see if you can figure out the following Italian holidays.

> *6 dicembre: La Festa di San Nicola*
>
> *8 dicembre: L'immacolata Concezione*
>
> *13 dicembre: La Festa di Santa Lucia*
>
> *24 dicembre: La Vigilia di Natale*
>
> *25 dicembre: Natale*
>
> *26 dicembre: La Festa di Santo Stefano*
>
> *1 gennaio: Capodanno*
>
> *6 gennaio: La Befana*

From What Realm Are You?

It is said by some that if you reach for the stars, you might arrive at the moon. Not a bad place to be. But how would da Vinci or Galileo discuss such ethereal topics? Although it ends in –*a*, the Italian word for planet is masculine, as in *il pianeta*.

La Bella Lingua

Whether you're into *l'astronomia* or *l'astrologia*, the following words will help you stargaze from anywhere.

astrology	*l'astrologia*	sun	*il sole*
astronomy	*l'astronomia*	universe	*l'universo*
constellation	*la costellazione*	Big Dipper	*l'Orsa Maggiore*
galaxy	*la galassia*	Little Dipper	*l'Orsa Minore*
moon	*la luna*	Milky Way	*la Via Lattea*
star (stars)	*la stella (le stelle)*		

Planets

Planet	Il Pianeta	Planet	Il Pianeta
Mercury	*Mercurio*	Saturn	*Saturno*
Venus	*Venere*	Uranus	*Urano*
Earth	*Terra*	Neptune	*Nettuno*
Mars	*Marte*	Pluto	*Plutone*
Jupiter	*Giove*		

What's Your Sign?

If the weather isn't your thing, you can go to another plane and ask about someone's background—astrologically speaking. Find out if you are compatible by asking some-one *Che segno sei?* (What's your sign?)

Astrological Signs

Simbolo	Segno	Elemento	Caratteristiche	Periodo	English
♈	*ariete*	*fuoco*	*indipendente, aggressivo, impulsivo*	*21 marzo– 19 aprile*	Aries
♉	*toro*	*terra*	*determinato, testardo, fedele, tollerante*	*20 aprile– 20 maggio*	Taurus
♊	*gemelli*	*aria*	*intelligente, ambizioso, capriccioso*	*21 maggio– 21 giugno*	Gemini
♋	*cancro*	*acqua*	*sensibile, simpatico, impressionabile*	*22 giugno– 22 luglio*	Cancer
♌	*leone*	*fuoco*	*generoso, nobile, entusiasta*	*23 luglio– 22 agosto*	Leo
♍	*vergine*	*terra*	*intellettuale, passivo, metodico*	*23 agosto– 22 settembre*	Virgo
♎	*bilancia*	*aria*	*giusto, organizzato, simpatico*	*23 settembre– 23 ottobre*	Libra
♏	*scorpione*	*acqua*	*filosofo, fedele, dominante*	*24 ottobre– 21 novembre*	Scorpio
♐	*sagittario*	*fuoco*	*pragmatico, maturo, creativo*	*22 novembre– 21 dicembre*	Sagittarius

Simbolo	*Segno*	*Elemento*	*Caratteristiche*	*Periodo*	English
♑	*capricorno*	*terra*	*ambizioso, fedele, perseverante*	*22 dicembre– 19 gennaio*	Capricorn
♒	*acquario*	*aria*	*generoso, idealistico, originale*	*20 gennaio– 18 febbraio*	Aquarius
♓	*pesci*	*acqua*	*timido, simpatico, sensibile*	*19 febbraio– 20 marzo*	Pisces

Like a Fish to Water

Imagine that you are reading the horoscopes for some very well-known *personaggi storici* (historical figures). Next to their names is a brief description of them and their key accomplishments. You might want to go back to Chapter 10, "Tell Me About Your Childhood," to review some adjectives to help you describe the different characteristics that make up each sign.

Did the individuals in the following table live up to their astrological inclinations?

Historical Figures

Personaggio Storico	*Compimento*	*Data di Nascità*	*Segno Astrologico*
Leonardo da Vinci	*pittore:* La Gioconda, *scultore, ingegnere, scienziato*	*15 aprile 1452*	*ariete*
Niccolò Machiavelli	*scrittore, politico:* Il Principe	*3 maggio 1469*	*toro*
Michelangelo Buonarroti	*pittore:* La Cappella Sistina, *scultore, architetto*	*5 marzo 1475*	*pesci*
Caterina de' Medici	*moglie di Enrico II, figlia di Lorenzo de' Medici (Urbino)*	*13 aprile 1519*	*ariete*
Galileo Galilei	*astronomo, matematico, fisico:* "parabola"	*15 febbraio 1564*	*capricorno*
Giuseppe Garibaldi	*"il Risorgimento" 1860*	*4 luglio 1807*	*cancro*
Giacomo Puccini	*compositore:* La Bohème	*22 dicembre 1858*	*capricorno*
Luigi Pirandello	*drammaturgo:* Sei Personaggi in Cerca d'Autore	*28 giugno 1867*	*cancro*
Benito Mussolini	*fascista, dittatore;* "Il Duce"	*28 luglio 1883*	*leone*

Did You Know?

The Medici family was enormously influential during the Renaissance. Having settled in Florence during the twelfth century, its reign of power lasted well into the seventeenth century. These powerful merchants and bankers later developed strong ties to royalty, bringing two popes and two queens into power, including **Caterina de' Medici** (1519–1589). The daughter of Lorenzo de' Medici, the Duke of Urbino, she later became the wife of Henry II of France and was mother to Francis II, Charles IX, and Henry III.

The Least You Need to Know

➤ Use the third person of the verb *fare* (*fa*) to express weather conditions and the temperature, and use it for idiomatic expressions.

➤ To express the date, use the number of the day plus the month and the year.

➤ Use the words *dopo Cristo* to describe a historical event that occurred after the death of Christ but before the beginning of the second millennium; use *avanti Cristo* to describe an event before the birth of Christ.

Part 3
Fun and Games

Part 3 is the meal after a hard day's work. You'll learn how to shop for your dinner, make a simple soup using an Italian recipe from the Tuscan countryside, and order a bottle of vino *from a restaurant.*

Maybe it's time to visit a bookstore and pick up a book that specializes in Italian grammar or culture. Why not borrow tapes from your local library (they're free!)?

Chapter 15, "I Can't Believe My Eyes!" starts you with a few more irregular verbs and a chance to review your present-tense conjugations. It then introduces a new tense used to talk about the moment: the present progressive.

Chapter 16, "Shop 'Til You Drop," will have special appeal for those of you combing the streets in search of treasure and precious objects.

Chapters 17, "Bread, Wine, and Chocolate," and 18, "Shall We Dine?" are stuffed with delightful food terms and interesting morsels, including the introduction of a new verb—piacere—that allows you to express your likes and dislikes.

In Chapter 19, "Having Fun Italian Style," you'll be offered the vocabulary you need to discuss the things you love the most: l'arte, la musica, and il cinema. In the meantime, you'll see how easy it is to talk about the past with the introduction of the passato prossimo *(present perfect).*

Perhaps it's time to make those reservations and reward yourself with a visit to the Madre Patria!

Chapter 15

I Can't Believe My Eyes!

In This Chapter

➤ Sights for your eyes

➤ Verbs for sightseeing: *rimanere, venire, uscire,* and *dire*

➤ How to make suggestions and plans

➤ Geography

➤ The present progressive

A lifetime wouldn't be long enough to see all there is in *Italia*. You can breeze through the boot from top to bottom or camp out in a corner and get intimate. There are so many things to see and do—but how? Read on; this chapter will give you the tools to set your own agenda.

Seeing Is Believing

There's a mystery to *Italia* and the people who live there that plucks at the strings of every heart. Just as *Roma* wasn't built in *un giorno,* nor should it be seen in one. Since you can't do everything, think about what is most important to you and start from there.

Where to Go and What to Do

Il Luogo	L'Attività	The Place	The Activity
l'acquario	*vedere i pesci*	the aquarium	see the fish
l'azienda vinicola	*fare un "picnic"*	the winery	have a picnic
il castello	*fare le foto*	the castle	take pictures
la cattedrale	*vedere le vetrate colorate*	the cathedral	see the stained-glass windows
la chiesa	*vedere l'architettura; accendere una candela*	the church	see the architecture; light a candle
il cinema	*vedere un film*	the cinema	see a film
il circo	*guardare lo spettacolo*	the circus	watch the show
la discoteca	*danzare/ballare*	the discothèque	dance
l'enoteca	*bere il vino*	the wine bar	drink wine
il giardino	*sentire i profumi dei fiori*	the garden	smell the flowers
il mercato	*fare la spesa*	the market	go shopping
il museo	*vedere le opere d'arte*	the museum	see the art
il parco	*fare una passeggiata*	the park	take a stroll
la piazza	*andare in giro*	the public square	wander around
lo stadio	*guardare una partita*	the stadium	watch a game
il teatro	*vedere una commedia*	the theater	see a play
lo zoo	*guardare gli animali*	the zoo	look at the animals

La Bella Lingua

Quel che l'occhio vede, il cuor crede. (What the eye sees, the heart believes.)

There are two verbs used to describe the act of using your eyes: *vedere* (to see) and *guardare* (to look at/watch). Both are regular verbs that follow the rules of their particular verb family.

Let's Go Visit, Find, See, Look At ...

In one form or another, many of these verbs and expressions have been presented in earlier chapters and should sound familiar. Notice how some of the verbs require a preposition when followed by an infinitive. When a verb is used as part of an *espressione,* the verb in (parentheses) needs to be conjugated.

Verbs for Sightseeing

Verbi e Espressioni	Verbs and Expressions
andare	to go
(andare) a trovare	to go visit
(andare) a vedere	to go see
(fare) un giro	to take a spin/to go around
(fare) una passeggiata	to take a walk
(fare) vedere	to show (literally, "to make see")
girare	to go around
passeggiare	to stroll
passare a	to pass by
restare	to rest/stay
rimanere	to remain
ritornare	to return
uscire	to go out/exit
venire	to come
visitare	to visit

Perché non facciamo un giro della città?	Why don't we take a spin around the city?
Vado a vedere lo spettacolo a teatro.	I am going to see the show at the theatre.
Fammi vedere le tue foto!	Show me your photos!
Passa a trovarmi!	Pass by to visit me!

Critters

In Italy, even the animals have a saint: San Francesco d'Assisi (1182–1226). Italy's patron saint, this gentle man wrote *Il Cantico delle Creature* (Canticle of Created Things) praising all living things.

Animal	*L'Animale*	Animal	*L'Animale*
alligator	*l'alligatore*	antelope	*l'antilope*
ant	*la formica*	bat	*il pipistrello*

continues

continued

Animal	L'Animale	Animal	L'Animale
bear	*l'orso*	lizard	*la lucertola*
bird	*l'uccello*	mole	*la talpa*
boar	*il cinghiale*	monkey	*la scimmia*
bull	*il toro*	mosquito	*la zanzara*
butterfly	*la farfalla*	mouse	*il topo*
cat	*il gatto*	ostrich	*lo struzzo*
chicken	*la gallina*	owl	*la civetta, il gufo*
cow	*la mucca*	pig	*il maiale*
crocodile	*il coccodrillo*	pigeon	*il piccione*
crow	*il merlo*	porcupine	*il porcospino*
deer	*il cervo*	rabbit	*il coniglio*
dog	*il cane*	raccoon	*il procione*
dolphin	*il delfino*	rooster	*il gallo*
donkey	*l'asino*	shark	*il pescecane, lo squalo*
duck	*l'anatra*	sheep	*la pecora*
eagle	*l'aquila*	skunk	*la moffetta*
elephant	*l'elefante*	snail	*la lumaca*
fish	*il pesce*	snake	*il serpente*
fly	*la mosca*	spider	*il ragno*
fox	*la volpe*	squirrel	*lo scoiattolo*
frog	*la rana*	swan	*il cigno*
giraffe	*la giraffa*	tiger	*la tigre*
goat	*la capra*	turtle	*la tartaruga*
gorilla	*il gorilla*	turkey	*il tacchino*
hare	*il lepre*	whale	*la balena*
hippopotamus	*l'ippopotamo*	wolf	*il lupo*
horse	*il cavallo*	worm	*il baco, il bruco, il verme*
leopard	*il gattopardo*	zebra	*la zebra*
lion	*il leone*		

More Irregular Verbs

You may already be familiar with the following irregular verbs used to get around town.

Uscire *(to Go Out/Exit)*

You're ready to paint the town red. The verb *uscire* will get you out of your hotel room and into the heart of the action.

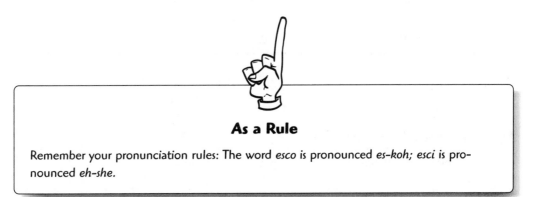

As a Rule

Remember your pronunciation rules: The word *esco* is pronounced *es-koh*; *esci* is pronounced *eh-she*.

The Verb *Uscire:* to Go Out/Exit

Italian	English
io esco	I go out
tu esci	you go out
lui/lei/Lei esce	he/she goes out; You go out
noi usciamo	we go out
voi uscite	you go out
loro escono	they go out

Stefano esce ogni sera.	Stefano goes out every evening.
Usciamo alle tre e un quarto.	We're going out at 3:15.

Venire *(to Come)*

Eventually, you have to come down to earth. The irregular verb *venire* may help you find your way.

The Verb *Venire:* to Come

Italian	English
io vengo	I come
tu vieni	you come
lui/lei/Lei viene	he/she comes; You come

continues

The Verb *Venire:* to Come   (continued)

Italian	English
noi **veniamo**	we come
voi **venite**	you come
loro **vengono**	they come

Vieni con noi?	Are you coming with us?
Sì, vengo fra cinque minuti.	Yes, I'm coming in five minutes.

Rimanere *(to Remain)*

The verb *rimanere* has similar endings to the verb *venire*.

The Verb *Rimanere:* to Remain

Italian	English
io **rimango**	I remain
tu **rimani**	you remain
lui/lei/Lei **rimane**	he/she remains; You remain
noi **rimaniamo**	we remain
voi **rimanete**	you remain
loro **rimangono**	they remain

La Bella Lingua

The verb *rimanere* can also be used idiomatically to express a state or condition, as in *rimanere male* (to be disappointed) or *rimanere soddisfatto* (to be satisfied). Among other things, it can also mean "to be situated," as in *Dove rimane la stazione?* (Where is the station?)

Rimango in albergo stasera.	I'm remaining in the hotel this evening.
Rimangono in campagna.	They are remaining in the country.

Your Turn

How are you doing with the verbs? Check out your progress by filling in the appropriate conjugations for the following verbs. Keep in mind that some may be irregular.

1. *Trovare:* to find/visit

Subject	Trovare
io	_____
tu	_____
lui/lei/Lei	_____
noi	_____
voi	_____
loro	_____

2. *Andare:* to go (irregular)

Subject	Andare
io	_____
tu	_____
lui/lei/Lei	_____
noi	_____
voi	_____
loro	_____

3. *Passare:* to pass

Subject	Passare
io	_____
tu	_____
lui/lei/Lei	_____
noi	_____
voi	_____
loro	_____

4. *Fare:* to do/make (irregular)

Subject	Fare
io	_____
tu	_____
lui/lei/Lei	_____

continues

continued

Subject	*Fare*
noi	_____
voi	_____
loro	_____

5. *Ritornare:* to return

Subject	*Ritornare*
io	_____
tu	_____
lui/lei/Lei	_____
noi	_____
voi	_____
loro	_____

As a Rule

All geographical terms, including continents, countries, cities, states, towns, and islands, require the definite article:

> *Quest'estate, noi visitiamo l'Italia, la Spagna, la Francia e la Grecia.*

The only exception occurs when the term comes after the preposition *in* and is feminine, singular:

> *Noi andiamo in Italia, in Albania e in Africa.*

All countries, regions, states, towns, and so on are capitalized. Nationalities are not capitalized.

Practice Makes Perfetto

You're no couch potato. Conjugate the highlighted verb in the present tense using the subject in parenthesis.

Example: **andare** *a vedere il Colosseo* (noi)

Answer: **Andiamo** *a vedere il Colosseo.*

1. **fare** *una passeggiata in piazza* (Pasquale)
2. **andare** *a vedere un film* (io)
3. **andare** *ad ascoltare l'opera* (noi)
4. **fare** *una foto del castello* (Giuseppe *and* Maria)
5. **fare** *un giro in macchina* (Voi)
6. **prendere** *l'autobus* (tu)

Dire (to Say/Tell)

You've already seen the phrase *Come si dice ... in italiano?* and know that it means "How do you say ... in Italian?"

Dire is another useful irregular verb. Note in the following table that the stem changes to *dic–* in all persons except the second plural.

The Verb *Dire:* to Say

Italian	English
io **dico**	I say
tu **dici**	you say
lui/lei/Lei **dice**	he/she says; You say
noi **diciamo**	we say
voi **dite**	you say
loro **dicono**	they say

Come si dice ... in italiano?	How do you say ... in Italian?
Che cosa dici?	What do you say?
Che ne dici?	What do you think? (idiomatic)

The Power of Suggestion

The gorgeous Italian you sat next to on the plane phoned you at your *albergo,* and you've made a date to go sightseeing. Although you haven't even left your hotel room, you've already planned your beautiful wedding. Sometimes a hint will not do; you have to come right out and make a suggestion.

Perché non?

The easiest way to make a suggestion is to ask this simple question using the words *perché non ...* (why not ...):

> ***Perché non*** + the verb in the first-person plural form (*noi*)?

For example:

Perché non andiamo in Italia?	Why don't we go to Italy?
Perché non partiamo domani?	Why don't we leave tomorrow?

If you want to ask what someone thinks of the idea, use these phrases:

Che ne pensi/pensa?	What do you think (of it)?
Che ne dici/dice?	What do you say (about it)?

Let's ...

To suggest the English "Let's ...," use the first-person plural form (*noi*) of the verb:

andare (to go)	*Andiamo al cinema.*	Let's go to the movies.
mangiare (to eat)	*Mangiamo.*	Let's eat.
partire (to leave)	*Partiamo stasera.*	Let's leave this evening.
viaggiare (to travel)	*Viaggiamo in Italia.*	Let's travel to Italy.

La Bella Lingua

In English, you "make" a suggestion. In Italian, you "give" a suggestion, as in *dare un suggerimento.*

How About ...?

Shape the phrases in the following table to to suggest doing whatever you want. After each *espressione*, simply add the infinitive of the verb that best expresses your suggestion.

Notice how the object pronouns change, depending on who is being addressed. The pronouns most commonly used are: *ti* ("you," familiar), *Le* ("You," polite), and *vi* ("you," plural). You'll learn more about these in Chapter 16, "Shop 'Til You Drop."

Getting Suggestive

Le va di ...?	Are you in the mood to ...?
Ti interessa ...?	Are you interested in ...?
Vi piacerebbe ...?	Would you like ...?

Notice how the examples you just saw apply in the following suggestions:

> *Le va di andare al cinema?*   Are you in the mood to go to the movies?
>
> *Ti interessa fare un viaggio in Italia?*   Are you interested in taking a trip to Italy?

Using Non to Make Suggestions

Italians often add the word *non* in front of a suggestion. These examples use the third person form of the verb.

> *Non vi piacerebbe … vedere il castello?*   Wouldn't you all like to see the castle?
>
> *Non Le interessa … guardare la partita?*   Aren't you interested in seeing the game?

Yes or No

Respond to the suggestions offered by changing the object pronoun accordingly.

1. *Ti va di andare al cinema?*   No, non _____ va di andare al cinema.
2. *Le interessa fare un viaggio in Italia.*   Sì, _____ interessa fare un viaggio in Italia.
3. *Le piacerebbe vedere il castello.*   No, non _____ piacerebbe vedere il castello.
4. *Ti interessa accompagnarmi al negozio?*   No, non _____ interessa accompagnar _____ al negozio, grazie.
5. *Ti piacerebbe mangiare un gelato?*   Sì, _____ piacerebbe mangiare un gelato!

Did You Know?

After performing several experiments on the nature of motion and velocity, **Galileo Galilei** (1564–1642) confirmed Copernicus's theory: The Earth revolved around the Sun.

The Roman Catholic Church charged Galileo with heresy and, with a threat of torture, "urged" him to denounce his thoughts, which Galileo wisely did. In exchange, Galileo's life was spared, but he was ordered to spend the rest of his days under house arrest in the Arcetri Villa outside *Firenze*.

Using Volere to Make Suggestions

Of course, you can always state what you want by using the verb *volere* (to want), using both the present indicative and the conditional tenses. Study the following examples, comparing the different tenses. All suggestions use the polite form (third-person singular) of the verb:

Vuole andare in Italia?	**Do You want** to go to Italy?
Vorrebbe andare in Italia?	**Would You like** to go to Italy?
Sì, *voglio* andare in Italia.	Yes, **I want** to go to Italy.
Sì, *vorrei* andare in Italia.	Yes, **I would like** to go to Italy.

The Big, Blue Marble

Back in Chapter 9, "Being There," you learned about different nationalities and religions. The following table tells you how to say the different countries and continents in Italian.

Countries

Country	*Paese*	Country	*Paese*
Belgium	*Il Belgio*	North Korea	*La Corea del nord*
China	*La Cina*	South Korea	*La Corea del sud*
Denmark	*La Danimarca*	Lebanon	*Il Libano*
Egypt	*L'Egitto*	Libya	*La Libia*
England	*L'Inghilterra*	Mexico	*Il Messico*
Ethiopia	*L'Etiopia*	Norway	*La Norvegia*
Finland	*La Finlandia*	Poland	*La Polonia*
France	*La Francia*	Portugal	*Il Portogallo*
Germany	*La Germania*	South Africa	*Il Sud Africa*
Great Britain	*La Gran Bretagna*	Spain	*La Spagna*
Greece	*La Grecia*	Sweden	*La Svezia*
Ireland	*L'Irlanda*	Switzerland	*La Svizzera*
Israel	*L'Israele*	Turkey	*La Turchia*
Italy	*L'Italia*	USA	*Gli Stati Uniti d'America*
Japan	*Il Giappone*	Vatican City	*La Città del Vaticano*

Name That Nation

The following countries all have the same name (or almost exactly) in Italian.

Afghanistan	*Argentina*	*Botswana*	*Costa Rica*
Albania	*Australia*	*Bulgaria*	*Cuba*
Algeria	*Austria*	*Canada*	*El Salvador*
Angola	*Belize*	*Colombia*	*Ghana*
Antigua	*Bolivia*	*Congo*	*Grenada*

Guatemala	*Kuwait*	*Romania*	*Taiwan*
Guinea	*Liberia*	*Russia*	*Tunisia*
Haiti	*Liechtenstein*	*San Marino*	*Uruguay*
Honduras	*Madagascar*	*Scandinavia*	*Venezuela*
India	*Malasia*	*Senegal*	*Vietnam*
Indonesia	*Nepal*	*Sierra Leone*	*Zaire*
Iran	*Nicaragua*	*Siria*	*Zambia*
Iraq	*Pakistan*	*Somalia*	*Zimbabwe*
Kenya	*Panama*	*Sudan*	

Did You Know?

As one of the world's smallest countries, *La Republica di San Marino*, is a land-locked independent city-state located on the slope of Mount Titano (near the Italian city of Rimini). Like any self-respecting country, it has its own mint, postal system, and football team.

I Continenti

As air travel becomes more common, the world shrinks exponentially. How many continents have you hopped?

L'Africa	*L'Asia*
L'America del Nord	*L'Australia*
L'America del Sud	*L'Europa*
L'Antartide	

Once Upon a Time

Before its unification in 1862, the peninsula now known as Italy was once a cluster of city-states ruled by powerful families. Although Italy is now a unified state, each of its 20 regions has a distinctive character. Refer to Appendix C, "Map of Italy," to see these regions outlined in the map of Italy.

Attenzione!

Use the preposition *in* before the name of a country and the preposition *a* before the name of a city.

Andiamo in Italia a Venezia.

Did You Know?

In 1492, **Cristoforo Colombo** bumped into North America, thinking he had found a route to India.

Ten years later, the Florentine **Amerigo Vespucci**—a skilled navigator and cartographer—was commissioned by King Ferdinand of Spain to do some fact checking. In addition to the colorful letters he wrote that described his findings, Vespucci's well-charted maps became the rage all over Florence, leading the new continent to be named in his honor.

Until his dying day, Columbus refused to accept the possibility that he had not reached India.

The regions of Italy are …

L'Abruzzo	*Il Molise*
La Basilicata	*Il Piemonte*
La Calabria	*La Puglia*
La Campania	*La Sardegna*
L'Emilia-Romagna	*La Sicilia*
Il Friuli-Venezia Giulia	*La Toscana*
Il Lazio	*Il Trentino-Alto Adige*
La Liguria	*L'Umbria*
La Lombardia	*La Val d'Aosta*
Le Marche	*Il Veneto*

A Refresher

In Chapter 9, you learned about showing possession using the preposition *di*. Remember that nationalities are considered to be adjectives, reflecting gender and number.

Tell someone you are from the following countries and what your nationality is. To say you have a particular origin, you must use *sono d'origine* + the nationality in its feminine form:

Sono d'origine italiana.   I'm of Italian origin.

Sono d'origine tedesca.   I'm of German origin.

Sono d'origine irlandese.   I'm of Irish origin.

Example: *Italia*

Answer: *Sono italiano. Sono d'origine italiana.*

1. *Gli Stati Uniti d'America*
2. *La Francia*
3. *La Spagna*
4. *La Grecia*
5. *L'Irlanda*

Did You Know?

In the Italian northern region of Trentino-Alto Adige just outside the Austrian border, the majority of people speak *il tedesco* (German), which is taught in schools and is one of the two official languages used in public and legal documents.

Present Progressive Tense (*–ing*)

In Italian, the present progressive tense is used to describe an action in progress.

Because the Italian present tense can serve as both the simple present and the progressive, native Italian, French, and Spanish speakers have difficulty distinguishing the difference between "I am going to the store now" and "I go to the store now." In English, we use the present progressive much more often than the simple present tense.

To form the present progressive, you'll need the verb *stare* that you learned back in Chapter 9. This helping verb does most of the work since the present participle does not change.

To create the present participle, simply slice off the infinitive ending of the verb and add the progressive endings in the following table.

Notice how the *–ere* and the *–ire* progressive tense endings are the same.

Present Progressive

Infinitive Verb		Present Progressive	English
studiare	→	*studiando*	studying
scrivere	→	*scrivendo*	writing
finire	→	*finendo*	finishing

The following table takes the verb *studiare* and shows what happens when we attach the auxiliary verb *stare* to the present progressive.

Forming the Present Progressive

Studiare	To Study
io sto studiando	I am studying
tu stai studiando	you are studying
lui/lei/Lei sta studiando	he/she is studying
noi stiamo studiando	we are studying
voi state studiando	you are studying
loro stanno studiando	they are studying

Making Progress

Turn the following sentences into the present progressive. (Hint: You need to determine the infinitive of the verb before you can find the appropriate progressive form. If you can't remember the verb families to which they belong, flip back to Chapter 8, "An Action-Packed Adventure.")

1. *Guardiamo il film.*
2. *Scrivi una lettera.*
3. *Nicola cucina la cena.*
4. *I bambini dormono.*
5. *Leggo il libro.*
6. *Pulisco la camera.*

That's the Fact, Giacomo

What makes an Italian? From joker to singer to lover to good fella, it's not an easy thing to define a people made up of so many individuals.

La Bella Lingua

The last queen of Italy, Maria José of Savoy, was regent for only 27 days before Italians voted to abolish the monarchy in 1946. Maria was labeled the "rebel queen" after defying Mussolini's dictate that she Italianize her name to Maria Giuseppina.

The daughter of Albert I (of the Belgians), Maria married Prince Umberto II, whose father was King Vittorio Emanuele III. Two years later, a law was passed banning any male member of the Savoy family from ever stepping foot in Italy again. The law is still in force, despite lobbying from Maria's oldest son Vittorio Emanuele.

Some statistics about the Republic of Italy are given in the following table:

The Republic of Italy

Area	116.320 sq. miles
Language	Italian
Capital	Rome
Currency	Lira (US$1 = approx. L1.800)
GNP/capita	L31.775.000
Religion	Roman Catholic
Population	58.000.000
Life expectancy	Females: 81
	Males: 74
Government	Parliamentary republic
Head of state	President
Head of government	Prime minister
Legislature	Bicameral legislature (Chamber of Deputies, Senate)
Voting age	18

> ### The Least You Need to Know
>
> ➤ To suggest an activity ("Let's ..."), use the first-person plural (*noi*) form of the verb.
>
> ➤ Countries and other geographical locations always take the definite article and are capitalized. Nationalities are not capitalized.
>
> ➤ The verbs *venire* (to come), *uscire* (to go out), *rimanere* (to remain), and *dire* (to say/tell) are all irregular.
>
> ➤ The present progressive tense is used to indicate an action that is occurring in the moment. It requires the use of the present participle (the verb form ending in *–ing*).

Chapter 16

Shop 'Til You Drop

In This Chapter

➤ Stores and their wares

➤ Bejeweled and bedazzled—Italian style

➤ Clothing: colors, sizes, and materials

➤ Direct and indirect object pronouns

The word *Italian* is synonymous with style, and whether you bring back hand-blown wine glasses from the famous Venetian island Murano, a Fendi bag from Milano, or an expressive cameo made in Florence, Italy is a place you definitely want to shop.

Stores Galore

As you meander through the *strade* of Italia, you might find some *licorizia* lozenges in a small *tabaccheria*, a silk scarf gently blowing in the wind at the *mercato,* or a small hand-painted porcelain doll staring blankly in a *vetrina.* Whatever you discover, there's no question about it: Shopping for new delights is one of life's greatest pleasures. The following table will help you find your way to the stores that carry the merchandise you're looking for.

Stores

Il Negozio	La Merce	The Store	The Merchandise
la bottega	*tutto*	shop	everything
la cartoleria	*la carta, le cartoline, i giochi, le sigarette*	stationery store	paper, postcards, toys, cigarettes
la farmacia	*le medicine*	pharmacy	medicine
il fioraio	*i fiori, le piante*	florist	flowers, plants
la gioielleria	*i gioielli*	jewelry store	jewelry
il giornalaio	*i giornali, le riviste, le cartoline*	newspaper stand	newspapers, magazines, postcards
il grande magazzino	*i gioielli, i giochi, i mobili, i profumi, i vestiti*	department store	jewelry, toys, magazines, furnishings, perfumes, clothing
la libreria	*i libri*	bookstore	books
il mercato	*tutto*	market	everything
il negozio d'abbigliamento	*l'abbigliamento, i vestiti*	clothing store	clothing
il negozio d'arredamento	*i mobili*	furniture store	furniture
il negozio di scarpe	*le scarpe*	shoe store	shoes
la pasticceria	*le paste, le torte, i biscotti*	pastry shop	pastries, cakes, cookies
la pelletteria	*le giacche, le borse, le valigie*	leather store	jackets, purses, luggage
la profumeria	*i profumi, i cosmetici*	cosmetics shop	perfumes, cosmetics
la tabaccheria	*le sigarette, i sigari, i fiammiferi*	tobacco shop	cigarettes, cigars, matches

Did You Know?

If you're more inclined to spend your time sightseeing but still need to pick up a few items, you can visit a *grande magazzino* (department store). Found throughout many Italian cities, several chains like *La Rinascente, Standa,* and *Upim* offer a wide selection of merchandise for that one-stop-shopping experience.

The Stationery Store: *La Cartoleria*

In addition to office supplies, stationery, candy, and cigarettes, *la cartoleria* often sells stamps and bus tickets. It's also a good place to find inexpensive gift items.

La Cartoleria

Stationery	*La Cartoleria*	Pronunciation
candy	*le caramelle*	*leh kar-ah-meh-leh*
cigarettes	*le sigarette*	*leh see-gah-reh-teh*
cigars	*i sigari*	*ee see-gah-ree*
gift	*il regalo*	*eel reh-gah-loh*
guidebook	*una guida*	*oo-nah gwee-dah*
lighter	*l'accendino*	*lah-chen-dee-noh*
map	*la pianta, la cartina, la mappa*	*lah pee-ahn-tah, lah kar-tee-nah, lah mah-pah*
matches	*i fiammiferi*	*ee fee-ah-mee-feh-ree*
notebook	*il quaderno*	*eel kwah-der-noh*
paper	*la carta*	*lah kar-tah*
pen	*la penna*	*lah peh-nah*
pencil	*la matita*	*lah mah-tee-tah*
postcard	*la cartolina*	*lah kar-toh-lee-nah*
stamp	*il francobollo*	*eel fran-koh-boh-loh*
ticket	*il biglietto*	*eel beel-yeh-toh*
… for the bus	*… per l'autobus*	*per lau-toh-boos*
… for the metro	*… per la metro*	*per lah meh-troh*

La Bella Lingua

Tobacco shops can be identified by a large white "T" on a black background. Matches must be purchased separately from cigarettes. At *la tabaccheria* (the tobacconist), you can also purchase *i biglietti per l'autobus*, stamps, and phone cards.

Did You Know?

Most stores will ship major purchases for you. Some purchases made with a credit card will be covered for loss or damage. The VAT (value-added tax) is a sales tax attached to all major purchases. Save your receipts—non-European travelers receive VAT refunds once they leave the country.

Posso avere la ricevuta, per favore?   May I have a receipt, please?

Diamonds Are a Girl's Best Friend

It could be a sapphire ring, a gold watch, or a silver chain that catches your eye. Throughout Italy, you'll find a *tradizione* of fine gold- and silversmithing, with some of the most exquisite jewelry in the world. The following table shows you how to ask for it.

Jewelry

Object	Oggetto	Pronunciation
amethyst	*l'ametista*	*lah-meh-tees-tah*
aquamarine	*l'acquamarina*	*lah-kwah-mah-ree-nah*
bracelet	*il braccialetto*	*eel brah-chah-leh-toh*
cameo	*il cammeo*	*eel kah-meh-oh*
chain	*la catena*	*lah kah-teh-nah*
cufflinks	*i gemelli*	*ee jeh-meh-lee*
diamond	*il diamante*	*eel dee-ah-mahn-teh*
earrings	*gli orecchini*	*ylee oh-reh-kee-nee*
enamel	*lo smalto*	*loh smal-toh*
gold	*l'oro*	*loh-roh*
jade	*la giada*	*lah jah-dah*
jewelry	*i gioielli*	*ee joh-yeh-lee*
mother-of-pearl	*la madreperla*	*lah mah-dreh-per-lah*
onyx	*l'onice*	*loh-nee-cheh*
pearls	*le perle*	*leh per-leh*
pendant	*il ciondolo*	*eel chon-doh-loh*
pewter	*il peltro*	*eel pel-troh*

Object	*Oggetto*	Pronunciation
platinum	*il platino*	*il plah-tee-noh*
precious stone	*la pietra preziosa*	*lah pee-eh-trah pre-zee-oh-zah*
ring	*l'anello*	*lah-neh-loh*
… engagement ring	*… l'anello di fidanzamento*	*lah-neh-loh dee fee-dahn-zah-men-toh*
… wedding ring	*… la fede*	*lah feh-deh*
ruby	*il rubino*	*eel roo-bee-noh*
sapphire	*lo zaffiro*	*loh zah-fee-roh*
silver	*l'argento*	*lar-jen-toh*
topaz	*il topazio*	*eel toh-pah-zee-oh*
turquoise	*il turchese*	*eel toor-keh-zeh*

It's in the Jeans

Italians seem to be born knowing how to dress. If the body is a blank canvas, they sure know how to paint! Maybe it's in part because Italians are used to being watched—and to watching each other. Some would say it's all in *le scarpe* (the shoes), the finely woven fabrics, and the tailoring.

Whatever the reason, *la moda* is a refined *eleganza* that has deep and powerful roots, permeating Italian culture. If you're hoping some of that Italian style will rub off on you, the following table gives you some helpful words to get you started.

L'Abbigliamento (Clothing)

Clothing Item	Italian	Pronunciation
article	*l'articolo*	*lahr-tee-koh-loh*
bathing suit	*il costume di bagno*	*eel kohs-too-meh dee bahn-yoh*
bra	*il reggiseno*	*eel reh-jee-seh-noh*
clothing	*l'abbigliamento*	*lah-beel-yah-men*
… women's	*… per donna*	*per doh-nah*
… men's	*… per uomo*	*per woh-moh*
… children	*… per bambini*	*per bam-bee-nee*
coat	*il cappotto/il giubotto*	*eel kah-poh-toh/eel joo-boh-toh*
dress	*l'abito*	*lah-bee-toh*
… evening dress	*… l'abito da sera*	*lah-bee-toh dah seh-rah*
jeans	*i jeans*	*ee jeens*
jacket	*la giacca*	*lah jah-kah*
lining	*la fodera*	*lah foh-deh-rah*
model	*il modello*	*eel moh-deh-loh*

continues

L'Abbigliamento (Clothing)   (continued)

Clothing Item	Italian	Pronunciation
pajamas	*il pigiama*	*eel pee-jah-mah*
pants	*i pantaloni*	*ee pahn-tah-loh-nee*
pullover	*il golf*	*eel golf*
raincoat	*l'impermeabile*	*leem-per-mee-ah-bee-leh*
robe	*l'accappatoio*	*lah-kah-pah-toh-yoh*
skirt	*la gonna*	*lah goh-nah*
suit	*il completo*	*eel kom-pleh-toh*
sweat suit	*la tuta da ginnastica*	*lah too-tah dah jee-nah-stee-kah*
sweater	*la maglia*	*lah mah-lyah*
t-shirt	*la maglietta*	*lah mah-lyeh-tah*
undershirt	*la canottiera*	*lah kan-oh-tee-yeh-rah*
underwear	*gli slip*	*ylee sleep*
... panties	*... le mutandine*	*leh moo-tahn-dee-neh*
... briefs	*... le mutande*	*leh moo-tahn-deh*

La Bella Lingua

Note the subtle shift in meaning when the noun (and its article) is made plural:

*Fare **la** spesa* (singular) generally means you are shopping for the household (groceries).

*Fare **le** spese* (plural) refers to shopping in general, as in "shop 'til you drop"!

Accessories

By adding *gli accessori* that best complement your wardrobe, you can look like a million bucks without spending a million *lire*.

Accessories

Clothing Item	Italian	Pronunciation
accessories	*gli accessori*	*ylee ah-chess-oh-ree*
belt	*la cintura*	*lah cheen-too-rah*

Clothing Item	Italian	Pronunciation
boots	*gli stivali*	*ylee stee-vah-lee*
cosmetics	*i cosmetici*	*ee kos-meh-tee-chee*
gloves	*i guanti*	*ee gwahn-tee*
handkerchief	*il fazzoletto*	*eel fah-tsoh-leh-toh*
hat	*il cappello*	*eel kah-peh-loh*
lingerie	*la biancheria intima*	*lah bee-an-keh-ree-yah een-tee-mah*
pantyhose	*i collant*	*ee koh-lant*
purse	*la borsa*	*lah bor-sah*
sandals	*i sandali*	*ee sahn-dah-lee*
scarf	*la sciarpa*	*lah shar-pah*
shoes	*le scarpe*	*leh skar-peh*
slippers	*le pantofole*	*leh pahn-toh-foh-leh*
sneakers	*le scarpe da tennis*	*leh skar-peh dah teh-nees*
socks	*le calze, i calzini*	*leh kal-zeh, ee kal-zee-nee*
stockings	*le calze*	*leh kal-zeh*
umbrella	*l'ombrello*	*lohm-breh-loh*

How Do I Look?

The helpful expressions in the following table will make your shopping even more enjoyable.

Phrases for Shopping 'Til You Drop

Espressione	Expression
Che taglia porta?	What size do you wear?
Porto la misura ...	I wear size ...
Che numero di scarpe?	What size shoe?
Porto il numero ...	I wear a size ...
Dov'è il camerino?	Where is the fitting room?
Sto solo dando un'occhiata.	I'm just looking.
Questo è (troppo) ...	This is (too) ...
... caro.	... expensive, dear.
... classico.	... classical.
... corto.	... short.
... di moda.	... in fashion.
... economico.	... inexpensive.

continues

Phrases for Shopping 'Til You Drop   (continued)

Espressione	Expression
… fuori stagione.	… out of season.
… grande.	… big.
… lungo.	… long.
… stretto.	… tight.
il commesso/la commessa	the sales clerk
la misura, la taglia	the size
il numero di scarpe	the shoe size
il prezzo	the price
lo sconto	discount
la svendita	sale
la taglia: piccola, media, grande	size: small, medium, large
la vetrina	shop window

As a Rule

You use the verb *portare* to describe the wearing of clothes, such as, *Gina porta la taglia quarantaquattro.* (Gina wears size 44.) Two additional verbs may come in handy when you go clothes shopping in Italy: *provare* (to try) and *vestire* (to dress).

One Size Does Not Fit All

The following table will help you determine what *misura* you are.

Conversion Tables for Clothing Sizes

Italy	USA	Italy	USA
Women—Clothing		Men—Clothing	
38	4	44	34
40	6	46	36
42	8	48	38

Italy	USA	Italy	USA
Women—Clothing		Men—Clothing	
44	10	50	40
46	12	52	42
48	14	54	44
50	16	56	46
52	18	58	48
		60	50
Women—Shoes		Men—Shoes	
35	5	38	5
36	6	39	6
37	7	40	7
38	8	41	8
39	9	42	9
40	10	43	10
41	11	44	11
		45	12
		46	13

La Bella Lingua

Keep in mind that there are two ways to express size in Italian: *la misura* (as in "measure") or *la taglia* (as in "cut").

Sizes vary, so make sure to try on something before you spend any of your hard-earned money. You should also make sure you have a basic knowledge of size lingo. Let's begin with the basics:

piccola	small
media	medium
grande	large

The Florist

Flowers are often associated with particular occasions or with certain emotions. For example, red roses are traditionally used to make a declaration of love. Chrysanthemums are given at funerals. There's nothing like *un campo di fiori* (a field of flowers) to arouse your senses. For a little flowery inspiration, look for the poem by the Italian poet Eugenio Montale titled, *Portami Il Girasole Ch'io Lo Trapianti* ("The Sunflower"). Regardless of whether you're giving flowers, reading about them, or just stopping to smell the roses, the following table will give you some sweet-smelling help.

Flowers

Flower	*Il Fiore*
carnation	*il garofano*
chrysanthemum	*il crisantemo*
daffodil	*la giunchiglia*
dandelion	*il dente di leone*
daisy	*la margherita*
flower	*il fiore*
lily	*il giglio*
orchid	*l'orchidea*
pansy	*la viola del pensiero*
petunia	*la petunia*
poppy	*il papavero*
rose	*la rosa*
sunflower	*il girasole*
violet	*il viola*

Smooth as Seta

Fine Italian cloth, such as silks, cashmeres, wools, cottons, and chiffons, are practically a national treasure. Rather than spend a fortune on designer clothing, you might consider buying the fabrics and having a *sarto* (tailor) sew something custom-made to your style and fit. The following table will give you the *abilità* to describe *esattamente* what you want (and if you review colors in Chapter 10, "Tell Me About Your Childhood," you'll be designing yourself a new outfit in no time).

What's What

Go back to Chapter 10, and study the demonstrative adjectives and pronouns for "this" (*questo*) and "that" (*quello*). It'll be helpful when you want to say, "I'll take this" (or that, these, and those).

Fabric

Fabric	Italian	Pronunciation
acetate	*l'acetato*	*lah-cheh-tah-toh*
cashmere	*il cachemire*	*eel kah-sheh-mee-reh*
chiffon	*lo chiffon*	*loh shee-fohn*
cotton	*il cotone*	*eel koh-toh-neh*
flannel	*la flanella*	*lah flah-neh-lah*
gabardine	*il gabardine*	*eel gah-bar-dee-neh*
knit	*la maglia*	*lah mah-lyah*
lace	*il merletto*	*eel mer-leh-toh*
	il pizzo	*eel pee-tsoh*
leather	*il cuoio*	*eel kwoy-yoh*
	la pelle	*lah peh-leh*
linen	*il lino*	*eel lee-noh*
nylon	*il nylon*	*eel ny-lon*
rayon	*il rayon*	*eel ray-on*
silk	*la seta*	*lah seh-tah*
taffeta	*il taffettà*	*eel tah-feh-tah*
velvet	*il velluto*	*eel veh-loo-toh*
wool	*la lana*	*lah lah-nah*

Sock It to Me!

Imagine you're shopping for clothes and see the following items in the shop window. See how many you can identify and write in Italian.

La Bella Lingua

Whether you need to raise, lower, loosen, or tighten your clothes, a visit to *il sarto* or *la sarta* (tailor) may be required. Start with *Vorrei* (I would like) + the appropriate expression + the item you want mended.

aggiustare	to mend
cucire	to sew
fare l'orlo a	to hem
modificare	to alter
rammendare	to mend

Pants: _____

Belt: _____

Pullover: _____

Shoes: _____

Socks: _____

Umbrella: _____

Coat: _____

Scarf: _____

Skirt: _____

Gloves: _____

Hat: _____

Shoes: _____

Stockings: _____

Purse: _____

Objection!

In this chapter, you've learned all about shopping and how to ask for what you want. Since we're on the subject of precious objects, this is as good an *opportunità* as any to introduce objects and object pronouns. Although not as exciting as shopping for new shoes, understanding object pronouns can certainly help you purchase them ("I want those and those and these and those ...").

A Little Review

As a reminder: An object pronoun sits in place of the object in a sentence. In Italian, it must agree in gender and number with the noun it is replacing. There are direct and indirect object pronouns. The key is to understand what an object is.

A direct object indicates who or what is affected by the verb's action. When you say, "I love *my mother*," the object of your love (and the verb) is Mommie Dearest. You can replace the object "my mother" with a direct object pronoun and simply say, "I love *her.*"

An indirect object answers the question "to whom" or "for whom." Indirect objects refer only to people (and pets) and are generally preceded by the preposition "to" or "for." When you say, "I talk *to my parents* every week," you could replace "*to my parents*" with an indirect object pronoun, as in "I talk *to them* every week."

In Italian, you also use double object pronouns, like when you say, "Give it to her." These will be covered in Chapter 18, "Shall We Dine?"

Stressed pronouns are used to emphasize and highlight certain nouns or pronouns. These are briefly covered in Chapter 20, "You're Not Having *Un Buon Giorno.*"

Objectify Me, Baby

The object pronouns may be confusing for the non-native speaker because of their similarity to each other as well as to the articles and other words in Italian. This is why it is so important to listen to the context of a sentence. One trick is to remember that direct and indirect object pronouns are all the same except in the third-person singular and plural forms. As shown in the table, *gli* is commonly used to replace *loro* primarily in the spoken language.

The following table outlines the object pronouns in Italian. It may help you to see how the direct and indirect object pronouns correspond to the subject pronouns.

Direct and Indirect Object Pronouns

Subject Pronouns	Direct Object Pronouns		Indirect Object Pronouns	
io	*mi*	me	*mi*	to me
tu	*ti*	you	*ti*	to you
lui	*lo*	he/it	*gli*	to him
lei	*la*	she/it	*le*	to her
Lei	*La*	You	*Le*	to You
noi	*ci*	us	*ci*	to us
voi	*vi*	you	*vi*	to you
loro	*li/le*	them (m./f.)	*a loro/gli**	to them

Follow the Rules

The following rules will make it easier to understand Italian object pronouns. Study the examples:

1. All Italian object pronouns agree in gender and number with the nouns they replace. The referred object is given in parentheses:

   Direct object pronouns:

La vedo ogni giorno. (Maria)	I see **her** every day. (Maria)
Li vedo ogni settimana. (i ragazzi)	I see **them** every week. (the boys)

   Indirect object pronouns:

Gli offro una mano. (a mio fratello)	I offer **him** a hand. (to my brother)
Le mando un bacio. (alla ragazza)	I send **her** a kiss. (the girl)

2. Both direct and indirect object pronouns are usually placed immediately before a conjugated verb.

Leopoldo compra il giornale e *lo legge a Mario.*	Leopoldo buys the newspaper and reads **it** to Mario. (direct)
Giulia gli legge una storia.	Giulia reads **him** a story. (indirect)

3. When an infinitive verb depends on the verbs *dovere* (to have to, to must), *potere* (to be able to), or *volere* (to want), the object pronoun can come before the conjugated verb. You'll also see it attached to the end of the infinitive (minus the final *–e*):

Ti voglio accompagnare al cinema.	I want to accompany **you** to the movies.
Voglio accompagnarti al cinema.	I want to accompany **you** to the movies.

When to Use the Direct Object Pronoun

"The next time I go to Italy, my friend Sofia asked me to buy a book for Sofia." You would probably never say something so awkward. You'd say something like, "The next time I go to Italy, my friend Sofia asked me to buy a book for *her.*" As you can see, direct object pronouns can make your life a lot easier when you use them to re-place the direct object in a sentence:

> *Bacio **il ragazzo.** → **Lo** bacio.*
>
> I kiss **the boy.** → I kiss **him.**
>
> *Leggo **i libri.** → **Li** leggo.*
>
> I read **the books.** → I read **them.**

Easy, right? You don't even have to add a preposi-tion (as in "to look *at*" or "to wait *for*"). In Italian, the commonly used verbs *guardare* (to look at), *cer-care* (to look for), and *aspettare* (to wait for) have a built-in preposition:

> *Cerco **il teatro.** → **Lo** cerco.*
>
> I am searching for **the theatre.** →
> I am searching for **it.**
>
> *Guardo **la ragazza.** → **La** guardo.*
>
> I am looking at **the girl.** → I am looking at **her.**

La Bella Lingua

Whenever you hear someone use the expression *Non lo so,* (I don't know it), the speaker is using the direct object pronoun *lo.*

When to Use Indirect Object Pronouns

"Congratulations! If you have the winning num-ber, a check for $1 billion will be sent *to you!*" Lucky you—you're the indirect object of the billion-dollar sweepstakes. As you can see here, the indirect object of a sentence tells to whom or for whom the action is done. Indirect objects are often replaced by indirect object pronouns:

> *Marco offre un bicchiere di vino **a Marina**. →*
> *Marco **le** offre un bicchiere di vino.*
>
> Marco offers a glass of wine **to Marina**. →
> Marco offers **her** a glass of wine.
>
> *Elisabetta scrive **a Francesco** una lettera. →*
> *Elisabetta **gli** scrive una lettera.*
>
> Elisabetta writes a letter **to Francesco**. →
> Elisabetta writes **him** a letter.

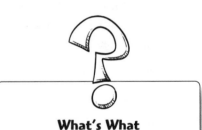

What's What

Are you confused over whether to use a direct or an indirect ob-ject pronoun? Remember that most indirect object pronouns are preceded by a preposition. Think of the preposition as a lit-tle bridge that must be crossed to get to the object. There is no "direct" way to get there—you must take the "indirect" way, over the bridge.

Verbs That May Use an Indirect Object

Some verbs that take a direct object in English take an indirect object in Italian:

> *Telefono a **Dario** stasera.* → ***Gli** telefono stasera.*
>
> I am calling **Dario** this evening. → I am calling **him** this evening.

The following Italian verbs may use an indirect object or its pronoun in Italian:

chiedere	to ask	*parlare*	to speak
dare	to give	*portare*	to bring
dire	to say	*preparare*	to prepare
domandare	to question	*presentare*	to present
donare	to give	*prestare*	to lend
fare sapere	to let know	*regalare*	to give
insegnare	to teach	*rendere*	to render
leggere	to read	*rispondere*	to respond
mandare	to send	*scrivere*	to write
mostrare	to show	*telefonare*	to telephone
offrire	to offer	*vendere*	to sell

> *Joel telefona **ai suoi amici**.* → *Joel telefona a **loro**.*
>
> Joel telephones **his friends**. → Joel telephones **them**.
>
> *Faccio sapere **a Silvia** la data.* → ***Le** faccio sapere la data.*
>
> I'm letting **Silvia** know the date. → I'm letting **her** know the date.

Attenzione!

The indirect object pronoun *loro* is often replaced with **gli** in modern spoken Italian.

> *Giovanni telefona **loro**.* → *Giovanni **gli** telefona.*
>
> *Chiede **loro** di uscire.* → ***Gli** chiede di uscire.*

In an imperative, *gli* is attached to the end of the verb:

> *Telefona **loro**!* → *Telefona**gli**!*

Who's in Command?

The indirect object pronoun follows the imperative (a command) when you use the *tu, noi,* or *voi* form of the verb and can usually be attached to the end of the verb to form one word.

> *Compra il libro per **Giovanni**!* → *Compra**gli** il libro!*
>
> Buy the book for **Giovanni**! → Buy **him** the book!
>
> *Invitate **la vostra amica** a casa!* → *Invita**tela** a casa!*
>
> Invite your **friend** home! → Invite **her** home.

The exception is *loro,* which must always remain separate.

> *Telefona ai tuoi **amici**!* → *Telefona a **loro**.*
>
> Call your **friends**! → Call **them**!
>
> *Non date una risposta a **Carlo e Maria**.* → *Non date **loro** una risposta.*
>
> Don't give a response to **Carlo and Maria**. → Don't give **them** a response.

Who's Who

Replace the direct object in each sentence with the direct object pronoun. Translate the sentences.

> Example: *Leggo il giornale.*
>
> Answer: *Lo leggo.*

1. *Mangiamo la pasta.*
2. *Dante e Boccaccio vogliono mangiare la pizza.*
3. *Prendo l'autobus.*
4. *Mario scrive un libro.*
5. *Vedo Giuseppe e Mario.*
6. *Giovanni bacia la sua ragazza.*
7. *Comprate una macchina.*
8. *Lei capisce la materia?*

What's What

Verbs that take a direct object are called **transitive** (I eat an *apple,* you *speak* Italian). Verbs that do not take a direct object are called **intransitive** (I *go,* you *return*).

La Bella Lingua

In Chapter 9, "Being There," you learned about the expression *Ecco!* To say "Here it is!" or "Here they are!" simply attach the appropriate object pronoun to *ecco,* as in *Eccolo!* (*Ecco il libro*) or *Eccoli!* (*Ecco i pantaloni*).

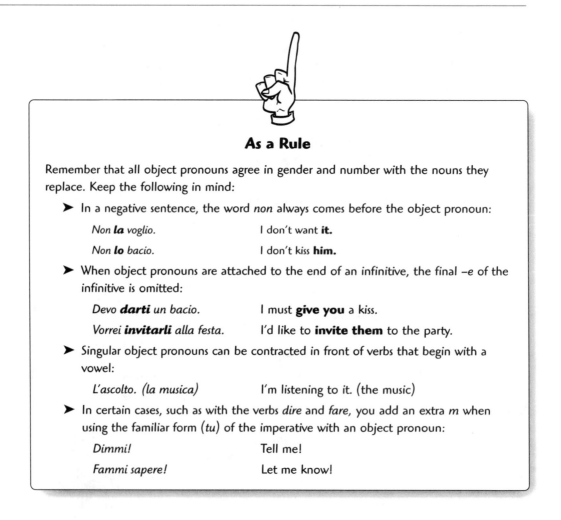

As a Rule

Remember that all object pronouns agree in gender and number with the nouns they replace. Keep the following in mind:

➤ In a negative sentence, the word *non* always comes before the object pronoun:

*Non **la** voglio.*	I don't want **it.**
*Non **lo** bacio.*	I don't kiss **him.**

➤ When object pronouns are attached to the end of an infinitive, the final *–e* of the infinitive is omitted:

*Devo **darti** un bacio.*	I must **give you** a kiss.
*Vorrei **invitarli** alla festa.*	I'd like to **invite them** to the party.

➤ Singular object pronouns can be contracted in front of verbs that begin with a vowel:

L'ascolto. (la musica)	I'm listening to it. (the music)

➤ In certain cases, such as with the verbs *dire* and *fare*, you add an extra *m* when using the familiar form (*tu*) of the imperative with an object pronoun:

Dimmi!	Tell me!
Fammi sapere!	Let me know!

Who's Who II

Replace the indirect object with its appropriate pronoun.

Example:	*Beatrice scrive una lettera a Dante.*
Answer:	*Beatrice gli scrive una lettera.*

1. *Desideriamo parlare a voi.*
2. *Maria e Giorgio danno un regalo a te.*
3. *Carlo telefona ad Anna.*
4. *Lo studente fa una domanda al professore.*
5. *Offro un caffè a Caterina.*

6. *I nonni danno le caramelle ai bambini.*

7. *Offro una birra a Dominick.*

8. *Augurano a noi una buona notte.*

Who's Who—Final Round

Determine which kind of object pronoun should go in the following sentences where it is bold.

1. *Guardate **il film**.*

2. *Regalo a Lorenzo **un mazzo di fiori**.* (bunch of flowers)

3. *Vede la **bella ragazza**?*

4. *Regalo **a Lorenzo** un mazzo di fiori.*

5. *Danno i libri **ai bambini**.*

6. *Conosco **il signor Spadone** molto bene.*

7. *Danno **i libri** ai bambini.*

8. *Accettiamo **l'invito** con piacere.*

The Least You Need to Know

➤ Italians use the metric system, so make sure you know what your proper *misura* is.

➤ The verb *portare* is used to express "to wear."

➤ A direct object answers the question, "*What* or *whom* is the subject acting upon?"

➤ An indirect object answers the question, "*To what* or *to whom* is the subject acting for?"

➤ Use object pronouns to replace the object in a sentence. Object pronouns are usually placed before the conjugated verb, except in an affirmative command, when they come after the verb.

Chapter 17

Bread, Wine, and Chocolate

In This Chapter

➤ Different foods and where to buy them

➤ Using *ne* and expressing quantity

➤ The verb *piacere* (to be pleasing to)

Food. Italy. The two are inseparable. It's *gastronomia* brought to the level of *arte*. What makes Italy so special is the *attenzione* it gives to the everyday elements of successful living; it's *naturale* that food plays an important *ruolo* in the Italian lifestyle. Italians know that fine cuisine is a precursor to living *la dolce vita*.

Many different kinds of stores cater to food, although a great deal of crossover occurs. Make sure you eat something before reading this chapter, or you won't be able to *concentrare* on anything. *Buon appetito!*

To Market, to Market

Imagine that you are staying with your *famiglia* in a rented villa for a month. The tomatoes are ripe and the *basilico* is fresh. Maybe you want to *fare un picnic*. Whatever your *preferenza*, in Italy there's something delicious for everyone. First, you'll have to do the shopping—and you'll need to know what all those delectables are called.

Dal Negozio (at the Store)

The words in the following table should help you on your next shopping expedition. To tell someone you would like to take something, use the verb *prendere* (to take), as in *Prendo un chilo di pomodori.* (I'll take a kilo of tomatoes.)

Did You Know?

The word *carnevale* (meaning "carnival" and source of the English word "carnal") is no different from the infamous Mardi Gras (in Italian, *Martedì Grasso*—literally, "fat Tuesday"). This was the last night one was permitted to eat meat before beginning the period of Lent. In Italy, two of the most famous *carnevale* celebrations take place in Venice and Viareggio, where tens of thousands show up to participate in the festivities and watch the parades.

Dal Negozio

Negozio	Store	*Il Prodotto*	The Product
il bar	bar	*il caffè, i liquori, gli alcolici*	coffee, liquors, alcohol
la drogheria	grocery store	*tutto*	everything
l'enoteca	wine bar	*il vino*	wine
il fornaio	bakery	*il pane*	bread
la gelateria	ice cream shop	*il gelato*	ice cream
la latteria	dairy store	*il formaggio, il latte, le uova*	cheese, milk, eggs
la macelleria	butcher	*la carne, il pollo*	meat, chicken
il mercato	market	*tutto*	everything
il fruttivendolo	green grocer	*la frutta, le verdure, i legumi*	fruit, vegetables, legumes
la pasticceria	pastry shop	*la pasta, i dolci*	pastry, sweets
la pescheria	fish store	*il pesce*	fish
il supermercato	supermarket	*tutto*	everything
il vinaio	wine store	*il vino*	wine

I Love Olives

In Italy, the *il commesso* or *la commessa* will carefully choose the best, ripest, most succulent produce you could want. The following table gives you the terms to express your needs.

Le Verdure

Vegetable	*La Verdura*	Pronunciation
anise	*l'anice*	*lah-nee-cheh*
artichoke	*il carciofo*	*eel kar-choh-foh*
asparagus	*gli asparagi*	*ylee ah-spah-rah-jee*
beans	*i fagioli*	*ee fah-joh-lee*
cabbage	*il cavolo*	*eel kah-voh-loh*
carrots	*le carote*	*leh kah-roh-teh*
cauliflower	*il cavolfiore*	*eel kah-vol-fee-yoh-reh*
corn	*il mais*	*eel mais*
eggplant	*la melanzana*	*lah meh-lan-zah-neh*
garlic	*l'aglio*	*lah-lyoh*
green beans	*i fagiolini*	*ee fah-joh-lee-nee*
legumes	*i legumi*	*ee leh-goo-mee*
lettuce	*la lattuga*	*lah lah-too-gah*
mushrooms	*i funghi*	*ee foon-ghee*
olive	*l'oliva*	*loh-lee-vah*
onion	*la cipolla*	*lah chee-poh-lah*
peas	*i piselli*	*ee pee-zeh-lee*
potato	*la patata*	*lah pah-tah-tah*
rice	*il riso*	*eel ree-zoh*
spinach	*gli spinaci*	*ylee spee-nah-chee*
tomato	*il pomodoro*	*ee poh-moh-doh-roh*
vegetable/greens	*la verdura*	*lah ver-doo-rah*
zucchini	*gli zucchini*	*ylee zoo-kee-nee*

La Bella Lingua

Reading food labels can be *difficile* in any language. It's wise to be familiar with these important expressions you may see written on perishables:

da consumarsi entro ...	best consumed before ...
la data di scadenza	expiration date

La Bella Lingua

Since eating is a favorite pastime of most self-respecting Italians, you're going to need a few verbs to get through any decent meal. Some food-oriented verbs include these:

assaggiare (to taste)　　　　　*fare* colazione* (to have breakfast, lunch)

bere* (to drink)　　　　　　　*mangiare* (to eat)

cenare (to dine)　　　　　　　*pranzare* (to eat lunch)

comprare (to buy)　　　　　　*preparare* (to prepare)

cucinare (to cook)

　*These verbs are irregular.

The idiomatic expression *fare la **prima** colazione* (to eat breakfast) differs slightly from *fare colazione*. Both can be used to eat breakfast, while the latter can also be used to eat lunch. Don't forget *fare la spesa* (to go food shopping).

An Apple a Day

In Rome, a favorite summertime treat is *il cocomero,* also called *l'anguria* (watermelon), which can be bought at brightly lit *bancarelle* (stands). It's so sweet your teeth will hurt, and as wet as a waterfall (get extra napkins). Somehow, the Italians manage to eat the thickly sliced pieces with a plastic spoon (good luck!). Another fruit fact: Italians rarely bite into an apple. They peel it with a knife in one long curl and then slice it into bite-sized chunks to share with everyone at the table. The following table provides a list of the Italian for various fruits and nuts.

La Frutta e La Nocciola

English	Italian	Pronunciation
almond	*la mandorla*	*lah mahn-dor-lah*
apple	*la mela*	*lah meh-lah*
apricot	*l'albicocca*	*lal-bee-koh-kah*
banana	*la banana*	*lah bah-nah-nah*
cherry	*la ciliegia*	*leh chee-leh-jah*
chestnut	*la castagna*	*lah kah-stah-nyah*

English	Italian	Pronunciation
date	*il dattero*	*eel dah-teh-roh*
figs	*i fichi*	*ee fee-kee*
fruit	*la frutta*	*lah froo-tah*
grapefruit	*il pompelmo*	*eel pom-pehl-moh*
grapes	*l'uva*	*loo-vah*
hazelnut	*la nocciola*	*lah noh-choh-lah*
lemon	*il limone*	*eel lee-moh-neh*
melon	*il melone*	*eel meh-loh-neh*
orange	*l'arancia*	*lah-rahn-chah*
peach	*la pesca*	*lah pes-kah*
pear	*la pera*	*lah peh-rah*
pineapple	*l'ananas*	*lah-nah-nas*
pistachio nut	*il pistacchio*	*eel pee-stah-kee-yoh*
pomegranate	*la melagrana*	*lah meh-lah-grah-nah*
raisin	*l'uva secca*	*loo-vah seh-kah*
raspberry	*il lampone*	*eel lam-poh-neh*
walnut	*la noce*	*lah noh-cheh*

As a Rule

Fruit is usually feminine, with a few exceptions. The fruit tree is masculine. *La mela* (the apple) becomes *il melo* (the apple tree), *l'arancia* becomes *l'arancio* (the orange tree), *la pera* becomes *il pero* (the pear tree), and so on.

La frutta refers to all fruit in general. *Un frutto* refers to a piece of fruit, as in *Vuole un frutto?* (Do you want a piece of fruit?)

In Macelleria *(at the Butcher)*

Italian food is fresh. Most perishables are bought and cooked immediately. You will find the terms for different types of meat in the following table.

La Macelleria

Meat and Poultry	*La Carne e Pollame*	Pronunciation
beef	*il manzo*	*eel mahn-zoh*
chicken	*il pollo*	*eel poh-loh*
cold cuts	*i salumi*	*ee sah-loo-mee*
cutlet	*la costoletta*	*lah koh-stoh-leh-tah*
duck	*l'anatra*	*lah-nah-trah*
fillet	*il filetto*	*eel fee-leh-toh*
ham	*il prosciutto*	*eel proh-shoo-toh*
lamb	*l'agnello*	*lah-nyeh-loh*
liver	*il fegato*	*eel feh-gah-toh*
meat	*la carne*	*lah kar-neh*
meatballs	*le polpette*	*leh pol-peh-teh*
pork	*il maiale*	*eel mah-yah-leh*
pork chop	*la braciola*	*lah brah-choh-lah*
quail	*la quaglia*	*lah kwah-lyah*
rabbit	*il coniglio*	*eel koh-nee-lyoh*
salami	*il salame*	*eel sah-lah-meh*
sausage	*la salsiccia*	*lah sal-see-chah*
steak	*la bistecca*	*lah bee-steh-kah*
tripe	*la trippa*	*lah tree-pah*
turkey	*il tacchino*	*eel tah-kee-noh*
veal	*il vitello*	*eel vee-teh-loh*
veal shank	*l'osso buco*	*loh-soh boo-koh*

La Bella Lingua

Meats and poultry are best when selected by your local *macellaio* (butcher), who will ask you how you would like it cut. In Italy, if you order a *fettina*, you are given a thinly sliced portion of meat, either *di manzo* (beef) or *di vitello* (veal). *Il filetto* is thicker. You can also order *una costoletta* (cutlet).

La Bella Lingua

L'agriturismo is an increasingly popular way for families to vacation abroad. Guests stay in the countryside on working farms or vineyards and eat the cheeses, meats, and vegetables produced at the establishment.

Why not take a cooking vacation? Eat, live, and drink Italian as you go from the market to the kitchen to the vineyard to the table!

Got Milk? La Latteria

The only real *parmigiano* comes from Parma, Italy. There are so many wonderful cheeses in Italy that you'll want to *fare un picnic*. Nothing beats fresh *pane, una bottiglia di vino,* and good company. Most *supermercati* carry a wide selection of cheeses and wines, but you can check your neighborhood stores as well for the products described in the following table.

La Bella Lingua

Some delicious food-related books include:

The Fine Art of Italian Cooking, Giuliano Bugialli (Random House)

The Harry's Bar Cookbook, Arrigo Cipriani (Bantam Doubleday Dell Publishing Group)

In Nonna's Kitchen, Carol Field (HarperCollins Publishers)

From the Tables of Tuscan Women, Anne Bianchi (HarperCollins Publishers)

Combine your word worship with your passion for petunias in *Edith Wharton's Italian Gardens,* by Vivian Russell.

La Latteria

Dairy Product	Il Prodotto	Pronunciation
butter	il burro	eel boo-roh
cheese	il formaggio	eel for-mah-joh
cream	la panna	lah pah-nah
eggs	le uova	leh woh-vah
milk	il latte	eel lah-teh
yogurt	lo yogurt	loh yoh-gurt

Di Bocca Buona

The Italians have a saying for everything. Read the idiomatic expressions related to food and eating, and draw a line connecting them to the appropriate translation.

Bere come una spugna.	A good mouth (a good eater).
Di bocca buona.	A hard bone.
Una ciliegia tira l'altra.	I don't care one dry fig's worth.
Non me ne importa un fico secco.	Of good pasta (good-natured).
Fare la frittata.	One cherry pulls the other. (One thing leads to another.)
Fino al midollo.	Red as a pepper.
Liscio come l'olio.	Smooth as oil.
Un osso duro.	To be a sack of potatoes.
Dire pane al pane e vino al vino.	To call bread bread and wine wine (to call a spade a spade).
Mangiare pane e cipolla.	To drink like a sponge (to drink like a fish).
Togliersi il pane di bocca.	To eat bread and onion (to live on bread and water).
Di pasta buona.	To give bread from your mouth.
Avere lo spirito di patata.	To have a potato's sense of humor.
Essere un sacco di patate.	To make an omelette of things.
Fare polpette di …	To make meatballs of …
Rosso come un peperone.	To the marrow.

Fruit of the Sea: La Pescheria

Ahh, *i frutti di mare!* Go to any seaside village in Italy, and you're guaranteed to eat some of the best seafood you've ever had. The following table gives you a little taste.

La Pescheria

Fish and Seafood	*I Pesci e Frutti di Mare*	Pronunciation
anchovies	*le acciughe*	*leh ah-choo-gheh*
cod	*il merluzzo*	*eel mer-loo-stoh*
crab	*il granchio*	*eel gran-kee-yoh*
fish	*il pesce*	*eel peh-sheh*
flounder	*la passera*	*lah pah-seh-rah*
halibut	*l'halibut*	*lah-lee-boot*
herring	*l'aringa*	*lah-reen-gah*
lobster	*l'aragosta*	*lah-rah-gohs-tah*
mussel	*la cozza*	*lah koh-tsah*
oyster	*l'ostrica*	*loh-stree-kah*
salmon	*il salmone*	*eel sahl-moh-neh*
sardines	*le sardine*	*leh sar-dee-neh*
scallop	*la cappasanta*	*lah kah-pah-sahn-tah*
shrimp	*i gamberetti*	*ee gahm-beh-reh-tee*
sole	*la sogliola*	*lah soh-lyoh-lah*
squid	*i calamari*	*ee kah-lah-mah-ree*
swordfish	*il pesce spada*	*eel peh-sheh spah-dah*
trout	*la trota*	*lah troh-tah*
tuna	*il tonno*	*eel toh-noh*
whities	*i bianchetti*	*ee bee-ahn-keh-tee*

What's in a Name?

When you're talking about food, what often sounds slightly exotic almost invariably derives from a simple description of its shape or taste. Look at the word *capellini*, referring to a type of spaghetti that is as thin as *capelli* (in English, you call this angel-hair pasta), or *orecchiette*, which literally means "little ear." And what about those wonderful, ricotta-filled *calzones* you treat yourself to at the local pizza parlor? When you bite into one, you're not really eating socks for dinner!

The pasta known as *conchiglie* are named after the sea shells they resemble. *Bombarde* describe the huge "bomb-like" tubes of pasta that are stuffed with cheese and meat fillings. The word for the popular *ziti* may find its origins in the word *zitellone*, referring to an old bachelor (*zitella* was used to describe a spinster). And let's not forget the cork-screw–shaped pasta *fusilli*, perhaps finding its origins in the word *fusello*, meaning "spindle" or "bobbin."

Study these popular types of pasta and see how well you can ascertain their origins.

i rigatoni	*i tortellini*
le penne	*i cannelloni*
le orecchiette	*i ravioli*
le farfalle	*le linguine*
le fettuccine	

This Drink's on Me

As is the Italian way, certain times befit certain beverages. *Il cappuccino* is generally consumed in the morning with a *cornetto* (similar to a croissant). *L'espresso* can be consumed any time of the day but is usually taken after meals (never *cappuccino*).

To whet your appetite, you can have an *aperitivo,* and to help you digest, a *digestivo* or *amaro.* As an afternoon pick-me-up, you can indulge in a *spremuta* (freshly squeezed juice). The following table lists different kinds of things you can drink. You should be able to pronounce these words without the guide—just sound them out like you see them.

I Bibiti

Drinks	Le Bibite
beer	*la birra*
coffee	*il caffè*
drink	*la bibita, la bevanda*
freshly squeezed juice	*la spremuta*
freshly squeezed grapefruit juice	*la spremuta di pompelmo*
freshly squeezed orange juice	*la spremuta d'arancia*
fruit juice	*il succo di frutta*
hot chocolate	*la cioccolata calda*
iced tea	*il tè freddo*
lemon soda	*la limonata*
milk	*il latte*
mineral water	*l'acqua minerale*
nonalcoholic beverage	*l'analcolico*
noncarbonated mineral water	*l'acqua minerale naturale*
orange soda	*l'aranciata*
sparkling mineral water	*l'acqua minerale gassata/frizzante*
sparkling wine	*lo spumante*
tea	*il tè*
wine	*il vino*

Dolcezza!

The word *dolcezza* is a term of endearment meaning "sweetheart." Do you have a sweet tooth? Italians love their *caramelle,* and if you're a chocolate addict, you definitely want to check out Perugina's *Baci* (kisses), which come in a silver wrapper and always include a fortune. The following table lists a number of treats.

For Your Sweet Tooth

The Candy	*La Caramella*
chocolate	*la cioccolata*
cough drop	*una caramella per la tosse*
gum	*la gomma americana*
licorice	*la liquirizia*
mint	*la menta*

Expressing Quantity

You want a little of this and a little of that. You'll take some olives, a loaf of bread, and a couple of boxes of pasta. Maybe you'll also get a slice of cheese, and since you're there, why not a chicken cutlet or two? Once you're out there shopping, you'll need to know how to express how much you want of something. There are a few ways of doing this.

It's the Quantity That Counts

Different measurements can lead to confusion. The following table will help make the metric system much easier to follow. These comparisons are approximate but close enough to get roughly the right amount.

Measuring

Solid Measures		Liquid Measures	
U.S. System	*Metrico*	U.S. System	*Metrico*
1 oz.	28 *grammi*	1 oz.	30 *millilitri*
¹/₄ lb.	125 *grammi (un etto)**	16 oz. (1 pint)	475 *millilitri*
¹/₂ lb.	250 *grammi*	32 oz. (1 quart)	*circa un litro*
³/₄ lb.	375 *grammi*	1 gallon	3.75 *litri*
1.1 lbs.	500 *grammi*		
2.2 lbs.	1 *chilogrammo (un chilo)*		

*Prices are often quoted by the etto *(a hectogram).*

It might be just as easy to indicate a little of this, a little of that, and then say when enough is enough using the expression, *Basta così*. Italy uses the metric system; instead of asking for "a dozen," you can also ask for "ten of." Some helpful ways of expressing quantity are listed in the following table.

Quantities

Amount	La Quantità
a bag of	*un sacchetto di*
a bottle of	*una bottiglia di*
a box of	*una scatola di*
a can of	*una lattina*
a container of	*un barattolo di*
a dozen of	*una dozzina di*
a drop of	*una goccia di*
a jar of	*un vasetto di*
a kilo of	*un chilo di*
a pack of	*un pacchetto di*
a piece of	*un pezzo di*
a quarter pound of	*un etto di*
a sack (lot) of	*un sacco di*
a slice of	*una fetta di*
a ten of	*una decina di*

La Bella Lingua

The words *qualche* and *alcuni* (or *alcune* [f.]) can mean "some" or "any" and can be used when there are *a few* or *several*. Note that *qualche* and the noun it modifies is always used in the singular even if the meaning is plural.

qualche volta	sometimes
alcuni amici	several friends
alcune lingue	a few languages

You Asked for It; You Got It!

You want to prepare a wonderful meal. You're planning to start with a light *brodo di tortellini,* then you want to roast a *pollo,* and for dessert, some *fragole fresche,* covered with *panna.* Here are some useful verbs and expressions you can use to make your meal:

Vorrei del (della)…	I would like some …
Per favore mi dia …	Please give me …
Mi può dare …	Can you give me …
Prendo …	I'll take …
Quanto viene?	How much does it come to?
Quanto ne serve per (il numero delle persone)?	How much is necessary for (the number of people)?
Quanto pesa?	How much does it weigh?
Avete una bustina di plastica?	Do you have a plastic bag?

Give Me Some!

To indicate that you would like "some of" a larger quantity, you can use the preposition *di* + the noun (with its appropriate definite article) to create the partitive. Refer back to Chapter 11, "Finally, You're at the Airport," to refresh your memory of contractions. Take a look at the following examples:

*Vorrei **del** pane.*	I'd like some bread.
*Prendo **della** frutta.*	I'll take some fruit.
*Ho anche bisogno **dello** zucchero.*	I also need some sugar.

Some or Any: The Partitive **Ne**

Imagine that someone asks you whether you want some ice cream. You're stuffed to the gills, though. If you eat one more bite, you'll explode, so you say, "Nah, I don't want any, thanks." It is assumed that *any* refers to the ice cream.

You've learned how to indicate some or any by using the preposition *di* plus *l'articolo.* The partitive pronoun *ne* comes in handy when used to ask for a "part of" or "some of" a greater quantity. It can be translated to mean "some," "any," "of it," "of them," "some of them," "any of it," and "any of them." It is especially used in response to a question, when the object has already been indicated.

Like most object pronouns, *ne* usually precedes the verb but attaches itself to the infinitive form (minus the final *–e*).

Vuole della frutta?	Would you like some fruit?
No grazie, non ne voglio.	No, thanks; I don't want any.
Non voglio mangiarne.	I don't want to eat any.

273

Some Practice

Answer the following questions with the pronoun *ne* using the affirmative and the negative:

> Example: *Vuole un frutto?* (Do you want a piece of fruit?)
>
> Answer: *No, non ne voglio.* (No, I don't want any.)

1. *Hanno dei soldi?* (Do they have money?)
   Sì, _____.

2. *Avete del pane?* (Do you [all] have some bread?)
   Sì, _____.

3. *Bevi vino?* (Do you drink wine?)
   Sì, _____.

4. *C'è del gelato?* (Is there any ice cream?)
   No, _____.

La Bella Lingua

If you want to indicate that you would like "more of" or "less of" something, just ask:

Di più, per favore.	More, please.
Di meno, grazie.	Less, thank you.

Facciamo La Spesa

In Italian, you use the expression *fare la spesa* to refer to shopping for household items such as food. Put together a shopping list in Italian for the following items you'll need for a picnic:

> *La Spesa*
>
> mineral water   a little prosciutto
> a bottle of red wine   some fruit
> some bread   a corkscrew
> a little cheese   a knife
> olives

What's Your Pleasure? The Verb *Piacere*

One of the first things an Italian will ask is *Le piace l'Italia?* (Do you like Italy?) What's not to like?

You need to understand the verb *piacere* (to be pleasing to) to express your likes and dislikes in Italian. In Italian, you don't say, "I like pizza." Using the verb *piacere*, you would say the equivalent of, "Pizza is pleasing to me," as in *Mi piace la pizza.* If you were talking about *gli spaghetti*, because the word *spaghetti* is plural in Italian, you would say, *Mi piacciono gli spaghetti.*

Unlike English, in Italian, the thing that is pleasing is the subject of the sentence. The person who is pleased is the indirect object.

Because the subject of the sentence dictates how the verb is conjugated, *piacere* is rarely used in anything other than the third-person singular and plural. Those two forms are shown here:

piace (it is pleasing/it pleases)

piacciono (they are pleasing/they please)

On rare occasions, you might find it necessary to use the verb in the first or second persons, in which case it is conjugated as follows:

The Verb *Piacere:* to Please

Italian	English
io **piaccio**	I am pleasing
tu **piaci**	you are pleasing
lui/lei/Lei **piace**	he/she (it) is pleasing; You are pleasing
noi **piacciamo**	we are pleasing
voi **piacete**	you are pleasing
loro **piacciono**	they are pleasing

Using Piacere

Expressing your likes and dislikes in Italian is much easier if you reprogram your brain. Instead of saying, "I like …," reword the expression to say "… is pleasing to me."

Some rules about the verb *piacere* are outlined here. In the first few examples, the **indirect object** (or pronoun) is in **bold** and the subject is underlined:

1. *Piacere* is almost always used in third person (singular and plural) and is always used with an indirect object or indirect object pronoun. Refer to Chapter 16, "Shop 'Til You Drop," to review your indirect objects and their pronouns:

Mi piace <u>la pizza</u>.	I like pizza. (<u>Pizza</u> is pleasing **to me**.)
Mi piacciono <u>gli spaghetti</u>.	I like spaghetti. (<u>Spaghetti</u> is pleasing **to me**.)
*Bambini, **vi** piace <u>la pizza</u>?*	Children, do you like pizza? (Is <u>pizza</u> pleasing **to you**?)
*Sì, **ci** piacciono la pizza e gli spaghetti!*	Yes, we like pizza and spaghetti. (Yes, pizza and spaghetti are pleasing **to us**.)

2. When used as the subject, the <u>infinitive</u> is singular.

Mi piace <u>mangiare</u> la pizza.	I like <u>eating</u> pizza.
Ti piace <u>studiare</u>?	Do you like <u>to study</u>?

3. When you're not using an indirect object pronoun, you must use the preposition *a* (or its contraction, *a* + the article) before the noun.

A Marcello piace bere il vino.	Marcello likes to drink wine. (Drinking wine is pleasing **to Marcello**.)
Ai bambini piace la cioccolata.	The children like chocolate. (Chocolate is pleasing **to the** children.)

4. The word order is somewhat flexible. The indirect object (the recipient of the verb's action) of the verb can come before or after the conjugated form of *piacere*.

*A **Giovanni** piace il pane.*	To Giovanni, bread is pleasing.
*Piace il pane **a Giovanni**?*	Is bread pleasing to Giovanni?

5. To make a negative statement, *non* goes in front of the indirect object pronoun.

***Non** mi piace il fegato.*	I don't like liver.

However, when the indirect object of the verb is a noun (and not a pronoun), *non* goes in front of the conjugated form of *piacere*.

*Ai bambini **non** piace il fegato.*	The children don't like liver.

6. The indirect object pronoun *loro* (to them) generally precedes the verb.

*A **loro** piacciono le caramelle.*	They like the candies.

7. The verb *dispiacere* means "to be sorry" (not "to be displeasing") as well as "to mind." It is used exactly like the verb *piacere*:

Mi dispiace.	I'm sorry.
Le dispiace attendere un momento?	Do you mind holding for a moment?

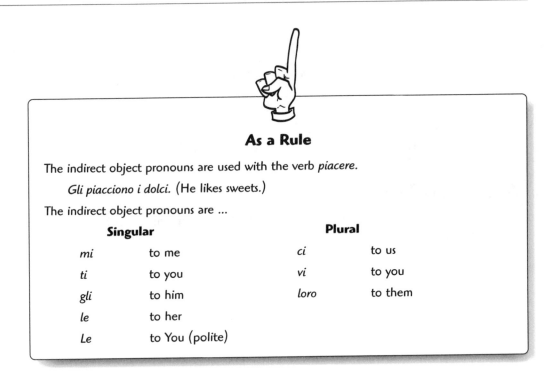

As a Rule

The indirect object pronouns are used with the verb *piacere.*

   Gli piacciono i dolci. (He likes sweets.)

The indirect object pronouns are ...

Singular		**Plural**	
mi	to me	*ci*	to us
ti	to you	*vi*	to you
gli	to him	*loro*	to them
le	to her		
Le	to You (polite)		

Using the Verb Piacere

Ask someone if he or she likes the following. Remember that the thing that is liked is the subject and that the verb *piacere* must reflect number.

   Example: *Le* _____ *il vino bianco?*

   Answer: *Le piace il vino bianco?*

1. *Ti* _____ *la frutta?*
2. *Signora, Le* _____ *il vino?*
3. *Vi* _____ *gli spaghetti?*
4. *Ti* _____ *cucinare?*
5. *Mamma, ti* _____ *le caramelle?*
6. *L'Italia* _____ *loro?*

Using the Verb Piacere II

Imagine that you are asking your partner if he or she likes something from the following list. Give both an affirmative and a negative response.

Example: *Ti piacciono i biscotti?*

Answer: *Sì, mi piacciono i biscotti.*

No, non mi piacciono i biscotti.

1. *i dolci*
2. *la pasta*
3. *gli spaghetti*

4. *le acciughe*
5. *i fichi*
6. *il fegato*

A Special Treat

There's nothing like good old-fashioned cooking. Here's an opportunity to apply your new Italian skills with a special recipe. The following words will help your dish turn out *perfetto:*

aggiungere	to add
bollire	to boil
cuocere	to cook
girare	to mix
mettere	to put
versare	to pour

Minestra di Riso e Limone

Ingredienti:

8 tazze di brodo

1 tazza di riso Arborio

3 tuorli di uova

¼ tazza formaggio Parmigiano-Reggiano, grattugiato

1 cucchiaino di scorza di limone grattugiata

1 cucchiaino di succo di limone

1. Mettete il brodo in un tegame e portatelo al punto di ebollizione. Aggiungete il riso, coprite il tegame e fatelo cuocere 20 minuti.

2. Nel frattempo battete le uova, aggiungete il formaggio, il limone grattugiato e il succo di limone.

3. Quando il riso è cotto, versate le uova nella minestra, sbattendo in continuazione. Riscaldate la minestra e servitela subito.

Per 4 persone.

The Least You Need to Know

➤ You need to do two things to eat well in Italy: work up a good appetite and learn a few gastronomical verbs: *mangiare* (to eat), *bere* (to drink), *assaggiare/ gustare* (to taste), *cenare* (to dine), *comprare* (to buy), *cucinare* (to cook), *pranzare* (to eat lunch), and *preparare* (to prepare).

➤ The pronoun *ne* is used to express that you want a "part of" or "some of" a greater quantity.

➤ To say that you like something, you must use the verb *piacere* (to be pleasing).

➤ You must use indirect object pronouns with *piacere.*

Chapter 18

Shall We Dine?

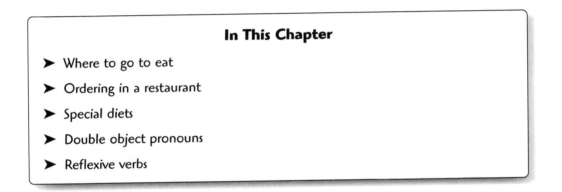

In This Chapter

➤ Where to go to eat

➤ Ordering in a restaurant

➤ Special diets

➤ Double object pronouns

➤ Reflexive verbs

You're on vacation and don't want to do dishes. Why not take a break? Sit back, relax, and let someone else do the running around for a change. If you want to understand the menu, or if you have special needs, this chapter will help you ask for what you want.

So Many Restaurants

You don't need to go to a five-star restaurant to eat well in Italy—there are restaurants for every palate and every pocket. Some of the smaller, family-run joints have the best food in town. Choose the place that best fits your needs:

Il bar: Apart from serving drinks of all kinds, bars serve *i panini* (sandwiches), *le merende* (snacks), and assorted *paste* (pastries).

La caffeteria: Pick and choose from whatever you see behind the glass counter, find an empty table, and eat. The food here is inexpensive and nourishing.

La mensa: Like a cafeteria, here you'll find wholesome food on a fixed-price basis; these places are usually frequented by *gli studenti*.

L'osteria: No different from a *taverna,* it's often family-run and frequented by locals.

La paninoteca: Here you can order sandwiches and beverages, good "on-the-go" food.

La pizzeria: Just like it sounds, at the pizzeria you can get your own personal pizza the size of a dinner plate, or a square cut from a large tray. Whatever the shape, the taste is unbeatable.

Il ristorante: This can range in *qualità* and *costo;* usually it has a more formal *ambiente.*

Self-service: Increasingly popular with young people; like a cafeteria, here you grab a tray and pick your *piatto.*

La tavola calda: Literally, this is a "hot table"— ready-to-eat food that you can take out as well.

La trattoria: Similar to *la taverna,* this local establishment offers home-style cooking in an intimate environment.

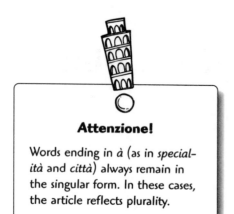

Attenzione!

Words ending in *à* (as in *specialità* and *città*) always remain in the singular form. In these cases, the article reflects plurality.

Two for Dinner, Please

The next time you are in an Italian *ristorante,* you may hear the following:

A che ora vorrebbe* mangiare?	At what time would you like to eat?
Vuole fare una prenotazione?	Would you like to make a reservation?
Per quante persone?	For how many people?
Va bene questo tavolo?	Is this table all right?
Tutto bene?	Is everything all right?
Le specialità del giorno sono …	Today's specials are …
Si accomodi.	Make yourself comfortable.

*Third-person conditional tense of volere *(to want).*

What's the House Special?

The following expressions will help you ask for what you want.

Dal Ristorante

L'Espressione	Expression
Cameriere!	Waiter!
Vorrei fare una prenotazione …	I'd like to make a reservation …
… per stasera.	… for this evening.
… per domani sera.	… for tomorrow evening.
… per sabato sera.	… for Saturday evening.

L'Espressione	Expression
... per due persone.	... for two people.
... alle otto.	... for 8:00.
Possiamo sederci ...	May we sit ...
... vicino alla finestra?	... near the window?
... sul terrazzo?	... on the terrace?
C'è una zona per non fumatori?	Is there a nonsmoking section?
Quanto tempo si deve aspettare?	How long is the wait?
Qual è la specialità della casa?	What is the house special?
Qual è il piatto del giorno?	What is the special for the day?
Che cosa ci consiglia?	What do you recommend?
Vorrei una porzione di ...	I'd like one portion of ...
Il conto, per favore.	The check, please.
Abbiamo mangiato* molto bene.	We ate very well.

*Past participle of mangiare.

A Table Setting

Prior to the fifteenth century, most food was eaten with the hands or from the point of a knife. Although it did not come to be commonly used until the seventeenth century, it appears that *i napoletani* created the four-pronged fork to aid them in eating spaghetti. Nowadays, it is considered *maleducato* (rude) to eat with your hands unless you're eating bread. The following table provides terms for the eating implements and other useful items.

Did You Know?

Il tavolo refers to a table in a restaurant; *la tavola* refers to a table at home.

At the Table

At the Table	Al Tavolo	Pronunciation
bowl	*la ciotola*	*lah choh-toh-lah*
	la scodella	*lah skoh-deh-lah*
carafe	*la caraffa*	*lah kah-rah-fah*
cup	*la tazza*	*lah tah-tsah*
dinner plate	*il piatto*	*eel pee-ah-toh*
fork	*la forchetta*	*lah for-keh-tah*
glass	*il bicchiere*	*eel bee-kee-yeh-reh*

continues

At the Table   (continued)

At the Table	*Al Tavolo*	Pronunciation
knife	*il coltello*	*eel koh-teh-loh*
menu	*il menù*	*eel meh-noo*
napkin	*il tovagliolo*	*eel toh-vah-lyoh-loh*
oil	*l'olio*	*loh-lee-yoh*
pepper	*il pepe*	*eel peh-peh*
pitcher	*la brocca*	*lah broh-kah*
salad bowl	*l'insalatiera*	*leen-sah-lah-tee-yeh-rah*
salt	*il sale*	*eel sah-leh*
silverware	*l'argenteria*	*lar-jen-teh-ree-ah*
spoon	*il cucchiaio*	*eel koo-kee-ay-yoh*
sugar bowl	*la zuccheriera*	*lah zoo-keh-ree-yeh-rah*
table	*il tavolo*	*eel tah-voh-loh*
tablecloth	*la tovaglia*	*lah toh-vah-lyah*
teapot	*la teiera*	*lah teh-yeh-rah*
teaspoon	*il cucchiaino*	*eel koo-kee-ay-ee-noh*
vinegar	*l'aceto*	*lah-cheh-toh*

In the Kitchen

Why not tape the following kitchen-related terms to your refrigerator?

In the Kitchen

In the Kitchen	*Nella Cucina*
basket	*il cesto*
bowl	*la ciotola*
box/container	*la scatola*
can opener	*l'apriscatole*
canister	*il barattolo*
colander	*il colapasta*
counter	*il piano di lavoro*
cupboard	*l'armadietto*
curtains	*le tende, le tendine*
cutting board	*il tagliere*
dishwasher	*la lavastoviglie*
faucet	*il rubinetto*
frying pan	*la pentola*

In the Kitchen	*Nella Cucina*
funnel	*l'imbuto*
grill	*la griglia*
measuring cup	*il misurino*
microwave oven	*il forno a microonde*
oven	*il forno*
oven mitt	*il guanto da forno*
pitcher	*la lattiera*
recipe	*la ricetta*
recipe book	*il libro di cucina*
refrigerator	*il frigorifero*
rolling board	*la spianatoia*
rolling pin	*il matterello*
sauce pan	*la padella*
saucer	*il piattino*
sink	*il lavandino*
stove	*il fornello*
stove burner	*la piastra*
straw	*la cannuccia*
toaster	*il tostapane*
tray	*il vassoio*
vase	*il vaso*

Did You Know?

One toasts (*fare un brindisi*) another to celebrate victory or an important accomplishment.

Alla salute!   *Cincin!* (pronounced *cheen-cheen*)

Il Bar

In Italy, the bar is a very different place than it is in other countries. At *il bar*, you can meet friends, have a *caffè*, grab a *panino* (sandwich, which literally comes from the word *pane*, meaning "little bread"), or sip an *amaro* after dinner. You must go to the

La Bella Lingua

Traditionally, Italians drink their coffee *in piedi* (standing up). Anytime you sit down for service, you're going to pay up to four times the amount you would otherwise. Some smaller, local establishments have courtesy tables—it's polite to bring your *tazza* back up to the bar after you've finished drinking.

cassa (cashier), pay for your choice, take your *scontrino* (receipt) to the bar, and pick up your order. It is customary to leave *una mancia* of 100 *lire* or so as a gesture of good will.

Il bar is usually well lit and very clean. No Italian bar would be the same without the familiar sound of milk being steamed for *il cappuccino*.

Il Caffè

In Italy, people take their *caffè* very seriously, and it is served in a variety of manners. If you must drink American coffee, which by Italian standards is considered weak and without flavor, ask for *un caffè americano*. If you are in a small town, you should indicate this as *un caffè molto lungo*.

The following table illustrates the different kinds of *caffè* you can order. Practice reading your Italian. Remember to use the verb *prendere* (to take) to ask for what you want, as in *Prendo un espresso*.

Coffee, Coffee Everywhere

Il Tipo di Caffè	La Descrizione
un espresso	*caffè normale*
un espresso lungo	*caffè con molta acqua*
un espresso ristretto	*caffè concentrato*
un cappuccino	*un espresso con latte vaporizzato* (steamed)
un latte macchiato	*molto latte, poco caffè*
un caffè macchiato	*caffè con una goccia* (a drop) *di latte*
un caffè latte	*caffè fatto* (made) *a casa con latte*
un caffè corretto	*caffè con un liquore*
un caffè decaffeinato	*caffè senza caffeina*
un caffè Hag	*caffè senza caffeina come* (like) *la Sanka*
un caffè freddo	*caffè freddo*

Etiquette for Idiots

Italians are not big snackers; when they eat, they really eat. Although nothing is written in stone, to enhance your dining *esperienza*, a few guidelines won't hurt.

For example, in Italy, almost everything is *alla carta*—that is, ordered individually. If you want *un contorno* (a side) of veggies, you'll get a separate *piattino* because Italians almost never have more than one kind of food on a plate unless you're eating from a buffet, usually referred to as either *la tavola fredda* or *la tavola calda*.

The order of the meal is important. Generally, you order a *primo piatto* (first course), which is usually a pasta dish or soup, and then you eat your *secondo piatto* (main course). *L'insalata* is usually eaten with *il secondo piatto*. Finally, when you order *un caffè*, it is assumed that you mean *espresso*. (Remember, Italians never drink cappuccino after a meal, and grated cheese is never offered for pasta dishes that include fish.)

The Courses

Be creative; unless you're in a formal establishment, why not order several *antipasti* and give everything a taste? The following table outlines the different courses.

Did You Know?

Contrary to popular belief, Marco Polo wasn't the first to introduce spaghetti to Italy. Evidence that the Romans had various forms of pasta predates Marco Polo's adventure, although tomatoes weren't introduced to Italy until the fifteenth century from South America. It was believed that the yellow and red fruit (yes, the tomato is a fruit—the Italian word *pomodoro* literally means "golden apple") was poisonous unless cooked for a long time.

Courses

L'Italiano	La Definizione	English	The Definition
l'antipasto	*un assaggio per stimolare l'appetito*	appetizer	a taste to stimulate the appetite
il primo piatto	*la pasta, il risotto, o la zuppa*	first course	a pasta, risotto, or soup
il secondo piatto	*la carne, il pollo, o il pesce*	second course	meat, chicken, or fish
il contorno	*di solito le verdure: gli spinaci, i fagioli, le melanzane, ecc.*	side dish	usually vegetables: spinach, beans, eggplant, and so on

What's on the Menu?

Italian food can be found in restaurants all over the world. You are probably already familiar with a lot of *piatti*. The following three tables help you interpret some of what you might find.

I Primi Piatti

Il Primo Piatto	What It Is
brodo	broth
gnocchi al sugo di pomodoro	potato pasta with tomato sauce
lasagna	lasagna
linguine alle vongole	spaghetti in clam sauce
minestrone	vegetable soup
orecchiette ai broccoli e aglio	ear-shaped pasta with broccoli and garlic
pasta e fagioli	pasta with beans
penne alla vodka	tubes of pasta with tomato, vodka, cream, and hot peppers
ravioli di zucca e ricotta	pumpkin ravioli with ricotta cheese
risotto di mare	seafood risotto
spaghetti alla bolognese	spaghetti in meat sauce
spaghetti alla carbonara	spaghetti with bacon, egg, and Parmesan
stracciatella	eggdrop soup
tortellini prosciutto e piselli	tortellini with prosciutto and peas
zuppa di verdura toscana	Tuscan country soup

I Secondi Piatti

Il Secondo Piatto	What It Is
pollo al limone	lemon chicken
pollo ai funghi	chicken with mushrooms
polpette al ragù	meatballs in tomato sauce
cotoletta alla milanese	breaded cutlet
pollo alla francese	chicken cooked in wine and lemon sauce
involtini di vitello	veal rolls cooked in wine with mushrooms
calamari alla marinara	squid in tomato sauce
salsiccia affumicata	smoked sausage
pollo alla griglia	grilled chicken
bistecca	steak
ossobuco alla milanese	oxtail or veal shanks with lemon, garlic, and parsley
agnello arrosto al rosmarino	roast lamb spiced with rosemary
anatra con vinsanto	duck with holy wine (sherry)
coda di rospo con carciofi	monkfish with artichokes

I Contorni e Gli Antipasti

Il Contorno e L'Antipasto	What It Is
la bruschetta lucchese	bruschetta with tomatoes, beans, and herbs
calamari fritti	fried calamari
cuori di carciofo marinati	marinated artichoke hearts
fagioli alla veneziana	beans, anchovies, and garlic
finocchi al cartoccio	baked fennel (literally "in a bag")
formaggi vari	various cheeses
funghi trifolati	sautéed mushrooms, garlic, onion, and parsley
prosciutto con melone	prosciutto with melon
insalata alla cesare	Caesar salad
insalata di pomodoro e cipolla	tomato and onion salad
insalata verde	green salad
melanzana alla griglia	grilled eggplant
patate bollite	boiled potatoes
spiedini di gamberi alla griglia	skewered, grilled shrimp
spinaci saltati	spinach tossed with garlic
zucchini fritti	fried zucchini

Ho Una Fame Da Lupo *(I'm as Hungry as a Wolf)*

There's no better way to understand what's on a menu than to look at one. Take a look and see how much you can understand.

La Pizza e Il Formaggio

Italians like to have their own pizza, which are about as big as a plate and ordered individually. The crust is crunchy, and the pizza is lightly covered with melted cheeses ranging from *gorgonzola*, a sharp cheese; *mozzarella*, a soft delicate cheese made from the milk of water buffalo; *Parmigiano-Reggiano*, a sharp cheese and one of Italy's finest; *pecorino*, a sharp cheese made from sheep milk; *provolone*, a sharp cheese often grated; and *ricotta* (literally meaning "recooked"), which is made from the whey produced in the cheese-making process, resulting in a soft, almost sweet cheese. The following tables describes some of the pizza you can order.

Did You Know?

In Italy, each region has its own bread. For example, *il pane toscano* is found throughout Tuscany and Umbria; here the bread has no salt, stemming back to the thirteenth century when a salt tax was imposed on the people.

Ristorante Gabriella

La Lista

Antipasti: *Insalata di Sedano, Funghi e Formaggio 8.000*

Frutti di Mare 10.500

Bruschetta al Pomodoro 4.000

Carpaccio con Rucola e Parmigiano 11.000

Primi Piatti: *Vermicelli alle Vongole 12.000*

Polenta con Porcini 10.000

Spaghetti alla Bolognese 10.000

Minestrone 8.000

Secondi Piatti: *Spiedino Misto 15.000*

Bistecca Marinata alla Griglia 20.000

Coniglio alla Contadina 18.000

Frutti di Mare 17.000

I Contorni: *Insalata Mista 6.000*

Melanzana alla Griglia 8.000

Fiori di Zucca Ripieni 6.000

Pane e Coperto 3.000

Per gruppi di oltre sei persone sarà aggiunto 8% di servizio.

Le Pizze

La Pizza	English
bianca	"white" pizza; plain (no tomato, no cheese; just crust)
ai funghi	tomato, mozzarella, and mushrooms
margherita	tomato, mozzarella, basil, and olives
napoletana	tomato, mozzarella, anchovies, capers, and olives
quattro formaggi	four cheeses: mozzarella, fontina, swiss, and gorgonzola
quattro stagioni	represents the four seasons: artichokes (spring), olives (summer), mushrooms (autumn), prosciutto (winter)
alle verdure	vegetables: tomato, mozzarella, zucchini, spinach, eggplant, and mushrooms

That's the Way I Like It

Do you want your eggs scrambled or poached? Your meat cooked rare, or well-done? A poached egg is called *le uova in camicia* because the white of the egg surrounds the yolk, like a shirt. Italians generally eat eggs for lunch or dinner as a *secondo piatto*. The terms in the following table will allow you to express exactly how you like it.

Proper Preparation of Meats and Vegetables (*La Carne e La Verdure*)

Preparation	La Preparazione	Pronunciation
baked	*al forno*	*ahl for-noh*
boiled	*bollito*	*boh-lee-toh*
breaded	*impanato*	*eem-pah-nah-toh*
fried	*fritto*	*free-toh*
grilled	*alla griglia*	*ah-lah gree-lyah*
marinated	*marinato*	*mah-ree-nah-toh*
medium	*normale*	*nor-mah-leh*
poached	*in camicia*	*een kah-mee-chah*
rare	*al sangue*	*ahl sahn-gweh*
steamed	*al vapore*	*ahl vah-poh-reh*
well-done	*ben cotto*	*ben koh-toh*
fried (eggs)	*le uova fritte*	*leh woh-vah free-teh*
hard-boiled (eggs)	*le uova bollite*	*leh woh-vah boh-lee-teh*
poached (eggs)	*le uova in camicia*	*leh woh-vah een kah-mee-chah*
scrambled (eggs)	*le uova strapazzate*	*leh woh-vah strah-pah-tsah-the*
soft-boiled (eggs)	*le uova alla coque*	*leh woh-vah ah-lah koh-kay*
omelette	*la frittata*	*lah free-tah-tah*

Spice Up Your Life

Italian food is generally flavored with a variety of spices that are subtly blended to create the dishes you love. If you want it hot, ask for *piccante*. Need a little salt? Tell your dining companion to pass *il sale*. The following table describes some of the spices you'll encounter while eating Italian cuisine.

Spices and Seasonings

Spices	Le Spezie	Spices	Le Spezie
basil	*il basilico*	caper	*il cappero*
bay leaf	*la foglia di alloro*	chive	*il cipollino, la cipollina*

continues

Spices and Seasonings (continued)

Spices	Le Spezie	Spices	Le Spezie
dill	*l'aneto*	oregano	*l'origano*
garlic	*l'aglio*	paprika	*la paprika*
ginger	*lo zenzero*	parsley	*il prezzemolo*
honey	*il miele*	pepper	*il pepe*
ketchup	*il ketchup*	rosemary	*il rosmarino*
mint	*la menta*	saffron	*lo zafferano*
mustard	*la senape*	salt	*il sale*
nutmeg	*la noce moscata*	sugar	*lo zucchero*

La Bella Lingua

After you order your food, your *cameriere* may acknowledge your request with the simple word *prego*. In addition to meaning "you're welcome," *prego* is also used to mean "Please," "Pardon," "After you," "I'm all yours," and "Don't mention it!"

Special People Have Special Needs

You're in great shape and have eliminated certain things from your diet. There's no reason to destroy all your hard work with one visit to Italy. The phrases in the following table will help you stick to your diet.

Special Needs

Phrase	La Frase
I am on a diet.	*Faccio la dieta/Sto in dieta.*
I'm a vegetarian.	*Sono vegetariano(a).*
Do you serve Kosher food?	*Servite del cibo Kosher?*
I can't have any ...	*Non posso prendere ...*
... dairy products.	*... i latticini.*
... alcohol.	*... l'alcol.*

Phrase	*La Frase*
… saturated fat.	… *i grassi saturi.*
… shellfish.	… *i frutti di mare.*
I'm looking for a dish …	*Cerco un piatto …*
… high in fiber.	… *con molta fibra.*
… low in cholesterol.	… *con poco colesterolo.*
… low in fat.	… *con pochi grassi.*
… low in sodium.	… *poco salato.*
… without preservatives.*	… *senza conservanti.*

Be sure to use the Italian word conservanti *and not the false cognate* preservativi, *which means "prophylactics"!*

La Bella Lingua

Whenever you go into *un ristorante italiano*, ask if they have a menu you can take home to begin a collection. There's no better way to learn Italian than by starting with the thing you love most: food!

You Call This Food?

You asked for a rare steak, but you received what looks like a shoe. There's a small nail in your pizza (don't worry, you won't be charged extra), a hair in your spaghetti, or cheese in the pasta (when you specifically asked for none). Keep your calm and tell the waiter. The following table gives you the terms.

Take It Away!

English	*L'Italiano*
This is …	*Questo è …*
… burned.	… *bruciato.*
… dirty.	… *sporco.*
… overcooked.	… *troppo cotto.*
… spoiled.	… *andato a male.*

continues

Take It Away! (continued)

English	L'Italiano
… too cold.	… *troppo freddo.*
… too rare.	… *troppo crudo.*
… too salty.	… *troppo salato.*
… too spicy.	… *troppo piccante.*
… too sweet.	… *troppo dolce.*
… unacceptable.	… *inaccettabile.*

La Bella Lingua

Italian standards for wine are very high. The next time you go for a *degustazione vini* (wine tasting), it might help you to know a little about how Italian wines are classified.

Finer wines are classified as *denominazione di origine controllata* (DOC) or *denominazione di origine controllata e garantita* (DOCG), which you'll see on the wine label.

Other wines are simply classified as *vino da tavola* (table wine), which range in quality and are served by many restaurants as *il vino della casa* (the house wine).

Fine Wine

Italian wines are among the best in the world, fulfilling one fifth of the total production. Wine talk is presented in the following table.

Bottle o' Wine, Fruit of the Vine

Wine	Il Vino
red wine	*il vino rosso*
rosé wine	*il rosé*
white wine	*il vino bianco*
dry wine	*il vino secco*
sweet wine	*il vino dolce*
sparkling wine	*lo spumante*

A Bellini *Please*

One of Italy's most popular cocktails is the *Bellini,* created by Giuseppe Cipriani of Harry's Bar in Venice. This light, refreshing drink is perfect before a meal:

Bellini

> ²/₃ *tazza (160 ml.) di purè di pesca*
> *1 cucchiaino di purè di lampone*
> *1 bottiglia di Prosecco (o Asti Spumante o champagne)*

In ogni bicchiere di vino o spumante, versate 1 cucchiaini di purè di pesca. Aggiungete 2-3 goccie di pur di lampone. Aggiungete il vino e servite subito.

What's Your Fancy?

Gli aperitivi (aperitifs) and *gli amari* (digestives) are a lovely part of a meal. Try something new, and bring back a bottle of Cynar (made from artichokes) to share with your friends. A common practice is to drink Sambuca with a couple of coffee beans (*grani di caffè*). In some parts, they are called *le mosche* (flies) because of their resemblance to the little pests. Word has it that this controls garlic breath (and you're going to be eating *a lot* of garlic). You'll find many drinks to try in the following table.

Gli Alcolici

Gli Aperitivi	*Gli Amari*
Aperol	*Fernet*
Campari (bevuto con/senza acqua)	*Jeigermeister (Germania minerale frizzante)*
Cynar (di carciofo)	*Lucano*
Martini (bianco o rosso)	*Petrus (Olanda)*
Negroni	*Averna*

La Dolce

Italians don't fool around when it comes to dessert. Many *dolci* are peculiar to a particular region and cannot be found elsewhere.

The following brief list mentions some of the sweets you can find in Italy. If baked goods, such as *biscotti* (cookies, literally meaning "twice-baked") and *torte* (cakes), don't trip your trigger, dip into *un gelato* (ice cream) at a *gelateria* where you are given up to three flavors in any *porzione* (portion). If you're not sure of a flavor, ask for *un assaggio* (a taste).

Bavarese (as in "Bavarian")	*Panettone*
Biscotti di mandorle (almond cookies)	*Panforte* (Tuscan)
Cannolo (Sicilian)	*Profiterole*
Colomba	*Ricciarelli* (Tuscan)
Cornetto	*Sfogliatella della Nobilità* (noble's pastry)
Danese ("Danish")	*Torta di Frutta Fresca*
Diplomatico (literally, "diplomat")	*Tiramisù* (literally, "pick me up")
Macedonia di frutta (mixed fruit)	*Ventaglio*
Maritozzo	*Zuppa Inglese* (English trifle)
Millefoglie (literally, "1,000 sheets")	

Double Object Pronouns

After your feast, it's time to get back to business. You've learned your object pronouns and remember that they must reflect the gender and number of the objects they replace.

In Italian, unlike English, it is possible to join the object pronouns together to form one word. In the following table, notice how the indirect object pronouns *mi, ti, ci, vi* and *si* change to *me, te, ce, ve* and *se*. Also note that the indirect object pronouns *gli, le,* and *Le* change to *glie–* before direct object pronouns, creating one word.

Double Object Pronouns

Pronoun	Indirect Object		Direct Object		
	lo	*la*	*li*	*le*	*ne*
mi	*me lo*	*me la*	*me li*	*me le*	*me ne*
ti	*te lo*	*te la*	*te li*	*te le*	*te ne*
gli, le, Le	*glielo*	*gliela*	*glieli*	*gliele*	*gliene*
ci	*ce lo*	*ce la*	*ce li*	*ce le*	*ce ne*
si	*se lo*	*se la*	*se li*	*se le*	*se ne*
vi	*ve lo*	*ve la*	*ve li*	*ve le*	*ve ne*
si	*se lo*	*se la*	*se li*	*se le*	*se ne*

Keep in mind the following:

➤ When the same verb has two object pronouns, the indirect object always precedes the direct object.

*Mandi la lettera al signor Rossi? Sì, **gliela** mando.*

Are you sending the letter to Mr. Rossi? Yes, I'm sending it to him.

*Restituiscono i soldi alla signora? Sì, **glieli** restituiscono.*

Are they giving back the money to the woman? Yes, they are giving it back to her.

➤ After an infinitive, the final *–e* is dropped and the double object pronoun is attached to the end of the infinitive forming one word:

*Posso spedir**tela**?*   Can I send it to you?

*Vuole dar**celo**.*   He wants to give it to us.

La Bella Lingua

You can avoid double object pronouns altogether by replacing them with nouns.

Me lo dà.   He gives it to me. (two object pronouns)

Mi dà il libro.   He gives the book to me. (one object pronoun)

You've Got Good Reflexes

Whenever you tell someone *Mi chiamo* (I call myself), you are using a reflexive verb. In Italian, when you enjoy yourself, get dressed, or comb your hair, you are using a reflexive verb.

Reflexive verbs are easily identified by the *–si* attached at the end of the infinitive. Conjugation of the reflexive verbs follows the same rules as any other Italian verb, with one exception: Reflexive verbs require the use of reflexive pronouns. These pronouns show that the subject is performing (or reflecting back) an action upon itself. In other words, the subject and the reflexive pronoun both refer to the same persons or things, as in the phrases "We enjoyed ourselves" and "I hurt myself."

The reflexive pronouns differ only from the direct object pronouns in the third-person singular and plural. Study the following reflexive pronouns.

Attenzione!

When dealing with double object pronouns, it is assumed that the speaker has already referred to the object of the sentence. In certain cases, the gender of the indirect object is not always obvious:

Presti la macchina a Silvia?
Sì, gliela do.
Are you lending the car to Silvia?
Yes, I'm lending it to her.

Reflexive Pronouns

Reflexive Pronoun	English Equivalent
mi	myself
ti	yourself
si	himself/herself; Yourself
ci	ourselves
vi	yourselves
si	themselves

I Call Myself

Look at the reflexive verb *chiamarsi* in the following table to see how the reflexive pronouns work with the conjugated verb.

Chiamarsi (to Call Oneself)

Italian	English
mi chiamo	I call myself
ti chiami	you call yourself
si chiama	he/she calls him/herself; You call yourself
ci chiamiamo	we call ourselves
vi chiamate	you call yourselves
si chiamano	they call themselves

Come ti chiami?	How do you call yourself?
Mi chiamo Gabriella.	I call myself Gabriella.

Attenzione!

In Italian, you are responsible for your own boredom because the verb *annoiarsi* (to be bored) is reflexive, literally translating to "I bore myself."

The verb *truccarsi* is the verb used "to put on makeup." It's interesting to note that the noun *trucco* means "trick" in Italian.

Flexing Those Muscles

Look at some common reflexive verbs in the following table.

Reflexive Verbs

Il Verb Riflessivo	Meaning	Il Verb Riflessivo	Meaning
accorgersi	to notice	*lavarsi*	to wash
addormentarsi	to fall asleep	*mettersi*	to put on
alzarsi	to get up	*pettinarsi*	to comb one's hair
annoiarsi	to be bored	*rendersi*	to realize
arrabbiarsi	to get angry	*ricordarsi*	to remember/to remind
conoscersi	to know each other	*sentirsi*	to feel
chiamarsi	to call	*sposarsi*	to get married
diplomarsi	to obtain a diploma	*svegliarsi*	to get up
divertirsi	to enjoy	*truccarsi*	to make up
fermarsi	to stop	*vestirsi*	to dress oneself
laurearsi	to graduate		

Vi conoscete da molto tempo?	Do you know each other for a long time?
Federico si laurea a giugno.	Federico is graduating in June.
Ricorda di lavarti la faccia!	Remember to wash your face!
I bambini si divertono al parco.	The children enjoy themselves in the park.
Come ti chiami?	What do you call yourself?

La Bella Lingua

What's in a name? If you're one of the many to possess a little Italian *sangue* in your veins, why not do some research and learn more about your family name? The study of genealogy has come a long way with the help of the Internet. A number of Web sites are devoted to helping people learn more about their family tree while helping them find long-lost relatives. Try doing a search and see what interesting tidbits come up. Many Italian names describe vocations (such as the English name Smith) or were taken from the names of the towns where people lived. For example, my last name, Euvino, originally meant "fine wine." Leonardo Da Vinci's name implies he came from the town of Vinci. You can probably guess *di dove* came San Francesco d'Assisi!

A Little Reflection

Some rules applying to reflexive verbs might make them easier to master:

1. When talking about parts of the body or clothing, a possessive adjective is not required when using a reflexive verb:

    Mi lavo il viso.   I wash my face.

    Si toglie la giacca.   He/she takes off the jacket.

2. The reflexive pronoun can be placed before the verb or after the infinitive when preceded by a form of the verb *potere, dovere,* or *volere*:

    Non voglio alzarmi troppo presto. I don't want to wake up too early.

    Devo lavarmi i capelli.   I must wash my hair.

Attenzione!

Because reflexive pronouns are not gender-specific, if you want to specify who is doing what, you'll have to use a proper name or noun:

Si lava il viso. → **Isabella** *si lava il viso.*

Si alzano alle otto. → **I ragazzi** *si alzano alle otto.*

Mirror, Mirror

Some verbs greatly change their meaning when made reflexive. The regular verb *sentire* can mean "to hear" or "to smell."

    Sento la musica.   I hear the music.

    Sento il profumo.   I smell the perfume.

As a reflexive verb, *sentirsi* means "to feel."

    Mi sento bene.   I feel well.

    Come si sente?   How do you feel?

The verbs in the following table exemplify the pliable nature of these flexible reflexives.

What's in a Name

Verb	English	Reflexive Verb	English
annoiare	to annoy	*annoiarsi*	to get bored
arrestare	to arrest	*arrestarsi*	to pause, to stop
battere	to beat	*battersi*	to fight
chiedere	to ask	*chiedersi*	to wonder
comportare	to entail	*comportarsi*	to behave
giocare	to play	*giocarsi*	to risk
infuriare	to infuriate	*infuriarsi*	to get angry
lamentare	to mourn	*lamentarsi*	to complain
licenziare	to dismiss/to fire	*licenziarsi*	to resign/to quit
offendere	to offend	*offendersi*	to take offense (at)
onorare	to honor	*onorarsi*	to take pride (in)
perdere	to lose	*perdersi*	to get lost
scusare	to excuse	*scusarsi*	to apologize
sentire	to hear/to smell	*sentirsi*	to feel

Mi perdo nelle città nuove.	I get lost (I lose myself) in new cities.
Giovanni si annoia quando va all'opera.	Giovanni is bored when he goes to the opera.

Test Your Reflexes

Use the reflexive verbs in parentheses in the following sentences with the appropriate reflexive pronoun:

Example: *Noi _____ spesso. (vedersi)*

Answer: *Noi ci vediamo spesso.*

1. *Io _____ alle nove. (alzarsi)*
2. *Luciano e Marcello _____ da nove anni. (conoscersi)*
3. *Tu _____ in palestra? (divertirsi)*
4. *Giulia deve _____ i capelli ogni giorno. (lavarsi)*
5. *Tu, come _____ ? (chiamarsi)*
6. *Noi _____ una volta la settimana. (telefonarsi)*
7. *Come _____ la nonna di Sandra? (sentirsi)*
8. *Antonella e Marco _____ lunedì prossimo. (sposarsi)*

Reciprocity

Every time you say to someone *Arrivederci!* you are using a reflexive. The expression literally translates as "to re-see each other." The same goes for the expression *Ci vediamo!* (We'll see one another), which comes from the infinitive *vedersi*.

You have seen all of the verbs in the following table as nonreflexive verbs. By simply being made reflexive, these verbs can all express reciprocity.

Do Unto Others

Reflexive Verb	English
abbracciarsi	to hug one another
baciarsi	to kiss one another
capirsi	to understand one another
conoscersi	to know one another
guardarsi	to look at one another
incontrarsi	to meet one another/to run into
salutarsi	to greet each other
vedersi	to see one another

Ci abbracciamo ogni volta che ci vediamo.
We hug one another every time we see each other.

Madre e figlia si capiscono senza parole.
Mother and daughter understand one another without words.

The Least You Need to Know

➤ You can read an Italian menu if you know the right terms for the food you love (and hate).

➤ Ask to make a reservation using the expression *Vorrei fare una prenotazione* or *Vorrei prenotare un tavolo*. Do not use the cognate *riservare*, which means "to keep" or "to put aside."

➤ There are several parts to an Italian meal: *gli antipasti, i contorni, i primi piatti, i secondi piatti,* and *i dolci.*

➤ When dealing with double object pronouns, the indirect object pronoun always precedes the direct object pronoun.

➤ Reflexive verbs, identified by the pronoun *–si* attached to the end of the infinitive, require the use of one of the reflexive pronouns: *mi, ti, si* (singular), *ci, vi,* and *si* (plural).

➤ Many regular verbs can become reflexive. In some cases, the meaning changes dramatically.

Chapter 19

Having Fun Italian Style

In This Chapter

➤ Sports and games

➤ Cinema, music, and art

➤ The present perfect tense

➤ Using double object pronouns in the past

This chapter covers many of the pastimes that make up the Italian lifestyle. Whether you are a sport's buff, a film fanatic, an opera lover, or an art appreciator, there's a little bit of everything and something for everyone.

In addition, you'll learn a very important new verb tense: *il passato prossimo*. Use of this tense allows you to talk about your sordid past. Let the fun begin!

Name Your Game

In Italian, *il football*—also known as *il calcio*—refers to soccer. The touchy-feely version played in the Super Bowl is aptly called *football americano*. Italians refer to baseball, golf, hockey, tennis, and windsurfing, however, in English.

There are three things you should never dare take away from an Italian: *la mamma, la pasta,* and *il calcio*. Expect anarchy if you dare.

La Bella Lingua

If you like to play *scacchi* (chess), you may get a rise out of playing one of the many accomplished players you'll find in some local establishments. You'll need a little chess terminology to get you started understanding *i pezzi* (the pieces) on your *scacchiera* (chess board):

Check!	*Scacco!*
Checkmate!	*Scacco Matto!*
the king	*il re*
the queen	*la regina*
the rook	*la torre* (the tower)
the bishop	*l'alfiere*
the knight	*il cavallo* (the horse)
the pawn	*il pedone*

Game Time

Sport	*Lo Sport*	Pronunciation
aerobics	*aerobica*	*lay-eh-roh-bee-kah*
basketball	*pallacanestro*	*pah-lah-kah-neh-stroh*
bicycling	*il ciclismo*	*eel chee-kleez-moh*
boating	*il canottaggio*	*eel kah-noh-tah-joh*
boxing	*il pugilato*	*eel poo-jee-lah-toh*
fencing	*la scherma*	*lah sker-mah*
fishing	*pescare*	*peh-skah-reh*
game	*la partita*	*lah par-tee-tah*
horseback riding	*l'equitazione*	*leh-kwee-tah-zee-oh-neh*
jogging	*il footing*	*fah-reh footing*
karate	*il karatè*	*fah-reh kah-rah-teh*
rock climbing	*l'alpinismo*	*lahl-pee-nee-zmoh*
sailing	*la vela*	*lah veh-lah*
score	*il punteggio*	*eel poon-teh-joh*
skating	*il pattinaggio*	*eel pah-tee-nah-joh*

Sport	Lo Sport	Pronunciation
skiing	lo sci	loh shee-ah-reh
... cross-country skiing	... lo sci di fondo	loh shee dee fon-doh
... water skiing	... lo sci acquatico	loh shee ak-wah-tee-koh
soccer	il calcio, il football	eel kahl-choh
swimming	il nuoto	eel nwoh-toh
team	la squadra	lah skwah-drah
volleyball	il pallavolo	lah pah-lah-voh-loh
wrestling	la lotta libera	lah loh-tah lee-beh-rah

You're Playing with My Head

If you're looking for less exertion, a few games allow you to use more brain power than brawn. *Briscola* and *Scopa* are two popular card games. *Giochiamo!*

Games for the Brain

backgammon	backgammon
Briscola	Briscola
cards	carte
checkers	dama
chess	scacchi
dice	dadi
dominoes	domino
hide-and-seek	cu-cù
poker	poker
Scopa (a popular card game)	Scopa
tarot	tarocchi

Out in Left Field

Each sport or activity has its own particular playing field, as shown in the following table.

Beach Blanket Bingo

The Place	Il Posto	Pronunciation
beach	la spiaggia	lah spee-ah-jah
casino	il casinò	eel kah-see-noh
court/field	il campo	eel kam-poh

continues

Beach Blanket Bingo   (continued)

The Place	Il Posto	Pronunciation
golf course	*il campo da golf*	*eel kam-poh dah golf*
gym	*la palestra*	*lah pah-leh-strah*
mountain	*la montagna*	*lah mohn-tan-yah*
ocean	*l'oceano*	*loh-sheh-ah-noh*
park	*il parco*	*eel par-koh*
path	*il sentiero*	*eel sen-tee-eh-roh*
pool	*la piscina*	*lah pee-shee-nah*
rink	*la pista da pattinaggio*	*lah pees-tah dah pah-tee-nah-joh*
sea	*il mare*	*eel mah-reh*
ski slope	*la pista da sci*	*lah pees-tah dah shee*
stadium	*lo stadio*	*loh stah-dee-yoh*
track	*la corsa*	*lah kor-sah*

La Bella Lingua

In Italian, there are many ways of expressing "to play." The verb *giocare* (to play) is used when playing sports or games. (Think of the English word "joker.")

The verb *suonare* (to play) is used when playing an instrument. (Think of the English word "sound.")

The verbs *andare* (to go) and *fare* (to do/to make) are often used when participating in a sport or activity.

Make a Date

This exercise will help you remember how to *fissare un'appuntamento* (make an appointment). See how well you are able to translate the following sentences into Italian:

1. Why don't we meet at 3:00 tomorrow?

2. Are you in the mood to go swimming? (idiomatic—a hint: *Ti va di …*)

3. Let's go to the mountains next week.

4. Why not visit the museum?

5. Do you want to play tennis with me?

Did You Know?

The infamous *Palio* is a horse race that has been taking place in Siena since medieval times. The entire city closes down to watch the various *contrade* (districts)—each represented by a flag and often an animal such as *il porcospino* (porcupine) or *la giraffa* (giraffe)—vie for their own jockeys as the horses race around the town square. Afterward, long tables are set in the streets and miles of spaghetti are cooked to feed the excited masses.

The Arts

Ah, *la Madre Patria!* The Italians have an emotional relationship to *la politica, la famiglia,* and *l'amore.* It is no surprise that their art reflects these powerful forces. The following sections are meant as a taster, or *antipasto,* to whet your appetite.

Il Cinema

There's no better way to practice your Italian than by watching films (next to visiting Italy, that is). Italy started as one of the world's major film producers. *Cinecittà* (the Hollywood of Italy), in *Roma,* has spawned some of the best filmmakers in the world, including Bernardo Bertolucci, Vittorio De Sica, Federico Fellini, Pier Paolo Pasolini, and Luchino Visconti, to name a few. And who hasn't heard of the noted Italian actors Sofia Loren, Marcello Mastroianni, Giancarlo Giannini, Gina Lollobrigida, Alberto Sordi, and Roberto Benigni?

The word *il cinema* is an abbreviated version of *cinematografo.* The terms in the following table can help you discuss whether a film deserves the thumbs up or thumbs down.

La Bella Lingua

The narrative plays of Venetian **Carlo Goldoni** (1707–1793) dealt with many of the same issues portrayed in modern stories: love, sex, and money. His play *La Locandiera* inspired an opera by **Antonio Salieri** (1750–1825) and reflected the social mores of his time.

Did You Know?

La carrellata (tracking shot) was pioneered on the set of Giovanni Pastrone's film *Cabiria* in 1914. The intertitles (they didn't have talkies yet) were written by the popular soldier-poet Gabriele D'Annunzio.

Movie Talk

The Cinema	Il Cinema
actor	*l'attore*
actress	*l'attrice*
camera	*la cinepresa, la macchina fotografica*
cinema	*il cinema*
close-up	*primo piano*
director	*il/la regista*
dissolve	*dissolvenza*
film	*il film, la pellicola*
long-shot	*campo lungo*
panning	*panoramica*
plot	*la trama*
producer	*il produttore*
scene	*la scena*
screen	*lo schermo*
theater	*la sala cinematografica*
video camera	*la telecamera*
to hear	*sentire, udire*
to listen	*ascoltare*
to see	*vedere*
to watch/look	*guardare*

Did You Know?

Check out the following "must sees" of Italian cinema. The director's last name is in parentheses next to the movie title.

The White Sheik (Fellini)

Bicycle Thief (De Sica)

Roma: Open City (Rossellini)

Kaos (Taviani Brothers)

Caro Diario (Moretti)

The Human Voice (Rossellini)

L'Amerika (Amelio)

Big Deal on Madonna Street (Monicelli)

The Conformist (Bertolucci)

Ossessione (Visconti)

La Dolce Vita (Fellini)

Seven Beauties (Wertmuller)

Hands Over the City (Rosi)

L'Avventura (Antonioni)

Before the Revolution (Bertolucci)

La Musica

Nothing soothes the savage breast like music. The great violin maker Antonio Stradivari (1644–1747) came from Cremona. Is there a musical instrument that makes you swoon every time you hear it? Find it in the following table, or find your favorite Italian composer in the timeline.

The Sound of Music

Instrument	Lo Strumento
accordion	*la fisarmonica*
cello	*il violoncello*
clarinet	*il clarinetto*
drum	*il tamburo, la batteria*
flute	*il flauto*
guitar	*la chitarra*
harp	*l'arpa*
horn	*il corno*
oboe	*l'oboe*

continues

The Sound of Music (continued)

Instrument	*Lo Strumento*
piano	*il pianoforte*
piccolo	*il piccolo*
saxophone	*il sassofono*
trombone	*il trombone*
trumpet	*la tromba*
viola	*la viola*
violin	*il violino*

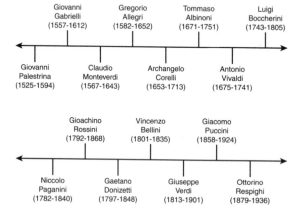

A Note on Opera

Opera. It's an Italian word—some would say the most beautiful Italian word. By the time Giuseppe Verdi (1813–1901)—who at the age of 20 was already performing at Milano's famous opera house *La Scala*—came onto the scene, opera had spread across Europe. During the course of his long career, the patriotic composer wrote 26 operas, including *Otello*, *Rigoletto*, and *La Traviata* (meaning "the corrupted").

It's All About the Story

Opera has as much drama as any Spielberg film, and the stories told are filled with unrequited love, betrayal, and revenge. To fully appreciate any opera, you need to understand the plot behind the rolled *R*'s and high *C*'s.

Did You Know?

Until the late eighteenth century, female lead parts were sung by men, often by *castrati* (eunuchs). Not unlike some of today's pop stars, many *castrati* used a single name for the stage. Farinelli (born Carlo Broschi) is by far the most famous of the eighteenth-century eunuchs.

That's where *il libretto* comes in. Literally meaning "little book" in Italian, *il libretto* tells the story, outlines the plot, and paints the picture that will be so passionately expressed by the singers. Without *il libretto,* opera loses half its meaning.

Sing It to Me!

You don't need to speak Italian to appreciate opera, but a quick glossary of terms might help:

a cappella: voices without music; no instruments

aria: a song or melody sung by a single voice

belcanto: "beautiful song" in Italian

cadenza: a passage toward the end of a song designed for the singer alone to strut his or her stuff

canzone: literally "song" in Italian

coloratura: describes the "color" in a passage, including those difficult trills and sparkling arpeggios that singers train all their lives to sing

duet: two people singing simultaneously, often with different words and melodies

forte/mezzo forte: loud/not so loud

piano/mezzo piano: soft/not so soft

falsetto: the high part for a man's voice

fuga: a baroque style passage in which three or more distinct musical lines are tossed from voice to voice

libretto: literally "little book" in Italian, the script for the piece

opera buffa: comic, "buffoon" opera

opera seria: serious, more formal opera

operetta: a cross between *opera buffa* and *opera seria*; usually very light

overture: an instrumental composition introducing the entire opera

prelude: a shorter overture

prima donna: a female opera star

recitative: sung dialogue between arias, to help advance the story

vibrato: a slight wavering in pitch used to enhance notes

La Bella Lingua

The Venetian composer **Giovanni Gabrielli** (1557–1612) was one of the first to use the term *concerto* (bringing into agreement), a classical term describing music that uses many different voices to form one.

Did You Know?

The old ebony and ivory derives from the Italian *piano-forte,* meaning "soft-strong," named because the piano, unlike its predecessor the harpsichord, allows the player to sustain the sounds she makes.

Life Imitates Art

Le belle arti attempt to interpret the real world, glorify God (or gods), or express something without words. As ideas about the world have changed, so has the *arte* that depicts these notions. Ultimately, you know what you like and what you don't, and that is often the only criterion necessary to appreciate a piece.

You may have seen countless reproductions of Botticelli's *Birth of Venus* on everything from greeting cards to coffee mugs, but there's still nothing like seeing her up close. If you want to be an artist, these verbs can help: *disegnare* (to draw/to design), *dipingere* (to paint), and *scolpire* (to sculpt).

Adding to Your Palette

English	Italian	English	Italian
abstract	*astratto*	masterpiece	*il capolavoro*
acrylic	*acrilico*	the Middle Ages	*il Medioevo*
architecture	*l'architettura*	mosaic	*il mosaico*
background	*lo sfondo*	oil	*olio*
Baroque	*Barocco*	painter	*il pittore*
bronze	*il bronzo*	painting	*il quadro*
ceramic	*la ceramica*	pencil	*la matita*
classical	*classico*	pen	*la penna*
cubism	*il cubismo*	perspective	*la prospettiva*
depth	*la profondità*	picture	*la pittura, il quadro*
drawing	*il disegno*	pigments	*i colori*
Etruscan	*etrusco*	portrait	*il ritratto*
figure	*la figura*	realism	*realismo*
foreground	*il primo piano*	the Renaissance	*il Rinascimento*

English	Italian	English	Italian
fresco	*l'affresco*	restoration	*il restauro*
futurism	*il futurismo*	sculpture	*la scultura*
geometric	*geometrico*	shadow	*l'ombra*
granite	*il granito*	sketch	*lo schizzo*
human figure	*la figura umana*	statue	*la statua*
landscape	*il paesaggio*	still life painting	*una natura morta*
light	*la luce*	symbol	*il simbolo*
marble	*il marmo*	visual arts	*le belle arti*
master	*il maestro, la maestra*	work of art	*un'opera d'arte*

Did You Know?

A master should transcend a subject matter, expanding the viewer's concept of art. There's no better example of this than **Giotto Di Bondone** (1267–1337), who departed from stylized Byzantine conservatism and revolutionized the art world of his time by using fore-shortening to create the illusion of depth. His use of perspective paved the way for all masters that followed, making him one of the founders of Western painting as we know it today.

Il Passato Prossimo (the Present Perfect)

There are several ways of expressing the past in Italian. For now, you're going to learn about the *passato prossimo*. Equivalent in usage to the simple past tense in English, the *passato prossimo* is used to say "I forgot," "I ate," and "I was." In addition, the *passato prossimo* expresses "I have forgotten," "I have eaten," and "I had been."

A compound tense, the *passato prossimo* requires the use of the helping verbs *avere* and *essere* (see Chapter 9, "Being There"). You already saw how the verb *stare* is used in the present progressive tense (see Chapter 15, "I Can't Believe My Eyes"). In Italian, all *transitive verbs* (verbs that take a direct object) require the use of the auxiliary verb *avere*. All *intransitive verbs* (verbs taking an indirect object) require the use of *essere*.

As a Rule

When to use *avere:*

When forming compound tenses, most **transitive verbs** (verbs that take a direct object) use *avere* as an auxiliary verb.

Transitive verbs answer the question "what?" and include verbs such as *lavare* (to wash), *mangiare* (to eat), and *studiare* (to study). Transitive verbs also answer the question of "whom?" and include the verbs *cercare* (to look for), *conoscere* (to be acquainted with), and *invitare* (to invite).

When to use *essere:*

Intransitive verbs use *essere* as an auxiliary verb and include verbs of locomotion such as *andare* (to go), *arrivare* (to arrive), *entrare* (to enter), *uscire* (to go out/exit), and *venire* (to come). Other intransitive verbs include *morire* (to die) and *nascere* (to be born).

Constructing the Past Participle

When you use the *passato prossimo*, you need a past participle. For example, in English you use the helping verb *have* plus the participle (wished/finished/studied). Most of the time, this is regular, but English also has several irregular past participles (had/been/sang). The same goes for Italian.

As you recall from Chapter 8, "An Action-Packed Adventure," Italian has three principal verb families (*–are*, *–ere*, and *–ire*). To form the past participle from an infinitive, you hold on to the stem and add the appropriate ending, as shown in the following table.

Regular Endings for the Past Participle

Endings		Infinitive	Participle		
–are	→	–ato	*lavare*	→	*lavato*
–ere	→	–uto	*potere*	→	*potuto*
–ire	→	–ito	*capire*	→	*capito*

Forming the Past with Avere

It's easy to construct the *passato prossimo*. Once you understand how this works, you'll have no trouble learning all of the other compound tenses. It all starts with the helping verb *avere*. Once you've determined your subject, you only have to conjugate *avere* in the present tense. The past participle stays the same, regardless of the subject (unless accompanied by a direct object pronoun, which will be discussed in a bit). Study the verb *lavare* (to wash) to better understand how this works.

The Present Perfect of *Lavare*

Italian	English
io **ho lavato**	I have washed
tu **hai lavato**	you have washed
lui/lei Lei **ha lavato**	he/she has washed; You have washed
noi **abbiamo lavato**	we have washed
voi **avete lavato**	you have washed
loro **hanno lavato**	they have washed

Irregular Past Participles

Some commonly used irregular past participles with *avere* are shown in the following table.

Commonly Used Irregular Past Participles with *Avere*

Verb	Past Participle	Meaning
accendere	acceso	to turn on, to light
aprire	aperto	to open
ardere	arso	to burn
bere	bevuto	to drink
chiedere	chiesto	to ask
chiudere	chiuso	to close
conoscere	conosciuto	to know someone
correre	corso	to run
decidere	deciso	to decide
dire	detto	to say
leggere	letto	to read
mettere	messo	to put, to place, to wear
offrire	offerto	to offer
perdere	perso	to lose

continues

Commonly Used Irregular Past Participles with *Avere* (continued)

Verb	Past Participle	Meaning
permettere	*permesso*	to permit
prendere	*preso*	to take
rispondere	*risposto*	to respond
rompere	*rotto*	to break
scrivere	*scritto*	to write
spegnere	*spento*	to turn off, to extinguish
spendere	*speso*	to spend
togliere	*tolto*	to take from
vedere	*visto*	to see
vincere	*vinto*	to win

Abbiamo vinto la partita.	We won the game.
Hai scritto alla mamma?	Did you write to Mom?
Il ristorante ha chiuso presto.	The restaurant closed early.
Ci hanno chiesto un favore.	They asked us for a favor.

Forming the Past with Essere

Intransitive verbs always require the use of *essere* as their auxiliary. How can you remember what those verbs are? Think of a squirrel living in a tree, and imagine all the motions he does in and around his home, high up in the branches of a great old oak tree: up, down, in, out, coming, going, staying, remaining, and leaving.

Whenever *essere* is used as the auxiliary verb, the participle is still formed by adding the appropriate ending to the stem of the verb. However, in addition to conjugating your helping verb *avere*, your past participle must reflect both gender and number of the subject.

Study the verb *andare* in the following table.

The Present Perfect Using *Essere: Andare*

Lavare	English
io sono andato(a)	I have gone
tu sei andato(a)	you have gone
lui/lei Lei è andato(a)	he/she has gone; You have gone
noi siamo andati(e)	we have gone
voi siete andati(e)	you have gone
loro sono andati(e)	they have gone

La ragazza è andata all'università di Bologna.	The girl went to the university of Bologna.
Enrico V (quinto) è diventato matto.	Henry V went crazy.

As a Rule

The verb *avere* takes itself as an auxiliary verb.

> *Ho avuto un'idea buonissima.* — I had a great idea.

The verb *essere* also takes itself as an auxiliary verb.

> *Sono stata in Italia in estate.* — I was in Italy for the summer.

Verbs Taking Essere

The following table contains a list of the most commonly used intransitive verbs conjugated with *essere*. The *(a)* is there to remind you that they must reflect the gender (and number) of the subject. Irregular participles are indicated. (Note that irregular participles are also offered in the glossary.)

Intransitive Verbs Commonly Used with *Essere*

Verb	Past Participle	Meaning
andare	*andato(a)*	to go
apparire	*apparso(a)**	to appear
arrivare	*arrivato(a)*	to arrive
bastare	*bastato(a)*	to be enough
cadere	*caduto(a)*	to fall
dimagrire	*dimagrito(a)*	to lose weight
dispiacere	*dispiaciuto(a)**	to be sorry
diventare	*diventato(a)*	to become
entrare	*entrato(a)*	to enter
esistere	*esistito(a)*	to exist
essere	*stato(a)**	to be
ingrassare	*ingrassato(a)*	to gain weight
morire	*morto(a)**	to die
nascere	*nato(a)**	to be born

continues

Intransitive Verbs Commonly Used with *Essere* (continued)

Verb	Past Participle	Meaning
partire	*partito(a)*	to leave
piacere	*piaciuto(a)**	to be pleasing
restare	*restato(a)*	to stay
rimanere	*rimasto(a)**	to remain
ritornare	*ritornato(a)*	to return
salire	*salito(a)*	to go up/to get on
scendere	*sceso(a)**	to get off
sembrare	*sembrato(a)*	to seem
stare	*stato(a)**	to stay
succedere	*successo(a)**	to happen
tornare	*tornato(a)*	to return
uscire	*uscito(a)*	to go out
venire	*venuto(a)*	to come
vivere	*vissuto(a)**	to live

*Irregular participle.

Sono uscita alle otto.	I went out at 8:00.
Roberto è nato nel 1967.	Roberto was born in 1967.
Siamo andati al cinema.	We went to the movies.
Le studentesse sono partite.	The students have left.

Attenzione!

Although considered transitive, all **reflexive verbs** require *essere* as their auxiliary verb. Reflexives are most easily identified by their endings, and include the verbs *alzarsi* (to get up), *arrabbiarsi* (to get angry), and *chiamarsi* (to call oneself).

Reflexive verbs always take *essere* as their auxiliary verb:

Il bambino si è divertito.	The baby enjoyed himself.
Mi sono alzata prestissimo.	I woke up very early.
Ci siamo baciati.	We kissed each other.

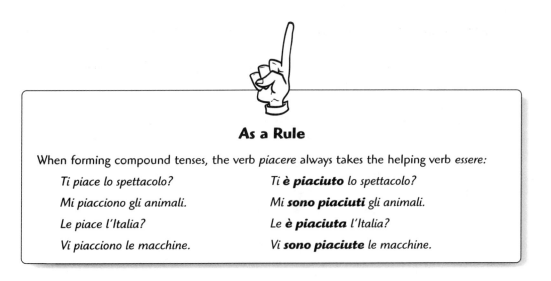

As a Rule

When forming compound tenses, the verb *piacere* always takes the helping verb *essere:*

Ti piace lo spettacolo?	*Ti **è piaciuto** lo spettacolo?*
Mi piacciono gli animali.	*Mi **sono piaciuti** gli animali.*
Le piace l'Italia?	*Le **è piaciuta** l'Italia?*
Vi piacciono le macchine.	*Vi **sono piaciute** le macchine.*

Adverbs in Compound Tenses

In this beautiful *sinfonia* (symphony) of words, it's time to add a few more notes. Refer back to Chapter 10, "Tell Me About Your Childhood," for a review of your adverbs. For now, keep in mind the following:

➤ Most adverbs are placed after the past participle in compound sentences, such as in the *passato prossimo.*

*Abbiamo mangiato **bene**.*	We ate **well**.
*Isabella ha studiato **regolarmente**.*	Isabella studied **regularly**.

➤ Adverbs related to time, such as *ancora, già, mai,* and *sempre,* are placed between the auxiliary verb and the past participle:

*Hai **già** mangiato?*	Have you **already** eaten?
*Lei è **mai** stato in Italia?*	Have you **ever** been to Italy?
*Abbiamo **sempre** passato l'estate al mare.*	We **always** passed the summer by the sea.

➤ When negating something in the past, the word ***non*** comes before the helping verb:

***Non** ho mangiato molto.*	I did **not** eat much.

Direct Object Pronouns in Compound Tenses

Transitive verbs take a direct object and are conjugated with the verb *avere*. When using direct object pronouns in compound tenses, including the *passato prossimo*, the ending of the participle must reflect gender and plurality of the direct object. Note that the singular direct object pronouns meaning "it" (*lo/la*) drop the final vowel and elide with the auxiliary verb *avere*. The plural object pronouns don't change.

The following table illustrates this for you. The direct object and direct object pronouns (DOP) are in bold.

Passato Prossimo with Direct Object Pronouns

Question	DOP	Answer
Hai spedito la lettera?	*la*	*Sì, l'ho spedita.*
Did you send the letter?	it	Yes, I sent it.
Hai mangiato il pane?	*lo*	*Sì, l'ho mangiato.*
Did you eat the bread?	it	Yes, I ate it.
Hai ricevuto le lettere?	*le*	*No, non le ho ricevute.*
Did you receive the letters?	them	No, I didn't receive them.
Hai letto i libri?	*li*	*Sì, li ho letti.*
Did you read the books?	them	Yes, I read them.

Indirect Object Pronouns and the Passato Prossimo

Both transitive and intransitive verbs can take an indirect object pronoun. In compound tenses, to distinguish the indirect and direct object pronouns from one another, the gender and number of indirect object pronouns—unlike the direct object pronouns—do not affect the participle. In the following table, the indirect object and indirect object pronouns (IOP) are in bold.

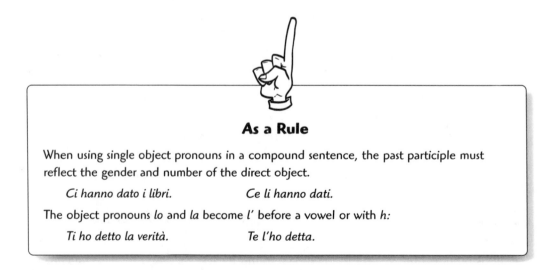

As a Rule

When using single object pronouns in a compound sentence, the past participle must reflect the gender and number of the direct object.

Ci hanno dato i libri.   *Ce li hanno dati.*

The object pronouns *lo* and *la* become *l'* before a vowel or with *h:*

Ti ho detto la verità.   *Te l'ho detta.*

Passato Prossimo **with Indirect Object Pronouns**

Question	IOP	Answer
Hai parlato alla ragazza?	*le*	*Sì, le ho parlato.*
Did you speak to the girl?	to her	Yes, I spoke to her.
Hai spedito la lettera a Paolo?	*gli*	*Sì, gli ho spedito la lettera.*
Did you send the letter to Paolo?	to him	Yes, I sent him a letter.
Hai offerto ai signori un caffè?	*loro/gli*	*Sì, ho offerto loro un caffè.* *
		Sì, gli ho offerto un caffè. *
Did you offer the men coffee?	to them	Yes, I offered them coffee.
Hanno mandato un pacco a noi?	*ci*	*Sì, ci hanno mandato un pacco.*
Did they send a package to us?	to us	Yes, they sent us a package.

*Both of these are correct. If you recall, loro *can be replaced with the pronoun* gli.

The **Passato Prossimo** *and Double Object Pronouns*

Everything here is detail. If you don't always remember to make things agree, you won't be locked into a tower and fed stale bread until you die. However, if you want to be a master, you've got to pay special attention to the little things.

When the same verb has two object pronouns, the indirect object pronoun always precedes the direct object pronoun. The following examples illustrate how double object pronouns work with the *passato prossimo*. Notice how the participle ending reflects the number and gender of the direct object.

Attenzione!

When dealing with double object pronouns, it is necessary to infer the gender of the indirect object (to him/to her).

Hai dato la lettera alla signora?	*Sì **gliel'**ho data.*
Did you give the letter to the lady?	Yes, I gave it to her.
Hai dato la lettera al ragazzo?	*Sì **gliel'**ho data.*
Did you give the letter to the boy?	Yes, I gave it to him.

Double Object Pronouns

Question	Answer
Hai mandato la lettera al signor Rossi?	*Sì, gliel'ho mandata.*
Did you send the letter to Mr. Rossi?	Yes, I sent it to him.
Hanno restituito i soldi alla signora?	*Sì, glieli hanno restituiti.*
Did they give back the money to the woman?	Yes, they gave it back to her.

The Least You Need to Know

➤ The verbs *andare* and *fare* are often used to describe participation in a sport.

➤ Use the verb *giocare* to play games and the verb *suonare* to play an instrument.

➤ The past participle is created by adding the appropriate ending to the stem of a verb. The three regular forms are –*ato*, –*uto*, and –*ito*.

➤ Many past participles are irregular, such as *chiuso* (closed) and *stato* (was).

➤ The two helping verbs used to form the *passato prossimo* are *essere* and *avere*.

➤ Intransitive verbs and reflexive verbs require *essere* as their auxiliary verb.

➤ The past participle must agree in gender and number with the preceding direct object pronoun.

➤ Double object pronouns often form one word and are used to refer to something already mentioned.

Part 4

Getting Down to Business

This part deals with the darker side of traveling and the problems that often crop up when you least expect them. Little did you know that you were opening Pandora's box when you unclicked the latch on your brand-new suitcase.

Chapter 20, "You're Not Having Un Buon Giorno,*" helps you deal with life's details, whether you need to replace the battery in your camera or want to have some clothes laundered. Chapter 21, "Is There a Doctor in the House?" gives you body language you can use at the doctor's office or when you visit the* farmacia. *You'll also learn the* imperfetto *(imperfect), a tense used to talk about how things were and used to be.*

In Chapter 22, "Can You Read Me?" you'll learn how to make a telephone call and deal with l'ufficio postale. *You'll study the future tense to ask when someone will return or when something will arrive.*

Chapter 23, "Home Sweet Home," introduces the conditional tense and gives you vocabulary used to talk about your home. This is the tense you could use to talk about what you would do if you lived in Italy.

In Chapter 24, "Money Matters," you'll learn practical money and banking terms followed by a glimpse of that most elusive of moods, il congiuntivo *(the subjunctive). This is followed by a brief introduction of another highly irregular tense used to talk about the distant past:* il passato remoto.

And finally, you'll be given a little riddle. If you've been paying attention, you should be able to figure it out.

Even though you're almost fluent, why not start the book from scratch to see how much you have learned? È stata un'avventura! A presto!

Chapter 20

You're Not Having *Un Buon Giorno*

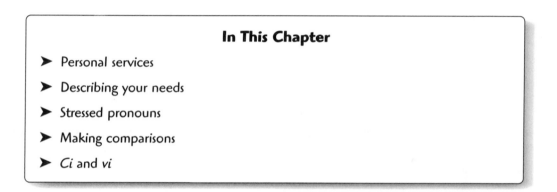

In This Chapter

➤ Personal services

➤ Describing your needs

➤ Stressed pronouns

➤ Making comparisons

➤ *Ci* and *vi*

Your e-mail isn't working on your laptop computer. Your perfect Prada pumps couldn't handle the cobblestone streets, and you need to have a heel replaced. You spilled tomato sauce all over your favorite silk tie. Your camera has suddenly developed mechanical problems. You've lost a contact lens and can't see without it. This chapter helps you solve life's little nuisances.

Get Down to the Basics

Before you can get anything done, you must be able to find someone who can help you. Your guidebook probably won't help, but a copy of *le pagine gialle* (the Yellow Pages) might. To locate one, ask your concierge or visit any TELECOM (phone center). Speaking on the telephone is elaborated on in Chapter 22, "Can You Read Me?" but for now, a couple of tips might help.

As a Rule

When calling any establishment open to the public, whether a *parrucchiere* (hair dresser), a *sarto* (tailor), or a *calzolaio* (shoemaker), it is often appropriate to use the second person plural (*voi*) form of the verb:

Avete ...?	Do you have ...?
Potete ...?	Are you able to ...?
A che ora aprite?	At what time do you open?
A che ora chiudete?	At what time do you close?

Tip #1: Know what your needs are, and write down the appropriate questions before you make the call. Having something written in front of you will help you focus.

Tip #2: Let the establishment know that you do not speak Italian very well, and ask the person to speak slowly. If you want to take the easy way out, ask if they speak English:

Non parlo l'italiano molto bene.	I don't speak Italian very well.
Parlate lentamente, per favore.	Speak slowly, please.
Parlate l'inglese?	Do you speak English?

Tip #3: Keep it simple. Basic statements such as *Ho bisogno ...* (I need ...) can go a long way.

The sentences in the following table will help you find out *if* someone can help you, *when* they are open, *how* to get there, and *what* your needs are.

Help!

La Frase	The Phrase
Ho bisogno di ...	I need ...
Mi potete aiutare?	Can you help me?
Siete aperti	Are you open
... adesso?	... now?
... fino a che ora?	... until what time?
... la domenica?	... Sundays?

326

La Frase	The Phrase
Dov'è ...	Where is ...
Conosce ...	Do you know ...
... un buon parrucchiere?	... a good hairdresser?
... un buon sarto?	... a good tailor?
... un buon calzolaio?	... a good shoemaker?
... una buona tintoria?	... a good dry cleaner?

Mirror Mirror on the Wall ...

Between packing, notifying your credit card companies, bringing the dog to the pound, paying your bills, and making sure your passport is valid, you didn't have time to make it to the hairdresser for a little shampoo, cut, and tint. Women in Italy usually go to *la parrucchiere,* whereas men visit the *il barbiere.*

Some verbs and idiomatic expressions you might find useful appear in the following table. You see *farsi,* which is a reflexive verb (*fare + si*) used when one is having something done to themselves. If you need to, review reflexive verbs in Chapter 18, "Shall We Dine?"

Getting Gorgeous (the Italian Way)

English	*L'Italiano*
to blow-dry	*asciugare i capelli*
to color	*tingere i capelli*
to curl	*fare i riccioli*
to cut	*tagliare*
to get a haircut	*farsi tagliare i capelli*
to get a manicure	*farsi fare il manicure*
to get a pedicure	*farsi fare il pedicure*
to get a permanent	*farsi la permanente*
to shampoo	*farsi lo shampoo*
to shave	*farsi la barba*
to wax	*farsi la ceretta*

Build up your grooming vocabulary with the terms in the following table.

Well Groomed

English	L'Italiano
bald	*calvo*
bangs	*la frangia*
beard	*la barba*
brush	*la spazzola*
comb	*il pettine*
conditioner	*il balsamo*
cut	*il taglio*
face	*il viso*
gel	*il gel*
hair	*i capelli*
hairspray	*la lacca*
head	*la testa*
mud	*il fango*
mustache	*i baffi*
nail	*l'unghia*
nail file	*la limetta*
nail polish	*lo smalto per le unghie*
razor	*il rasoio*
shampoo	*lo shampoo*

Do Blondes Really Have More Fun?

There's a revolution happening inside as the "real" you comes forth: Maybe you'd rather be a bobbed redhead, a permed brunette, or a cropped blond. The following table offers the lowdown on stylists' lingo. Remember that the word *capelli* is plural, and your adjectives (given here in the masculine, plural form) must agree:

Preferisco i miei capelli ...	I prefer my hair ...
Li vorrei ...	I'd like them ...

Get Rid of That Gray

Style	Lo Stile
auburn	*castani*
black	*mori*
blond	*biondi*
brunette	*bruni*

Style	Lo Stile
curly	*ricci*
darker	*più scuri*
highlights	*i colpi di sole*
layered	*scalati*
lighter	*più chiari*
like this photo	*come questa foto*
long	*lunghi*
medium	*ledi*
red	*rossi*
retouched	*ritoccati*
straight	*lisci*
the same	*uguali*
trimmed	*spuntati*
wavy	*ondulati*

In Tintoria *(at the Dry Cleaner's)*

Perhaps you went out last night, and now your favorite silk shirt has Chianti stain on it. Then there's that grass smudge on your pants from the picnic you had in the *parco* the other day. The following table gives you the dirt on dirt.

The Dirt on Dirt (and Other Mishaps)

Italian	English
C'è ...	There is ...
... una macchia.	... a stain.
... una bottone che manca.	... a missing button.
... uno strappo.	... a tear.
Mi potete lavare a secco questo (questi ...)?	Can you dry clean this (these ...) for me?
Mi potete rammendare questo (questi ...)?	Can you mend this (these ...) for me?
Mi potete stirare questo (questi ...)?	Can you iron this (these ...) for me?
Mi potete inamidare questo (questi ...)?	Can you starch this (these ...) for me?
Quando sarà pronto?	When will it be ready?
L'ho bisogno il più presto possibile.	I need it as soon as possible.

Dal Calzolaio *(at the Shoemaker's)*

You've never walked this much before, and every step takes you deeper into the mystery of *Italia*. Maybe you want to have your *scarpe* stretched, a heel replaced, or a new shoelace added. The phrases in the following table will help you.

If the Shoe Fits

English	L'Italiano
boot	*lo stivale*
heel	*il tacco*
shoe	*la scarpa*
shoelace	*il laccio da scarpe*
shoemaker	*il calzolaio*
sole	*la suola*
to stretch	*allargare*
to shine	*lucidare*
to repair	*riparare*

Dall'Ottica *(at the Optician's)*

You just sat on your glasses and need to have them repaired. Perhaps you want to invest in Italian designer frames. The terms in the following table will let you see things through new eyes (or at least improved ones).

The Better to See You With

English	L'Italiano
astigmatism	*l'astigmatismo*
contact lens	*le lenti a contatto*
eyes	*gli occhi*
far-sighted	*presbite*
frame	*la montatura*
glasses	*gli occhiali*
lens	*le lenti*
near-sighted	*miope*
prescription	*la ricetta medica*
sunglasses	*gli occhiali da sole*

Dal Negozio di Fotografia *(at the Camera Shop)*

You bought what you thought was enough film for your camera, but now you need more. You want to buy a cap for your lens before it gets scratched—and it could also use a good cleaning.

Say "Mozzarella"

English	L'Italiano
battery	*la batteria, la pila*
camera	*la macchina fotografica*
exposure	*l'esposizione*
film	*la pellicola, il film*
filter	*il filtro*
flash	*il "flash"*
lens	*l'obiettivo*
transformer	*il trasformatore*
to develop	*sviluppare*

In Gioiellleria *(at the Jeweler's)*

Maybe your watch came off during a gondola ride and you need to get another, or perhaps the battery just ran out of juice. If you need to go the jeweler to have something fixed or replaced, the words in the following table will help you get things ticking again. Refer back to Chapter 16, "Shop 'Til You Drop," for a list of jewelery terms. If you've broken a chain and need it repaired, or have lost a stone and want to have it replaced, ask the salesperson, *Può riparare questo?* (Can you fix this?)

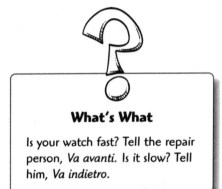

What's What

Is your watch fast? Tell the repair person, *Va avanti.* Is it slow? Tell him, *Va indietro.*

Fix It Again, Tony

English	L'Italiano
battery	*la batteria, la pila*
chain	*la catena*
clasp	*il gancio*
watch	*l'orologio*
watch band	*il cinturino*

Nel Negozio Elettronico *(at the Electronics Store)*

You've brought over your laptop computer and have been furiously tapping away at the keys, trying to recall every detail for the book you're going to write about Italy. Perhaps the battery has died and you need to replace it. If your computer just won't work, you'll have to bring it in and explain, *Il mio computer non funziona,* and pray you haven't lost any material. A few of the terms in the following table might also help you get your point across.

Vocabulary for the Information Superhighway

English	L'Italiano
adapter	*l'adattatore*
battery	*la batteria, la pila*
computer	*il computer*
disks	*i dischetti*
e-mail	*la posta elettronica*
keyboard	*la tastiera*
laptop computer	*il computer portatile*
mouse	*il mouse*
screen	*lo schermo*

Attenzione!

You'll learn all the telephone talk you need in Chapter 22. In case of an emergency, keep these helpful contact numbers handy:

General SOS (free from any telephone): 113

Carabinieri (police; free): 112

Automobile Club d'Italia (car accidents and break-downs): 116

Help, I Lost My Passport!

It could happen to anyone, so don't feel like a total idiot if you lose your passport. Hopefully, you have written down the number—or better yet, made a photocopy of the front page with all your vital statistics. You'll want to advise the embassy as soon as *possibile,* and it wouldn't hurt to let the police know where you are staying in case the missing passport miraculously turns up.

Don't Leave Home Without It (but If You Do ...)

English	L'Italiano
Where is ...	Dov'è ...
... the police station?	... la stazione di polizia?
... the American embassy?	... l'ambasciata americana?
... the American consul?	... il console americano?
I lost ...	Ho perso ...
... my passport.	... il mio passaporto.
... my wallet.	... il mio portafoglio.
... my purse.	... la mia borsa.
... my head.	... la mia testa.

Stressed Out

Disjunctive, or stressed, pronouns—called *i pronomi tonici* in Italian—must follow a preposition or verb. They are also used to emphasize certain facts and highlight or replace certain nouns or pronouns. Study how they correspond to the object pronouns you have learned so far.

Disjunctive Pronouns

Subject	Direct Object	Indirect Object	Disjunctive (Stressed)	
io	mi	mi	*me*	me
tu	ti	ti	*te*	you
lui	lo	gli	*lui/esso*	him/it
lei	la	le	*lei/essa*	her/it
Lei	La	Le	*Lei*	You
			sè	himself, herself, itself, oneself, yourself
noi	ci	ci	*noi*	us
voi	vi	vi	*voi*	you
loro	li/le	a loro/gli	*loro*	them
			sè	yourselves, themselves

The following points may help you remember when to use a disjunctive pronoun:

➤ Disjunctive pronouns must always follow a verb or preposition:

*Vuoi venire **con** me?*	Do you want to come with me?
*Aspetto una telefonata **da** lei.*	I am waiting for a phone call from her.
*Sono fiero **di** te.*	I am proud of you.
*Questi fiori sono **per** voi.*	These flowers are for you.
*Lui parte prima **di** me.*	He is leaving before me.

➤ The disjunctive pronoun *sè* is used to indicate *oneself, himself, herself,* and *themselves* as well as *itself:*

Caterina parla sempre di sè.	Caterina always talks about herself.
La luce si spegne da sè.	The light goes out by itself.
Anna lavora per sè.	Anna works for herself.

➤ The disjunctive pronoun is most commonly used when there are two direct or indirect objects in a phrase:

*Daniela scrive **a me** e **a te**.*	Daniela writes to me and to you.
*Telefonano **a lui** e **a lei**.*	They are telephoning him and her.

➤ Disjunctive pronouns are used after a verb to emphasize the object (direct or indirect).

Emphatic	Unemphatic	English
*Aspetto **lui**.*	***Lo** aspetto.*	I'm waiting **for him**.
*Do un regalo **a te**.*	***Ti** do un regalo.*	I give **you** a gift.
*Telefona **a me**.*	***Mi** telefona.*	Call (telephone) **me**.

Stressful Exercise

Use the appropriate stressed pronoun in the following sentences:

1. *Senza di ____, non posso vivere.* (you, informal)
2. *Mario parla sempre di ___.* (himself)
3. *Vuole parlare a ____?* (me)
4. *Questa lettera è per ____.* (Cristina)
5. *Passiamo la sera alla casa di ____.* (Robert)
6. *Viene con ____ o con ____?* (me, her)

Comparatives and Superlatives

In Chapter 10, "Tell Me About Your Childhood," you learned all about adjectives and adverbs. In addition to describing nouns and verbs, you use adjectives and adverbs to compare things. Often, you can add *–er* or *–est* to an adjective in English to indicate that something is more (or less) beautiful, big, sweet, tall, and so on, as in, "She is sweeter than honey; in fact, she is the sweetest person I have ever met." Use the following table to help you compare things.

Comparison of Adjectives: Inequality

	Italian	English
Adjective	*dolce*	sweet
Comparative	*più dolce*	sweeter
	meno dolce	less sweet
Superlative	*il/la* più dolce*	the sweetest
	il/la* meno dolce	the least sweet

*Note: The same rules apply using the plural articles i, gli, *and* le.

➤ To compare one thing as being either more or less than another, place the word *più* (more) or *meno* (less) before the adjective:

Questo ristorante è più caro.	This restaurant is more expensive.
Quel ristorante è meno caro.	That restaurant is less expensive.

➤ To express the English "than," use the preposition *di* (or its contraction) in front of nouns and pronouns.

Ho più amici di te.	I have more friends than you.
Il gatto è più piccolo del cane.	The cat is smaller than the dog.
I cani sono più grandi dei gatti.	Dogs are bigger than cats.

➤ The comparative and superlative forms of the adjectives must agree in gender and number with the nouns they describe:

La luna è meno grande della terra.	The moon is smaller than the earth.
I tuoi occhi sono i più belli.	Your eyes are the most beautiful.

➤ *Che* is used when making comparisons of quantity, when comparing two qualities pertaining to the same person or thing, or when comparing two infinitive verbs:

più ... di (che)	more ... than
meno ... di (che)	less ... than

Tu sei più alto di me.	You are taller than I.
Io sono meno alta di te.	I am less tall than you.
Di sera fa più freddo che di giorno.	The evening is colder than the day.
Meglio tardi che mai.	Better late than never.
È più facile giocare che studiare.	It's easier to play than study.

➤ To make a relative comparison between two things, simply add *più* (more) or *meno* (less) before the adjective or adverb.

Questo è il ristorante più caro.	This restaurant is the most expensive.
Quello è il ristorante meno caro.	That restaurant is the least expensive.

Attenzione!

You've seen *che* used as an interrogative adjective meaning "what." It is also used with the subjunctive signifying "that" and "than." Look for clues in a sentence that can help you determine its meaning. The following examples illustrate the different uses of this word:

Che significa?	What does it mean?
È più bello cantare che urlare.	Singing is more beautiful than shouting.
Penso che Giulia sia simpatica.	I think that Giulia is nice.

Better Than the Best

In addition to having regular forms, some adjectives have irregular comparative and superlative forms. Are you good? Getting better? Or the best?

Irregular Adjective Comparatives and Superlatives

Adjective	Comparative	Relative Superlative
buono (good)	*migliore* (better)	*il/la migliore* (the best)
cattivo (bad)	*peggiore* (worse)	*il/la peggiore* (the worst)
grande (big/great)	*maggiore* (bigger/greater)	*il/la maggiore* (the biggest/greatest)
piccolo (small)	*minore* (smaller/lesser)	*il/la minore* (the smallest/least)

What's What

Maggiore and *minore* are often used to reference family members, such as younger sister or older brother. The superlative is used to indicate "the oldest" or "the youngest."

> *Mio fratello minore si chiama Roberto.*   My younger brother is called Robert.

The superlatives *migliore, peggiore, maggiore,* and *minore* drop the final *-e* before nouns, except with nouns beginning with *s* + consonant or *z:*

> *Tu sei la mia miglior amica!*   You are my best friend!

Irregular Comparisons

How are you doing? Well? A perfect illustration of an irregular adverb is the English word "well." In Italian, irregular adverbs are easily learned. The following table outlines some of the most commonly used adverbs.

Irregular Adverb Comparatives and Superlatives

Adverb	Comparative	Absolute Superlative
bene (well)	*meglio* (better)	*benissimo* (best)
male (badly)	*peggio* (worse)	*malissimo* (worse)
molto (much/a lot)	*più, di più* (more)	*moltissimo* (very much)
poco (little)	*meno, di meno* (less)	*pochissimo* (very little)

Oggi sto meglio.	I am better today.
Devi studiare di più.	You must study more.
Anna lavora moltissimo in questi giorni.	Anna is working very much these days.

To make the relative superlative, simply add the definite article in front of the comparative:

Arrivo il più presto possibile.	I'm arriving as soon as possible.
Faccio del mio meglio.	I'm doing my best.

La Bella Lingua

Give all that you have to give! To say this in Italian, use the following *espressione:*

Farò del mio meglio.   I will do my best.

Comparisons of Equality

To say that something is as good as another is called a comparison of equality.

➤ To say that two things are equal:

*(tanto) ... **quanto*** + adjective or adverb	as ... as + adjective or adverb
*(così) ... **come*** + adjective or adverb	as ... as + adjective or adverb

➤ *Tanto* and *così* can also be omitted.

Jessica è (tanto) alta quanto Gabriella.	Jessica is as tall as Gabriella.
Tu sei (così) bello come tuo padre.	You are as handsome as your father.
Mi piace sciare (tanto) quanto giocare a tennis.	I like skiing as much as playing tennis.
L'insegnante impara (tanto) quanto insegna.	The teacher learns as much as she teaches.

➤ Personal pronouns following *come* or *quanto* are always stressed:

Io sono intelligente come te.	I am as intelligent as you are.
Tu sei come me.	You are like me.

Absolutely, Totally Superlative

If something is really extraordinary, you can use the adverb *veramente* (truly) or *molto* (very) in front of your adjective or adverb. Or, to show the extreme of something, a poetic, commonly used ending is *–issimo*. The following table looks at a few adjectives (which must always reflect gender and number) used in this manner:

Above Average

Adjective	"Very"	"Extremely"
bello	*molto bello*	*bellissimo*
buono	*molto buono*	*buonissimo/ottimo**
cattivo	*molto cattivo*	*cattivissimo/pessimo**
grande	*molto grande*	*grandissimo*
piccolo	*molto piccolo*	*piccolissimo*
vecchio	*molto vecchio*	*vecchissimo*
veloce	*molto veloce*	*velocissimo*

*Irregular.

As a Rule

Ottimo is often used in addition to *buonissimo* when something is really great, as in the best. *Pessimo* is used to describe something that is as bad as bad can get, as in *Questo ristorante è pessimo.* (This restaurant is the worst.)

Sto benissimo!	I am very well!
La macchina è velocissima.	The car is really fast.

Ci and Vi

In Chapter 9, "Being There," you learned about the adverb *ci* and saw how it works with the verb *essere*. Besides being object pronouns, *ci* and *vi* are used as adverbs of place, meaning "here" and "there." Modern Italian tends to use *ci* more often, although the two are interchangeable.

They often replace nouns or prepositional phrases preceded by *a*, *in*, and *su*, saving the speaker unnecessary repetition.

Denoting place:

Vai spesso in piazza?	Do you often go to the piazza?
Sì, ci vado.	Yes, I go there.
Abiti a New York?	Do you live in New York?
No, non ci abito.	No, I don't live there.

339

Denoting things or ideas:

Credi in Dio?	Do you believe in God?
Sì, ci credo.	Yes, I do.
Pensi ai tuoi amici?	Do you think about your friends?
Sì, ci penso.	Yes, I do.

Go On and Brag a Little

Translate the following sentences into Italian.

1. You are the most beautiful woman in the world.
2. The view is gorgeous.
3. He is as nice as he is handsome.
4. I'm feeling better, thank you.
5. Are you going to Italy this summer? Yes, I'm going there.

The Least You Need to Know

➤ Asking for what you need starts with being able to describe your problem.

➤ Use stressed pronouns when you want to emphasize a point or after the preposition *a*.

➤ Use *meno* (less) or *più* (more) before adjectives and adverbs to make comparisons or express the superlative.

➤ Use *(tanto) quanto* or *(così) come* to express that things are equal.

➤ Use the ending *–issimo* to form the absolute superlative of adverbs and adjectives.

➤ Use *ci* or *vi* in lieu of a prepositional phrase.

Chapter 21

Is There a Doctor in the House?

In This Chapter

➤ Your body

➤ Symptoms, complaints, and illnesses

➤ The imperfect tense

You're probably more prone to getting sick while in a foreign country than any other time. You're in a new environment, you're eating different foods, your daily rituals have been altered, and you're having a great time. Those little bugs know just when to crash a party. In this chapter, you'll learn how to feed your cold, starve your fever, and get back on your feet. You'll also learn about the imperfect tense, another way to talk about the past.

What a Bod!

You've only got one, so you might as well love it. Just like people, the names of body parts (and their plurals) are often irregular. Start at your toes and work up.

La Bella Lingua

A little schmoozing can go a long way. To give someone a compliment, use the word *che* + the appropriate form of *bello* + the body part, as in *Che begli occhi!* (What beautiful eyes!)

The Sum of Your Parts

The Body	*Il Corpo*	The Body	*Il Corpo*
ankle	*la caviglia*	hand	*la mano (le mani)*
appendix	*l'appendice*	head	*la testa*
arm	*il braccio (le braccia)*	heart	*il cuore*
back	*la schiena*	joint	*l'articolazione*
bladder	*la vescica*	knee	*il ginocchio (le ginocchia)*
blood	*il sangue*	leg	*la gamba*
body	*il corpo*	ligament	*il legamento*
bone	*l'osso (le ossa)*	mouth	*la bocca*
brain	*il cervello*	muscle	*il muscolo*
breast	*il seno*	nail	*l'unghia*
buttock	*il sedere*	neck	*il collo*
chest	*il petto*	nose	*il naso*
chin	*il mento*	skin	*la pelle*
ear	*l'orecchio*	shoulder	*la spalla*
elbow	*il gomito*	stomach	*lo stomaco*
eye	*l'occhio*	throat	*la gola*
face	*il viso*	toe	*il dito (le dita)*
finger	*il dito (le dita)*	tongue	*la lingua*
foot	*il piede*	tooth	*il dente*
gland	*la ghiandola*	wrist	*il polso*

Farsi

The reflexive and highly idiomatic verb *farsi* comes from the verb *fare* (to do/to make) and can be used in several manners. *Farsi* is used to talk about when something hurts.

In this case, the subject of the sentence is the troublesome body part (or parts). If what is hurting you is singular—for example, your head—so is your verb; if your feet hurt you, because they are plural, your verb must also be plural. You may want to refer back to Chapter 16, "Shop 'Til You Drop," to review your indirect object pronouns again.

Mi fa male la testa.	My head hurts. (My head is hurting me.)
Mi fanno male i piedi.	My feet hurt. (My feet are hurting me.)

A doctor or pharmacist will ask you what hurts by changing the indirect object pronoun. The verb stays the same.

Ti fa male il braccio?	Does your arm hurt?
Le fa male lo stomaco?	Does your stomach hurt?
Le fanno male i piedi?	Do your feet hurt?

La Bella Lingua

If you have a medical condition, it's not a bad idea to bring a copy of your *anamnesi* (medical history) when traveling abroad.

Speaking of medical history: Several ancient medical instruments were discovered by archeologists at the House of the Surgeon in Pompeii, including tweezers, speculums, scalpels, probes, needles, and forceps. If you're interested in knowing more, visit the *Istituto di Storia della Medicina* in Rome. Entry is free, but you're best off calling for hours.

Express Yourself

When talking about your body, you use the verb *avere* to describe any kind of ache, whether it's in your head or your stomach. You'll also use the reflexive verb *sentirsi* (to feel) to describe your various ailments, as in, *Mi sento male* (I feel badly). When using the idiomatic expression *avere mal di*, the final *–e* is dropped from the word *male*. The following expressions will help you describe your discomfort or pain.

Ho ...	I have ...
... mal di testa.	... a headache.
... mal di stomaco/pancia.	... a stomachache.
... mal di gola.	... sore throat.

Mi fa male …	(The body part) … hurts me.
Mi fa male il ginocchio.	My knee hurts.
Mi fanno male i piedi.	My feet hurt.
Mi sento male.	I feel bad.
Non mi sento bene.	I don't feel well.

As a Rule

The preposition *da* is used in the present tense to indicate an action that began in the past that is still occurring in the present, much like the English word "since."

Da quanto tempo soffre?	(For) How long have you been suffering?
Soffro da due giorni.	I've been suffering for (since) two days.

What Ails You?

Sickness can be especially exasperating in a foreign country where you don't know the names of your medicines and you have to explain to a *dottore* or *farmacista* exactly what the problem is.

There's no need to be shy about what you're experiencing. Italians have the same kinds of ailments you do. The doctor will ask you a few questions. Naturally, the *Lei* form of the verb is used to maintain a professional relationship.

Qual è il problema?	What is the problem?
Come si sente?	How do you feel?
Quanti anni ha?	How old are you?
Da quanto tempo soffre?	(For) How long have you been suffering?
Prende delle medicine?	Are you taking any medications?
Ha delle allergie?	Do you have any allergies?
Soffre di …?	Do you suffer from …?
Ha avuto …?	Have you had …?
Che cosa Le fa male?	What hurts you?

Tell Me Where It Hurts

Imagine that you are telling a doctor what your aches and pains are. If you are using the expression *mi fa male,* don't forget to account for number if what hurts you is plural.

Example: your head

Answer: *Mi fa male la testa* or *Ho mal di testa.*

1. your knee
2. your shoulders
3. your feet
4. your throat
5. your tooth
6. your ankle

As a Rule

If you want the indirect object pronoun to clearly and specifically express who is in pain, you may add the preposition *a* plus the name of the person or a prepositional phrase:

A Fabio fanno male le braccia.   Fabio's arms hurt.

It is not necessary to use the possessive adjective before a body part because it is already indicated by the indirect object pronoun.

This Isn't Funny Anymore

If you have a serious medical condition that warrants immediate attention, don't hesitate to contact a doctor should you feel the need for one.

The following table will help you describe what's going on.

Symptoms and Conditions

Symptom	*Il Sintomo*	Symptom	*Il Sintomo*
abscess	*l'ascesso*	bump	*la tumefazione*
blister	*la vescica*	burn	*la scottatura*
broken bone	*un osso rotto*	chills	*i brividi*
bruise	*il livido*	constipation	*la stitichezza*

continues

Symptoms and Conditions (continued)

Symptom	Il Sintomo	Symptom	Il Sintomo
cough	*la tosse*	headache	*il mal di testa*
cramps	*i crampi*	indigestion	*l'indigestione*
diarrhea	*la diarrea*	insomnia	*l'insonnia*
dizziness	*le vertigini*	lump (on the head)	*il bernoccolo*
exhaustion	*l'esaurimento*	migraine	*l'emicrania*
fever	*la febbre*	nausea	*la nausea*
fracture	*la frattura*	pain	*il dolore*
rash	*un'irritazione*	swelling	*il gonfiore*
sprain	*la distorsione*	toothache	*il mal di denti*
stomachache	*il mal di stomaco*	wound	*la ferita*

Attenzione!

You may think you've taken care of everything by bringing your own little medicine chest filled with leftover pills from prescriptions for one thing or another, but self-medicating could make things worse, especially in a foreign country.

Feeling Funny

Some particularly unattractive verbs and other useful phrases describing conditions are outlined in the following table. With idiomatic expressions, the verb in parentheses needs to be conjugated.

How Are You Feeling?

Italian	English	Example	English
(avere) la febbre	to have a fever	*Ho la febbre.*	I have a fever.
(avere) la nausea	to be nauseous	*Ho la nausea.*	I am nauseous.
(avere) la tosse	to cough	*Ho la tosse.*	I am coughing.
(avere) mal di	to have pain	*Ho mal di ...*	I have pain in my ...
(essere) esaurito	to be exhausted	*Sono esaurito/a.*	I am exhausted.

Italian	English	Example	English
sanguinare	to bleed	*Sanguino.*	I am bleeding.
(soffrire) di	to suffer from	*Soffro di …*	I am suffering from …
starnutire	to sneeze	*Starnutisco.*	I am sneezing.
vomitare	to vomit	*Vomito.*	I am vomiting.

La Bella Lingua

Tired and troubled? There's a saint for just about every ailment. Got a hangover? Pray to Saint Bibiana, a virgin who was martyred in Rome in c. 361 A.D. She is also invoked against epilepsy and headaches.

Here are a few more saints you may want to invoke should the need arise:

St. Aldegonda: cancer

St. Ignatius: sore throats

St. Antoninus: fever

St. Lucy: blindness

St. Stephen: headaches

St. Valentine: heartache

This Is What You Have

The word "disease" literally means "not at ease." Should you have to visit the doctor, he or she is going to ask you to fill out a form, tell about any medications you're taking, and answer questions about pre-existing medical conditions. The following table offers you some helpful, if unpleasant, terms to describe health.

Conditions and Diseases

Illness	*La Malattia*	Illness	*La Malattia*
angina	*l'angina*	hemophilia	*l'emofilia*
appendicitis	*l'appendicite*	hepatitis	*l'epatite*

continues

Conditions and Diseases   (continued)

Illness	*La Malattia*	Illness	*La Malattia*
asthma	*l'asma*	measles	*il morbillo*
bronchitis	*la bronchite*	mumps	*gli orecchioni*
cancer	*il cancro*	pneumonia	*la polmonite*
cold	*il raffreddore*	polio	*la poliomielite*
diabetes	*il diabete*	smallpox	*il vaiolo*
drug addiction	*la tossicodipendenza*	stroke	*il colpo apoplettico*
dysentry	*la dissenteria*	sunstroke	*il colpo di sole*
flu	*l'influenza*	tetanus	*il tetano*
German measles	*la rosolia*	tuberculosis	*la tubercolosi*
gout	*la gotta*	whooping cough	*la pertosse*
heart attack	*l'infarto*		

Your doctor may give you *una ricetta medica* (prescription) to be filled at the *farmacia*.

Alla Farmacia *(at the Pharmacy)*

A visit to the *farmacia* will provide you with prescriptions, vitamins, and assorted sundries. Pick up some *vitamina C* to get your system back in sync, buy some *aspirina* for your head, or smooth some moisturizer all over your body.

Drugstore Items

English	Italian	English	Italian
ace bandage	*la fascia elastica*	deodorant	*il deodorante*
antibiotics	*gli antibiotici*	depilatory wax	*la ceretta depilatoria*
antiseptic	*l'antisettico*	diapers	*i pannolini*
aspirin	*l'aspirina*	eye drops	*le gocce per gli occhi*
Band-Aids	*i cerotti*	floss	*il filo interdentale*
body lotion	*la lozione*	gauze bandage	*la fascia*
baby bottle	*il biberon*	heating pad	*l'impacco caldo*
castor oil	*l'olio di ricino*	ice pack	*la borsa del ghiaccio*
condoms	*i preservativi, i profilattici*	laxative	*il lassativo*
		mirror	*lo specchio*
cotton balls	*i batuffoli di ovatta*	needle and thread	*l'ago e filo*
cotton swabs (for ears)	*i tamponi per le orecchie*	nose drops	*le gocce per il naso*
		pacifier	*il ciuccio*
cough syrup	*lo sciroppo per la tosse*	pills	*le pastiglie*

English	Italian	English	Italian
prescription	*la ricetta medica*	talcum powder	*il talco*
razor	*il rasoio*	tampons	i tamponi
safety pin	*la spilla di sicurezza*	thermometer	*il termometro*
sanitary napkins	*gli assorbenti*	tissues	*i fazzoletti*
scissors	*le forbici*	toothbrush	*lo spazzolino da denti*
shaving cream	*la crema da barba*	toothpaste	*il dentifricio*
sleeping pill	*il sonnifero*	tweezers	*le pinzette*
soap	*il sapone*	vitamins	*le vitamine*
syringe	*la siringa*		

Questions

Suppose you can't find what you're looking for or the pharmacy is out of stock. The following sentences all express possible questions you may have for the pharmacist:

Mi serve una ricetta?	Do I need a prescription?
Sa dove posso trovare ...?	Do you know where I can find ...?
C'è un'altra farmacia qui vicino?	Is there another pharmacy nearby?
C'è una farmacia notturna?	Is there an all-night pharmacy?

La Bella Lingua

These nouns are always used in the plural:

le forbici	scissors
le pinze	tweezers
gli occhiali	eyeglasses

La Profumeria (The Cosmetics Store)

We all need a little help now and then. Make-up isn't called *il truco* (the trick) for nothing! Many toiletries, cosmetics, and perfume can be found at *la profumeria*.

349

English	Italian
blush	*il fard*
body lotion	*la crema per il corpo*
brush	*la spazzola*
eye shadow	*l'ombretto*
nail polish	*lo smalto per le unghie*
perfume	*il profumo*

I Was What I Was: The Imperfect

L'imperfetto (the imperfect) tense describes repeated actions that occurred in the past. Whenever you refer to something that used to be or describe a habitual pattern, you use the imperfect. *Mentre* (while), *quando* (when), *sempre* (always), *spesso* (often), and *di solito* (usually) are all key words you can look for to identify when the imperfect is being used.

The imperfect also expresses actions we were doing when something else happened. For example, "I was studying when the telephone rang." The phone interrupted your studies, which you had been doing for an indefinite amount of time.

Attenzione!

When using the past tense, be careful to use the appropriate tense. At times it may not always be clear whether you should use the present perfect or the imperfect.

As a Rule

Which tense should you use? The **present perfect** expresses an action that was completed at a specific time in the past; you did it once and now it's over and done with. The **imperfect** represents an action that continued to occur, that was happening, that used to happen, or that would (meaning used to) happen.

Andavamo al mare ogni estate.   We used to go to the sea every summer.

Formation of the Imperfect

The imperfect tense is one of the easiest tenses to remember. With the exception of the verb *essere*, there are hardly any irregularities—and when there are, they are usually consistent with stem changes in the present. The best part is that the endings are the same for all three verb families. Just drop the final *–re* from the infinitive and add the endings in the following table.

Imperfect Endings

Subject	Imperfect Endings
io	*–vo*
tu	*–vi*
lui/lei/Lei	*–va*
noi	*–vamo*
voi	*–vate*
loro	*–vano*

The verbs in the following table all share the same endings. Take a look at them.

Imperfect Examples

Subject	*Parlare*	*Leggere*	*Capire*
io	*parlavo*	*leggevo*	*capivo*
tu	*parlavi*	*leggevi*	*capivi*
lui/lei/Lei	*parlava*	*leggeva*	*capiva*
noi	*parlavamo*	*leggevamo*	*capivamo*
voi	*parlavate*	*leggevate*	*capivate*
loro	*parlavano*	*leggevano*	*capivano*

The only verb that completely changes form in the imperfect is the verb *essere*, shown in the following table.

Essere (to Be)

Italian	English
*io **ero***	I was
*tu **eri***	you were
*lui/lei/Lei **era***	he/she was; You were
*noi **eravamo***	we were
*voi **eravate***	you were
*loro **erano***	they were

Fill in the Spazio

Take a look at these stem-changing verbs and fill in the rest of the chart using the endings you just learned.

	Dire (to Say)	*Fare* (to Do/Make)	*Bere* (to Drink)
io	_____	*facevo*	_____
tu	*dicevi*	_____	_____
lui/lei/Lei	_____	_____	*beveva*
noi	*dicevamo*	_____	_____
voi	_____	*facevate*	_____
loro	_____	_____	*bevevano*

As a Rule

You use the imperfect when you want to say that something happened regularly. The imperfect also describes states of being (mental, emotional, and physical) that occurred in the past and is used to express age, time, and weather.

Quando ero piccola ...	When I was small ...
Quando avevo cinque anni ...	When I was five years old ...
Mi sentivo bene.	I felt well.
Faceva freddo.	It was cold.
Erano le sei.	It was 6:00.

La Pratica

Fill in the blanks with the verb in parenthesis, using the imperfect.

1. *Quando hai telefonato, (io)* _____ *(guardare) la televisione.*

2. *Quando (noi)* _____ *(essere) bambini,* _____ *(andare) spesso al mare.*

3. *Mentre Maria* _____ *(lavorare), Luigi* _____ *(preparare) la cena.*

4. *Mi* _____ *(piacere) ascoltare la radio ogni notte.*

5. *Quando Katerina* _____ *(avere) 18 anni, è andata in Italia per la prima volta.*

6. *(Loro)* _____ *(abitare) in Via Condotti quando è nata loro figlia.*

7. *Mio nonno* _____ *(fare) una passeggiata ogni giorno della sua vita. Lui* _____ *(essere) un'uomo forte.*

8. *(Io)* _____ *(tornare) a casa quando ho visto l'incidente.*

9. *(Noi) Ci* _____ *(vedere) spesso al lavoro.*

10. *Maurizio si* _____ *(alzare) sempre tardi la mattina.*

What's Done Is Done

It's awkward trying to speak in the present tense all the time. Replace the underlined verbs with the appropriate form of the past tense (present perfect or imperfect).

> *Arriviamo il 21 settembre, il primo giorno d'autunno. Il sole brilla e fa bel tempo. Viaggiamo spesso ma questa è la nostra prima volta in Italia. Prima andiamo a Roma dove vediamo il Vaticano, il Foro Romano e il Colosseo. Poi andiamo a Firenze per una settimana.*

A Review

You've seen these verbs before and should know them pretty well by now. Each verb has its participle in parentheses. Conjugate each verb in both the present perfect (simple past) and the imperfect tense using the helping verb *avere*.

1. *Scrivere (scritto)*

Subject	Present Perfect	Imperfect
io		
tu		
lui/lei/Lei		
noi		
voi		
loro		

2. *Spedire (spedito)*

Subject	Present Perfect	Imperfect
io		
tu		
lui/lei/Lei		
noi		
voi		
loro		

353

3. *Leggere* (*letto*)

Subject	Present Perfect	Imperfect
io	_____	_____
tu	_____	_____
lui/lei/Lei	_____	_____
noi	_____	_____
voi	_____	_____
loro	_____	_____

4. *Mandare* (*mandato*)

Subject	Present Perfect	Imperfect
io	_____	_____
tu	_____	_____
lui/lei/Lei	_____	_____
noi	_____	_____
voi	_____	_____
loro	_____	_____

The Least You Need to Know

➤ To tell someone that a certain part of your body doesn't feel well, use *Mi fa male* plus the body part.

➤ Certain body parts are irregular in the plural.

➤ The imperfect tense is used to indicate something that occurred in the past over a period of time or something that you *used to do.* It is also used to talk about a mental, emotional, or physical condition that happened in the past.

➤ The present perfect is used to indicate an isolated event that occurred in the past.

Chapter 22

Can You Read Me?

In This Chapter

➤ Using the telephone

➤ Visiting the post office

➤ Writing a letter

➤ The future tense

The twentieth century has brought us to levels of communication that a Roman living during Virgilio's time could not fathom. Satellites are beaming down signals through space. You drop a package off today, and it clears the *continente* by tomorrow.

You've become accustomed to these services and may require them in Italy. This chapter shows you how to make *una telefonata* (telephone call), send a fax, deal with the *ufficio postale* (post office), and write *una lettera*. You'll also take a look at what's to come in the *futuro*.

Il Telefono

Most telephone numbers in Italy start with 0 + the area code followed by the number. To get an operator, you must dial 15; to get an international operator, dial 170. For an emergency or to get the *la polizia*, dial 113, or for *i carabinieri*, dial 112. It's always a good idea to find out any local numbers that you might need in a quandary.

La Bella Lingua

Public telephones are easy to use in Italy. You can go to a telephone office, easily identified with a red or yellow sign that reads "TELECOM," or you can use any telephone you find in a bar, restaurant, or on the street. You can use a prepaid telephone card called a *scheda telefonica*, and most public telephones accept coins.

Types of Phone Calls

When speaking to an international operator, you can probably speak in English. What happens if you're in a small village and need to call back home? The vocabulary in the following table should help you reach out and touch someone. Review Chapter 3, "Sound Like an Italian," to remember how to spell your name in Italian.

Types of Calls

Type of Call	*La Telefonata*
collect call	*una telefonata a carico del destinatario*
credit-card call	*una telefonata con carta di credito*
intercontinental call	*una telefonata intercontinentale*
international call (Europe)	*una telefonata internazionale*
local call	*una telefonata urbana*
long-distance call	*una telefonata interurbana*
person-to-person call	*una telefonata con preavviso*

Reach Out

Le pagine gialle (the Yellow Pages) are a handy reference for more than phone numbers—check here for listings of museum hours, places to go, and things to do. Familiarize yourself with the terms related to the telephone in the following table.

The Telephone

The Telephone	Il Telefono
800 number (free)	*il numero verde*
answering machine	*la segreteria telefonica*
area code	*il prefisso*
booth	*la cabina telefonica*
cellular phone	*il telefonino/il cellulare*
coin return	*la restituzione monete*
cordless phone	*il telefono senza fili*
keypad	*la tastiera*
line	*la linea*
message	*il messaggio*
operator	*l'operatore*
phone card	*la scheda telefonica*
public phone	*il telefono pubblico*
receiver	*il ricevitore/la cornetta*
telephone book	*l'elenco telefonico*
telephone call	*la telefonata*
token	*il gettone*
touch-tone phone	*il telefono a tastiera*
Yellow Pages	*le pagine gialle*

Call Me Sometime!

Some useful verbs and expressions related to the telephone might come in handy. (Bonus: You've probably seen most of these verbs by now!)

Phone Phrases and Verbs

The Verb	Il Verbo
to call back	*richiamare*
to dial	*comporre il numero*
to drop a line/to buzz someone	*dare un colpo di telefono (idiomatico)*
to hang up	*attaccare, riagganciare*
to hold	*attendere*
to insert the card	*introdurre la carta*
to leave a message	*lasciare un messaggio*
to make a call	*fare una telefonata*
to pick up	*alzare il ricevitore*

continues

Phone Phrases and Verbs   (continued)

The Verb	Il Verbo
to press	*premere*
to receive a call	*ricevere una telefonata*
to ring	*suonare/squillare*
to speak to an operator	*parlare con un operatore*
to telephone	*telefonare*

Say What?

The following words and phrases should help you get your point across.

Ice Breakers

English	L'Italiano
Hello!	*Pronto!*
With whom do I speak?	*Con chi parlo?*
I would like to make a phone call.	*Vorrei fare una telefonata.*
Do you sell telephone cards?	*Vendete schede telefoniche?*
Is ... there?	*C'è ...?*
It's ...(your name).	*Sono ... (il tuo nome).*
I'd like to speak with ...	*Vorrei parlare con ...*
I'll call back later.	*Richiamo più tardi.*

Making Una Telefonata

Italians love their *telefonini,* also known as *cellulari,* which are constantly beeping and chirping. These can be rented from any airport, although it is just as easy to pick up a prepaid *scheda telefonica* (telephone card) for L5.000 or L10.000 and use public phones. After breaking off the corner at the dotted line, just slide it into any phone that accepts cards. You can check to see how much money you still have left on your card by looking at the small screen on top of the phone. Most phones also accept coins, but it can be cumbersome having to constantly feed the machine. A few older phones require the use of a *gettone* (token), but these are quickly disappearing.

Hello, Operator?

You can run into many problems when you're making a phone call. You may dial the wrong number or hear a recording telling you the number is no longer in service. The following are some phrases you might hear or want to say to an operator. They may be in the past tense, so keep an ear out for the auxiliary verbs and their participles.

What you might say:

È caduta la linea.	The line was disconnected.
La linea è sempre occupata.	The line is always busy.
Mi scusi, ho sbagliato numero.	Excuse me, I dialed the wrong number.
Non posso prendere la linea.	I can't get a line.
Posso parlare con un operatore internazionale?	May I speak with an international operator?
Mi può mettere in communicazione con ...?	Can you connect me with ...?

What the operator might say:

Attendere.	Hold.
Che numero ha fatto?	What number did you dial?
Non risponde.	No one is answering.
Questo (quel) numero di telefono è fuori servizio.	This (that) number is out of service.
Questo (quel) numero non funziona.	This (that) number does not work.

La Bella Lingua

When calling back home from Italy, it's always cheaper to charge your calls to your home phone. To contact MCI from anywhere in Italy, dial 172-1022. To contact AT&T, dial 172-1011. Although this is a toll-free call, you'll still need to use a calling card or L200 to get a line. Make sure you get your password *before* you leave for Italy.

Just the Fax

You might have some business to attend to while you are away or need directions to your next destination point. The following terms all relate to sending messages electronically or through the telephone lines.

Faxing Lingo

English	*L'Italiano*
fax/fax machine	*il facsimile/il fax*
fax number	*il numero di fax*
to send a fax	*inviare un fax/"faxare"*
fax modem	*il fax modem*
Internet	*l'internet*
e-mail	*la posta elettronica*
e-mail address	*l'indirizzo elettronico/internet*

Rain or Shine: The Post Office

A visit to *l'ufficio postale* (the post office) can bring the most reasonable person to the verge of insanity. All you want is a stamp, but you've got to wait in *la fila* (line) just like everyone else. If you want to send a *pacco*, you wait in one line only to find out you need to go to the other *sportello* (counter).

Take a deep breath and remember: You're not just in the post office, you're in the post office in *Italy*. Things could be worse.

The Post Office

English	*L'Italiano*
addressee	*il recipiente*
cardboard box	*la scatola di cartone*
counter/window	*lo sportello*
envelope	*la busta*
extra postage	*la soprattassa postale*
letter	*la lettera*
line	*la fila*
mail	*la posta*
mail carrier	*il postino*
mailbox	*la buca da lettere, la cassetta della posta*
money transfer	*il vaglia postale, il vaglia telegrafico*
package	*il pacco*
packing paper	*la carta da pacchi*
post office	*l'ufficio postale*
post office box	*la cassetta postale*
postage	*la tariffa postale*
postal worker	*l'impiegato(a) postale*

English	*L'Italiano*
postcard	*la cartolina*
receipt	*la ricevuta*
to send	*spedire, mandare*
sender	*il mittente*
stamps	*i francobolli*
telegram	*il telegramma*

Rain or Shine

There are many different ways to send something—some costing more, some taking longer than others. If you don't indicate how you want something to be shipped, chances are good that it will take the longest route. *Vorrei mandare questa lettera ...* (I'd like to send this letter ...).

Letter Perfect

English	*L'Italiano*
by air mail	*per posta aerea/per via aerea*
by C.O.D.	*con pagamento alla consegna*
by express mail	*per espresso*
by special delivery	*per corriere speciale*
registered mail	*per posta raccomandata*

Getting Service

Do you need to communicate your postal needs quickly? The following phrases should get you and your mail out the door as fast as possible.

Going Postal

English	*L'Italiano*
Where is the ...	*Dov'è ...*
... post office?	*... l'ufficio postale?*
... mailbox?	*... la buca da lettere?*
What is the postal rate?	*Qual è la tariffa postale?*
I would like to send this letter	*Vorrei spedire questa lettera ...*
... by airmail.	*... per posta aerea.*
... by express mail.	*... per espresso.*
... registered mail.	*... per posta raccomandata.*

continues

Going Postal   (continued)

English	L'Italiano
How much does this letter (this package) weigh?	*Quanto pesa questa lettera (questo pacco)?*
When will it arrive?	*Quando arriverà?*

As a Rule

Remember that cities take the preposition *a*, whereas countries take the preposition *in*. Remember to use the correct form of the demonstrative adjective (*questo/questa* and so on) before the noun you are using.

*Vorrei mandare questa lettera **a** Roma ma questo pacco va **in** Francia.*

Dear Gianni

Pick up some beautiful handmade marbleized paper from a *cartoleria* in Firenze. You don't have to write a lot; a couple of lines letting someone know you appreciate him or her goes a long way.

La Lettera

Letter	La Lettera
Dear (informal)	*Caro/a*
Dear (formal)	*Egregio/a*
Affectionately (informal)	*Affettuosamente*
Cordially (formal)	*Cordialmente*
Yours (formal)	*il Suo/la Sua*
Yours (informal)	*il tuo/la tua*
Sincerely (formal)	*Sinceramente*
A hug (informal)	*Un abbraccio*
Soon! (informal)	*A presto!*

Che Sarà Sarà: **The Future**

The future tense is quite easy. It is used in Italian in exactly the same manner as English. Some irregular verbs may change their stem (such as *potere, fare,* and *andare*), but future endings are all the same for all three verb families.

Unlike most verb conjugations, where you add the appropriate conjugated ending to the infinitive stem, the future endings are added to the end of the infinitive minus its final *–e.* Regular *–are* verbs must also change the final *–a* of the future stem to *–e,* except the verbs *dare, fare,* and *stare.*

Future Endings

Subject	Future Endings
io	*–ò*
tu	*–ai*
lui/lei/Lei	*–à*
noi	*–emo*
voi	*–ete*
loro	*–anno*

The following illustrates how the future works in all three verb families. Pay attention to what happens to the *–are* verb *parlare.*

Future Examples

Subject	Parlare	Scrivere	Capire
io	*parlerò*	*scriverò*	*capirò*
tu	*parlerai*	*scriverai*	*capirai*
lui/lei/Lei	*parlerà*	*scriverà*	*capirà*
noi	*parleremo*	*scriveremo*	*capiremo*
voi	*parlerete*	*scriverete*	*capirete*
loro	*parleranno*	*scriveranno*	*capiranno*

Ti parlerò domani.	I'll speak to you tomorrow.
Durante la sua vacanza,	During her vacation,
Maria scriverà molte lettere.	Maria will write many letters.

What Will Be Will Be

You may already be familiar with the old Italian adage *Che sarà sarà!* (What will be, will be!) The following table shows how you talk about the future. As usual, the irregular verb *essere* has its own set of rules.

Essere (to Be)

Italian	English
io **sarò**	I will be
tu **sarai**	you will be
lui/lei/Lei **sarà**	he/she/(it)* will be; You will be
noi **saremo**	we will be
voi **sarete**	you will be
loro **saranno**	they will be

*As you learned in Chapter 9, "Being There," Italian has no neuter "it" but uses the verb form alone to refer to things and animals.

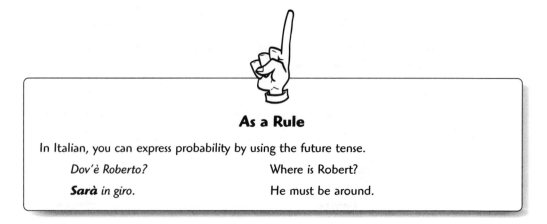

As a Rule

In Italian, you can express probability by using the future tense.

Dov'è Roberto?	Where is Robert?
Sarà *in giro.*	He must be around.

What Will You Have?

The following table shows how the irregular verb *avere* is conjugated in the future.

Avere (to Have)

Italian	English
io **avrò**	I will have
tu **avrai**	you will have
lui/lei/Lei **avrà**	he/she/You will have

Italian	English
noi **avremo**	we will have
voi **avrete**	you will have
loro **avranno**	they will have

Look for the Pattern

Verbs that end in *–care* or *–gare* (such as *cercare*, *giocare*, and *pagare*) add an *–h* before the *–er* base in order to maintain the original sound of their infinitives.

Verb		Stem	Future Conjugations
cercare	→	*cercher–*	*cercherò, chercherai, cercherà ...*
giocare	→	*giocher–*	*giocherò, giocherai, giocherà ...*
pagare	→	*pagher–*	*pagherò, pagherai, pagherà ...*

Many verbs that end in *–iare* (such as *cominciare*, *lasciare*, *mangiare*, and *noleggiare*) change *–ia* to *–e.*

Verb		Stem	Future Conjugations
cominciare	→	*comincer–*	*comincerò, comincerai, comincerà ...*
lasciare	→	*lascer–*	*lascerò, lascerai, lascerà ...*
mangiare	→	*manger–*	*mangerò, mangerai, mangerà ...*

As a Rule

Often it is not the endings that are irregular in the future tense, but the stems of the infinitives. Once you have memorized the stem, you will have no problem conjugating a verb into the future.

Irregular Stems

The following table shows a list of commonly used verbs with irregular future stems. However, once the stem has been changed, these verbs use regular future endings.

Verb	Stem	Future
andare (to go)	*andr–*	*andrò, andrai …*
bere (to drink)	*berr–*	*berrò, berrai …*
dare (to give)	*dar–*	*darò, darai …*
dovere (to have to)	*dovr–*	*dovrò, dovrai …*
fare (to do/make)	*far–*	*farò, farai …*
giocare (to play)	*giocher–*	*giocherò, giocherai …*
potere (to be able to)	*potr–*	*potrò, potrai …*
rimanere (to remain)	*rimarr–*	*rimarrò, rimarrai …*
sapere (to know)	*sapr–*	*saprò, saprai …*
stare (to stay)	*star–*	*starò, starai …*
tenere (to hold)	*terr–*	*terrò, terrai …*
vedere (to see)	*vedr–*	*vedrò, vedrai …*
vivere (to live)	*vivr–*	*vivrò, vivrai …*

Ti darò i soldi fra una settimana.	I'll give you the money in a week.
Staremo in vacanza per dieci giorni.	We will be on vacation for ten days.

Back to the Future

Fill in the blanks with the proper future conjugation of the following verbs. Look at the stems to determine the rest:

	Andare	Dovere	Potere	Sapere	Vedere
io	andrò	dovrò	potrò	saprò	vedrò
tu	_____	_____	_____	_____	_____
lui/lei/Lei	_____	_____	potrà	_____	_____
noi	andremo	_____	_____	_____	_____
voi	_____	_____	_____	_____	vedrete
loro	_____	_____	_____	sapranno	_____

Verbs such as *bere, rimanere, tenere, venire,* and *volere* double the final *–r* before the endings. See if you can fill in the conjugation for them:

	Bere	Rimanere	Tenere	Venire	Volere
io	berrò	rimarrò	terrò	verrò	vorrò
tu	berrai	_____	_____	_____	_____
lui/lei/Lei	_____	_____	_____	_____	_____

	Bere	*Rimanere*	*Tenere*	*Venire*	*Volere*
noi	_____	rimarremo	_____	_____	_____
voi	_____	rimarrete	_____	_____	_____
loro	_____	_____	_____	verranno	_____

Now let's put it all together. Replace the underlined verbs with the future tense.

> *Domani <u>ho</u> molto da fare. <u>Devo</u> fare la spesa per la cena. Prima <u>devo</u> comprare la frutta al mercato, poi <u>compro</u> il pane alla panetteria. <u>Vado</u> al supermercato per comprare la pasta e poi <u>voglio</u> andare alla pescheria per un bel filetto di sogliola. Probabilmente <u>sono</u> stanca; allora <u>prendo</u> l'autobus per tornare a casa. I miei amici <u>arrivano</u> alle otto.*

The Future Perfect

When you have finished this book, *you will have learned* the Italian language. The future perfect is a compound tense that indicates something *will have happened* in the future before another future action. You form the future perfect by using either the auxiliary verb *avere* or *essere* in the future and the past participle of a verb.

Per l'anno prossimo avrò imparato l'italiano.	I will have learned Italian by next year.
Sarai tornato dal lavoro alle otto?	Will you have returned from work by 8:00?

The Least You Need to Know

➤ The future endings are the same for all three verb families.

➤ Many verbs have irregular stems in the future tense.

➤ The verbs *avere* and *essere* are irregular in the future and must be memorized.

Chapter 23

Home Sweet Home

In This Chapter

➤ Apartments and houses

➤ Rooms, furnishings, and amenities

➤ The conditional tense

Some people visit Italy and never leave. If you're one of the many who have fallen in love with the beautiful panoramas, wonderful food, and warm people, you may want to invest in a house or villa (or maybe even a castle!) nestled deep within the Italian countryside. You'll also learn about the conditional tense!

Your Home Away from Home

Pick up a local paper and comb through the real estate section to search for your perfect home. How many bedrooms does it have? Is there a balcony? The following table lists the various features people look for in a home. Use the expression *Ce l'ha …* (Does it have …) to ask if it has what you're looking for.

Internal Affairs

English	L'Italiano	English	L'Italiano
air conditioning	*l'aria condizionata*	hallway	*il corridoio*
apartment	*l'appartamento*	heating	*il riscaldamento*
attic	*la soffitta*	electric	*elettrico*
balcony	*il balcone*	gas	*a gas*
basement	*la cantina*	house	*la casa*
bathroom	*il bagno*	kitchen	*la cucina*
bathtub	*la vasca da bagno*	laundry room	*la lavanderia*
bedroom	*la camera da letto*	lease	*il contratto di affitto*
building	*il palazzo, l'edificio*	living room	*il soggiorno*
ceiling	*il soffitto*	maintenance	*la manutenzione*
closet	*l'armadio, il guardaroba*	owner	*il padrone di casa*
condominium	*il condominio*	rent	*l'affitto*
courtyard	*il cortile*	roof	*il tetto*
day room	*il soggiorno*	room	*la stanza, la camera*
dining room	*la sala da pranzo*	security deposit	*il deposito cauzionale*
entrance	*l'ingresso*	shower	*la doccia*
elevator	*l'ascensore*	stairs	*le scale*
fireplace	*il camino*	storage room	*la cantina*
floor	*il pavimento*	tenant	*l'inquilino, l'affittuario*
floor (story)	*il piano*	terrace	*la terrazza*
garden	*il giardino*	villa	*la villa*
garage	*il garage*	window	*la finestra*
ground floor	*il pianterreno*		

Inside Your Home

Is the house furnished, or do you have to provide your own bed? Is there an eat-in kitchen? Curtains for the windows? Clothes dryers are quite uncommon in Italy; you'll have to *stendere* your clothes on a line just like the Italians do. The following table gives you the names of the basics you need to live comfortably.

Furniture and Accessories

Furniture	I Mobili	Furniture	I Mobili
armchair	*la poltrona*	carpet	*il tappeto*
bed	*il letto*	chair	*la sedia*
bookcase	*la libreria*	chest of drawers	*il cassettone*

Furniture	I Mobili	Furniture	I Mobili
desk	*la scrivania*	refrigerator	*il frigorifero*
dishwasher	*la lavapiatti, la lavastoviglie*	rug	*il tappeto*
dresser	*la cassettiera*	sideboard	*la credenza*
freezer	*il freezer*	sofa	*il divano*
furniture	*i mobili*	stereo	*lo stereo*
glass case	*la cristalliera*	stove	*la macchina del gas*
lamp	*la lampada*	table	*il tavolo*
microwave oven	*il forno a microonde*	television	*la televisione, il televisore*
mirror	*lo specchio*	trunk	*il baule*
night table	*il comodino*	VCR	*il videoregistratore*
oven	*il forno*	washing machine	*la lavatrice*

Buying or Renting

You'll have lots of questions for a real estate agent or management company. You don't want anyone to waste the agent's (or your) time looking at things that aren't consistent with your vision. Being able to say what your *esigenze* (needs) are will help you get exactly what you want.

Did You Know?

Current rent laws in Italy make it quite difficult for a landlord to reclaim a property once he has a renter, regardless of the circumstances. Also, if a piece of land has not been used for a long time, that land becomes public property and can be used for a variety of purposes, usually for agricultural or pastoral needs.

Oh, Give Me a Home ...

English	L'Italiano
I am looking for ...	*Sto cercando ...*
I need ...	*Ho bisogno di ...*

continues

Oh, Give Me a Home ... (continued)

English	L'Italiano
Where can I find ...	*Dove posso trovare ...*
... the classified ads?	*... gli annunci (immobiliari)?*
... a real estate agency?	*... un'agenzia immobiliare?*
I'd like ...	*Vorrei ...*
... to lease.	*... noleggiare.*
... to rent.	*... affittare.*
... to buy.	*... comprare.*
Is this house available to rent?	*È possibile affittare questa casa?*
Is there rent control?	*C'è l'equo cannone?*
How much is the rent ...	*Quanto è l'affitto ...*
... per week?	*... alla settimana?*
... per month?	*... al mese?*
Does it include ...	*Include ...*
... heat?	*... il riscaldamento?*
... water?	*... l'acqua?*
... electric?	*... la corrente?*
Do I have to leave a deposit?	*Devo lasciare un deposito?*
How many square meters?	*Quanti metri quadrati?*

Useful Verbs

It's always good to know your verbs. The following table contains a few you might find useful when shopping around for a home.

Verbs for Renting (or Buying)

Verb	Il Verbo
to buy	*comprare*
to lease	*noleggiare*
to move	*cambiare casa*
to rent	*affittare/prendere in affitto*
to sell	*vendere*
to share	*condividere*
to transfer	*trasferirsi*

Bright, Spacious, and Cheap

Is your concern light or space? Do you want something modern or old? The adjectives in the following table can help you describe just what you're looking for.

It Looks Like ...

Adjective	L'Aggettivo	Adjective	L'Aggettivo
antique	*antico*	new	*nuovo*
big	*grande*	noisy	*rumoroso*
bright	*luminoso*	old	*vecchio*
luxurious	*lussuoso*	quiet	*silenzioso*
modern	*moderno*	restored	*ristrutturato, restaurato*
modest	*modesto*	small	*piccolo*

How's Your Italian?

Read the following *annunci* (ads) in the real estate section and see how much you understand. If you're staying for a couple of weeks somewhere, why not rent a room in someone's apartment? Usually there's a maximum stay of three weeks, but if an owner likes you, you may be able to stay longer. Many ads indicate when you should call: *Ore pasti* refers to lunch and dinner hours. Other ads will tell you not to waste any time: *No perditempo.* Keep in mind that Italians use the metric system. *Metri quadrati* refers to square meters.

Trastevere
Appartamento in affitto. 40 mq. Secondo piano. Luminoso, ristrutturato. Referenze.
No perditempo.
06-34-56-32

Testaccio
Palazzo in vendita. 4 piani, 8 appartamenti: da ristrutturare. No agenzie.
06-45-16-22

Via Flaminia
Casa in vendita o affitto. Totale mq. 180. Giardino mq. 1500 con alberi alto fusto.
Migliore offerente. Dilazioni. Tel. ore pasti
06-78-53-10

Centro
Camera affittasi a turisti in ampio appartamento. Uso cucina. Massimo 3 settimane—
1 settimana di deposito.
06-99-45-12

That Would Be Nice: The Conditional Tense

When *should* you use the conditional tense? You *would* use it whenever you *would* like to express what *would* happen or what you *would* do under certain circumstances.

Forming the Conditional Tense

The conditional tense follows easy, idiot-proof rules that make it one of the easier tenses to learn. Verbs that are irregular in the present tense tend to be regular in the conditional. The same stems you learned for the future tense apply to the conditional tense.

As you saw with the future tense, simply drop the final *–e* of the infinitive and add the endings. Regular *–are* verbs, except the verbs *dare, fare,* and *stare,* must again change the final *–a* of their base to *–e*.

The conditional tense is often used in conjunction with another tense, the subjunctive. You'll see how that works in the next chapter.

Conditional Endings

Subject	Conditional Endings
io	*–ei*
tu	*–esti*
lui/lei/Lei	*–ebbe*
noi	*–emmo*
voi	*–este*
loro	*–ebbero*

The following examples illustrate how the conditional works.

Conditional Examples

Subject	*Parlare*	*Vendere*	*Capire*
io	*parlerei*	*venderei*	*capirei*
tu	*parleresti*	*venderesti*	*capiresti*
lui/lei/Lei	*parlerebbe*	*venderebbe*	*capirebbe*
noi	*parleremmo*	*venderemmo*	*capiremmo*
voi	*parlereste*	*vendereste*	*capireste*
loro	*parlerebbero*	*venderebbero*	*capirebbero*

Non gli parlerei per nessun motivo.	I wouldn't talk to him for any reason.
Per quattro soldi venderebbe anche sua madre.	For money, he would even sell his mother.

The verb *essere* maintains the same stem as it did for the future tense.

Essere (to Be)

Italian	English
io **sarei**	I would be
tu **saresti**	you would be
lui/lei/Lei **sarebbe**	he/she/You would be
noi **saremmo**	we would be
voi **sareste**	you would be
loro **sarebbero**	they would be

Andare in Italia sarebbe una buona idea.	Going to Italy would be a good idea.
Sareste interessati a fare un viaggio?	Would you be interested in taking a trip?

As a Rule

The conditional tense uses the same stems as the future. Once you have learned the stems, you simply add the appropriate conditional ending. Note that the first person plural in the future should not be confused with the conditional, which has an extra *–m:*

> Future: *Vorremo* (we will want)
>
> Conditional: *Vorremmo* (we would like)

What Would You Have?

The following table shows how the verb *avere* is conjugated in the conditional.

Avere (to Have)

Italian	English
io **avrei**	I would have
tu **avresti**	you would have
lui/lei/Lei **avrebbe**	he/she/You would have

continues

Avere (to Have) (continued)

Italian	English
noi **avremmo**	we would have
voi **avreste**	you would have
loro **avrebbero**	they would have

Look for the Pattern II

Just like you saw in the future tense, verbs that end in *–care* or *–gare* (such as *cercare*, *giocare*, and *pagare*) add an *–h* before the *–er* base to maintain the original sound of their infinitives:

Verb		Stem	Conditional Conjugations
cercare	→	*cercher–*	*cercherei, cercheresti, cercherebbe* …
giocare	→	*giocher–*	*giocherei, giocheresti, giocherebbe* …
pagare	→	*pagher–*	*pagherei, pagheresti, pagherebbe* …

Many verbs that end in *–iare,* (such as *cominciare, lasciare, mangiare,* and *noleggiare*) change *–ia* to *–e.*

Verb		Stem	Conjugations
cominciare	→	*comincer–*	*comincerei, cominceresti, comincerebbe* …
lasciare	→	*lascer–*	*lascerei, lasceresti, lascerebbe* …
mangiare	→	*manger–*	*mangerei, mangeresti, mangerebbe* …

What's What

The conditional tense of the verbs *dovere, potere,* and *volere* express "should," "could," and "would like."

Stem Changing Verbs

Let's look at some of those stem changing verbs again. Try finishing the conjugations.

Verb	Stem	Conditional
andare (to go)	*andr–*	*andrei, andresti …*
bere (to drink)	*berr–*	*berrei, berresti …*
dare (to give)	*dar–*	*darei, daresti …*
fare (to do/make)	*far–*	*farei, faresti …*
rimanere (to remain)	*rimarr–*	*rimarrei, rimarresti …*
sapere (to know)	*sapr–*	*saprei, sapresti …*
stare (to stay)	*star–*	*starei, staresti …*
tenere (to hold)	*terr–*	*terrei, terresti …*
vedere (to see)	*vedr–*	*vedrei, vedresti …*
venire (to come)	*verr–*	*verrei, verresti …*

As a Rule

The verb *piacere* is used in the conditional to indicate that something would be pleasing to you.

Ti piacerebbe andare al cinema?	Would you like to go to the movies?
Sì, mi piacerebbe andarci.	Yes, I'd like to go (there).

Coulda, Shoulda, Woulda

The verbs *dovere* (to have to), *potere* (to be able to), and *volere* (to want) are often used in the conditional tense. When you should do something, you use the verb *dovere*. When you could do something, use the verb *potere*. When you would like something, use *volere*. These verbs in the conditional are often used with the infinitive form of another verb.

Dovere, Potere, and Volere

Subject	Dovere	Potere	Volere
io	dovrei	potrei	vorrei
tu	dovresti	potresti	vorresti
lui/lei/Lei	dovrebbe	potrebbe	vorrebbe
noi	dovremmo	potremmo	vorremmo
voi	dovreste	potreste	vorreste
loro	dovrebbero	potrebbero	vorrebbero

Dovresti studiare di più.	You should study more.
Andare in Italia potrebbe essere una buona idea.	Going to Italy could be a good idea.
Vorresti bere un tè?	Would you like to drink a tea?

La Bella Lingua

To form the conditional past tense, as in "I would have gone" or "He would have eaten," simply use the conditional form of the appropriate helping verb *avere* or *essere* + the past participle. The past conditional is most often used in conjunction with the subjunctive mood.

Practice Makes Perfetto

Translate the following sentences into Italian:

1. I'd like to go to Italy for the summer.
2. We should leave; it's getting late.
3. I could come later.
4. Sofia, would you like to see a film?
5. I'd like a big house in the country.
6. I would be rich with a million dollars.

The Least You Need to Know

➤ The conditional is formed by adding the conditional endings to the stem of the verbs.

➤ Many irregular stems are the same as used in the future tense.

➤ To express that you should, could, or would like, you must use the conditional form of the verbs *dovere, potere,* and *volere.*

➤ The verb *piacere* is used in the conditional to indicate that something would be pleasing to you and is used like the verb *volere,* as in "would like."

Chapter 24

Money Matters

In This Chapter

➤ Banking terms

➤ Business lingo and titles

➤ The subjunctive

➤ The past absolute

Money can't buy you love, but you sure can have fun spending it. For people doing business in Italy and for those fortunate enough to have the opportunity to stay in Italy for an extended *periodo,* this chapter gives you the terms you need to open a bank account, take out a mortgage, or make an investment. It also teaches you the subjunctive, a tense used most often when one is thinking about a hypothetical situation (such as, you guessed it, living in Italy).

Bank on It

Let's face it, banking terms are neither sexy nor fun, but they are absolutely *necessario.* Money talks, and so do you.

Did You Know?

Founded in 1472, Monte dei Paschi di Siena is one of the oldest banks in the world. The official currency used at the time was the *florin* (named after Florence), but credit as we know it today was an alien concept until the creation of the *cambiale*—the first example of an official document stating one's debt to another. In today's world, we call this a check.

Mini Dictionary of Banking Terms

The Bank	**La Banca**
account	*il conto*
… checking account	*… il conto corrente*
… savings account	*… il conto di deposito*
amount due (balance)	*corrispettivo non pagato*
amount paid	*corrispettivo riscosso*
automated teller machine	*Bancomat/lo sportello*
balance	*l'estratto conto*
bank	*la banca*
… savings bank	*… la cassa di risparmio*
bank account	*il conto bancario*
bill	*la bolletta, il conto, la fattura*
bill of sale	*l'atto di vendita*
bills payable	*gli effetti passivi*
bills receivable	*gli effetti attivi*
to borrow	*prendere in prestito*
branch	*la filiale*
cash	*i contanti*
cashier	*il cassiere*
change	*gli spiccioli*
change (transaction)	*il cambio*
check	*l'assegno*
checkbook	*il libretto degli assegni*
checking account	*il conto corrente*
coins	*le monete*
credit	*il credito*
currency (foreign)	*la valuta*

The Bank	La Banca
customer	*il cliente*
debt	*il debito*
deposit	*il deposito*
down payment	*l'anticipo*
employee	*l'impiegato*
endorse	*la girata*
exchange rate	*il tasso di scambio*
final payment	*il saldo*
guarantee	*la garanzia*
holder	*il titolare*
installment plan	*il piano di pagamento*
interest	*l'interesse*
... compound	*... composto*
... rate	*... tasso di*
investment	*l'investimento*
invoice	*la fattura*
loan	*il prestito*
long term	*a lungo termine*
monthly statement	*l'estratto conto*
mortgage	*il mutuo*
overdrawn account	*il conto scoperto*
overdrawn check	*l'assegno scoperto*
payment	*il pagamento*
percentage	*la percentuale*
promissory note	*la cambiale*
quarter	*il trimestre*
rate	*la rata*
receipt	*la ricevuta*
revenue	*i ricavi*
safe	*la cassaforte*
sale	*la vendita*
savings book	*il libretto di risparmio*
short term	*a breve termine*
signature	*la firma*
stock	*l'azione*
sum	*la somma*
teller	*l'impiegato di banca*
total	*il totale*
traveler's check	*travel check*
window	*lo sportello*

Do you need to cancel a check? Open an account? Take out a loan to continue your fabulous Italian vacation? You may need to know the verbs in the following table. Verbs used in idiomatic expressions are in parenthesis to remind you they need to be conjugated.

Banking Lingo

Verb	*Il Verbo*
to annul/cancel	*annullare*
to balance the accounts	*(fare) tornare i conti*
to cash	*incassare*
to change money	*(cambiare) i soldi*
to close an account	*(chiudere) il conto*
to deposit	*depositare*
to do the accounting	*(tenere) i conti*
to endorse	*girare*
to fill out (a form)	*riempire, compilare*
to go to the bank	*(andare) in banca*
to invest	*investire*
to loan	*prestare*
to manage	*occuparsi*
to open an account	*(aprire) un conto*
to pay by check	*(pagare) con assegno*
to pay cash	*(pagare) in contanti*
to save	*risparmiare*
to sign	*firmare*
to take out a loan	*(prendere) in prestito*
to transfer	*trasferire*
to withdraw	*ritirare*

Transactions

You already have all the skills you need to express your needs at the bank, so let's practice a little. Use the conditional of *volere* (*Vorrei ...*) to tell the nice folks at the bank you would like to do the following:

1. Open a checking account
2. Take out a loan
3. Change some money
4. Cash a check
5. Make a deposit
6. Make a withdrawal

La Bella Lingua

If you're in business, these titles will help you know who's who:

Chief Executive Officer	*Amministratore Delegato*
President	*Presidente*
Vice president	*Vice Presidente*
Director	*Direttore*
Consultant	*Consulente*
Manager	*Manager*
Sales representative	*Commesso*

The Wheel of Life

These days, with multitasking as the norm, it's more difficult to pinpoint professions. The terms in the following table will help you talk about where you fit in.

Trades

Trade	Mestiere	Trade	Mestiere
banking	*banca*	insurance	*assicurazioni*
communications	*comunicazioni*	law	*legge*
computers	*computer*	manufacturing	*produzione*
construction	*costruzioni*	marketing	*marketing*
design	*design*	medicine	*medicina*
development	*sviluppo*	public relations	*pubbliche relazioni*
education	*istruzione, pedagogia*	publishing	*editoria*
engineering	*ingegneria*	real estate	*immobiliari*
fashion	*moda*	retail	*vendita al dettaglio*
finance	*finanza*	sales	*vendite*
food services	*alimentazione*	software	*software*
government	*governo*		

Everyone Has Needs: *Il Congiuntivo* (The Subjunctive)

Il congiuntivo is not pink eye; it's the subjunctive. The subjunctive is a mood, not a tense, and it expresses wishes, feelings, and doubt. It's the mood you use to express your hunches, your dreams, and your musings. As opposed to describing what is, the subjunctive describes what might be.

La Bella Lingua

Several English business terms have made their way into Italian, including the words for "business," "computer," "software," and "fax."

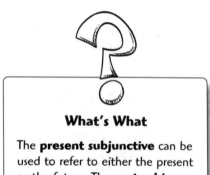

What's What

The **present subjunctive** can be used to refer to either the present or the future. The **past subjunctive** talks about things you "wished had happened."

You use the subjunctive every time you express your opinion or describe a hypothetical situation. When the fiddler on the roof starts singing, he's using the subjunctive mood in the imperfect tense: "If I *were* a rich man ...."

Using the Subjunctive

The subjunctive is most often used in dependent clauses introduced by *che*, (meaning "that," as in "I think that ..." or "It's important that ...").

> *Penso che Marcello arrivi domani.*
> I think that Marcello is arriving tomorrow.
>
> *È importante che lui parli con un dottore.*
> It's important that he speak to a doctor.

The present subjunctive is formed by adding the subjunctive endings to the stem of the verb. Unlike future and conditional stems, most subjunctive stems change little from the infinitive.

Unless you are using a proper noun, you need to use the singular subject pronouns (*io, tu, lui/lei/Lei*) to distinguish the singular forms from one another. The pronouns are not necessary for the plural forms. The examples presented in the following three tables are given with *che* to familiarize you with this construction.

Present Subjunctive Examples

Parlare	*Vendere*	*Offrire*	*Capire*
che io parli	*che io venda*	*che io offra*	*che io capisca*
che tu parli	*che tu venda*	*che tu offra*	*che tu capisca*
che lui/lei/Lei parli	*che lui/lei/Lei venda*	*che lui/lei/Lei offra*	*che lui/lei/Lei capisca*
che parliamo	*che vendiamo*	*che offriamo*	*che capiamo*

Parlare	*Vendere*	*Offrire*	*Capire*
che parliate	*che vendiate*	*che offriate*	*che capiate*
che parlino	*che vendano*	*che offrano*	*che capiscano*

È difficile che lui venda la casa a quel prezzo.	It's difficult for him to sell the house at that price.
Non penso che Maria capisca.	I don't think that Maria understands.

As a Rule

The subjunctive is used when

1. Two different clauses exist (dependent and independent) pertaining to two different subjects.

2. Those clauses are joined by **che**.

3. One of these clauses expresses need, emotion, doubt, or an opinion:

Need: *È necessario che lui vada da un dottore.* It's necessary for him to go to the doctor.

Doubt: *Dubito che vinca la nostra squadra.* I doubt that our team will win.

Opinion: *Credo che tu sia la più bella donna del mondo.* I think that you are the most beautiful woman in the world.

Emotion: *Ho paura che sia troppo tardi per andarci.* I am afraid it's too late to go there.

The verbs *essere* and *avere* are both irregular.

Essere (to Be)

Essere	
che io **sia**	*che* **siamo**
che tu **sia**	*che* **siate**
che lui/lei/Lei **sia**	*che* **siano**

Penso che Luisa sia bella.	I think that Luisa is beautiful.
Credo che siano a casa.	I believe that they are at home.

387

Avere (to Have)

Avere	
che io **abbia**	*che* **abbiamo**
che tu **abbia**	*che* **abbiate**
che lui/lei/Lei **abbia**	*che* **abbiano**

Penso che Tiziana **abbia** *ragione.*	I think that Tiziana is right.
È un peccato che non **abbiano** *il tempo di venire.*	It's a shame that they don't have time to come.

Oh, So Moody

Oh, those irregularities. It should be no surprise at this point that there are several verbs with irregular subjunctive forms.

Irregular Verbs in the Present Subjunctive

Verb	Irregular Present Subjunctive
andare	*vada, vada, vada, andiamo, andiate, vadano*
dare	*dia, dia, dia, diamo, diate, diano*
dire	*dica, dica, dica, diciamo, diciate, dicano*
dovere	*debba, debba, debba, dobbiamo, dobbiate, debbano*
fare	*faccia, faccia, faccia, facciamo, facciate, facciano*
mantenere	*mantenga, mantenga, mantenga, manteniamo, manteniate, mantengano*
piacere	*piaccia, piaccia, piaccia, piacciamo, piacciate, piacciano*
potere	*possa, possa, possa, possiamo, possiate, possano*
rimanere	*rimanga, rimanga, rimanga, rimaniamo, rimaniate, rimangano*
salire	*salga, salga, salga, saliamo, saliate, salgano*
sapere	*sappia, sappia, sappia, sappiamo, sappiate, sappiano*
stare	*stia, stia, stia, stiamo, stiate, stiano*
tenere	*tenga, tenga, tenga, teniamo, teniate, tengano*
venire	*venga, venga, venga, veniamo, veniate, vengano*
volere	*voglia, voglia, voglia, vogliamo, vogliate, vogliano*

Dependent Clauses and the Subjunctive

The following expressions are all dependent clauses requiring the subjunctive mood. What makes a dependent clause? If a phrase cannot stand on its own, it is dependent. "I think that …" depends on the independent clause, something like, "… it's raining." You use the subjunctive when you're not sure of something. It could be raining or not.

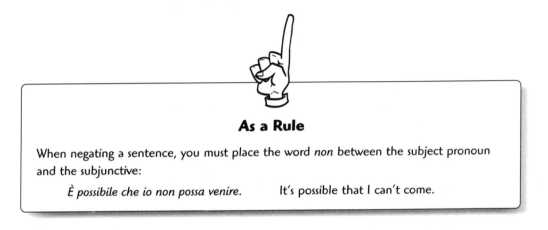

As a Rule

When negating a sentence, you must place the word *non* between the subject pronoun and the subjunctive:

È possibile che io non possa venire.   It's possible that I can't come.

Express Yourself

Expression	L'Espressione

Expressions of Wishing, Emotion, Need, and Doubt

I am happy that ...	*Sono contento che ...*
I am sorry that ...	*Mi dispiace che ...*
I believe that ...	*Credo che ...*
I desire that ...	*Desidero che ...*
I doubt that ...	*Dubito che ...*
I imagine that ...	*Immagino che ...*
I think that ...	*Penso che ...*
I want that ...	*Voglio che ...*

Impersonal Expressions and Conjunctions

although ...	*sebbene ...*
before ...	*prima che ...*
even though ...	*benché ...*
in case ...	*nel caso che ...*
It seems that ...	*Sembra che ...*
It's difficult that ...	*È difficile che ...*
It's easy that ...	*È facile che ...*
It's good/bad that ...	*È bene/male che ...*
It's important that ...	*È importante che ...*
It's incredible that ...	*È incredibile che ...*

continues

Express Yourself (continued)

Expression	*L'Espressione*
Impersonal Expressions and Conjunctions	
It's likely (probable) that ...	*È probabile che ...*
It's necessary that ...	*Bisogna che ...*
It's not important that ...	*Non importa che ...*
It's possible/impossible that ...	*È possibile/impossibile che ...*
It's strange that ...	*È strano che ...*
provided that ...	*purché ...*
so that ...	*affinché ...*
unless ...	*a meno che ...*
until ...	*finché non ...*
without ...	*senza che ...*

Mi sembra che tu sia intelligente.	It seems to me that you are intelligent.
Sebbene io non possa uonare il violino, mi piace ascoltarlo.	Although I can't play the violin, I like listening to it.

Attenzione!

You can avoid the subjunctive altogether when the subject is the same for both the dependent and the independent clauses by using *di* plus the infinitive:

Penso di andare al cinema.   I'm thinking of going to the movies.

Practice Makes *Perfetto*

Paolo hopes she can go to Italy this summer to study the language. She wants her friend Silvia to join her on an excursion. Fill in the blanks with the appropriate form of the subjunctive.

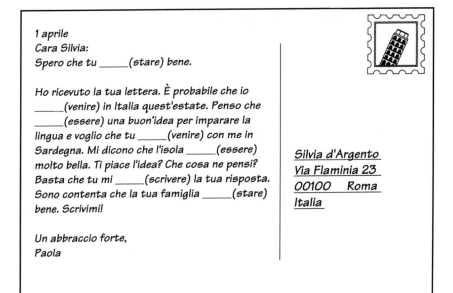

1 aprile
Cara Silvia:
Spero che tu _____(stare) bene.

Ho ricevuto la tua lettera. È probabile che io
_____(venire) in Italia quest'estate. Penso che
_____(essere) una buon'idea per imparare la
lingua e voglio che tu _____(venire) con me in
Sardegna. Mi dicono che l'isola _____(essere)
molto bella. Ti piace l'idea? Che cosa ne pensi?
Basta che tu mi _____(scrivere) la tua risposta.
Sono contenta che la tua famiglia _____(stare)
bene. Scrivimi!

Un abbraccio forte,
Paola

Silvia d'Argento
Via Flaminia 23
00100   Roma
Italia

The Past (Present Perfect) Subjunctive

To make the past subjunctive (*passato del congiuntivo*), you'll need to use the present subjunctive form of the auxiliary verbs *avere* or *essere* + the past participle of your verb. Remember that verbs requiring *essere* as their auxiliary reflect gender and number in the participle. You use the past (or "perfect") subjunctive when the action expressed by the verb of the dependent clause occurred before the action expressed by the verb in the independent clause. Study the following examples.

Past Subjunctive

Avere + Telefonare	*Essere + Andare*
che io abbia telefonato	*che io sia andato(a)*
che tu abbia telefonato	*che tu sia andato(a)*
che lui/lei/Lei abbia telefonato	*che lui/lei/Lei sia andato(a)*
che noi abbiamo telefonato	*che siamo andati(e)*
che voi abbiate telefonato	*che siate andati(e)*
che loro abbiano telefonato	*che siano andati(e)*

Sono contenta che tu abbia telefonato.	I am happy that you telephoned.
Sembra che lui sia diventato pazzo.	It seems that he has gone crazy.

391

Purely Speculation: The Imperfect Subjunctive

The imperfect subjunctive (*imperfetto del congiuntivo*) is most often used when someone is talking about what they *would* do *if*, as in "If I *were* rich, I would buy a villa," or "If I *had* more time, I would stay in better shape."

Imperfetto

Parlare	Vendere	Offrire	Capire
che io parlassi	che io vendessi	che io offrissi	che io capissi
che tu parlassi	che tu vendessi	che tu offrissi	che tu capissi
che lui/lei/Lei parlasse	che lui/lei/Lei vendesse	che lui/lei/Lei offrisse	che lui/lei/Lei capisse
che parlassimo	che vendessimo	che offrissimo	che capissimo
che parlaste	che vendeste	che offriste	che capiste
che parlassero	che vendessero	che offrissero	che capissero

The Past Was Perfect

The possibilities are endless once you start mixing and matching auxiliary verbs in compound tenses. The past perfect subjunctive (*trapassato del congiuntivo*) is created by using the imperfect subjunctive of your auxiliary verb (*avere* or *essere*) + the past participle of the verb you are conjugating.

Trapassato

Parlare	Partire
che io avessi parlato	che io fossi partito(a)
che tu avessi parlato	che tu fossi partito(a)
che lui/lei/Lei avesse parlato	che lui/lei/Lei fosse partito(a)
che avessimo parlato	che fossimo partiti(e)
che aveste parlato	che foste partiti(e)
che avessero parlato	che fossero partiti(e)

Once Upon a Time: Il Passato Remoto

The *passato remoto* (also called the past definite and the past absolute) is a tense that goes so far back that it doesn't even have an equivalent in English. Although it translates to the simple past, as in "I went," the *passato remoto* requires you to look at time differently.

The *passato remoto* is the tense you hear when a story begins, "Once upon a time ...." It is the tense used in literature, fables, and historical references to describe an event that took place at a specific time in the distant past. A highly irregular verb tense, at times it is difficult to determine the infinitive of a conjugation. Although rarely used in daily speech, an understanding of the *passato remoto* is necessary in order to read Italian literature and poetry (which you definitely don't want to miss!).

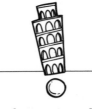

Attenzione!

The *passato remoto* is used almost exclusively in written language. You will occasionally hear it spoken in place of the *passato prossimo* as part of various dialects.

Past Absolute Examples

Subject	*Parlare*	*Vendere*	*Capire*
io	parlai	vendei	capii
tu	parlasti	vendesti	capisti
lui/lei/Lei	parlò	vendè	capì
noi	parlammo	vendemmo	capimmo
voi	parlaste	vendeste	capiste
loro	parlarono	venderono	capirono

Dante scrisse La Divina Commedia *nel 1307.*

Dante wrote *The Divine Comedy* in 1307.

Ci Fu Una Volta *(Once Upon a Time)*

The *passato remoto* is used in *fiabe* (fables) and *racconti* (stories). These ancient forms of the verbs *essere* and *avere* are virtually unrecognizable from the present-tense conjugations.

Essere (to Be)

Italian	English	Italian	English
io **fui**	I was	noi **fummo**	we were
tu **fosti**	you were	voi **foste**	you were
lui/lei/Lei **fu**	he/she was; You were	loro **furono**	they were

Avere (to Have)

Italian	English	Italian	English
io **ebbi**	I had	noi **avemmo**	we had
tu **avesti**	you had	voi **aveste**	you had
lui/lei/Lei **ebbe**	he/she/You had	loro **ebbero**	they had

Cose Da Vedere

The following has been excerpted from a travel brochure promoting the *la bellissima città di* San Gimignano. See if you can identify the use of the *passato remoto*.

> ### Cose Da Vedere
>
> *San Gimignano prende il nome dal vescovo di Modena morto nel 387. Nel 1099 divenne libero Comune. Combattè contro i vescovi di Volterra e le città vicine. La peste del 1348 e la successiva crisi portarono San Gimignano nel 1353 alla sottomissione a Firenze.*

What Am I?

After all your hard work, you should be able to make sense of this *indovinello toscano* (Tuscan riddle).

> *Son la bella del palazzo;*
> *Casco in terra e non mi ammazzo;*
> *Faccio lume al gran Signore,*
> *Son servita con amore.*

What am I?

Hint: I'm edible. (The answer is in Appendix A, "Answer Key.")

The Least You Need to Know

➤ If you need to open a bank account or deal with money matters, it's helpful to have the terms.

➤ The subjunctive is a mood, not a tense, and it is used to express opinions, thoughts, feelings, and desires.

➤ The absolute past is used primarily in the written language and is very irregular.

Answer Key

Chapter 2

Practice Makes Perfetto

1. dentro
2. stomaco
3. entro
4. informazioni riservate
5. interno

Chapter 4

How Intelligente You Are

1. posizione
2. incredibile
3. nazione
4. presenza
5. identità
6. pessimismo
7. prudente
8. continente
9. religioso
10. differenza

Masculine Nouns

1. airplane
2. anniversary
3. arch
4. actor
5. bus
6. coffee
7. color
8. communism
9. continent
10. cotton
11. director
12. dictionary
13. doctor
14. elephant
15. fact
16. group
17. idiot
18. lemon
19. mechanic
20. motor
21. museum
22. nose
23. odor
24. paradise
25. president
26. perfume
27. program
28. respect
29. salary
30. service
31. socialism
32. spirit
33. student
34. taxi
35. tea
36. telephone
37. train

Feminine Nouns

1. art
2. bicycle
3. carrot
4. guitar
5. class
6. condition
7. conversation
8. culture
9. curiosity
10. depression
11. diet
12. difference
13. discussion
14. emotion
15. experience
16. expression
17. holiday, party, festivity
18. figure
19. fountain
20. form
21. fortune
22. idea
23. identity
24. inflation
25. salad
26. lamp
27. letter
28. list
29. medicine
30. music
31. nation
32. person
33. possibility
34. probability
35. profession
36. region
37. religion
38. rose
39. sculpture
40. temperature
41. tourist
42. university
43. violence

How Much Do You Understand Already?

1. The city is beautiful.
2. The restaurant is terrible.
3. The jacket is big.
4. The museum is interesting.
5. The service is good.
6. The mountain is high (tall).

A Piece of Cake

1. to allude
2. to attribute
3. to fall, to drop
4. to consist
5. to change, to convert
6. to correspond
7. to deliberate
8. to detest
9. to defend
10. to descend
11. to discuss
12. to disgust
13. to dissolve
14. to examine
15. to form
16. to function
17. to glorify
18. to imply
19. to indicate
20. to intend
21. to navigate
22. to occupy
23. to offend
24. to offer
25. to operate
26. to pronounce
27. to recommend
28. to represent
29. to resist
30. to receive
31. to respond

Translation Please

1. Italy is part of the continent of Europe.
2. The student studies mathematics and history.
3. The actor is very famous in the movies.
4. The mechanic repairs the automobile.
5. The cook prepares a salad and an appetizer.
6. The doctor speaks with the patient.
7. The family desires a modern and big apartment.
8. The Japanese tourist visits the museum and the cathedral.
9. The president presents the plan (the program).
10. Robert prefers classical music.

What's Your Take?

1. La cioccolata è deliziosa.
2. Il ristorante è eccellente.
3. La città è splendida e magnifica.
4. Il profumo è elegante.
5. La conversazione è interessante.
6. Il dottore è sincero.
7. Lo studente è intelligente.
8. Il museo è importante.
9. La cattedrale è alta.
10. Il treno è veloce.

Are You Well Read?

Dante—*The Divine Comedy*
Di Lampedusa—*The Leopard*
Eco—*The Name of the Rose*

Machiavelli—*The Prince*
Morante—*History*
Pirandello—*6 Characters in Search of an Author*

Chapter 5

Did You Know Trivia

July and August

Chapter 6

Practice Makes Perfetto

1. la casa (f.)
2. il cane (m.)
3. l'albero (m.)
4. il piatto (m.)
5. la lezione (f.)
6. l'estate (f.)
7. la chiesa (f.)
8. lo straniero (m.)
9. la cattedrale (f.)
10. il pianeta (m./irregular)

La Pratica

1. i libri
2. i gatti
3. le ragazze
4. le stazioni
5. gli amici
6. le amichi

What Does It Mean?

1. gli aeroplani (airplanes)
2. i bambini (children)
3. la birra (beer)
4. i dollari (dollars)
5. l'invenzione (invention)
6. il libro (book)
7. il nome (name, noun)
8. la notte (night)
9. l'odore (odor)
10. le ragazze (girls)
11. le scuole (schools)
12. gli stranieri (foreigners)
13. i supermercati (supermarkets)
14. le tavole (tables)
15. la vacanza (vacation)
16. i viaggi (the trips)

Practice Those Plurals

1. Cerco le cartoline.
2. Cerco le riviste.
3. Cerco le collane.
4. Cerco i profumi.
5. Cerco le cravatte.
6. Cerco le penne.

What Have You Learned About Gender?

1. Mature actress (40 to 50 years old) sought with the ability to speak English and French for interpreting the role of countess. Distinct look. Send resume with photo to Via Garibaldi 36, Roma.
2. Strong actor, athletic, young with light hair sought to interpret the role of Caesar. Present yourself on June 25 at 9:00 at Superforte gym, second floor.
3. Very sexy men and women sought to appear nude in beach scene: various ages. No experience necessary. Telephone 06/040357.

Chapter 7

Name That Subject

1. The stars (they)
2. Jessica (she)
3. Leslie (she)
4. My mother (she)
5. Louis (he)
6. The food (it)
7. Italian (it)
8. Anna (she)

Subject to Interpretation

1. Davide: David takes the bus.
2. Io: I eat fish.
3. Patrizia e Raffaella: Patrizia and Raffaella study art.
4. L'insalata: The salad is fresh.
5. La farmacia: The pharmacy is open.
6. Lo studente: The student speaks with the professor.
7. Io e Gianni: Gianni and I are going to Italy.
8. La ragazza: The girl is going home.

Hey You!

1. tu
2. voi
3. loro
4. voi, Lei (singular)

5. Loro
6. tu
7. Lei, tu (depending on your relationship)

Chapter 8

Practice Makes Perfetto

1. lavora
2. aspettiamo
3. abiti

4. parlo
5. passate
6. preparano

Practice Makes Perfetto II

1. spendono
2. scrivo
3. accendi

4. vediamo
5. risolve
6. prendete

Chapter 9

Come Sei Intelligente!

1. è
2. sei
3. sono

4. sono
5. siete

Chitchat

1. stiamo
2. sta
3. sto

4. sono
5. è
6. è

Fill In the Blanks

1. C'è
2. Ci sono
3. Ci sono
4. C'è

5. Ci sono
6. Ci sono
7. Ci sono
8. c'è

Express Yourself

1. ho fame
2. ho freddo
3. sono stanco, sono stanca, ho sonno
4. ho ____ anni
5. ho vergogna

Back to Your Roots

1. Olivier è francese e abita a Parigi.
2. Patrizia è cattolica e ha cinque sorelle.
3. Primo Levi è ebreo.
4. Massimo è di origine italiana.
5. Ci sono molti turisti giapponesi in Italia.

Eureka!

1. il museo: Eccolo!
2. il ristorante: Eccolo!
3. la banca: Eccola!
4. il negozio: Eccolo!
5. la strada: Eccola!
6. la stazione: Eccola!
7. l'albergo: Eccolo!
8. il bar: Eccolo!
9. l'ospedale: Eccolo!
10. l'autobus: Eccolo!
11. lo stadio: Eccolo!
12. il supermercato: Eccolo!

Chapter 10

A Sense of Belonging

1. la sua casa
2. la mia scuola
3. i suoi libri
4. i suoi libri
5. il tuo amico

One Yellow Banana, Please

1. bianca; pulita (The white house is clean.)
2. vecchio (The Colosseo is very old.)
3. alte (The mountains in Switzerland are high.)
4. chiuso (The store is closed on Sundays.)
5. economico (This hotel is inexpensive.)
6. tirchio (The Scrooge is a very cheap man.)

Make the Connection

Definite Article	Translation	Quello	Translation
1. il libro	the book	quel libro	that book
2. i libri	the books	quei libri	those books
3. la penna	the pen	quella penna	that pen
4. le penne	the pens	quelle penne	those pens
5. l'articolo	the article	quell'articolo	that article
6. gli articoli	the articles	quegli articoli	those articles
7. lo studente	the student	quello studente	that student
8. gli studenti	the students	quegli studenti	those students

The More Things Change

1. dolcemente
2. sinceramente
3. intelligentemente
4. necessariamente
5. velocemente
6. regolarmente
7. difficilmente
8. probabilmente
9. solamente
10. gentilmente

Chapter 11

In the Comfort Zone

Available to passengers on board are Italian and foreign magazines, blankets and pillows, medicine, stationery, toys for children, pens, postcards, cigarettes, Italian sparkling wines, wine, beer, and various beverages.

Going, Going, Gone

1. vanno
2. vado
3. vai
4. andiamo
5. andate; vanno

All Verbed Up and Everywhere to Go

1. prendo
2. andiamo
3. prendono
4. vai
5. prendete
6. va

Switcharoo

1. alla festa
2. in piazza
3. in macchina
4. nell'armadio
5. degli spaghetti

Tell Me What to Do

aiutare: Aiuta! Aiuti!

mangiare: Mangia! Mangi!

portare: Porta! Porti!

telefonare: Telefona! Telefoni!

La Dogana (Customs)

Form I-94

Immigration

You are kindly asked to respond to the following questions (surname, name, birthdate, nationality, etc.). Please fill out only the front of the form. You are also kindly asked to keep this form in your passport. One form is necessary for every member of the family. Please fill it out using capital letters.

1. Last Name	6. Passport Number
2. Name	7. Airline and Flight Number
3. Date of Birth: Day/Month/Year	8. Place of Residence
4. Citizenship	9. City from which visa was obtained
5. Sex: Male/Female	10. Date of visa: Day/Month/Year

Chapter 12

Time Will Tell

1. Andiamo al cinema alle sei.
2. Il volo parte alle otto e venticinque di mattino.
3. La cena è alle sette.
4. C'è l'autobus per Verona a mezzogiorno.
5. Sono le quattro e quarantaquattro. (That's a mouthful, isn't it?)
6. C'è il treno per Roma alle due e trentatrè.
7. Andiamo a fare la colazione alle sette e mezzo.

Ask Away

(Cinzia)

Come ti chiami? Dove abiti? Perché sei in Italia? Cosa studi? Come viaggi? Con chi? Quanto tempo passate in Italia? Dove andate? Quando ritorni?

(Il Signore Pesce)

Come si chiama? Qual è la Sua professione? Parla l'inglese? Di dov'è Lei? Quanti figli ha? Come si chiamano i figli? Quando venite a New York?

Practice Those Conjugations

(chiedere) chiedo, chiedi, chiede, chiediamo, chiedete, chiedono
(prendere) prendo, prendi, prende, prendiamo, prendete, prendono
(prenotare) prenoto, prenoti, prenota, prenotiamo, prenotate, prenotano
(ritornare) ritorno, ritorni, ritorna, ritorniamo, ritornate, ritornano
(scendere) scendo, scendi, scende, scendiamo, scendete, scendono

What to Do, What to Do

1. facciamo: Why don't we take a spin?
2. fare: I'm going to the supermarket to do the shopping.
3. fa: The tourist takes a picture.
4. fa: The student is asking a question at the information booth.
5. fa: The child makes the bed.

Chapter 13

Room Service Please

1. Mi serve della carta da lettera.
   Vorrei la carta de lettera.
2. Mi serve la chiave.
   Vorrei la chiave.
3. Mi serve un asciugamano in più.
   Vorrei un asciugamano in più.
4. Mi serve la sveglia.
   Vorrei la sveglia.
5. Mi serve una saponetta in più.
   Vorrei una saponetta in più.

Practice Makes Perfetto

1. due coperte
2. cuscino
3. un asciugacapelli, un fon
4. chiave
5. ristoranti
6. una camera, una stanza
7. una bottiglia d'acqua minerale

Feeling Moody: The Modal Verbs

Any one of the answers given is sufficient.

1. voglio, devo, posso
2. vuoi
3. deve, vuole
4. voglio
5. vogliono, devono
6. possiamo, vogliamo, dobbiamo
7. volete
8. può
9. vuole, deve

Learning by Example

1. Avete bisogno di
2. Impari a
3. Cristoforo continua a
4. Andiamo a
5. Smetto di
6. Finiscono di

Practice Makes Perfetto II

1. voglio
2. finisce di
3. aiutano a
4. credete di
5. devi
6. fare

Chapter 14

Give Your Mind a Trip

1. b
2. e
3. f
4. b
5. a
6. g
7. d

The Dating Game

1. Il mese scorso
2. L'anno scorso
3. L'anno prossimo
4. Fra dieci anni
5. La primavera scorsa
6. L'inverno prossimo
7. Sette anni fa
8. Ieri notte
9. Ieri sera
10. Stamattina

Dating Dilemmas

1. Christmas
2. New Year's
3. Your birthday
4. Your parent's anniversary

Quando Quando Quando?

1. Il mio compleanno è ...
2. Vado in vacanza ...
3. L'anniversario dei miei è il ...

Quale Festa?

December 6: San Nicola's day
December 8: The Immaculate Conception
December 13: Santa Lucia's day
December 24: Christmas Eve

December 25: Christmas
December 26: Santo Stefano's day
January 1: New Year's day
January 6: The Epiphany

Chapter 15

Your Turn

1. trovare: trovo, trovi, trova, troviamo, trovate, trovano
2. andare: vado, vai, va, andiamo, andate, vanno
3. passare: passo, passi, passa, passiamo, passate, passano
4. fare: faccio, fai, fa, facciamo, fate, fanno
5. ritornare: ritorno, ritorni, ritorna, ritorniamo, ritornate, ritornano

Practice Makes Perfetto

1. Pasquale **fa** una passaggiata in piazza.
2. **Vado** a vedere un film.
3. **Andiamo** ad ascoltare l'opera.
4. Giuseppe e Marta **fanno** una foto del castello.
5. **Fate** un giro in macchina.
6. **Prendi** l'autobus.

Yes or No

1. mi
2. mi
3. mi
4. mi, ti
5. mi

A Refresher

1. Sono americano(a). Sono d'origine americana.
2. Sono francese. Sono d'origine francese.
3. Sono spagnolo(a). Sono d'origine spagnola.
4. Sono greco(a). Sono d'origine greca.
5. Sono irlandese. Sono d'origine irlandese.

Making Progress

1. Stiamo guardando.
2. Stai scrivendo.
3. Sta cucinando.
4. Stanno dormendo.
5. Sto leggendo.
6. Sto pulendo.

Chapter 16

Man

1. i pantaloni
2. la cintura
3. la maglia, il golf
4. le scarpe
5. l'ombrello

Woman

1. il cappotto, il giubotto
2. la sciarpo
3. la gonna
4. i guanti
5. il cappello
6. le calze
7. la borsa

Who's Who

1. La mangiamo.
2. Dante e Boccaccio vogliono mangiarla.
3. Lo prendo.
4. Mario lo scrive.
5. Li vedo.
6. La bacia.
7. La comprate.
8. La capisce?

Who's Who II

1. Desideriamo parlarvi.
2. Mario e Giorgio ti danno un regalo.
3. Carlo le telefona.
4. Lo studente gli fa una domanda.
5. Le offro un caffè.
6. I nonni danno le caramelle a loro.
7. Gli offro una birra.
8. Ci augurano una buona notte.

Who's Who—Final Round

1. Lo guardate.
2. Lo regalo a Lorenzo.
3. La vede?
4. Gli regalo un mazzo di fiori.
5. Danno i libri a loro.
6. Lo conosco molto bene.
7. Li danno ai bambini.
8. Lo accettiamo con piacere.

405

Chapter 17

Di Bocca Buona

Bere come una spugna.	To drink like a sponge.
Di bocca buona.	A good mouth (a good eater).
Una ciliegia tira l'altra.	One cherry pulls the other.
Non me ne importa un fico secco.	I don't care one dry fig's worth.
Fare la frittata.	To make an omelette of things.
Fino al midollo.	To the marrow.
Liscio come l'olio.	Smooth as oil.
Un osso duro.	A hard bone.
Dire pane al pane e vino al vino.	To call bread bread and wine wine (to call a spade a spade).
Mangiare pane e cipolla.	To eat bread and onion. (To live on bread and water.)
Togliersi il pane di bocca.	To give bread from your mouth.
Di pasta buona.	Of good pasta (good natured).
Avere lo spirito di patata.	To have a potato's sense of humor.
Essere un sacco di patate.	To be a sack of potatoes.
Fare polpette di ...	To make meatballs of ...
Rosso come un peperone.	Red as a pepper.

Some Practice

1. Sì, ne hanno. No, non ne hanno.
2. Sì, ne abbiamo. No, non ne abbiamo.
3. Sì, ne bevo. No, non ne bevo.
4. Sì, c'è ne. No, non c'è ne.

Facciamo La Spesa

l'acqua minerale
una bottiglia di vino rosso
del pane
un po' di formaggio
le olive

un po' di prosciutto
della frutta
un cavatappi
un coltello

Using the Verb Piacere

1. piace
2. piace
3. piacciono
4. piace
5. piacciono
6. piace

Using the Verb Piacere II

1. Ti piacciono i dolci?
   Sì, mi piacciono i dolci.
   No, non mi piacciono i dolci.

2. Ti piace la pasta?
   Sì, mi piace la pasta.
   No, non mi piace la pasta.

3. Ti piacciono gli spaghetti?
   Sì, mi piacciono gli spaghetti.
   No, non mi piacciono gli spaghetti.

4. Ti piacciono le acciughe?
   Sì, mi piacciono le acciughe.
   No, non mi piacciono le acciughe.

5. Ti piacciono i fichi?
   Sì, mi piacciono i fichi.
   No, non mi piacciono i fichi.

6. Ti piace il fegato?
   Sì, mi piace il fegato.
   No, non mi piace il fegato.

Minestra di Riso e Limone

Ingredients

8 cups of broth
1 cup of Arborio rice
3 egg yolks

¼ cup of grated Parmigiano-Reggiano
1 teaspoon of grated lemon rind
1 teaspoon of lemon juice

1. Place broth in pan and bring to boil point. Add the rice; cover the pan and allow it to cook for 20 minutes.

2. In the meantime, beat the eggs, add the cheese, grated lemon rind, and lemon juice.

3. When the rice is cooked, mix the eggs into the soup, beating continually. Warm the soup and serve immediately (serves four people).

Chapter 18

A Bellini Please

⅔ cup (160 ml.) of peach purée
1 teaspoon of raspberry purée
1 bottle of Prosecco (or Asti Spumante or champagne)

In every glass of wine or sparkling wine, mix 7 teaspoons of the peach purée. Add 2–3 drops of the raspberry purée. Add wine and serve immediately.

Test Your Reflexes

1. mi alzo
2. si conoscono
3. ti diverti
4. lavarsi
5. ti chiami
6. ci telefoniamo
7. si sente
8. si sposano

Chapter 19

Make a Date

1. Perché non ci incontriamo domani alle tre?
2. Ti va di nuotare?
3. Andiamo in montagna la settimana prossima.
4. Perchè non andare al museo?
5. Vuoi giocare a tennis con me?

Chapter 20

Stressful Exercise

1. te
2. sè
3. me

4. lei
5. lui
6. me, lei

Go On and Brag a Little

1. Tu sei la più bella donna del mondo.
2. Il panorama è bellissimo.
   La vista è bellissima.
3. Lui è tanto simpatico quanto bello.

4. Mi sento meglio, grazie.
5. Va in Italia quest'estate? Sì, ci vado.

Chapter 21

Tell Me Where It Hurts

1. Mi fa male il ginocchio.
2. Mi fanno male le spalle.
3. Mi fanno male i piedi.

4. Mi fa male la gola/Ho mal di gola.
5. Mi fa male il dente/Ho mal di denti.
6. Mi fa male la caviglia.

Fill in the Spazio

dire: dicevo, diceva, dicevate, dicevano
fare: facevi, faceva, facevamo, facevano
bere: bevevo, bevevi, bevevamo, bevevate

La Pratica

1. guardavo
2. eravamo, andavamo
3. lavorava, preparava
4. piaceva
5. aveva

6. abitavano
7. faceva, era
8. tornavo
9. vedevamo
10. alzava

What's Done Is Done

siamo arrivati, brillava, faceva, viaggiavamo, era, siamo andati, abbiamo visto, siamo andati

A Review

1. Scrivere

ho scritto	scrivevo
hai scritto	scrivevi
ha scritto	scriveva
abbiamo scritto	scrivevamo
avete scritto	scrivevate
hanno scritto	scrivevano

2. Spedire

ho spedito	spedivo
hai spedito	spedivi
ha spedito	spediva
abbiamo spedito	spedivamo
avete spedito	spedivate
hanno spedito	spedivano

3. Leggere

ho letto	leggevo
hai letto	leggevi
ha letto	leggeva
abbiamo letto	leggevamo
avete letto	leggevate
hanno letto	leggevano

4. Mandare

ho mandato	mandavo
hai mandato	mandavi
ha mandato	mandava
abbiamo mandato	mandavamo
avete mandato	mandavate
hanno mandato	mandavano

Chapter 22

Back to the Future

andrai, andrà, andrete, andranno

dovrai, dovrà, dovremo, dovrete, dovranno

potrai, potremo, potrete, potranno

saprai, saprà, sapremo, saprete

vedrai, vedrà, vedremo, vedranno

berrà, berremo, berrete, berranno

rimarrai, rimarrà, rimarranno

terrai, terrà, terremo, terrete, terranno

verrai, verrà, verremo, verrete

vorrai, vorrà, vorremo, vorrete, vorrano

In the Future

avrò, dovrò, dovrò comprerò andrò, vorrò, sarò, prenderò, arriveranno

Chapter 23

How's Your Italian?

Trastevere. Apartment for rent. 40 square meters. 2nd floor. Lots of light, renovated. References required. Don't waste my time.

Testaccio. Building for sale. 4 floors, 8 apartments: needs restoration. No agencies.

Via Flaminia. House for sale or rent. Total square meters 180. Shaded garden 1500 square meters. Best offer. Installment plan. Call during meal times.

Downtown. Room for rent for tourists in large apartment. Use of kitchen. Maximum stay 3 weeks—1 week deposit.

Practice Makes Perfetto

1. Vorrei andare in Italia per l'estate.
2. Dovremmo partire; è tardi.
3. Potrei venire più tardi.
4. Sofia, vorresti vedere un film?
5. Vorrei una grande casa in campagna.
6. Sarei ricco(a) con un milione di dollari.

Chapter 24

Transactions

1. Vorrei aprire un conto corrente.
2. Vorrei prendere in prestito.
3. Vorrei cambiare i soldi.
4. Vorrei incassare un assegno.
5. Vorrei depositare i soldi.
6. Vorrei ritirare i soldi.

Cara Silvia

1. stia
2. venga
3. sia
4. venga or venissi (the imperfect subjunctive)
5. sia
6. scriva
7. stia

April 1

Dear Silvia:

I hope that everything is going well.

I received your letter. I will probably come to Italy this summer. I think it's necessary for learning the language. I would be so pleased if you came with me to Sardegna. They tell me the island is very beautiful. What do you think? Do you like the idea? It's enough if you write me your response. I am happy your family is well.

Write me!

A big hug,

Paola

Cose Da Vedere

San Gimignano took its name from the Bishop of Modena who died in 387 A.D. In 1099 it became a free Township. It fought against the bishops of Volterra and bordering cities. The plague of 1348 and successive crisis brought San Gimignano to the submission of Florence in 1353.

What Am I?

The following is an adaptation of the poem, altered slightly to recreate the rhyme.

I am the beauty of the palace;
I fall on the ground without malaise;
I shine for the Grand Lord above,
I am always served with love.

What am I?—un'oliva (an olive)

Glossary

All feminine nouns (f.), irregular masculine nouns (m.), and plural (pl.) nouns are indicated. Irregular past participles are given in parentheses.

English to Italian

A

a, an: un, uno, un', una
abandon, to: abbandonare
abbey: l'abbazia (f.)
able: capace
able, to be (can): potere
aboard: bordo, a
abolish, to: abolire
about: circa
about: di
above all: soprattutto
above, on: sopra
abroad: all'estero
absolutely: assolutamente
academy: l'accademia (f.)
accent: l'accento
accept, to: accettare
access: l'accesso
accident: l'incidente (m.)
accompany, to: accompagnare
accomplish, to: compiere, superare
accountant: il/la contabile (m./f.)
achieve, to: realizzare
acoustic: acustico
acquire, to: acquistare
across: attraverso
action: l'azione (f.)
active: attivo
activity: l'attività (f.)
actor: l'attore
actress: l'attrice (f.)
ad: l' annuncio pubblicitario
add, to: aggiungere (aggiunto)
address: l'indirizzo
adjective: l'aggettivo
admire, to: ammirare
admission charge: il prezzo d'entrata
adorable: adorabile
adult: l'adulto
advance, in: in anticipo
advantage: il vantaggio
adventure: l'avventura (f.)
adverb: l'avverbio

advise, to: consigliare
aerobics: l'aerobica (f.)
affection: l'affetto
affectionate: affettuoso, affezionato
affirm, to: affermare
after: dopo
afternoon: il pomeriggio
again: ancora
against: contro
age: l'età (f.)
agency: l'agenzia (f.)
agent: l'agente (m./f.)
aggressive: aggressivo
agile: agile
ago: fa
agreement: l'accordo
agriculture: l'agricoltura (f.)
air: l'aria (f.)
air conditioning: l'aria condizionata (f.)
airplane: l'aereo
airport: l'aeroporto
alarm clock: la sveglia (f.)
alcohol: l'alcol (m.)
alcoholic: alcolico
alive: vivo
All Saint's Day (Nov. 1): Ognissanti
allergic: allergico
allergy: l'allergia (f.)
alley: il vicolo
almost: quasi
alms: l'elemosina (f.)
alone: solo
alphabet: l'alfabeto
already: già
also: anche, inoltre, pure
although: benché, sebbene
always: sempre
ambition: l'ambizione (f.)
ambulance: l'ambulanza (f.)
American: americano
amphitheater: l'anfiteatro
ample: ampio
analysis: l'analisi (f.)
ancestor: l'antenato
anchovy: l'acciuga (f.)
ancient: antico
and: e, ed (before vowels)

angry: arrabbiato
animal: l'animale (m.)
animated, lively: animato
announce, to: annunciare
answer: la risposta (f.)
antibiotics: gli antibiotici (m. pl.)
antiques: l'antiquariato
any: qualsiasi
any: qualunque
apartment: l'appartamento
aperitif: l'aperitivo
apologize, to: scusarsi
appetizer: l'antipasto
applaud, to: applaudire
apple: la mela (f.)
appreciate, to: apprezzare
approach, to: avvicinarsi
approve of, to: approvare
apricot: l'albicocca (f.)
April: aprile
aquarium: l'acquario
archeology: l'archeologia (f.)
architect: l'architetto/ l'architetta (f.)
architecture: l'architettura (f.)
area: l'area (f.)
area code: il prefisso
argue, to: discutere (discusso), litigare
aria, air, appearance: l'aria (f.)
aristocratic: aristocratico
arm: il braccio (pl. le braccia)
aroma: l'aroma (m.), l'odore (m.)
around: intorno a
arrival: l'arrivo
arrive, to: arrivare
art: l'arte (f.)
arthritis: l'artrite (f.)
artichoke: il carciofo
article: l'articolo
artist: l'artista (m./f.)
ashtray: il portacenere (m.)
ask, to: chiedere (chiesto)
aspirin: l'aspirina (f.)
assault, to: assaltare
assistance: l'assistenza (f.)
association: l'associazione (f.)
Assumption Day (August 15): Ferragosto
astrology: l'astrologia (f.)

astronaut: l'astronauta (m./f.)
at: a, in
at least: almeno
athlete: l'atleta (m./f.)
athletics: l'atletica (f.)
ATM: il Bancomat
atrium: l'atrio (m.)
attach, to: attaccare
attack: l'attacco (m.)
attention!/warning!: attenzione!
attitude: l'atteggiamento
attract, to: attirare
attribute, to: attribuire
August: agosto
aunt: la zia (f.)
Australian: australiano
Austrian: austriaco
authoritarian: autoritario
automatic: automatico
automobile: la macchina (f.),
    l'automobile (f.), l'auto (f.)
autumn: l'autunno (m.)
available: disponibile
avalanche: la valanga (f.)
avoid, to: evitare
awaken, to: svegliarsi
away: via

B

baby: il bambino
baby bottle: il biberon (m.)
bachelor: lo scapolo
back, behind: indietro
backpack: lo zaino
backward: arretrato
bacon: la pancetta (f.)
bad: male
bag: (purse) la borsa (f.)
baker: il fornaio
balcony: il balcone (m.)
ball: la palla (f.)
bank: la banca (f.)
bar: il bar (m.)
barber: il barbiere (m.)
Baroque: barocco
bartender: il/la barista (m./f.)
base: la base (f.)
basement: la cantina (f.)
basketball: la pallacanestro, il
basket
bathroom: il bagno
battery: la batteria (f.), la pila (f.)
bay: la baia (f.)
be, to: essere (stato), stare (stato)
beach: la spiaggia (f.)
bean: il fagiolo
bear: l'orso
beard: la barba (f.)

beast: la bestia (f.)
beat, to: battere
beauty: la bellezza (f.)
because: perché
bed: il letto
beef: il manzo
beer: la birra (f.)
before: prima
begin, to: iniziare, cominciare
beginning: l'inizio
behave, to: comportarsi
behavior: il comportamento
behind: dietro
believe, to: credere
bell: la campana (f.)
bell pepper: il peperone (m.)
bell tower: il campanile (m.)
belong, to: appartenere
belt: la cintura (f.)
bench: la panchina (f.)
beneath: sotto
berth: la cuccetta (f.)
beside, next to: accanto a
best: il/la migliore
best wishes!: auguri!
bet, to: scommettere
    (scommesso)
better: meglio
between: tra
beverage: la bibita (f.)
Bible: la Bibbia (f.)
big, large: grande
bill: il conto
biodegradable: biodegradabile
biology: la biologia (f.)
bird: l'uccello
birth: la nascita (f.)
birthday: il compleanno
bishop: il vescovo
bitter: amaro
black: nero
blanket: la coperta (f.)
blind: cieco
blond: biondo
blood: il sangue (m.)
blouse: la camicetta (f.)
blue: blu
boarding: l'imbarco
boat: la barca (f.)
body: il corpo
boil, to: bollire
bone: l'osso (pl. le ossa)
book: il libro
bookstore: la libreria (f.)
boot: lo stivale (m.)
border: la frontiera (f.)
boring: noioso
born, to be: nascere (nato)
boss: il padrone/la padrona (f.)
both: entrambi, tutt'e due

bottle: la bottiglia (f.)
bottom: il fondo
boulevard: il viale (m.)
box: la scatola (f.)
box (theater): il palco
boy: il ragazzo
bra: il reggiseno
bracelet: il braccialetto
brain: il cervello
brand: la marca (f.)
brass: l'ottone
bread: il pane (m.)
break, to: rompere (rotto)
breakdown: il guasto
breakfast: la prima colazione (f.)
breath: il respiro
bridge: il ponte (m.)
brief: breve
briefs: gli slip (m. pl.)
bring, to: portare
British: inglese
broadcast, to: trasmettere
    (trasmesso)
broken: rotto
bronchitis: la bronchite (f.)
bronze: il bronzo
brooch: la spilla (f.)
broth: il brodo
brother: il fratello
brother-in-law: il cognato
brown: castano, marrone
bruise: la contusione (f.), il livido
brush: la spazzola (f.)
buffoon: il buffone (m.)
build, to: costruire
building: l'edificio, il palazzo
bulletin: il bollettino
burn, to: bruciare
bus: l'autobus (m.), la corriera (f.),
    il pullman (m.)
busy: impegnato, occupato
but: ma, però
butcher: il macellaio
butcher shop: la macelleria (f.)
butter: il burro
button: il bottone (m.)
buy, to: comprare
by: da, in

C

cabin: la cabina (f.)
cable: il cavo
cable car: la funivia (f.)
cafeteria: la mensa (f.)
cake: la torta (f.)
call oneself, to: chiamarsi
call, to: chiamare
calm: calmo, sereno

calm, to: calmare
camera: la macchina fotografica (f.)
camping: il campeggio
Canadian: canadese
cancer: il cancro
candidate: il candidato
candle: la candela (f.)
candy: la caramella (f.)
canyon: il burrone (m.)
cap: il berretto
capable: capace
cape: il mantello
car: *See* automobile.
car rental: l'autonoleggio
card: la carta (f.)
care: la cura (f.)
career: la carriera (f.), il lavoro
careful: attento
carnation: il garofano
carpenter: il falegname (m.)
carrot: la carota (f.)
cash: i contanti (m. pl.)
cash register: la cassa (f.)
castle: il castello
cat: il gatto
catalogue: il catalogo
category: la categoria (f.)
cathedral: la cattedrale (f.)
Catholic: cattolico
cave: la grotta (f.)
ceiling: il soffitto
celebrate, to: celebrare, festeggiare
cemetery: il cimitero
center: il centro
central: centrale
century: il secolo
ceramic: la ceramica (f.), la terracotta (f.)
certain: certo
certificate: il certificato
chain: la catena (f.)
chair: la sedia (f.)
challenge, to: sfidare
championship: il campionato
change, to: cambiare
channel: il canale (m.)
chaotic: caotico
chapel: la cappella (f.)
character: il carattere (m.), il personaggio
characteristic: caratteristico
check: l'assegno
check, to: controllare
cheek: la guancia (f.)
cheese: il formaggio
cherry: la ciliegia (f.)
chess: gli scacchi (m. pl.)
chest: il petto

chimney: il camino
chin: il mento
China: la Cina
Chinese: cinese
chocolate: la cioccolata (f.)
choose, to: scegliere (scelto)
chorus (choir): il coro
Christian: cristiano
Christmas, Merry: Natale, Buon
church: la chiesa (f.)
cigar: il sigaro
cigarette: la sigaretta (f.)
cinema: il cinema (m.)
circle: il circolo
circus: il circo
citizen: il cittadino/la cittadina (f.)
citizenship: la cittadinanza (f.)
city: la città
civic: civico
civil: civile
class: la classe (f.)
classical: classico
classification: la classificazione (f.)
clause: la clausola (f.)
clean, to: pulire
clear: chiaro
clever: furbo (slang), intelligente
client: il/la cliente (m./f.)
cliff: la costiera (f.), la rupe (f.)
climate: il clima (m.)
cloakroom: il guardaroba
clock: l'orologio
close, to: chiudere (chiuso)
closed: chiuso
clothing: l'abbigliamento
cloud: la nuvola (f.)
coast: la costa (f.)
coat: il cappotto, il giubbotto
coffee: il caffè (m.)
coin: la moneta (f.)
cold: freddo (adj.), il raffreddore (m.)
collaborate, to: collaborare
colleague: il/la collega (m./f.)
colony: la colonia (f.)
color: il colore (m.)
comb, to: pettinare
come, to: venire
comfort: il conforto
commandment: il comandamento
communicate, to: comunicare
communism: il comunismo
community: la comunità (f.)
company: l'azienda (f.), la ditta (f.), la società (f.)
comparison: il paragone (m.)
complain, to: lamentarsi
compliment: il complimento
compose, to: comporre (composto)
composition: la composizione (f.)

concentration: la concentrazione (f.)
concept: il concetto
conception: la concezione (f.)
concert: il concerto
conclude, to: concludere (concluso)
condition: la condizione (f.)
condom: il profilattico, il preservativo
condominium: il condominio
conference: la conferenza (f.), il congresso
confess, to: confessare
conflict: il conflitto
congratulations!: congratulazioni! auguri!
conjugate, to: coniugare
conjugation: la coniugazione (f.)
connection: la coincidenza (f.)
conquest, to: conquistare
consecutive: consecutivo
consequence: la conseguenza (f.)
consider, to: considerare
console, to: consolare
consonant: la consonante (f.)
constitution: la costituzione (f.)
consumption: il consumo
contact: il contatto
contact, to: contattare
contain, to: contenere
contemporary: contemporaneo
contest: il concorso, la gara (f.)
continent: il continente (m.)
continue, to: continuare
contraceptive: il contraccettivo
contrast: il contrasto
convenient: comodo, pratico
convent: il convento
conversation: la conversazione (f.)
convince, to: convincere (convinto)
cook, to: cucinare, cuocere (cotto)
cooked: cotto
cookie: il biscotto
copper: il rame
copy: la copia (f.)
cork: il tappo
corkscrew: il cavatappi (m.)
corn: il mais (m.)
cornmeal: la polenta (f.)
correct: corretto
correct, to: correggere (corretto)
correspond, to: corrispondere (corrisposto)
cosmetics: i cosmetici (m. pl.)
cosmetics shop: la profumeria (f.)
cost: il costo, il prezzo
cost, to: costare
costly: costoso

413

costume: il costume (m.)
cotton: il cotone (m.)
cough: la tosse (f.)
count: il conte, il conto
count, to: contare
counter: il banco, lo sportello
countess: la contessa (f.)
country: la campagna (f.),
    il paese (m.)
couple: la coppia (f.)
courage: il coraggio
course: il corso
court: la corte (f.)
courteous: cortese
cousin: il cugino/la cugina (f.)
cover charge: il coperto
cow: la vacca (f.)
crazy: matto, pazzo
cream: la crema (f.), la panna (f.)
create, to: creare
creation: la creazione (f.)
credit: il credito
credit card: la carta di credito (f.)
crib: la culla (f.)
crisis: la crisi (f.)
cross: la croce (f.)
cross, to: attraversare
cross-country skiing: lo sci
    di fondo
crossing: l'incrocio
crowded: affollato
cruise: la crociera (f.)
crunchy: croccante
cry, to: piangere (pianto)
Cuban: cubano
cube: il cubo
cultivate, to: coltivare
cultural: culturale
culture: la cultura (f.)
cup: la coppa (f.), la tazza (f.)
curiosity: la curiosità (f.)
curious: curioso
curly: riccio
currency: la valuta (f.),
    la moneta (f.)
current event: l'attualità (f.)
curtain: la tenda (f.)
curve: la curva (f.)
customs: la dogana (f.)
cut, to: tagliare
cute, pretty: carino
cutlet: la braciola (f.),
    la costoletta (f.)
cycling: il ciclismo

D

daddy: papà, babbo
dairy store: la latteria (f.)

dam: la diga (f.)
damaged: danneggiato
damned: dannato
dance: il ballo, la danza (f.)
danger: il pericolo
dangerous: pericoloso
dark: il buio, scuro (adj.)
darn!: accidenti!
date: la data (f.)
daughter: la figlia (f.)
daughter-in-law: la nuora (f.)
day: il giorno, la giornata
dead: morto
deaf: sordo
dear: caro
death: la morte (f.)
December: dicembre
decide, to: decidere (deciso)
decision: la decisione (f.)
declare, to: dichiarare
decrease, to: diminuire
dedicate, to: dedicare
defect: il difetto
defend: difendere (difeso)
define, to: definire
definition: la definizione (f.)
degree: il grado (temp.), la laurea
    (f.) (diploma)
delay: il ritardo
delicious: delizioso
democracy: la democrazia (f.)
democratic: democratico
demonstrate, to: dimostrare
Denmark: la Danimarca (f.)
density: la densità (f.)
dentist: il/la dentista (m./f.)
depart, to: partire
department: il dipartimento
department store: il grande
    magazzino
departure: la partenza (f.)
depend, to: dipendere (dipeso)
descend, to (get off): scendere
    (sceso)
deserve, to: meritare
desk: la scrivania (f.)
dessert: il dolce
destination: la destinazione (f.)
destiny: il destino
destroy, to: distruggere (distrutto)
detergent: il detersivo
detour: la deviazione (f.)
develop, to: sviluppare
diabetes: il diabete (m.)
dialogue: il dialogo, il discorso
diamond: il diamante (m.)
diaper: il pannolino
diarrhea: la diarrea (f.)
dictatorship: la dittatura (f.)
diction: la dizione (f.)
dictionary: il dizionario

die, to: morire (morto)
diet: la dieta (f.)
difference: la differenza (f.)
different: differente, diverso
difficult: difficile
digest, to: digerire
digestion: la digestione (f.)
dine, to: cenare
dining room: la sala da pranzo (f.)
dinner: la cena (f.)
direct: diretto
direction: la direzione (f.),
    l'indicazione (f.)
director: il direttore/la direttrice
    (f.), il/la regista (m./f.)
dirty: sporco
discothèque: la discoteca (f.)
discount: lo sconto
discover, to: scoprire (scoperto)
discuss, to: discutere (discusso)
discussion: il discorso,
    la discussione (f.)
distance: la distanza (f.)
distinguish, to: distinguere
    (distinto)
distracted: distratto
dive: il tuffo
divide, to: dividere (diviso)
division: la divisione (f.)
divorced: divorziato
do, to: fare (fatto)
dock: il molo
doctor: il dottore/la dottoressa (f.)
    il medico
document: il documento
dog: il cane (m.)
dollar: il dollaro
dolphin: il delfino
dome: la cupola (f.), il duomo
door: la porta (f.)
doorbell: il campanello
double: doppio
down: giù
dozen: la dozzina (f.)
draw, to (design): disegnare
drawing: il disegno
dream, to: sognare
dress oneself, to: vestirsi
dress: il vestito
drink, to: bere (bevuto)
drive, to: guidare
driver's license: la patente (f.)
drown, to: annegare
drug: la droga (f.)
druggist: il droghiere
drugstore: la drogheria (f.)
drum: il tamburo
dry: asciutto, secco
dry cleaner: la lavanderia
    a secco, la tintoria (f.)

dub, to: doppiare
duchess: la duchessa (f.)
duck: l'anatra (f.)
duke: il duca (m.)
during: durante, mentre
dust: la polvere (f.)

E

each: ciascuno, ogni, ognuno
eagle: l'aquila (f.)
ear: l'orecchio
earn, to: guadagnare
earrings: gli orecchini (m. pl.)
earth: la terra (f.)
east: est, Oriente
Easter Monday: lunedì
    dell'Angelo, Pasquetta (f.)
Easter, Happy: Pasqua, Buona
easy: facile
eat, to: mangiare
eat breakfast, to: fare la prima
    colazione
eat dinner, to: cenare
eat lunch, to: pranzare
economy: l'economia (f.)
effect: l'effetto
efficient: efficiente
effort: la fatica (f.), lo sforzo
egg: l'uovo (pl. le uova)
eggplant: la melanzana (f.)
Egypt: l'Egitto
eighteen: diciotto
eighth: ottavo
eighty: ottanta
elderly: anziano
election: l'elezione (f.)
electricity: l'elettricità (f.)
elegant: elegante
element: l'elemento
elevator: l'ascensore (m.)
eleven: undici
eliminate, to: eliminare
embassy: l'ambasciata (f.)
embroider, to: ricamare
emergency: l'emergenza (f.)
emigrate, to: emigrare
empire: l'impero
empty: vuoto
end: la fine (f.)
enemy: il nemico
energetic: dinamico
engineer: l'ingegnere
England: l'Inghilterra (f.)
English: inglese
engraved: inciso
enjoy oneself, to: divertirsi
enormous: enorme
enough: abbastanza, basta!

enter, to: entrare
entrance: l'entrata (f.), l'ingresso
entrepreneur: l'imprenditore
envelope: la busta (f.)
environment: l'ambiente
Epiphany (Jan. 6): la Befana (f.),
    l'Epifania (f.)
equipped: attrezzato
error: l'errore (m.)
escape, to: scappare
essay: il saggio
essence: l'essenza (f.)
essential: essenziale
establish, to: stabilire
et cetera: eccetera
Europe: l'Europa (f.)
even: persino
evening: la sera (f.), la serata
event: l'avvenimento, l'evento
ever: mai
every: ogni
everybody: ognuno
everyone: tutti
everything, all: tutto
everywhere: dappertutto
evil: cattivo, il male
evoke, to: evocare
exact: esatto
exactly: esattamente
exaggerate, to: esagerare
exam: l'esame (m.)
exam , to: esaminare
excavate, to: scavare
excellent: eccellente, ottimo
except: eccetto
excerpt: la citazione (f.)
exchange: il cambio, lo scambio
exchange, to: scambiare
exclude, to: escludere (escluso)
excursion: l'escursione (f.),
    la gita (f.)
excuse me!: permesso!
excuse, to: scusare
exercise: la ginnastica (f.)
exist, to: esistere (esistito)
exit: l'uscita (f.)
exit, to: uscire
exotic: esotico
expense: la spesa (f.)
expensive: caro
experience: l'esperienza (f.)
expiration: la scadenza (f.)
explain, to: spiegare
explode, to: esplodere (esploso)
export, to: esportare
express: espresso
express, to: esprimere (espresso)
expression: l'espressione (f.)
eye: l'occhio (pl. gli occhi)
eyeglasses: gli occhiali (m. pl.)

F

fable: la favola (f.), la fiaba (f.)
fabric: la stoffa (f.), il tessuto
face: la faccia (f.), il viso
fact: il fatto
factory: la fabbrica (f.)
fair: la fiera (f.)
faith: la fede (f.)
fall in love, to: innamorarsi
fall, to: cadere
family: la famiglia (f.)
famous: famoso
fantasy: la fantasia (f.)
far: lontano
far-sighted: presbite
fare: la tariffa (f.)
farm: la fattoria (f.)
farmer: il contadino/
    la contadina (f.)
fascinate, to: affascinare
fascism: il fascismo
fasten, to: allacciare
fat: grasso
father: il padre (m.)
father-in-law: il suocero
faucet: il rubinetto
fear: la paura (f.)
Feast of the Assumption:
    l'Assunzione (f.)
feather: la piuma (f.)
February: febbraio
feel, to: sentirsi
feeling: il sentimento,
    la sensazione (f.)
felt: il feltro
ferry: il traghetto
fever: la febbre (f.)
fiancé: il fidanzato
fiancée: la fidanzata (f.)
field: il campo, il prato
fifteen: quindici
fifth: quinto
fifty: cinquanta
fight, to: combattere
filet: il filetto
fill out, to (a form): riempire
fill up, to (a gas tank): fare il
    pieno
film: il film (m.), la pellicola (f.)
filter: il filtro
finally: finalmente
finance: la finanza (f.)
finance, to: finanziare
find, to: trovare
fine: la multa (f.)
finger: il dito (pl. le dita)
finish, to: finire
fire: il fuoco

firefighter: il pompiere (m.),
il vigile del fuoco
fire, to: licenziare
fireplace: il caminetto
firm: fisso
first aid: pronto soccorso
first: primo
fiscal: fiscale
fish: il pesce (m.)
fish store: la pescheria (f.)
fist: il pugno
flea: la pulce (f.)
flight: il volo
floor: il pavimento, il piano
Florence: Firenze
florist: il fioraio
flour: la farina (f.)
flower: il fiore (m.)
flu: l'influenza (f.)
fly: la mosca (f.)
fly, to: volare
foam: la schiuma (f.)
fog: la nebbia (f.)
follow, to: seguire
food: il cibo
foot: il piede (m.)
for: per
foreigner: lo straniero/
la straniera (f.)
forest: la foresta (f.)
forgive, to: perdonare
fork: la forchetta (f.)
form: la forma (f.), il modulo
formal: formale
formulate, to: formulare
fortress: la fortezza (f.), la rocca (f.)
fortune: la fortuna (f.)
forty: quaranta
forward: avanti
founded: fondato
fountain: la fontana (f.)
fourteen: quattordici
fourth: quarto
fox: la volpe (f.)
fragile: fragile
France: la Francia (f.)
free: libero
free of charge: gratis
French: francese
frequent, to: frequentare
fresh: fresco
friar: il frate (m.)
Friday: venerdì
fried: fritto
friend: l'amico/l'amica (f.)
friendship: l'amicizia (f.)
frighten, to: spaventare
frog: la rana (f.)
from: di, da
fruit: la frutta (f.)

frying pan: la padella (f.)
fulfillment: l'adempimento
full: pieno
function, to: funzionare
funeral: il funerale (m.)
funny: buffo
fur: la pelliccia (f.)
furnishings: l'arredamento
furrier shop: la pelliceria (f.)
future: il futuro

G

gain weight, to: ingrassare
game: il gioco, la partita (f.)
game room: la sala giochi (f.)
garage: il garage (m.)
garden: il giardino, l'orto
garlic: l'aglio
gas pump: il distributore
di benzina
gas tank: il serbatoio
gasoline: la benzina (f.)
gate: il cancello
generous: generoso
genesis: la genesi (f.)
genre: il genere (m.)
geography: la geografia (f.)
German: tedesco
Germany: la Germania
gerund: il gerundio
get drunk, to: ubriacarsi
get on, to (climb): salire
get up, to: alzarsi
ghost: l'anima, il fantasma (m.)
gift: il regalo, il dono
girl: la ragazza (f.),
la fanciulla (f.) (Tuscany)
give, to (a present): regalare
give, to: dare
glad: contento
gladly!: volentieri!
glance: l'occhiata (f.)
glass (drinking): il bicchiere (m.)
glass (material): il vetro
gloves: i guanti (m. pl.)
go, to: andare
goat: la capra (f.)
god: il dio
goddess: la dea (f.)
godfather: il padrino
gold: l'oro
good: buono
good day: buon giorno
good: bravo
gothic: gotico
government: il governo
grace: la grazia (f.)
grade: il voto

gram: il grammo
grammar: la grammatica (f.)
granddaughter: la nipote (f.)
grandfather: il nonno
grandmother: la nonna (f.)
grandson: il nipote (m.)
grapefruit: il pompelmo
grapes: l'uva (f.)
grappa: la grappa (f.)
gravity: la gravità
gray: grigio
Greek: greco
green: verde
greengrocer's: il fruttivendolo
greet, to: salutare
grill: la griglia (f.)
grilled: alla griglia
groceries: gli alimentari (m. pl.)
ground: la terra
ground floor: il pianterreno
group: il gruppo
grow, to: crescere (cresciuto)
guarantee, to: garantire
guess, to: indovinare
guest: l'ospite (m./f.)
guide: la guida (f.)
guitar: la chitarra (f.)
gym: la palestra (f.)
gym suit: la tuta da ginnastica (f.)
gynecologist: il ginecologo/
la ginecologa (f.)

H

habit: l'abitudine (f.)
hair: il pelo
hair (on head): i capelli (m. pl.)
hair dryer: il fon (m.)
half: la metà, mezzo (adj.)
hall: la sala (f.)
ham: il prosciutto cotto
hand: la mano (f.) (pl. le mani)
handle: la maniglia (f.)
hanger: la gruccia (f.),
la stampella (f.)
happen, to: capitare, succedere
(successo)
happiness: l'allegria (f.),
la felicità (f.)
happy: allegro, felice
Happy Birthday!: Buon
Compleanno!
Happy Easter!: Buona Pasqua!
Happy Holidays!: Buone Feste!
Happy New Year!: Buon Anno!
harbor: il porto
hard: duro
haste: la fretta (f.)
hat: il cappello

hate, to: odiare
have to, to (must): dovere
have, to: avere
hazel nut: la nocciola (f.)
he: lui, egli
head: la testa (f.)
headlight: il faro
health: la salute (f.)
healthy: sano
hear, to: sentire, udire
heart: il cuore (m.)
heart attack: l'infarto
heat: il riscaldamento
heaven: il cielo, il paradiso
heavy: pesante
hectogram: l'ettogrammo
    (*abb.* l'etto)
height: l'altezza (f.)
helicopter: l'elicottero
hell: l'inferno
hello: ciao, buon giorno;
    pronto! (telephone)
helmet: il casco , l'elmetto
help!: aiuto!
help, to: aiutare
hen: la gallina (f.)
here: ecco, qua, qui
hernia: l'ernia (f.)
hide, to: nascondere (nascosto)
highway: l'autostrada (f.)
hill: la collina (f.)
hire, to: assumere (assunto)
history: la storia (f.)
hitchhiking: l'autostop (m.)
hobby: l'hobby (m.),
    il passatempo
holiday: la festa (f.)
Holland: l'Olanda
homeland: la patria (f.)
homemade: della casa,
    fatto in casa
homework: il compito
honest: onesto
honey: il miele (m.)
honeymoon: la luna di miele (f.)
honor: l'onore (m.)
hope: la speranza (f.)
hope, to: sperare
horoscope: l'oroscopo
horse: il cavallo
horse riding: l'equitazione (f.)
hospital: l'ospedale
hostel: l'ostello
hot: caldo
hotel: l'albergo, l'hotel (m.)
hour: l'ora (f.)
house: la casa (f.)
housewife: la casalinga (f.)

how: come
how much?: quanto?
however: comunque, tuttavia
hug, to: abbracciare
human: l'umano
humble: umile
humidity: l'umidità (f.)
humor: l'umore
hunger: la fame (f.)
husband: il marito
hymn: l'inno

I

I: io
ice: il ghiaccio
ice-cream: il gelato
ice-cream parlor: la gelateria (f.)
idea: l'idea (f.)
ideal: l'ideale (m.)
identification card: la carta
    d'identità (f.)
identify , to: identificare
identity: l'identità (f.)
idiom: l'idioma (f.)
idol: l'idolo
if: se
ignorant: ignorante
ignore, to: ignorare
illness: la malattia (f.)
illustrate, to: illustrare
illustration: l'illustrazione (f.)
image: l'immagine (f.)
imagination: l'immaginazione (f.)
imagine, to: immaginare
imitation: l'imitazione
immaculate: immacolato
immediately: subito
immense: immenso
immigration: l'immigrazione (f.)
imperative: l'imperativo
imperfect: l'imperfetto
import, to: importare
important: importante
impossible: impossibile
impression: l'impressione (f.)
improve, to: migliorare
in: a, in
in a hurry: in fretta
in care of (c/o): presso
in fact: infatti
in front of: davanti a
in season: della stagione
include, to: includere (incluso)
increase, to: aumentare
incredible: incredibile
indefinite: l'indefinito
independence: l'indipendenza (f.)
index: l'indice (m.)

India: l'India
Indian: indiano
indicate, to: indicare
indigestion: l'indigestione (f.)
indirect: indiretto
indispensable: indispensabile
indoor: dentro, al coperto
industry: l'industria (f.)
inexpensive: economico
infection: l'infezione (f.)
inferior: inferiore
infinitive: l'infinito
inflammation: l'infiammazione (f.)
inflation: l'inflazione (f.)
inform, to: informare
information: l'informazione (f.)
information office: l'ufficio
    informazioni
ingredient: l'ingrediente (m.)
inhabitant: l'abitante (m./f.)
injection: l'iniezione (f.),
    la puntura (f.)
injury: la ferita (f.)
inn: la pensione (f.),
    la locanda (f.)
insect: l'insetto
insect bite: la puntura (f.)
insecure: insicuro
insert, to: inserire
inside: dentro
insist, to: insistere
inspiration: l'ispirazione (f.)
instead: invece
institute: l'istituto
instruction: l'istruzione (f.)
insulin: l'insulina (f.)
insurance: l'assicurazione (f.)
insure, to: assicurare
intelligent: intelligente
intend, to: intendere (inteso)
intention: l'intenzione (f.)
interesting: interessante
intermission: l'intermezzo,
    l'intervallo
internal: interno, dentro
international: internazionale
interpret, to: interpretare
interpreter: l'interprete
interrupt, to: interrompere
    (interrotto)
interval: l'intervallo
interview: il colloquio
interview: l'intervista (f.)
introduce, to: introdurre
    (introdotto)
invitation: l'invito
invite, to: invitare
Ireland: l'Irlanda (f.)
Irish: irlandese

417

iron: il ferro (steel), il ferro da stiro
irregular: irregolare
is: è
island: l'isola (f.)
issue: la questione (f.)
issued: rilasciato
Italian: italiano
Italy: l'Italia (f.)
itinerary: l'itinerario
ivy: l'edera (f.)

J

jack (car): il cric (m.)
jacket: la giacca (f.)
jail: il carcere (m.)
January: gennaio
Japan: il Giappone
Japanese: giapponese
jeans: jeans
Jesus: Gesù
jeweler's: l'oreficeria (f.)
jewelry store: la gioielleria (f.)
Jewish: ebreo
joke: la barzelletta (f.)
joke, to: scherzare
journalist: il/la giornalista (m./f.)
joy: la gioia (f.)
judge, to: giudicare
juice: il succo
July: luglio
June: giugno
just: giusto, proprio

K

keep, to: tenere
ketchup: il ketchup
key: la chiave (f.)
kill, to: uccidere (ucciso)
kilogram: il chilogrammo (*abb.* il chilo)
kilometer: il chilometro
kind: gentile
kindergarten: l'asilo
kindness: la gentilezza (f.)
king: il re
kiss: il bacio
kiss, to: baciare
knife: il coltello
knock, to: bussare
know, to (someone): conoscere (conosciuto)
know, to (something): sapere
knowledge: la conoscenza (f.)
Kosher: Kosher

L

lace: il merletto
lack, to (be missing): mancare
lake: il lago
lamb: l'agnello
lamp: la lampada (f.)
land, to: sbarcare
landing: l'atterraggio
landlord: il padrone di casa
lane: la corsia (f.)
language: la lingua
large: grande, grosso
last: scorso, ultimo
last, to: durare
late: tardi
Latin: latino
laugh, to: ridere (riso)
laundry: il bucato
laundry service: la lavanderia (f.)
law: il Diritto, la giurisprudenza (f.) la legge (f.)
lawyer: l'avvocato
lazy: pigro
lead, to: condurre (condotto)
leaf: la foglia (f.)
learn, to: imparare
leather: il cuoio, la pelle (f.)
leave, to: partire
leave, to (behind): lasciare
left: sinistro
leg: la gamba (f.)
lemon: il limone (m.)
lemonade: la limonata (f.)
lend, to: prestare
length: la lunghezza (f.)
leopard: il leopardo
less: meno
lesson: la lezione (f.)
letter: la lettera (f.)
lettuce: la lattuga (f.)
level: il livello
liberty: la libertà (f.)
license: la patente (f.)
license plate: la targa (f.)
lie down, to: sdraiarsi
life: la vita (f.)
light: la luce (f.)
light bulb: la lampadina (f.)
light, to: accendere (acceso)
lightening flash: il lampo
line: la linea (f.)
linen: il lino
linguistics: la linguistica (f.)
lip: il labbro
liquor: il liquore (m.)
list: l'elenco
listen to, to: ascoltare

liter: il litro
literature: la letteratura (f.)
little: piccolo, (a little) un po'
live, to: abitare, vivere (vissuto)
lively: vivace
liver: il fegato
living room: il salotto, il soggiorno
load, to: caricare
loaf: la pagnotta (f.)
loan: il mutuo
lobster: l'aragosta (f.)
local: locale
lodge, to: alloggiare
logistics: la logistica (f.)
long: lungo
long-distance call: l'interurbana (f.)
look, to: guardare
lose weight, to: dimagrire
lose, to: perdere (perso)
lost and found: l'ufficio oggetti smarriti
lotion: la lozione (f.)
love: l'amore (m.)
love, to: amare
lunch: il pranzo
lung: il polmone (m.)
luxury: lusso

M

magazine: la rivista (f.)
magic: la magia (f.)
magnificent: magnifico
maid: la domestica (f.)
maiden name: il nome da nubile
mail: la posta (f.)
mail, to: inviare, spedire
mailbox: la cassetta postale (f.)
maintain, to: mantenere
majority: la maggioranza (f.)
man: l'uomo
manage, to: dirigere (diretto)
management: l'amministrazione (f.)
manager: il/la dirigente (m./f.)
manner: la maniera (f.), il modo
manufacture, to: fabbricare
map: la carta (f.), la mappa (f.)
marble: il marmo
March: marzo
marina: la marina (f.), il lido
mark, to: segnare
market: il mercato
marmalade: la marmellata (f.)
married: sposato
marry, to: sposare
marvelous: meraviglioso

masculine: maschile
mass: la messa (f.)
matches: i fiammiferi (m. pl.)
mathematics: la matematica (f.)
matrimony: il matrimonio
maximum: il massimo
May: maggio
maybe: forse
mayor: il sindaco
me: mi, a me
meadow: il prato
meal: il pasto
meaning: il significato, il senso
means: il mezzo
measure: la misura (f.)
meat: la carne (f.)
meatball: la polpetta (f.)
mechanic: il meccanico
medicine: la medicina (f.)
meet, to: incontrare
meeting: il congresso,
   la riunione (f.)
melon: il melone (m.)
mentality: la mentalità (f.)
menu: la lista (f.), il menù
merchandise: la merce (f.)
merchant: il/la mercante (m./f.)
message: il messaggio
messenger: il corriere
metal: il metallo
method: il metodo
Mexico: il Messico
Middle Ages: il Medioevo
midnight: la mezzanotte (f.)
migraine: l'emicrania (f.)
mile: il miglio (pl. le miglia)
milk: il latte (m.)
mind: la mente (f.)
minister: il ministro
minority: la minoranza (f.)
mint: la menta (f.)
minute: il minuto
mirror: lo specchio
misfortune: la disgrazia (f.)
misfortune, bad luck:
   la sfortuna (f.)
Miss, young lady: la signorina (f.)
mix, to: mischiare
model: il modello
modern: moderno
modest: modesto
mom, mother: la mamma (f.)
moment: l'attimo
moment: il momento
monastery: il monastero
Monday: lunedì
money: il denaro, i soldi (m. pl.)
money exchange office:
   l'ufficio cambio
money order: il vaglia
   postale (m.)

month: il mese (m.)
monthly: mensile
monument: il monumento
moon: la luna (f.)
more: più
more than, in addition to: oltre
morning: la mattina (f.)
morsel, nibble: il bocconcino
mosaic: il mosaico
mosquito: la zanzara (f.)
mother: la madre (f.)
mother-in-law: la suocera (f.)
motive: il motivo
motor: il motore (m.)
motorcycle: la motocicletta (f.)
mountain: la montagna (f.)
mourn, to: lamentare
mouse: il topo
mouth: la bocca (f.)
movie director: il/la regista (m./f.)
Mr.: il signore (m.)
Mrs.: la signora (f.)
much: molto
municipality: il comune (m.)
muscle: il muscolo
museum: il museo
mushroom: il fungo
music: la musica (f.)
musician: il/la musicista (m./f.)
Muslim: mussulmano
mustard: la senape (f.)
mute: muto
myth: il mito

N

name: il nome (m.)
name of spouse: il nome del
   coniuge
napkin: la salvietta (f.),
   il tovagliolo
narrative: la narrativa (f.)
nation: la nazione (f.)
nationality: la nazionalità (f.)
native language: la madrelingua
   (f.)
natural: naturale
nature: la natura (f.)
nature preserve: la riserva
   naturale (f.)
nausea: la nausea (f.)
near: vicino
near-sighted: miope
necessary: necessario
necessity: la necessità (f.)
neck: il collo
necklace: la collana (f.)
need: il bisogno
need, to: avere bisogno
negative: il negativo

neighbor: il vicino/la vicina (f.)
neighborhood: il quartiere (m.)
neither: neppure
neither … nor: né … né
nephew: il nipote
nervous: nervoso
nest: il nido
never: mai
new: nuovo
news: la notizia (f.)
news program: il telegiornale (m.)
newspaper: il giornale (m.),
   il quotidiano
newspaper vendor: il giornalaio
newsstand: l'edicola (f.)
next: prossimo
nice: simpatico
niece: la nipote
night: la notte (f.)
nightmare: l'incubo
nineteen: diciannove
ninety: novanta
ninth: nono
no entrance: vietato l'ingresso
no one: nessuno
no parking: divieto di sosta
nocturne: notturno
noisy: rumoroso
noon: mezzogiorno
normal: normale
north: nord
Norway: la Norvegia
nose: il naso
not: non
not even: neanche, nemmeno
notebook: il quaderno
nothing: niente, nulla
notwithstanding: nonostante
noun: il nome (m.)
novel: il romanzo
November: novembre
now: adesso, ora
number: il numero
nurse: l'infermiera (f.)

O

object: l'oggetto
obligation: l'obbligo
oblige, to: obbligare
obsession: la mania (f.)
obtain, to: ottenere
obvious: ovvio
occasion: l'occasione (f.)
occupy, to: occupare
ocean: l'oceano
October: ottobre
of: di
offer: l'offerta (f.)
office: l'ufficio

often: spesso
oil: l'olio
old: vecchio
olive: l'oliva (f.)
on: su
on board: a bordo
on purpose: apposta
one: uno
one hundred: cento
one-way street: senso unico
onion: la cipolla (f.)
only: solamente
open: aperto
open, to: aprire (aperto)
operation: l'operazione (f.)
opinion: l'opinione (f.)
opposite: il contrario
opposite: opposto
optician: l'ottico
or: o, oppure
orange: l'arancia (f.)
order: l'ordine (m.)
order, to: ordinare
ordinal: ordinale
oregano: l'origano
origin: l'origine (f.)
original: originale
other: altro
outdoor: all'aperto
outfit: l'abito
outside: fuori
oven: il forno
overcoat: il cappotto, il soprabito
overdone: scotto, troppo cotto
owner: il proprietario

P

package: il pacco
page: la pagina (f.)
pain: il dolore (m.)
paint: la vernice (f.)
paint, to: dipingere (dipinto)
painter: il pittore/la pittrice (f.)
painting: la pittura (f.), il quadro
pair: il paio (pl. le paia)
panorama: il panorama (m.)
pants: i pantaloni (m. pl.)
paper: la carta (f.)
paradise: il paradiso
parents: i genitori (m. pl.)
park: il parco
parking lot: il parcheggio
parsley: il prezzemolo
part: la parte (f.)
participate, to: partecipare
pass, to: passare
passing: il sorpasso
passion: la passione (f.)

passport: il passaporto
past: il passato
pasta: la pasta (f.)
pastry shop: la pasticceria (f.)
path: il sentiero, la via (f.)
paw: la zampa (f.)
pay, to: pagare
payment: il pagamento
pea: il pisello
peace: la pace (f.)
peach: la pesca (f.)
peak: il picco
peanut: la nocciolina (f.)
pear: la pera (f.)
pedagogy: la didattica (f.)
pen: la penna (f.)
penalty: la multa (f.), la pena (f.)
pencil: la matita (f.)
peninsula: la penisola (f.)
people: la gente (f.)
pepper: il pepe (m.)
percentage: il percento,
   la percentuale (f.)
perception: la percezione (f.)
perfume: il profumo
period: il periodo, il punto
permit, to: permettere (permesso)
person: la persona (f.)
pharmacy: la farmacia (f.)
phase: la fase (f.)
philosophy: la filosofia (f.)
phonetics: la fonetica (f.)
photocopy: la fotocopia (f.)
photograph: la fotografia (f.)
phrase: la frase (f.)
physics: la fisica (f.)
pie: la torta (f.)
piece: il pezzo
piece of furniture: il mobile (m.)
pig: il maiale
pill: la pillola (f.)
pillow: il cuscino
pink: rosa
pistol: la pistola (f.)
place: il locale (m.), il luogo,
   il posto
plain: la pianura (f.)
plan: il programma (m.)
planet: il pianeta (m.)
plant: la pianta (f.)
plastic: la plastica (f.)
plate: il piatto
plateau: l'altopiano
play, to: giocare
play, to (an instrument): suonare
please: per favore, per piacere
please hold!: attendere prego!
please, to (to like): piacere
   (piaciuto)
pleasing: piacevole

pleasure: il piacere (m.)
plural: plurale (m.)
pocket: la tasca (f.)
poem, poetry: la poesia (f.)
poet: il poeta (m.), la poetessa (f.)
poison: il veleno
police: la polizia (f.)
police headquarters:
   la questura (f.)
police officer: il carabiniere (m.),
   il poliziotto, il vigile
political party: il partito
politics: la politica (f.)
polluted: inquinato
pollution: l'inquinamento
pond: lo stagno
poor: povero
Pope: il Papa (m.)
population: la popolazione (f.)
pork: il maiale (m.), il porco
portion: la porzione (f.)
portrait: il ritratto
Portugal: Portogallo
position: la posizione (f.)
possibility: la possibilità
possible: possibile
post office: l'ufficio postale
postage stamp: il francobollo
postal carrier: il postino
postcard: la cartolina (f.)
potato: la patata (f.)
poultry: il pollame (m.)
poverty: la miseria (f.),
   la povertà (f.)
practice: la pratica (f.)
praise, to: lodare
pray, to: pregare
prayer: la preghiera (f.)
precise: preciso
prefer, to: preferire
preference: la preferenza (f.)
pregnant: incinta
prepare, to: preparare
prescription: la ricetta (f.)
present: il presente
present, to: presentare
preservatives: i conservanti
   (m. pl.)
president: il presidente
price: il prezzo
priest: il prete (m.)
prince: il principe (m.)
princess: la principessa (f.)
principal: principale
print: la stampa (f.)
printing: la tipografia (f.)
prison: il carcere (m.),
   la prigione (f.)
private property: la proprietà
   privata (f.)

problem: il problema (m.)
produce, to: produrre (prodotto)
product: il prodotto
production: la produzione (f.)
profession: la professione (f.)
professor: il professore/
   la professoressa (f.)
progress: il progresso
progressive: progressivo
prohibited: vietato, proibito
prohibition: il divieto,
   la proibizione (f.)
project: il progetto
promise, to: promettere
   (promesso)
pronoun: il pronome (m.)
pronounce, to: pronunciare
pronunciation: la pronuncia (f.)
propose, to: proporre (proposto)
protect, to: proteggere (protetto)
Protestant: protestante
proud: orgoglioso
proverb: il proverbio
provided that: purché
psychology: la psicologia (f.)
public: il pubblico
publicity: la pubblicità (f.)
pull, to: tirare
punctual: puntuale
pupil: l'allievo, lo scolaro
pure: puro
purple: viola
purse: la borsa (f.)
push, to: spingere (spinto)
put, to: mettere (messo)
pyramid: la piramide (f.)

Q

quality: la qualità (f.)
quantity: la quantità (f.)
queen: la regina (f.)
question, to: domandare
quickly, early: presto
quit, to: smettere (smesso)
quote, to: citare

R

Rabbi: il rabbino
rabbit: il coniglio
race: la corsa (f.)
racket: la racchetta (f.)
radiator: il radiatore (m.)
radio: la radio (f.)
rail car: il vagone (m.)
railroad: la ferrovia (f.)
rain: la pioggia (f.)

rain, to: piovere
raincoat: l'impermeabile (m.)
raise, to: alzare
rare: raro, al sangue
rarely: raramente
raspberry: il lampone (m.)
rather: piuttosto
raw: crudo
razor: il rasoio
read, to: leggere (letto)
ready: pronto
really: davvero, veramente
receipt: la ricevuta (f.),
   lo scontrino
receive, to: ricevere
recent: recente
reception: il ricevimento
recipe: la ricetta (f.)
recite, to: recitare
record: il disco
red: rosso
reflect, to: riflettere (riflesso)
reflexive: il riflessivo
refreshment: la bevanda (f.)
refrigerator: il frigorifero
refuge: il rifugio
refund: il rimborso
region: la regione (f.)
regret, to (to be sorry):
   dispiacersi (dispiaciuto)
relationship: il rapporto
relative: il/la parente (m./f.)
relaxing: rilassante
religion: la religione (f.)
remain, to: rimanere (rimasto)
remainder: il resto
remember, to: ricordare
Renaissance: il Rinascimento
render, to: rendere (reso)
rent: l'affitto
rent, to: affittare, noleggiare
repair, to: riparare
repeat, to: ripetere
report: la cronaca (f.), il rapporto
represent, to: rappresentare
reptile: il rettile (m.)
republic: la repubblica (f.)
request: la richiesta (f.)
reservation: la prenotazione (f.)
reserve, to: prenotare
reserved: riservato
reservoir: la riserva d'acqua (f.)
residence: il domicilio,
   la residenza (f.)
resident: l'abitante (m./f.)
resign, to: licenziarsi
resistance: la resistenza (f.)
resolve, to: risolvere (risolto)
respect, to: rispettare
respond, to: rispondere (risposto)

responsible: responsabile
restaurant: il ristorante (m.)
result: il risultato
return, to: ritornare, tornare
revision: la revisione (f.)
rheumatism: il reumatismo
rhythm: il ritmo
rib: la costola (f.)
rice: il riso
rich: ricco
riddle: l'indovinello
right: destro
right (legal): il diritto
ring: l'anello
ripe: maturo
river: il fiume (m.)
roasted: arrosto
robbery: la rapina (f.)
rock: la pietra (f.), la roccia (f.)
roll of film: il rullino
romantic: romantico
roof: il tetto
room: la camera (f.), la stanza (f.)
root: la radice (f.)
rope: la corda (f.)
rose: la rosa (f.)
round-trip (ticket): il biglietto
   d'andata e ritorno
route: il percorso, la via
row: la fila (f.)
ruckus: il baccano
ruins: le rovine (f. pl.)
run, to: correre (corso)
rush hour: l'ora di punta (f.)
Russia: la Russia (f.)
Russian: russo

S

sad: triste
safe: sicuro
sailboat: la barca a vela (f.)
saint: il santo/la santa (f.)
salad: l'insalata (f.)
salary: il salario
sale: i saldi (m. pl.), la svendita (f.)
sales clerk: il commesso/
   la commessa (f.)
salmon: il salmone (m.)
salt: il sale (m.)
same: stesso
sand: la sabbia (f.)
sandwich: il panino
Saturday: sabato
sauce: la salsa (f.)
saucepan: la casseruola (f.),
   il tegame (m.)
sausage: la salsiccia (f.)
say, to: dire (detto)

scarf: la sciarpa (f.)
scene: la scena (f.)
schedule: l'orario, la tabella (f.)
school: la scuola (f.)
science: la scienza (f.)
science fiction: la fantascienza (f.)
scissors: le forbici (f. pl.)
scooter: il motorino
Scotland: la Scozia
screwdriver: il cacciavite (m.)
sculpture: la scultura (f.)
sea: il mare (m.)
sea shell: la conchiglia (f.)
search, to: cercare
season: la stagione (f.)
seat: il posto, il sedile
seat belt: la cintura di
    sicurezza (f.)
second: secondo
secretary: il segretario/
    la segretaria (f.)
sedative: il sedativo
see you later!: arrivederci!
    ci vediamo!
see, to: vedere (visto)
seem, to: sembrare
sell, to: vendere
semester: il semestre (m.)
Senate: il Senato
send, to: inviare, mandare,
    spedire
sender: il/la mittente (m./f.)
sensation: la sensazione (f.)
sentence: la frase (f.)
sentiment: il sentimento
separate, to: separare
separated: separato
September: settembre
serenade: la serenata (f.)
serious: grave, serio
service: il servizio
set: fisso, fissato
set, to: apparecchiare
seventeen: diciassette
seventh: settimo
seventy: settanta
severe: severo
sex: il sesso
sexuality: la sessualità
shadow: l'ombra (f.)
shame: la vergogna (f.)
share, to: condividere (condiviso)
shave, to: radersi
she: lei, ella
sheet: il lenzuolo
sheet of paper: il foglio
shingle: la tegola (f.)
ship: la nave (f.)
shirt: la camicia (f.)
shoe: la scarpa (f.)

shoe repair: il calzolaio
shoe store: la calzoleria (f.)
shop: la bottega (f.), il negozio
shop window: la vetrina (f.)
short: basso, corto
shorten, to: accorciare
shorts: i calzoncini (m. pl.)
shout, to: gridare, urlare
show: lo spettacolo, la mostra (f.)
    (art)
shower: la doccia (f.)
shrimp: il gambero
shy: timido
Sicilian: siciliano
Sicily: la Sicilia
sick: ammalato
side: il lato, il fianco
side dish: il contorno
sidewalk: il marciapiede (m.)
sign: il cartello, il segno
signal: il segnale (m.)
signature: la firma (f.)
signify, to: significare
silence: il silenzio
silk: la seta (f.)
silver: l'argento
simple: semplice
since: poiché, da quando
sincere: sincero
sing, to: cantare
singer: il/la cantante (m./f.)
single: singolo
single room: il monolocale (m.)
singular: singolare
sink: il lavandino
sister: la sorella (f.)
sister-in-law: la cognata (f.)
sit, to: sedersi
situation: la situazione (f.)
sixteen: sedici
sixty: sessanta
size: la misura (f.), la taglia (f.)
sketch: lo schizzo
ski, to: sciare
skiing: lo sci (m.)
skirt: la gonna (f.)
sky: il cielo
sled: lo slittino
sleep: il sonno
sleep, to: dormire
sleeping bag: il sacco a pelo
sleeping pill: il sonnifero
slender: magro, snello
slide: la diapositiva (f.)
slope: la pista (f.), la discesa (f.)
slow down: rallentare
small: piccolo
small bag: il sacchetto
smell, to: odorare, sentire
smile, to: sorridere (sorriso)

smoke, to: fumare
snack: lo spuntino
snake: il serpente (m.)
snob: lo snob
snow: la neve (f.)
so: così
so-so: così così
soap: il sapone (m.)
soccer: il calcio, il football
soccer player: il calciatore (m.)
socks: le calze (f. pl.), i calzini
    (m. pl.)
sofa: il divano
soft: soffice
sold out: esaurito
soldier: il soldato
some: alcuni/alcune, qualche
some of: ne
someone: qualcuno
something: qualcosa
sometimes: qualche volta,
    talvolta
son: il figlio
son-in-law: il genero
soon: subito, presto
soul: l'anima (f.)
soup: la minestra (f.), la zuppa (f.)
south: sud
space: lo spazio
Spain: la Spagna (f.)
Spanish: spagnolo
sparkling wine: lo spumante (m.)
special: speciale
spend, to: spendere (speso)
spice: la spezia (f.)
spicy: piccante
spider: il ragno
spirit: l'anima, lo spirito
spiritual: spirituale
splendid: splendido
spoiled: guasto, rovinato
sponge: la spugna (f.)
spoon: il cucchiaio
sport: lo sport (m.)
sports ground: il campo sportivo
spouse: lo sposo/la sposa (f.)
spring: la sorgente (f.),
    la primavera (f.) (season)
squid: i calamari (m. pl.)
stadium: lo stadio
stage: il palcoscenico
stain: la macchia (f.)
stairs: la scala (f.), le scale (f. pl.)
stall: la bancarella (f.)
star: la stella (f.)
state: lo stato
statement: l'affermazione (f.)
station: la stazione (f.)
stationery store: la cartoleria (f.)
statue: la statua (f.)

steak: la bistecca (f.)
steal, to: rubare
steel: l'acciaio
step: il passo
stepfather: il patrigno
stepsister: la sorellastra (f.)
stewardess: la hostess (f.)
still (again): ancora
stingy: avaro, tirchio
stitch: il punto
stockings: le calze (f. pl.), i collant
stomach: lo stomaco, la pancia
stone: la pietra (f.), il sasso
stop: la fermata (f.)
stop, to: fermare
storm: la tempesta (f.)
story: la storia (f.)
stove: la stufa (f.)
straight: diritto
strange: strano
straw: la cannuccia (f.), il fieno
  (hay)
strawberry: la fragola (f.)
stream: il rio
stream: il ruscello
street: la strada (f.), la via (f.)
stress: lo stress
stress, to: stressare
strike: lo sciopero
stroll, to: passeggiare
strong: forte
struggle: la lotta (f.)
student: lo studente/
  la studentessa (f.)
study: lo studio
study, to: studiare
stuff: la roba (f.)
stuffed: ripieno
stupendous: stupendo
stupid: stupido
subject: la materia (f.),
  il soggetto
subscription: l'abbonamento
substitute, to: sostituire
subtitle: il sottotitolo
suburbs: la periferia (f.)
subway: la metropolitana (f.)
succeed, to: riuscire
such: tale
suffer, to: soffrire (sofferto)
suffice, to: bastare
sugar: lo zucchero
suit: l'abito, il vestito
suitable: adatto
summer: l'estate (f.)
sun: il sole (m.)
Sunday: domenica
sunrise: l'alba (f.)
sunset: il tramonto
supermarket: il supermercato
sure: sicuro

surgery: la chirurgia (f.)
surgeon: il chirurgo/la chirurga (f.)
surname: il cognome (m.),
  il nome di famiglia
surprise: la sorpresa (f.)
surprise, to: sorprendere
  (sorpreso)
surround, to: circondare
swallow: la rondine (f.)
swallow, to: inghiottire
swamp: la palude (f.)
swear, to: giurare
sweater: la maglia (f.)
Sweden: la Svezia (f.)
sweet: dolce
swim, to: nuotare
swimming pool: la piscina (f.)
Switzerland: la Svizzera
symbol: il simbolo
symphony: la sinfonia (f.)
symptom: il sintomo
synagogue: la sinagoga (f.)
synthetic: sintetica
system: il sistema (m.)

T

table: il tavolo (restaurant),
  la tavola
tablecloth: la tovaglia (f.)
tablet: la compressa (f.)
tag: l'etichetta (f.)
tailor: il sarto
take, to: prendere (preso)
tall: alto
tan, to: abbronzarsi
tape: l'adesivo, il nastro
task: il compito, l'impegno
taste: il gusto, il sapore (m.)
taste, to: assaggiare
tax: la tassa (f.)
taxi: il tassì
taxi meter: il tassametro
tea: il tè (m.)
teach, to: insegnare
teacher: l'insegnante (m./f.)
team: la squadra (f.)
telephone: il telefono
telephone call: la telefonata (f.)
telephone card: la carta
  telefonica (f.)
telephone, to: telefonare
tell, to: dire (detto), raccontare
temple: il tempio
tender: tenero
tent: la tenda (f.)
tenth: decimo
terrace: il terrazzo
thank you!: grazie!
thank, to: ringraziare

that: quello/quella
that which: ciò, quel che
theater: il teatro
theme: il tema (m.)
then: allora, poi
there: ci, lì/là
there is: c'è
therefore: perciò, quindi
thermometer: il termometro
they: loro
thief: il ladro
thin: magro
thing: la cosa (f.)
think, to: pensare
third: terzo
thirst: la sete (f.)
thirteen: tredici
thirty: trenta
this: questo
this evening: stasera
this morning: stamattina
thought: il pensiero
thousand: mille (pl. mila)
three: tre
throw, to: buttare
thunder: il tuono
Thursday: giovedì
thus: dunque
ticket: il biglietto
ticket counter: la biglietteria (f.)
tide: la marea (f.)
tie: la cravatta (f.)
tie, to: legare
tight: stretto
tile: la piastrella (f.)
time: l'ora (f.), il tempo
tip: la mancia (f.)
tire: il pneumatico
tired: stanco
tissue: il fazzoletto
to: a, in
tobacco shop: la tabaccheria (f.)
today: oggi
toe: il dito (pl. le dita)
together: insieme
toilet: il gabinetto, la toilette (f.)
toilet paper: la carta igienica (f.)
token: il gettone (m.)
tolerance: la tolleranza (f.)
toll: il pedaggio
toll-free number: il numero
  verde
tomato: il pomodoro
tomorrow: domani
tongue: la lingua (f.)
tonight: stanotte
too: troppo
tooth: il dente (m.)
toothbrush: lo spazzolino
  da denti
toothpaste: il dentifricio

423

topic: l'argomento, il soggetto
total: totale
touch, to: toccare
tour: il giro
tourism: il turismo
tourist: il/la turista (m./f.)
toward: verso
tower: la torre (f.)
town square: la piazza (f.)
toy: il giocattolo
track: il binario
tradition: la tradizione (f.)
traffic: il traffico
traffic light: il semaforo
tragic: tragico
train: il treno
transfer, to: trasferirsi
transform, to: trasformare
translate, to: tradurre (tradotto)
translation: la traduzione (f.)
transport, to: trasportare
trash: i rifiuti (m. pl.)
trash can: il bidone della
    spazzatura
travel, to: viaggiare
tree: l'albero
tremendous: tremendo
trip: il viaggio
tropical: tropicale
trouble: il guaio
truck: il camion (m.)
true: vero
trust: la fiducia (f.)
trust, to: fidarsi
truth: la verità (f.)
try, to: provare
tub: la vasca (f.)
Tuesday: martedì
tulip: il tulipano
tunnel: la galleria (f.),
    il sotterraneo
turn: il turno
turn off, to: spegnere (spento)
twelve: dodici
twenty: venti
two: due
type, kind: la specie (f.), il tipo

U

ugly: brutto
umbrella: l'ombrello
uncle: lo zio
uncomfortable: scomodo
understanding: la comprensione
    (f.)
understood!: capito!
underwear: la biancheria
    intima (f.)
unemployed: disoccupato

unfortunately: purtroppo
unhealthy: malato
unified: unificato
unique: unico
united: unito
United States: gli Stati Uniti
    (m. pl.)
unmarried: celibe (m.), nubile (f.)
unpleasant: antipatico, spiacevole
until: fino a
unusual: insolito
urgent: urgente
usage: l'uso
use, to: usare
useless: inutile
usual: solito

V

vacation: la vacanza (f.)
vaccination: la vaccinazione (f.)
vacuum cleaner: l'aspirapolvere
    (m.)
validate, to: convalidare
validated: convalidato
validity: la validità
valise: la valigia (f.)
valley: la valle (f.)
value: il valore (m.)
variation: la variazione (f.)
variety: la varietà (f.)
various: vario
vase: il vaso
VAT/sales tax: I.V.A. (Imposta
    Valore Aggiunto)
veal: il vitello
vegetables: la verdura (f.)
vegetarian: vegetariano
vehicle: il veicolo
velocity: la velocità
vengeance: la vendetta (f.)
verb: il verbo
very: molto
victim: la vittima (f.)
view: la vista (f.)
villa: la villa (f.)
village: il villaggio
vine: la vigna (f.)
vinegar: l'aceto
violence: la violenza (f.)
violet: la violetta (f.)
visible: visibile
visit: la visita (f.)
visit, to: visitare
vitamin: la vitamina (f.)
vocabulary: il vocabolario
voice: la voce (f.)
volleyball: la pallavolo (f.)
vote, to: votare
vowel: la vocale (f.)

W

wait, to: aspettare
waiter: il cameriere
waiting room: la sala d'attesa (f.)
waitress: la cameriera (f.)
walk, to: camminare, passeggiare
wall: il muro, la parete (f.)
wallet: il portafoglio
walnut: la noce (f.)
want, to: volere
war: la guerra (f.)
warm: caldo
warm, to: riscaldare
warn, to: avvertire
warning: l'avviso
wash, to: lavare
wasp: la vespa (f.)
watch: l'orologio
water: l'acqua (f.)
wave: l'onda (f.)
we: noi
weak: debole
wear, to: indossare, portare
weather: il tempo
Wednesday: mercoledì
week: la settimana (f.)
weekend: il fine settimana
weigh, to: pesare
weight: il peso
welcome! greetings!: benvenuto!
well (adv.): bene
well: il pozzo
west: ovest, l'Occidente
wet: bagnato
what: che, che cosa
wheel: la ruota (f.)
when: quando
where: dove
wherever: ovunque
which: quale
while: mentre
whistle, to: fischiare
white: bianco
who: chi
wholesale: all'ingrosso
why: perché
wide: largo
widespread: diffuso
widow: la vedova (f.)
widower: il vedovo
wife: la moglie (f.)
wild: selvaggio, selvatico
willing: disposto
win, to: vincere (vinto)
wind: il vento
window: la finestra (f.),
    il finestrino
windshield: il parabrezza (m.)

wine: il vino
wine bar: l'enoteca (f.)
winery: l'azienda vinicola (f.)
winter: l'inverno
wise: saggio
wish: il desiderio, la voglia (f.)
witch: la strega (f.)
with: con
within: fra
without: senza
wolf: il lupo
woman: la donna (f.),
    la femmina (f.),
    la signora (f.)
wood: il legno
woods: il bosco, la selva (f.)
wool: la lana (f.)
work: il lavoro
work, to: lavorare
worker: l'impiegato, l'operaio
world: il mondo
worm: il baco
worried: preoccupato
worry, to: preoccuparsi
worse: peggio
wrap, to: incartare
write, to: scrivere (scritto)
writer: lo scrittore/
    la scrittrice (f.)
wrong: il torto
wrong, to be: sbagliare

X–Y

x-ray: la radiografia (f.)

yawn, to: sbadigliare
year: l'anno
yell, to: gridare
yellow: giallo
yes: sì
yesterday: ieri
yoga: lo yoga (m.)
yogurt: lo yogurt (m.)
you: Lei (polite), tu (familiar),
    voi (plural)
you are welcome!: prego!
young: giovane

Z

zero: zero
zipper: la cerniera (f.)
zone: la zona (f.)
zoo: lo zoo

Italian to English

A

a, ad (before vowels): at, in,
    to, by
a bordo: on board
abbandonare: to abandon
abbastanza: enough
l'abbazia (f.): abbey
l'abbigliamento: clothing
l'abbonamento: subscription
abbracciare: to hug
abbronzarsi: to get tanned
l'abitante (m./f.): resident,
    inhabitant
abitare: to live
l'abito: outfit, suit
l'abitudine (f.): habit
abolire: to abolish
l'accademia (f.): academy
accanto a: beside, next to
accendere (acceso): to light,
    to turn on
l'accento: accent
l'accesso: access
accettare: to accept
l'acciaio: steel
accidenti!: darn!
l'acciuga (f.): anchovy
accompagnare: to accompany
accorciare: to shorten
accordo: agreement
l'aceto: vinegar
l'acqua (f.): water
acqua non potabile: do not
    drink water
l'acquario: aquarium
acquistare: to acquire
acustico: acoustic
adatto: suitable, appropriate
l'adempimento: fulfillment
adesso: now
adorabile: adorable
l'adulto: adult
l'aereo: airplane
l'affare (m.): business, deal
l'aeroporto: airport
affascinare: to fascinate
affermare: to affirm, to assert
l'affermazione (f.): statement
l'affetto: affection
affettuoso: affectionate
affittare: to rent
affittasi: for rent
l'affitto: rent
affollato: crowded
l'agente (m./f.): agent
l'agenzia (f.): agency

l'aggettivo: adjective
aggiungere (aggiunto): to add
aggressivo: aggressive
agile: agile
l'aglio: garlic
l'agnello: lamb
agosto: August
l'agricoltura (f.): agriculture
aiutare: to help
aiuto!: help!
al coperto: indoor
al forno: grilled
al sangue: rare
l'alba (f.): sunrise
l'albergo: hotel
l'albero: tree
l'albicocca (f.): apricot
l'alcol: alchohol (m.)
alcolico: alcoholic
alcuni/alcune: some
l'alfabeto: alphabet
gli alimentari (m. pl.): groceries
all'aperto: outdoor, open air
allacciare: to fasten, to buckle
l'allegria (f.): happiness
allegro: happy
allenarsi: to train (sports)
l'allergia (f.): allergy
allergico: allergic
l'allievo: pupil
alloggiare: to lodge
allora: then
almeno: at least
altezza (f.): height
alto: tall
l'altopiano: plateau
altro: other
alzare: to raise, lift
alzarsi: to get up
amare: to love
amaro: bitter
l'ambasciata (f.): embassy
l'ambiente: environment (m.)
l'ambizione: ambition
l'ambulanza (f.): ambulance
americano: American
l'amicizia (f.): friendship
l'amico/l'amica (f.): friend
ammalato: sick, ill
l'amministrazione (f.): manage-
    ment, administration
ammirare: to admire
l'amore (m.): love
ampio: ample
l'anatra (f.): duck
l'analisi (f.): analysis
anche: also
ancora: still, again, yet
andare: to go
andata e ritorno: round-trip
    (ticket)

l'anello: ring
l'anfiteatro: amphitheater
l'anima (f.): spirit
l'animale (m.): animal
animato: animated, lively
annegare: to drown
l'anno: year
l'anno bisestile: leap year
annoiarsi: to get bored
annunciare: to announce
l'antenato: ancestor
gli antibiotici (m. pl.): antibiotics
antico: ancient, antique
l'antipasto: appetizer
antipatico: unpleasant, disagreeable
l'antiquariato: antiques
anzi: and even, but rather
anziano: elderly
l'aperitivo: aperitif
aperto: open, (all'aperto) outside
apparecchiare: to set
appartamento: apartment
appartenere: to belong
applaudire: to applaud
apposta: on purpose, deliberately
apprezzare: to appreciate
approvare: to approve of
aprile: April
aprire (aperto): to open
l'aquila (f.): eagle
l'aragosta (f.): lobster
l'arancia (f.): orange
l'archeologia (f.): archeology
l'architettura (f.): architecture
l'area (f.): area
l'argento: silver
l'argomento: topic, subject
l'aria (f.): aria, air, appearance
l'aria condizionata (f.): air conditioning
aristocratico: aristocratic
l'aroma (f.): aroma
arrabbiarsi: to get angry
arrabbiato: angry
l'arredamento: furnishings
arretrato: backward
arrivare: to arrive
arrivederci!: see you later!
l'arrivo: arrival
arrosto: roasted
l'arte (f.): art
l'articolo: article
l'artista (m./f.): artist
l'artrite (f.): arthritis
l'ascensore (m.): elevator
asciutto: dry
ascoltare: to listen to
l'asilo: kindergarten, day-care center

aspettare: to wait for
l'aspirapolvere (m.): vacuum cleaner
l'aspirina (f.): aspirin
assaggiare: to taste
assaltare: to assault
l'assegno: check
assicurare: to ensure, insure
l'assicurazione (f.): insurance
l'assistenza (medica) (f.): assistance, insurance (health)
l'associazione (f.): association
assolutamente: absolutely
assumere (assunto): to hire, to assume
l'Assunzione (f.): Feast of the Assumption
l'astrologia (f.): astrology
l'astronauta (m./f.): astronaut
l'atleta (m./f.): athlete
l'atletica: athletics
l'atrio (m.): atrium
attaccare: to attach, to attack
l'attacco (m.): attack
l'atteggiamento: attitude
attendere prego!: please hold!
attento: careful, attentive
attenzione!: attention! warning!
l'atterraggio: landing
l'attimo: moment
attirare: to attract
l'attività (f.): activity
attivo: active
l'atto: document, record
l'attore: actor
attraversare: to cross
attraverso: across
attrezzato: equipped
attribuire: to attribute
l'attrice (f.): actress
attuale: actual, current
l'attualità (f.): current event
auguri!: best wishes!
aumentare: to increase
australiano: Australian
austriaco: Austrian
l'autobus (m.): bus
automatico: automatic
l'automobile (f.) (*abb.* auto): car
l'autonoleggio: car rental
l'autore: author
autoritario: authoritarian
l'autostop (m.): hitchhiking
l'autostrada (f.): highway
l'autunno (m.): autumn
avanti: forward
avaro: stingy
avere: to have
l'avvenimento (m.): event
avvenire: to happen

l'avventura (f.): adventure
l'avverbio (m.): adverb
avvertire: to warn
avvicinarsi: to approach, to get near
l'avvocato: lawyer
l'azienda (f.): firm, company
l'azione (f.): action
azzurro: light blue

B

il babbo: dad
il baccano: ruckus
baciare: to kiss
il bacio: kiss
il baco: worm
bagnato: wet
il bagno: bath
la baia (f.): bay
il balcone (m.): balcony
il ballo: dance
il bambino: baby, child
la banca (f.): bank
la bancarella (f.): stall, booth
il banco: counter
il Bancomat: ATM
il bar (m.): bar, café
la barba (f.): beard
il barbiere (m.): barber
la barca (f.): boat
la barca a vela (f.): sailboat
il/la barista (m./f.): bartender
barocco: Baroque
la barzelletta (f.): joke
la base (f.): base
basso: short, low
bastare: to be enough, to suffice
battere: to beat
la batteria (f.): battery
la bellezza (f.): beauty
benché: although
bene: well
benvenuto!: welcome! greetings!
la benzina (f.): gasoline
bere (bevuto): to drink
il berretto: cap
la bestia (f.): beast
la bevanda (f.): refreshment
la biancheria intima (f.): underwear
bianco: white
la Bibbia (f.): Bible
il biberon (m.): baby bottle
la bibita (f.): refreshment, beverage
il bicchiere (m.): glass
la biglietteria (f.): ticket counter
il biglietto: ticket
il binario: track, platform

biodegradabile: biodegradable
la biologia (f.): biology
biondo: blond
la birra (f.): beer
il biscotto: cookie
bisognare: to be necessary
la bistecca (f.): steak
blu: blue
la bocca (f.): mouth
il bocconcino: morsel, nibble
il bollettino: bulletin, news
bollire: to boil
bordo, a: aboard
la borsa (f.): bag, purse
la borsetta (f.): purse, bag
il bosco: woods
la bottega (f.): shop
la bottiglia (f.): bottle
il bottone (m.): button
il braccialetto: bracelet
il braccio; le braccia (pl.): arm
bravo: good, able
la braciola (f.): cutlet
breve: brief, short
la brioche (f.): brioche, croissant
britannico: British
il brodo: broth
la bronchite (f.): bronchitis
il bronzo: bronze
bruciare: to burn
bruno: brown haired
brutto: ugly
il bucato: laundry
buffo: funny
il buffone (m.): buffoon, clown, fool
il buio: dark
Buon Anno!: Happy New Year!
Buon Compleanno!: Happy Birthday!
Buon giorno!: Good day, hello!
Buon Natale!: Merry Christmas!
Buona Feste!: Happy Holidays!
Buona Pasqua!: Happy Easter!
buono: good
il burro: butter
il burrone (m.): canyon
bussare: to knock
la busta (f.): envelope
la bustina (f.): bag
buttare: to throw

C

c'è: there is
la cabina (f.): cabin
il cacciavite (m.): screwdriver
cadere: to fall
il caffè (m.): coffee, café

i calamari (m. pl.): squid
il calciatore (m.): soccer player
il calcio : soccer, kick
caldo: heat, hot (adj.)
calmare: to calm
le calze (f. pl.): stockings
i calzini (m. pl.): socks
il calzolaio: shoe repair
la calzoleria (f.): shoe store
i calzoncini (m. pl.): shorts
cambiare: to change, to exchange
il cambio: exchange
la camera (f.): room
la cameriera (f.): waitress, maid
il cameriere: waiter
la camicetta (f.): blouse
la camicia (f.): shirt
il caminetto: fireplace
il camino: chimney
il camion (m.): truck
camminare: to walk
la campagna (f.): country, countryside
la campana (f.): bell
il campanello: doorbell
il campanile (m.): bell tower
il campeggio: camping
il campionato: match, championship
il campo: field
il campo sportivo: sports ground
canadese: Canadian
il canale (m.): channel
il cancello: gate
il cancro: cancer
la candela (f.): candle
il candidato: candidate
il cane (m.): dog
la cannuccia (f.): drinking straw
il canottaggio: canoeing
il/la cantante (m./f.): singer
cantare: to sing
la cantina (f.): basement, cellar
caotico: chaotic
capace: capable
il capello: strand of hair
i capelli (m. pl.): hair (on head)
capitare: to happen
capito!: understood!
la cappella (f.): chapel
il cappello: hat
il cappotto: overcoat
la capra (f.): goat
il carabiniere (m.): police officer
la caramella (f.): candy
il carattere (m.): character
caratteristico: characteristic, typical
il carcere (m.): jail, prison

il carciofo: artichoke
caricare: to load
carino: cute, pretty
la carne (f.): meat
caro: dear, expensive
la carota (f.): carrot
la carriera (f.): career
la carta (f.): paper
la carta di credito (f.): credit card
la carta d'identità: identification card
la carta igienica (f.): toilet paper
la carta stradale (f.): map
la carta telefonica (f.): telephone card
il cartello: sign
la cartoleria (f.): stationery store
la cartolina (f.): postcard
la casa (f.): house, home
la casalinga (f.): housewife
il casco: helmet
la cassa (f.): cash register
la casseruola (f.): saucepan
la cassetta postale (f.): mailbox
castano: brown
il castello: castle
il catalogo: catalogue
la categoria (f.): category
la catena (f.): chain
la cattedrale (f.): cathedral
cattivo: bad, evil, naughty
cattolico: Catholic
il cavallo: horse
il cavatappi (m.): corkscrew
il cavo: cable
celebrare: to celebrate
celibe: unmarried, single (m.)
la cena (f.): dinner
cenare: to dine
cento: one hundred
centrale: central
il centro: center, downtown
la ceramica (f.): ceramic
cercare: to search, look for
la cerniera (f.): zipper
il certificato: certificate
certo: certain, sure, of course!
il cervello: brain
che: what, who, which, that
che cosa: what
chi: who? whom? the one who
la chiacchiera (f.): chat
chiacchierare: to chat
chiamare: to call
chiamarsi: to call oneself (to be named)
chiaro: clear, light
la chiave (f.): key
chiedere (chiesto): to ask
la chiesa (f.): church
il chilogrammo: kilogram

il chilometro: kilometer
la chirurgia (f.): surgery
il chirurgo/la chirurga (f.): surgeon
la chitarra (f.): guitar
chiudere (chiuso): to close
chiuso: closed
la chiusura festiva (f.): closed for the holidays
ci: there
ciao: hello, hi, bye
ciascuno: each, each one
il cibo: food
il ciclismo: cycling
cieco: blind
il cielo: sky, heaven
la ciliegia (f.): cherry
il cimitero: cemetery
la Cina: China
il cinema (m.): cinema
cinese: Chinese
cinquanta: fifty
la cintura (f.): belt
la cintura di sicurezza (f.): seat belt
ciò: that which
la cioccolata (f.): chocolate
la cipolla (f.): onion
circa: about, approximately
il circo: circus
il circolo: circle
circondare: to surround
citare: to quote
la citazione (f.): excerpt, quote
la città: city
la cittadinanza (f.): citizenship
il cittadino/la cittadina (f.): citizen
civico: civic
civile: civil
la classe (f.): class
classico: classical
la classificazione (f.): classification
il/la cliente (m./f.): client, customer
il clima (m.): climate
la cognata (f.): sister-in-law
il cognato: brother-in-law
il cognome (m.): surname
la coincidenza (f.): connection, coincidence
la colazione (f.): breakfast, lunch
collaborare: to collaborate
la collana (f.): necklace
i collant (m. pl.): stockings
il/la collega (m./f.): colleague
la collina (f.): hill
il collo: neck
il colloquio: interview
la colonia (f.): colony
il colore (m.): color

il coltello: knife
coltivare: to cultivate
il comandamento: commandment
combattere: to fight
come: how, like, as
cominciare: to begin, to start
il commesso/la commessa (f.): sales clerk
comodo: convenient, comfortable
compiere: to accomplish
il compito: homework, task, chore
il compleanno: birthday
il complimento: compliment
comporre (composto): to compose
il comportamento: behavior
comportarsi: to behave
la composizione (f.): composition
comprare: to buy
la comprensione (f.): understanding
la compressa (f.): tablet, pill
il comune (m.): municipality; common (adj.)
comunicare: to communicate
il comunismo: communism
la comunità: community
comunque: however, no matter how
con: with
la concentrazione (f.): concentration
il concerto: concert
il concetto: concept
la concezione (f.): conception
la conchiglia (f.): sea shell
concludere (concluso): to conclude
il concorso: contest, exam
la condizione (f.): condition
condividere (condiviso): to share
il condizionale (m.): conditional (verb mood)
il condominio: condominium
condurre (condotto): to lead, to carry out
la conferenza (f.): conference, lecture
confessare: to confess
il conflitto: conflict
il conforto: comfort, convenience
congratulazioni!: congratulations!
il congresso: meeting, conference
il coniglio: rabbit
coniugare: to conjugate
la coniugazione (f.): conjugation

la conoscenza (f.): knowledge, acquaintance
conoscere (conosciuto): to know someone
conquistare: to conquest
consecutivo: consecutive
la conseguenza (f.): consequence
i conservanti (m. pl.): preservatives
considerare: to consider
consigliare: to advise, to recommend
consolare: to console
la consonante (f.): consonant
il consumo: consumption, waste
il contadino/ la contadina (f.): farmer, peasant
i contanti (m. pl.): cash
contare: to count
contattare: to contact
il contatto: contact
il conte: count
contemporaneo: contemporary
contenere: to contain
contento: glad, satisfied
la contessa (f.): countess
contestare: to challenge, dispute
il continente (m.): continent
continuare: to continue
il conto: check, bill, account
il contorno: side dish
il contraccettivo: contraceptive
il contrario: opposite
il contrasto: contrast
contro: against
controllare: to check
il controllo: check, control
la contusione (f.): bruise
convalidare: to validate
convalidato: validated
il convento: convent
la conversazione (f.): conversation
convincere (convinto): to convince
la coperta (f.): blanket, cover
il coperto: cover charge
la copia (f.): copy
la coppa (f.): cup
la coppia (f.): couple
il coraggio: courage
la corda (f.): rope
il coro: chorus, choir
il corpo: body
correggere (corretto): to correct
correre (corso): to run
corretto: correct
il corriere: messenger, courier
la corriera (f.): bus
corrispondere (corrisposto): to correspond
la corsa (f.): race

la corsia (f.): lane
il corso: course
la corte (f.): court
cortese: courteous
la cosa: cosa c'è?: thing, what:
    what is it?
così: so, thus
così così: so-so
i cosmetici (m. pl.): cosmetics
la costa (f.): coast
il costo: cost, price
costare: to cost
la costiera (f.): cliff
la costituzione (f.): constitution
la costola (f.): rib
costoso: costly, expensive
la costoletta (f.): cutlet
costruire: to build, construct
il costume (m.): costume
il cotone (m.): cotton
cotto: cooked
la cravatta (f.): tie
creare: to create
la creazione (f.): creation
credere: to believe
il credito: credit
la crema (f.): cream
crescere (cresciuto): to grow
il cric (m.): jack (car)
la crisi (f.): crisis
cristiano: Christian
croccante: crunchy
la croce (f.): cross
la crociera (f.): cruise
la cronaca (f.): report
la crostata (f.): pie
crudo: raw, uncooked
cubano: Cuban
il cubo: cube
la cuccetta (f.): berth
il cucchiaio: spoon
cucinare: to cook
il cugino/la cugina (f.): cousin
cui: whom, that, which
la culla (f.): crib
la cultura (f.): culture
culturale: cultural
cuocere (cotto): to cook
il cuoio: leather
il cuore (m.): heart
la cupola (f.): dome
la cura (f.): care
curare: to care for, to look after
la curiosità (f.): curiosity
curioso: curious, strange
la curva (f.): curve
il cuscino: pillow

D

da: from, by
Danimarca: Denmark
dannato: damned
danneggiato: damaged
la danza (f.): dance
dappertutto: everywhere
dare: to give
la data (f.): date
davanti a: in front of
davvero: really
la dea (f.): goddess
debole: weak
decidere (deciso): to decide
decimo: tenth
la decisione (f.): decision
dedicare: to dedicate
definire: to define
la definizione (f.): definition
il delfino: dolphin
delizioso: delicious
della casa: homemade
della stagione: in season
democratico: democratic
la democrazia (f.): democracy
il denaro: money
la densità (f.): density
il dente (m.): tooth
il dentifricio: toothpaste
il/la dentista (m./f.): dentist
dentro: inside
il desiderio: wish, desire
la destinazione (f.): destination
il destino: destiny
destro: right
il detersivo: detergent
la deviazione (f.): detour
di: of, about, from
di solito: usually
il diabete (m.): diabetes
il dialogo: dialogue
il diamante (m.): diamond
la diapositiva (f.): slide
la diarrea (f.): diarrhea
dicembre: December
dichiarare: to declare
diciannove: nineteen
diciassette: seventeen
diciotto: eighteen
la didattica (f.): pedagogy,
    teaching
la dieta (f.): diet
dietro a: behind
difendere (difeso): to defend
il difetto: defect
la differenza (f.): difference
difficile: difficult
diffuso: widespread, diffuse

la diga (f.): dam
digerire: to digest
dimagrire: to lose weight
diminuire: to decrease
dimostrare: to demonstrate
la dimostrazione (f.):
    demonstration
dinamico: energetic
il dio: god
il dipartimento: department
dipendere (dipeso): to depend
dipingere (dipinto): to paint
dire (detto): to say, to tell
diretto: direct
il direttore/la direttrice (f.):
    director
la direzione (f.): direction
dirigere (diretto): to manage,
    to direct
diritto: straight (adv.)
il Diritto: law
il disco: record
il discorso: speech, discussion
la discoteca (f.) : discothèque
la discussione (f.): discussion
discutere (discusso): to discuss
disegnare: to draw
il disegno: drawing, design
la disgrazia (f.): misfortune
disoccupato: unemployed
dispiacere (dispiaciuto):
    to be sorry
disponibile: available
disposto: willing
la distanza (f.): distance
distinguere (distinto):
    to distinguish
distratto: distracted, absent
    minded
il distributore di benzina:
    gas pump
distruggere (distrutto): to destroy
il dito (pl. le dita): finger, toe
la ditta (f.): firm, business
la dittatura (f.): dictatorship
il divano: sofa
diverso: different
divertirsi: to enjoy oneself
dividere (diviso): to divide
divieto: prohibition
divieto di sosta: no parking
la divisione (f.): division
divorziare: to get divorced
divorziato: divorced
il dizionario: dictionary
la dizione (f.): diction
la doccia (f.): shower
il documento: document
dodici: twelve
la dogana (f.): customs

dolce: sweet
il dolce: dessert
il dollaro: dollar
il dolore (m.): pain
domandare: to question
domani: tomorrow
domenica: Sunday
la domestica (f.): maid
il domicilio: residence
la donna (f.): woman
dopo: after (prep.),
    afterward (adv.)
doppiare: to dub
doppio: double
dormire: to sleep
il dottore/la dottoressa (f.):
    doctor
dove: where
dovere: to have to, to must
la dozzina (f.): dozen
la droga (f.): drug
la drogheria (f.): grocery store
il duca (m.): duke
due: two
la duchessa (f.): duchess
il duomo: cathedral, dome
dunque: thus, then
durante: during
durare: to last
duro: hard, tough

E

e, ed (before vowels): and
è: is
ebbene: well then, so
ebreo: Hebrew, Jewish
eccellente: excellent
eccetera: et cetera
eccetto: except
ecco: here is, there is
l'economia (f.): economy
economico: inexpensive
l'edera (f.): ivy
l'edicola (f.): newsstand
l'edificio: building
l'effetto: effect
efficiente: efficient
Egitto: Egypt
elegante: elegant
l'elemosina (f.): alms
elementare: elementary
l'elenco: list, directory
l'elettricità (f.): electricity
l'elezione (f.): election
l'elicottero: helicopter
eliminare: to eliminate
l'emergenza (f.): emergency
l'emicrania (f.): migraine
emigrare: to emigrate

enorme: enormous
l'enoteca (f.): wine bar
entrambi: both
entrare: to enter
l'entrata (f.): entrance
l'Epifania (f.): Epiphany (Jan. 6)
l'equitazione (f.): horse riding
l'ernia (f.): hernia
l'errore (m.): error
esagerare: to exaggerate
l'esame (m.): exam
esaminare: to exam
esattamente: exactly
esatto: exact
esaurito: sold out
escludere (escluso): to exclude
l'escursione (f.): excursion
esistere (esistito): to exist
esotico: exotic
l'esperienza (f.): experience
esplodere (esploso): to explode
esportare: to export
l'espressione (f.): expression
espresso: express
esprimere (espresso): to express
l'essenza (f.): essence
essenziale: essential
essere (stato): to be
est: east
l'estate (f.): summer
l'estero: abroad
l'età (f.): age
l'etichetta (f.): tag, label
l'etto: hectogram
l'Europa (f.): Europe
l'evento: event
evitare: to avoid
evocare: to evoke

F

fa: ago
la fabbrica (f.): factory
fabbricare: to manufacture
la faccenda (f.): thing, matter,
    chore
la faccia (f.): face
facile: easy
la facoltà (f.): school
il fagiolo: bean
il falegname (m.): carpenter
la fame (f.): hunger
la famiglia (f.): family
famoso: famous
la fantascienza (f.): science fiction
la fantasia (f.): fantasy
il fantasma (m.): ghost, phantom
fare (fatto): to do, to make
la farina (f.): flour
la farmacia (f.): pharmacy

il faro: headlight, lighthouse
il fascismo: fascism
la fase (f.): phase
fastidio: bother, annoyance
la fatica (f.): effort
il fatto: fact
la fattoria (f.): farm
la favola (f.): fable
il fazzoletto: tissue
febbraio: February
la febbre (f.): fever
la fede (f.): faith
il fegato: liver
felice: happy
il feltro: felt
la femmina (f.): woman, female
la ferita (f.): injury
fermare: to stop
la fermata (f.): stop
fermo: still
Ferragosto: Assumption Day
    (Aug. 15)
il ferro: iron
la ferrovia (f.): railroad
la festa (f.): holiday
festeggiare: to celebrate
la fiaba (f.): fable, tale
i fiammiferi (m. pl.): matches
il fianco: side
fidarsi: to trust
la fidanzata (f.): fiancée
il fidanzato: fiancé
la fiducia (f.): trust
fiero: proud
la fiera (f.): fair
la figlia (f.): daughter
il figlio: son
la fila (f.): line, row
il filetto: filet
la filosofia (f.): philosophy
il filtro: filter
finalmente: finally
la finanza (f.): finance
finanziare: to finance
la fine (f.): end
il fine settimana: weekend
la finestra (f.): window
finire: to finish
fino a: until, as far as
il fioraio: florist
il fiore (m.): flower
Firenze: Florence
la firma (f.): signature
fisso: firm, fixed
fiscale: fiscal
fischiare: to whistle
la fisica (f.): physics
fissare: to set up
fisso: set, fixed
il fiume (m.): river
il fuoco: fire

la foglia (f.): leaf
il foglio: sheet of paper
il fon (m.): hair dryer
fondato: founded
il fondo: bottom
la fonetica (f.): phonetics
la fontana (f.): fountain
il football: soccer, football
le forbici (f. pl.): scissors
la forchetta (f.): fork
la foresta (f.): forest
la forma (f.): form
il formaggio: cheese
formale: formal
formulare: to formulate,
    to compose
il fornaio: baker
il forno: oven
forse: maybe
forte: strong
la fortezza (f.): fortress
la fortuna (f.): fortune
la fotocopia (f.): photocopy
la fotografia (f.): photograph
fra: within, in, between, among
fragile: fragile
la fragola (f.): strawberry
francese: French
la Francia (f.): France
il francobollo: postage stamp
la frase (f.): phrase, sentence
il frate (m.): friar
il fratello: brother
freddo: cold
frequentare: to frequent
fresco: fresh
la fretta (f.): haste, hurry
il frigorifero: refrigerator
fritto: fried
la frontiera (f.): border
la frutta (f.): fruit
il fruttivendolo: greengrocer's
fumare: to smoke
il fumetto: comic strip
il funerale (m.): funeral
il fungo: mushroom
la funivia (f.): cable car, gondola
funzionare: to function, to work
il fuoco: fire
fuori: outside
furbo: clever, sly (slang)
il futuro: future

G

il gabinetto: toilet
la galleria (f.): tunnel, gallery
la gallina (f.): hen
la gamba (f.): leg

il gambero: shrimp
la gara (f.): contest
il garage (m.): garage
garantire: to guarantee
il garofano: carnation
il gatto: cat
il gattopardo: leopard
la gelateria (f.): ice-cream parlor
il gelato: ice-cream
il genere (m.): genre, type
il genero: son-in-law
generoso: generous
la genesi (f.): genesis
i genitori (m. pl.): parents
gennaio: January
la gente (f.): people
gentile: kind, polite
la gentilezza (f.): kindness
la geografia (f.): geography
la Germania (f.): Germany
il gerundio: gerund
Gesù: Jesus
il gettone (m.): token
il ghiaccio: ice
già: already
la giacca (f.): jacket
giallo: yellow
la ginnastica (f.): gymnastics,
    exercise
il Giappone (m.): Japan
giapponese: Japanese
il giardino: garden
il ginecologo/la ginecologa (f.):
    gynecologist
giocare: to play
il giocattolo: toy
il gioco: game
la gioia (f.): joy
la gioielleria (f.): jewelry store
il giornalaio: newspaper vendor
il giornale (m.): newspaper
il/la giornalista (m./f.): journalist
la giornata (f.): day
il giorno: day
giovane: young
giovedì: Thursday
girare: to spin, to shoot (a film)
il giro: tour
la gita (f.): excursion
giù: down
il giubbotto: coat
giudicare: to judge
giugno: June
giurare: to swear
la giurisprudenza (f.): law
giusto: just, right, correct
la gonna (f.): skirt
gotico: gothic
il governo: government
la grammatica (f.): grammar
il grammo: gram

grande: big, large
la grappa (f.): grappa
grasso: fat
gratis: free of charge
grave: serious, grave
la gravità (f.): gravity
la grazia (f.): grace
grazie!: thank you!
la Grecia: Greece
greco: Greek
greggio: raw, crude
gridare: to yell, to shout
grigio: gray
la griglia (f.): grill
grosso: large
la grotta (f.): cave
la gruccia (f.): hanger
il gruppo: group
i guanti (m. pl.): gloves
guadagnare: to earn
il guaio: trouble
la guancia (f.): cheek
guardare: to look at, to watch
il guardaroba (m.): cloakroom
guasto: spoiled, rotten
il guasto: breakdown
la guerra (f.): war
la guida (f.): guide
guidare: to drive
gustare: to taste
il gusto: taste

H

l'hobby (m.): hobby
l'hockey (m.): hockey
la hostess (f.): stewardess
l'hotel (m.): hotel

I

I.V.A. (Imposta Valore Aggiunto):
    VAT/sales tax
l'idea (f.): idea
l'ideale (m.): ideal
identificare: to identify
l'identità (f.): identity
l'idioma (f.): idiom
l'idolo: idol
ieri: yesterday
ignorante: ignorant
ignorare: to ignore
illustrare: to illustrate
l'illustrazione (f.): illustration
l'imbarco: boarding
l'imitazione (f.): imitation
immacolato: immaculate
immaginare: to imagine

431

l'immaginazione (f.): imagination
l'immagine (f.): image
immenso: immense
l'immigrazione (f.): immigration
imparare: to learn
l'impegno: commitment, task
l'imperativo: imperative
l'imperfetto: imperfect
l'impermeabile: raincoat
l'impero: empire
l'impiegato: worker, employee, official
importante: important
importare: to import, to matter
impossibile: impossible
l'imprenditore: entrepreneur
l'impressione (f.): impression
imprestare: to lend
in: in, to, at
in fretta: in a hurry
incartare: to wrap
l'incidente (m.): accident
incinta: pregnant
inciso: engraved
includere (incluso): to include
incominciare: to begin, to start
incontrare: to meet
incredibile: incredible
l'incrocio: crossing
l'incubo: nightmare
l'indefinito: indefinite
indiano: Indian
indicare: to indicate
l'indicazione (f.): direction, indication
l'indice (m.): index
indietro: back, behind
l'indigestione (f.): indigestion
l'indipendenza (f.): independence
indiretto: indirect
l'indirizzo: address
indispensabile: indispensable
indossare: to wear
indovinare: to guess
l'indovinello: riddle
l'industria (f.): industry
l'infarto: heart attack
infatti: in fact
inferiore: inferior, lower
l'infermiera (f.): nurse
l'inferno: hell
l'infezione (f.): infection
l'infiammazione (f.): inflammation
l'infinito: infinitive
l'inflazione (f.): inflation
l'influenza (f.): flu
informare: to inform

l'informazione (f.): information
l'ingegnere: engineer
l'Inghilterra (f.): England
inghiottire: to swallow
inglese: English
ingrassare: to get fat
l'ingrediente (m.): ingredient
l'ingresso: entrance
l'ingrosso: wholesale
l'iniezione (f.): injection
iniziare: to begin
l'inizio: beginning
innamorarsi: to fall in love with
l'inno: hymn
inoltre: also
l'inquinamento: pollution
inquinato: polluted
l'insalata (f.): salad
l'insegnante (m./f.): teacher
insegnare: to teach
inserire: to insert
l'insetto: insect
insicuro: insecure
insieme: together
insistere (insisto): to insist
insolito: unusual
l'insulina (f.): insulin
intelligente: intelligent
intendere (inteso): to mean
l'intenzione (f.): intention
interessante: interesting
l'intermezzo: intermission
internazionale: international
interno: internal, inside
interpretare: to interpret
l'interprete: interpreter
interrogativo: interrogative
interrompere (interrotto): to interrupt
l'interurbana (f.): long-distance call
l'intervallo: interval
l'intervista (f.): interview
intorno a: around
introdurre (introdotto): to introduce
inutile: useless
invece: instead
l'inverno: winter
inviare: to mail, to send
invitare: to invite
l'invito: invitation
io: I
l'Irlanda: Ireland
irlandese: Irish
irregolare: irregular
l'iscritto: student, member
l'isola (f.): island
l'ispirazione (f.): inspiration
l'istituto: institute

l'istruzione (f.): instruction
l'Italia (f.): Italy
italiano: Italian
l'itinerario: itinerary

J–K

i jeans: jeans

Kosher: Kosher
il ketchup: ketchup

L

là: there
la Befana (f.): Epiphany (January 6)
il labbro: lip
il ladro: thief
lamentare: to mourn, to grieve
lamentarsi: to complain
il lago: lake
la lampada (f.): light
la lampadina (f.): light bulb
il lampo: lightening flash
il lampone (m.): raspberry
la lana (f.): wool
largo: wide
lasciare: to let, to leave behind
latino: Latin
il lato: side
il latte (m.): milk
la latteria (f.): dairy store
la lattuga (f.): lettuce
la laurea (f.): degree
la lavanderia (f.): laundry service
la lavanderia a secco: dry cleaner
il lavandino: sink
lavare: to wash
lavorare: to work
il lavoro: work
leccare: to lick
legare: to tie
la legge (f.): law
leggere (letto): to read
leggero: light
il legno: wood
lei: she, her
Lei (polite): you
il lenzuolo: sheet
la lettera (f.): letter
la letteratura (f.): literature
il letto: bed
la lezione (f.): lesson
lì: there
libero: free
la libertà (f.): liberty
la libreria (f.): bookstore
il libretto: libretto, little book

il libro: book
licenziare: to fire someone
licenziarsi: to resign
la limonata (f.): lemonade
il limone (m.): lemon
la linea (f.): line
la lingua (f.): language, tongue
la linguistica (f.): linguistics
il lino: linen
il liquore (m.): liquor
la lista (f.): list, menu
litigare: to argue, to fight
il litro: liter
il livello: level
locale: local
il locale (m.): place
lodare: to praise
la logistica (f.): logistics
lontano: far
loro: they
la lotta (f.): struggle
la lozione (f.): lotion
la luce (f.): light
luglio: July
lui: he, him
la luna (f.): moon
la luna di miele (f.): honeymoon
lunedì: Monday
lunedì dell'Angelo: Easter Monday
la lunghezza (f.): length
lungo: long
il luogo: place
il lupo: wolf
lusso: luxury

M

ma: but
la macchia (f.): stain
la macchina (f.): automobile,
    car, machine
la macchina fotografica (f.):
    camera
il macellaio: butcher
la macelleria (f.): butcher shop
la madre (f.): mother
la madrelingua (f.): native
    language
il magazzino: department store
maggio: May
la maggioranza (f.): majority
la magia (f.): magic
la maglia (f.): sweater, pullover
il magnetofono: tape recorder
magnifico: magnificent
magro: thin
mai: never, ever
il maiale (m.): pork, pig
il mais (m.): corn

malato: unhealthy, sick
la malattia (f.): illness
il male: evil; fa male: it hurts
la mamma (f.): mom, mother
la mancia (f.): tip
mancare: to lack, to be missing
mandare: to send
mangiare: to eat
la mania (f.): obsession
la maniera (f.): manner, way
la maniglia (f.): handle
la mano (f.; pl. le mani): hand
il mantello: cape
mantenere: to maintain
il manzo: beef
la marca (f.): brand, type
il marciapiede (m.): sidewalk
il mare (m.): sea
la marea (f.): tide
la marina (f.): marina
il marito: husband
la marmellata (f.): jam
il marmo: marble
marrone: brown
martedì: Tuesday
marzo: March
maschile: masculine
il massimo: maximum
la matematica (f.): mathematics
la materia (f.): subject
la matita (f.): pencil
il matrimonio: matrimony
la mattina (f.): morning
matto: crazy
maturo: ripe, mature
il meccanico: mechanic
la medicina (f.): medicine
il medico: doctor
il Medioevo: Middle Ages
meglio: better
la mela (f.): apple
la melanzana (f.): eggplant
il melone (m.): melon,
    cantaloupe
meno: less
la mensa (f.): cafeteria
mensile: monthly
la menta (f.): mint
la mentalità (f.): mentality
la mente (f.): mind
il mento: chin
mentre: while
il menù (m.): menu
meraviglioso: marvelous
il/la mercante (m./f.): merchant
il mercato: market
la merce (f.): merchandise
mercoledì: Wednesday
meritare: to deserve
il merletto: lace

il mese (m.): month
la messa (f.): mass
il messaggio: message
Messico (f.): Mexico
la metà: half
il metallo: metal
il metodo: method
la metropolitana (f.): subway
mettere (messo): to put, to place
la mezzanotte (f.): midnight
mezzo: half
il mezzo: means
mezzogiorno: noon
mi: me, to me
il miele (m.): honey
il miglio (pl. le miglia): mile
migliorare: to improve
il/la migliore: the best
mille (pl. mila): thousand
la minestra (f.): soup
il ministro: minister
la minoranza (f.): minority
minore: smaller, less
il minuto: minute
miope: near-sighted
mischiare: to mix
la miseria (f.): poverty
misto: mixed
la misura (f.): measure, size
il mito: myth
il/la mittente (m./f.): sender
il mobile (m.): piece of furniture
il modello: model
moderno: modern
modesto: modest
il modo: manner, method, way
il modulo: form
la moglie (f.): wife
il molo: dock
molto: a lot, much, very
il momento: moment
il monastero: monastery
il mondo: world
la moneta (f.): coin
monolocale (m.): single room,
    studio
la montagna (f.): mountain
il monumento: monument
morbido: soft, smooth
morire (morto): to die
la morte (f.): death
il mosaico: mosaic
la mosca (f.): fly (insect)
la mostra (f.): show (art)
il motivo: motive
la motocicletta (f.): motorcycle
il motore (m.): motor
il motorino: scooter
la multa (f.): fine, ticket
il muro: wall

433

il muscolo: muscle
il museo: museum
la musica (f.): music
il/la musicista (m./f.): musician
mussulmano: Muslim
muto: mute
il mutuo: loan

N

la narrativa (f.): narrative, story,
    fiction
nascere (nato): to be born
la nascita (f.): birth
nascondere (nascosto): to hide
il naso: nose
il nastro: tape
Natale, Buon: Christmas, Merry
la natura (f.): nature
naturale: natural
la nausea (f.): nausea
la nave (f.): ship
la nazionalità (f.): nationality
la nazione (f.): nation
ne: some of, about it
né ... né: neither ... nor
neanche: not even
la nebbia (f.): fog
la necessità (f.): need, necessity
necessario: necessary
il negativo: negative
il negozio: shop
il nemico: enemy
nemmeno: not even
neppure: neither, not even
nero: black
nervoso: nervous
nessuno: no one, nobody
la neve (f.): snow
il nido: nest
niente: nothing
il nipote: grandson, nephew
la nipote: granddaughter, niece
la nocciola (f.): hazelnut
la nocciolina (f.): peanut
la noce (f.): walnut
noi: we
noioso: boring
noleggiare: to rent
il nome (m.): noun, name
il nome da nubile: maiden name
il nome del coniuge: name
    of spouse
il nome di famiglia: surname
non: not
la nonna (f.): grandmother
il nonno: grandfather
nono: ninth
nonostante: notwithstanding
nord: north

normale: normal
la Norvegia: Norway
la notizia (f.): news
la notte (f.): night
il notturno: nocturne
novanta: ninety
novembre: November
la novità (f.): news
nubile: unmarried
nulla: nothing
il numero: number
il numero verde: toll-free number
la nuora (f.): daughter-in-law
nuotare: to swim
nuovo: new
la nuvola (f.): cloud

O

o: or
obbligare: to oblige
l'obbligo: obligation
l'occasione (f.): occasion, bargain
gli occhiali (m. pl.): eyeglasses
l'occhiata (f.): glance
l'occhio: eye
l'Occidente: West
occupare: to occupy
occupato: busy, occupied
l'oceano: ocean
odiare: to hate
odorare: to smell
l'odore (m.): aroma, odor
l'offerta (f.): offer
gli oggetti smarriti (m. pl.):
    lost property
l'oggetto: object
oggi: today
ogni: each, every
Ognissanti: All Saint's Day
    (Nov. 1)
ognuno: everybody
l'Olanda (f.): Holland
l'olio: oil
l'oliva(f.): olive
oltre: more than, in addition to
l'ombra (f.): shadow
l'ombrello: umbrella
l'onda (f.): wave
onesto: honest
l'onore (m.): honor
l'opera (f.): opera, work
l'operaio: worker
l'operazione (f.): operation
l'opinione (f.): opinion
opposto: opposite
oppure: or
l'ora (f.): hour, now
l'ora di punta (f.): rush hour
l'orario: schedule

ordinale: ordinal
ordinare: to order
l'ordine (m.): order
gli orecchini (m. pl.): earrings
l'orecchio: ear
l'oreficeria (f.): jeweler's,
    goldsmith's
orgoglioso: proud
Oriente: East, Orient
l'origano: oregano
originale: original
l'origine (f.): origin
l'oro: gold
l'orologio: watch, clock
l'oroscopo: horoscope
l'orso: bear
l'orto: garden
l'oscuro: dark, obscure
l'ospedale (m.): hospital
l'ospite (m./f.): guest
l'osso (pl. le ossa): bone
l'ostello: hostel
ottanta: eighty
ottavo: eighth
ottenere: to obtain
ottico: optician
ottimo: excellent, best
ottobre: October
l'ottone: brass
ovest: west
ovunque: wherever
ovvio: obvious

P

il pacco: package, parcel
la pace (f.): peace
la padella (f.): frying pan
il padre (m.): father
il padrino: godfather
il padrone/la padrona (f.): boss,
    landlord, owner
il paese (m.): country, town
il pagamento: payment
pagare: to pay
la pagina (f.): page
la pagnotta (f.): loaf
il paio (pl. le paia): pair
il palazzo: building, palace
il palco: box (theater)
il palcoscenico: stage
la palestra (f.): gym
la palla (f.): ball
la pallacanestro (f.): basketball
la pallavolo (f.): volleyball
la palude (f.): swamp, marsh
la pancetta (f.): bacon
la panchina (f.): bench
il pane (m.): bread
la panetteria (f.): bakery

il panino: sandwich
la panna (f.): cream
il pannolino: diaper
il panorama (m.): panorama, view
i pantaloni (m. pl.): pants
il Papa (m.): Pope
il papà (m.): daddy, pop
il parabrezza (m.): windshield
il paradiso: paradise
il paragone (m.): comparison
il parcheggio: parking lot
il parco: park
il/la parente (m./f.): relative
parere (parso): to seem, to appear
la parete (f.): inside wall
la parte (f.): part
partecipare: to participate
la partenza (f.): departure
partire: to depart, to leave
la partita (f.): game, match
il partito: political party
Pasqua: Easter
il passaporto: passport
passare: to pass
il passatempo: hobby
il passato: past
passeggiare: to stroll
la passeggiata (f.): stroll, walk
la passione (f.): passion
il passo: step
la pasta (f.): pasta, pastry
la pasticceria (f.): pastry shop
il pasto: meal
la patata (f.): potato
la patente (f.): driver's license
la patria (f.): homeland
il patrigno: stepfather
il patto: agreement, pact
la paura (f.): fear
il pavimento: floor
pazzo: crazy
peccato!: what a shame!
il pedaggio: toll
peggio: worse
il pelo: hair
la pelle (f.): skin, leather
la pelletteria (f.): furrier shop
la pelliccia (f.): fur
la pellicola (f.): film
la pena (f.): penalty
la penisola (f.): peninsula
la penna (f.): pen, feather
pensare: to think
il pensiero: thought, idea
la pensione (f.): inn
il pepe (m.): pepper
il peperone (m.): bell pepper
per: for, in order to

per favore: please
per piacere: please
la pera (f.): pear
il percento: percentage
la percezione (f.): perception
perché: why, because
perciò: therefore
il percorso: route
perdere (perso): to lose
perdonare: to pardon
il pericolo: danger
pericoloso: dangerous
la periferia (f.): suburbs
permesso!: excuse me!
il periodo: period
permettere (permesso): to permit
però: but, however
persino: even
la persona (f.): person
il personaggio: character, type (of person)
pesante: heavy
pesare: to weigh
la pesca (f.): peach
il pesce (m.): fish
la pescheria (f.): fish store
il peso: weight
pettinare: to comb
il petto: chest
il pezzo: piece
il piacere (m.): pleasure
piacersi (piaciuto): to be pleasing, to like
piacevole: pleasing
il pianeta (m.): planet
piangere (pianto): to cry
il pianterreno: ground floor
il piano: floor, (adv.) softly
la pianta (f.): plant
la pianura (f.) : plain
la piastrella (f.): floor tile
il piatto: plate
la piazza (f.): town square
piccante: spicy
il picco: peak
piccolo: small
il piede (m.): foot
pieno: full
la pietra (f.): stone
pigro: lazy
la pila (f.): battery
la pillola (f.): pill
la pioggia (f.): rain
piovere: to rain
la piramide (f.): pyramid
la piscina (f.): swimming pool
il pisello: pea
la pista (f.): track, trail, slope
la pistola (f.): pistol
la pittura (f.): painting

più: more
la piuma (f.): feather
piuttosto: rather
la plastica (f.): plastic
plurale (m.): plural
il pneumatico: tire
un po': a little
poco: not very much
la poesia (f.): poem, poetry
poi: then, afterward
poiché: since
la polenta (f.): corn meal
la politica (f.): politics
la polizia (f.): police
il poliziotto: police officer
il pollame (m.): poultry
il polmone (m.): lung
la polpetta (f.): meatball
la polvere (f.): dust
il pomeriggio: afternoon
il pomodoro: tomato
il pompelmo: grapefruit
il pompiere (m.): firefighter
il ponte (m.): bridge
la popolazione (f.): population
il porco: pig, pork
la porta (f.): door
il portabagagli (m.): porter
il portacenere (m.): ashtray
il portafoglio: wallet
portare: to bring, to carry
il porto: harbor, port
il Portogallo: Portugal
la porzione (f.): portion
la posizione (f.): position
possibile: possible
la possibilità (f.): possibility
la posta (f.): mail, post office
il postino: postal carrier
il posto: seat, place
potere: to be able to, to can
povero: poor
il pozzo: well
pranzare: to dine, to eat lunch
il pranzo: lunch, supper
la pratica (f.): practice
pratico: convenient, practical
il prato: field
preciso: precise
la preferenza (f.): preference
preferire: to prefer
il prefisso: area code
pregare: to pray, to beg, to ask
la preghiera (f.): prayer
prego!: you are welcome!
prendere (preso): to take
prenotare: to make a reservation
la prenotazione (f.): reservation
preoccuparsi: to worry
preoccupato: worried

435

preparare: to prepare
presbite: far-sighted
presentare: to present
il presente (m.): present
il presidente: president
presso: in care of (c/o)
presto: quickly, early
il prete (m.): priest
il prezzemolo: parsley
il prezzo: price
il prezzo d'entrata: admission
   charge
la prigione (f.): prison
prima: before
la primavera (f.): spring
primo: first, before
principale: principal, main
il principe: prince
la principessa (f.): princess
il problema (m.): problem
il prodotto: product
produrre (prodotto): to produce
la produzione (f.): production
la professione (f.): profession
il professore/la professoressa (f.):
   professor
il profilattico: condom
la profumeria (f.): cosmetics shop
il profumo: perfume
il progetto: project
il programma (m.): plan,
   program
progressivo: progressive
il progresso: progress
promettere (promesso):
   to promise
il pronome (m.): pronoun
pronto: ready, hello (telephone)
pronto soccorso: first aid
la pronuncia (f.): pronunciation
pronunciare: to pronounce
proporre (proposto): to propose
la proposizione (f.): clause
il proprietario: owner
la proprietà privata (f.):
   private property
proprio: just, really
il prosciutto: ham
prossimo: next
proteggere (protetto): to protect
protestante: Protestant
provare: to try, to experience
il proverbio: proverb
la psicologia (f.): psychology
la pubblicità (f.): publicity
il pubblico: public
il pugno: fist
la pulce (f.): flea
pulire: to clean
il pullman (m.): bus
il punto: period, point, stitch

la puntura (f.): injection,
   insect bite
puntuale: punctual
purché: provided that
pure: also
puro: pure
purtroppo: unfortunately

Q

qua: here
il quaderno: notebook
il quadro: painting, picture
qualche: some
qualche volta: sometimes
qualcosa: something
qualcuno: someone
quale: which
la qualità (f.): quality
qualsiasi: any
qualunque: any
quando: when
la quantità (f.): quantity
quanto?: how much?
quaranta: forty
il quartiere (m.): neighborhood
quarto: fourth, quarter
quasi: almost
quattordici: fourteen
quello/quella: that
la questione (f.): matter
questo: this one
la questura (f.): police
   headquarters
qui: here
quindi: therefore
quindici: fifteen
quinto: fifth
quotidiano: (adj.) daily
il quotidiano: daily paper

R

il rabbino: Rabbi
la racchetta (f.): racket
raccontare: to tell (a story)
radersi: to shave
il radiatore (m.): radiator
la radice (f.): root
la radio (f.): radio
la radiografia (f.): x-ray
il raffreddore (m.): cold
la ragazza (f.): girl
il ragazzo: boy
il ragno: spider
rallentare: slow down
il rame (m.): copper
la rana (f.): frog
il rapido: express train

la rapina (f.): robbery
il rapporto: relationship
rappresentare: to represent
raramente: rarely, seldom
raro: rare, scarce
il rasoio: razor
la razza (f.): breed, race
il re: king
realizzare: to achieve
recente: recent
recitare: to recite
regalare: to give a present
il regalo: gift, present
il reggiseno: bra
la regina (f.): queen
la regione (f.): region
il/la regista (m./f.): movie
   director
la religione (f.): religion
rendere (reso): to render,
   to give back
la repubblica (f.): republic
la residenza (f.): residence
la resistenza (f.): resistance
respiro: breath
responsabile: responsible
restare: to remain, to stay
il resto: remainder, rest
il rettile (m.): reptile
il reumatismo: rheumatism
la revisione (f.): revision
ricamare: to embroider
riccio: curly
ricco: rich
la ricetta (f.): recipe, prescription
ricevere: to receive
il ricevimento: reception
la ricevuta (f.): receipt
la richiesta (f.): request
ricordare: to remember
ridere (riso): to laugh
riempire: to fill out (a form)
i rifiuti (m. pl.): trash
il riflessivo: reflexive
riflettere (riflesso): to reflect
il rifugio: refuge
rilasciato: issued
rilassante: relaxing
rimanere (rimasto): to remain
il rimborso: refund
il Rinascimento: the Renaissance
ringraziare: to thank
il rio: stream
riparare: to repair
ripetere: to repeat
ripieno: stuffed, filled
il riscaldamento: heat
riscaldare: to warm, to heat
la riserva d'acqua (f.): reservoir
la riserva naturale (f.): nature
   preserve

riservato: reserved
il riso: rice
risolvere (risolto): to resolve
rispettare: to respect
rispondere (risposto): to respond
la risposta (f.): answer, response
il ristorante (m.): restaurant
il risultato: result
il ritardo: delay
il ritmo: rhythm
ritornare: to return
il ritratto: portrait
riuscire: to succeed
la rivista (f.): magazine
la roba (f.): stuff, things
la rocca (f.): fortress
la roccia (f.): rock
romantico: romantic
il romanzo: novel, fiction,
    romance
rompere (rotto): to break
la rondine (f.): swallow (bird)
rosa: pink
la rosa (f.): rose
rosso: red
rotto: broken
le rovine (f. pl.): ruins
rubare: to steal
il rubinetto: faucet
il rullino: roll of film
rumoroso: noisy
la ruota (f.): wheel
la rupe (f.): cliff
il ruscello: stream
russo: Russian

S

sabato: Saturday
la sabbia (f.): sand
il sacchetto: small bag
il sacco a pelo: sleeping bag
saggio: wise
il saggio: essay
la sala (f.): room, hall
la sala d'attesa (f.): waiting room
la sala da pranzo (f.): dining
    room
la sala giochi (f.): game room
il salario: salary
il saldo: sale, discount
il sale (m.): salt
salire: to climb, to mount
il salmone (m.): salmon
il salotto: living room, lounge
la salsa (f.): sauce
la salsiccia (f.): sausage
i salumi (m. pl.): cold cuts, meats
salutare: to greet

la salute (f.): health
la salvietta (f.): napkin
il sangue (m.): blood
il santo/la santa (f.): saint
sapere: to know something
il sapone (m.): soap
il sapore (m.): taste
il sarto: tailor
sbadigliare: to yawn
sbagliare: to be mistaken
sbarcare: to land,
    to disembark
gli scacchi (m. pl.): chess
la scadenza (f.): expiration
la scala (f.): stairs
scambiare: to exchange
lo scambio: exchange
lo scapolo: bachelor
scappare: to escape, to run away
la scarpa (f.): shoe
la scatola (f.): box
scavare: to excavate
scegliere (scelto): to choose
scemo: silly, idiotic
la scena (f.): scene
scendere: to descend, to get off
scherzare: to joke
la schiuma (f.): foam
lo schizzo: sketch
lo sci (m.): skiing
lo sci di fondo: cross-country
    skiing
sciare: to ski
la sciarpa (f.): scarf
la scienza (f.): science
lo sciopero: strike
scocciare: to bother, annoy
scommettere (scommesso): to bet
scomodo: uncomfortable
lo sconto: discount
lo scontrino: receipt
scoprire (scoperto): to discover
scorso: last, past
scotto: overdone
la Scozia (f.): Scotland
lo scrittore/la scrittrice (f.): writer
la scrivania (f.): desk
scrivere (scritto): to write
la scultura (f.): sculpture
la scuola (f.): school
scuro: dark
scusare: to excuse
scusarsi: to apologize
sdraiarsi: to lie down
se: if
sé: oneself (himself, herself ...)
sebbene: although
secco: dry
il secolo: century
secondo: second
il sedativo: sedative

sedersi: to sit down
la sedia (f.): chair
sedici: sixteen
il segnale (m.): signal, sign
segnare: to mark, to note
il segno: sign
la segretaria (f.): secretary
seguente: following
seguire: to follow
la selva (f.): woods, forest
selvaggio: wild, savage
selvatico: wild, untamed
il semaforo: traffic light
sembrare: to seem
il semestre (m.): semester
semplice: simple
sempre: always
la senape (f.): mustard
il Senato: Senate
la sensazione (f.): sensation,
    feeling
senso unico: one-way street
il sentiero: path, track
il sentimento: feeling, sentiment
sentire: to hear, to smell, to taste
sentirsi: to feel
senza: without
separare: to separate
separato: separated
la sera (f.): evening
il serbatoio: gas tank
la serenata (f.): serenade
sereno: calm, good weather
serio: serious
il serpente (m.): snake
il servizio: service
sessanta: sixty
il sesso: sex
la sessualità (f.): sexuality
la seta (f.): silk
la sete (f.): thirst
settanta: seventy
settembre: September
la settimana (f.): week
settimo: seventh
severo: severe, strict
sfidare: to challenge
la sfortuna (f.): misfortune,
    bad luck
lo sforzo: effort
si: oneself, each other, one, they
sì: yes
la Sicilia (f.): Sicily
siciliano: Sicilian
sicuro: safe, sure
la sigaretta (f.): cigarette
il sigaro: cigar
significare: to signify
il significato: meaning
la signora (f.): Mrs., Ms., woman
il signore (m.): Mr., Sir, man

437

la signorina (f.): Miss, young lady
il silenzio: silence
il simbolo: symbol
simpatico: nice, kind
la sinagoga (f.): synagogue
sincero: sincere
il sindaco: mayor
la sinfonia (f.): symphony
singolare: singular
singolo: single
sinistro: left
sintetica: synthetic
il sintomo: symptom
il sipario: curtain (theater)
il sistema (m.): system
la situazione (f.): situation
gli slip (m. pl.): briefs
lo slittino: sled
smettere (smesso): to quit
snello: slender
lo snob: snob
la società (f.): company
soffice: soft
il soffitto: ceiling
soffrire (sofferto): to suffer
il soggetto: subject
sognare: to dream
solamente: only
il soldato: soldier
i soldi (m. pl.): money
il sole (m.): sun
solito: usual
solo: alone
il sonnifero: sleeping pill
il sonno: sleep
sono: I am, they are
sopra: above, on
il soprabito: overcoat
soprattutto: above all
sordo: deaf
la sorella (f.): sister
la sorellastra (f.): stepsister, half-sister
la sorgente (f.): spring
il sorpasso: passing
sorprendere (sorpreso): to surprise
la sorpresa (f.): surprise
sorridere (sorriso): to smile
la sosta (f.): stop, pause
sostituire: to substitute
il sotterraneo: tunnel
sotto: beneath
il sottotitolo: subtitle
la Spagna (f.): Spain
spaventare: to scare, to frighten
lo spazio: space
la spazzatura (f.): trash can
la spazzola (f.): brush
lo spazzolino da denti: toothbrush

lo specchio: mirror
speciale: special
la specie (f.): type, kind
spedire: to send
spegnere (spento): to turn off
spendere (speso): to spend
la speranza (f.): hope
sperare: to hope
la spesa (f.): expense, shopping
spesso: often
lo spettacolo: show
la spezia (f.): spice
la spiaggia (f.): beach
spiegare: to explain
la spilla (f.): brooch, pin
spingere (spinto): to push
lo spirito: spirit
spirituale: spiritual
splendido: splendid
sporco: dirty
lo sport (m.): sport
lo sportello: counter, window
sposare: to marry
sposato: married
lo sposo/la sposa (f.): spouse
la spugna (f.): sponge
lo spumante (m.): sparkling wine
lo spuntino: snack
la squadra (f.): team
stabilire: to establish
lo stadio: stadium
la stagione (f.): season
lo stagno: swamp
stamattina: this morning
la stampa (f.): print, press
stanco: tired
stanotte: tonight
la stanza (f.): room
stare (stato): to be, to remain, to stay
stasera: this evening
lo stato: state, government, condition
gli Stati Uniti (m. pl.): United States
la statua (f.): statue
la stazione (f.): station
la stella (f.): star
stesso: same
lo stivale (m.): boot
la stoffa (f.): fabric, cloth
lo stomaco: stomach
la storia (f.): history, story
la strada (f.): street
lo straniero: foreigner, (adj.) foreign
strano: strange
la strega (f.): witch
stressare: to stress
stretto: tight

lo studente/la studentessa (f.): student
studiare: to study
lo studio: study
la stufa (f.): stove
stupendo: stupendous
su, sul, sulla: on top of, on, up
subito: soon, immediately
succedere (successo): to happen
il succo: juice
sud: south
la suocera (f.): mother-in-law
il suocero: father-in-law
suonare: to sound, to play
superare: to overcome, to accomplish
il supermercato: supermarket
la sveglia (f.): alarm clock
svegliarsi: to wake up
la svendita (f.): sale
la Svezia (f.): Sweden
sviluppare: to develop
la Svizzera (f.): Switzerland

T

la tabaccheria (f.): tobacco shop
la tabella (f.): schedule, time table
la taglia (f.): size
tagliare: to cut
tale: such, like, similar
talvolta: sometimes
il tamburo: drum
tanto: so much, so many, a lot
il tappo: cork
tardi: late
la targa (f.): license plate
la tariffa (f.): fare, charge
la tasca (f.): pocket
la tassa (f.): tax
il tassametro : taxi meter
il tassì (m.): taxi
la tavola (f.): dinner table
il tavolo: table (restaurant)
la tazza (f.): cup
te: you
il tè (m.): tea
il teatro: theater
tedesco: German
il tegame (m.): saucepan
la tegola (f.): shingle
telefonare: to telephone
la telefonata (f.): telephone call
il telefono: telephone
il telegiornale (m.): news program
il tema (m.): theme
la tempesta (f.): storm
il tempio: temple

il tempo: weather, time
la tenda (f.): tent
tenere: to hold, to keep
tenero: tender, affectionate
il termometro: thermometer
la terra (f.): earth, dirt
la terracotta (f.): ceramic
il terrazzo: terrace
terzo: third
la tessera (f.): card, ticket
la testa (f.): head
il tetto: roof
timido: shy
il tipo: type, kind
la tipografia (f.): printing
tirare: to pull
tirchio: stingy
toccare: to touch
la toilette (f.): toilet
la tolleranza (f.): tolerance
il topo: mouse
tornare: to return
la torre (f.): tower
la torta (f.): cake
il torto: wrong, fault
la tosse (f.): cough
totale: total
la tovaglia (f.): tablecloth
tovagliolo: napkin
tra: between
la tradizione (f.): tradition
tradurre (tradotto): to translate
la traduzione (f.): translation
il traffico: traffic
il traghetto: ferry
tragico: tragic
il tramonto: sunset
trasferirsi: to transfer, to move
trasformare: to transform
trasmettere (trasmesso):
    to broadcast
trasportare: to transport
trattare: to treat
tre: three
tredici: thirteen
tremendo: tremendous
il treno: train
trenta: thirty
triste: sad
tropicale: tropical
troppo: too
trovare: to find
tu: you (familiar)
il tuffo: dive
il tulipano: tulip
il tuono: thunder
il turismo: tourism
il/la turista (m./f.): tourist
il turno: turn
tutt'e due: both

tuttavia: however, yet
tutti: everyone
tutto: everything, all

U

ubriacarsi: to get drunk
l'uccello: bird
uccidere (ucciso): to kill
udire: to hear
l'ufficio: office
l'ufficio cambio: money
exchange office
l'ufficio informazioni: informa-
    tion office
l'ufficio oggetti smarriti:
    lost and found
l'ufficio postale: post office
ultimo: last
l'umano: human
l'umidità (f.): humidity
umile: humble
l'umore: humor, mood
un: a, an, one
una: a, an, one
undici: eleven
unico: unique, only
unificato: unified
unito: united
uno: one, a, an
l'uomo: man
l'uovo (pl. le uova): egg
urbano: city, local
urgente: urgent
urlare: to shout
usare: to use
uscire: to exit
l'uscita (f.): exit
l'uso: usage
l'uva (f.): grapes

V

la vacanza (f.): vacation
la vacca (f.): cow
la vaccinazione (f.): vaccination
il vaglia postale (m.): money
    order
il vagone (m.): rail car
la valanga (f.): avalanche
la validità (f.): validity
la valigia (f.): bag, valise, suitcase
la valle (f.): valley
il valore (m.): value
la valuta (f.): currency, money
il vantaggio: advantage
la variazione (f.): variation
la varietà (f.): variety

vario: various
la vasca (f.): tub
il vaso: vase
vecchio: old
vedere (visto): to see
la vedova (f.): widow
il vedovo: widower
il veicolo: vehicle
vegetariano: vegetarian
il veleno: poison
la velocità (f.): velocity
vendere: to sell
la vendetta (f.): vengeance
la vendita (f.): sale
venerdì: Friday
venire: to come
venti: twenty
il vento: wind
veramente: really
il verbo: verb
verde: green
la verdura (f.): vegetables
la vergogna (f.): shame
la verità (f.): truth
la vernice (f.): paint
vero: true, genuine
verso: toward, near, about
il vescovo: bishop
la vespa (f.): wasp
vestire: to dress
il vestito: dress, suit
la vetrina (f.): shop window
il vetro: glass
la vettura (f.): carriage,
    railroad car
vi: (adv.) there, to you
la via (f.): street, way
via: away
viaggiare: to travel
il viaggio: trip
il viale (m.): boulevard, avenue
vicino: neighbor, near (adj.)
il vicolo: alley, lane
vietato: prohibited
vietato di sosta: no parking
vietato l'ingresso: no entrance
il vigile: police officer
il vigile del fuoco: firefighter
la vigna (f.): vine
la villa (f.): villa
il villaggio: village
vincere (vinto): to win
il vino: wine
viola: purple
la violetta (f.): violet (flower)
la violenza (f.): violence
visibile: visible
la visita (f.): visit
visitare: to visit
il viso: face

439

la vista (f.): view
la vita (f.): life
la vitamina (f.): vitamin
il vitello: veal
la vittima (f.): victim
vivace: lively
vivere (vissuto): to live
vivo: alive
il vocabolario: vocabulary
la vocale (f.): vowel
la voce (f.): voice
la voglia (f.): wish, desire
voi: you (plural)
volare: to fly
volentieri!: gladly!
volere: to want
il volo: flight
la volpe (f.): fox
la volta (f.): time, occurrence
votare: to vote
il voto: grade
vuoto: empty

Y

lo yoga (m.): yoga
lo yogurt (m.): yogurt

Z

lo zaino: backpack
la zampa (f.): paw, leg
la zanzara (f.): mosquito
zero: zero
la zia (f.): aunt
lo zio: uncle
la zona (f.): zone, section
lo zoo: zoo
lo zucchero: sugar
la zuppa (f.): soup

Map of Italy

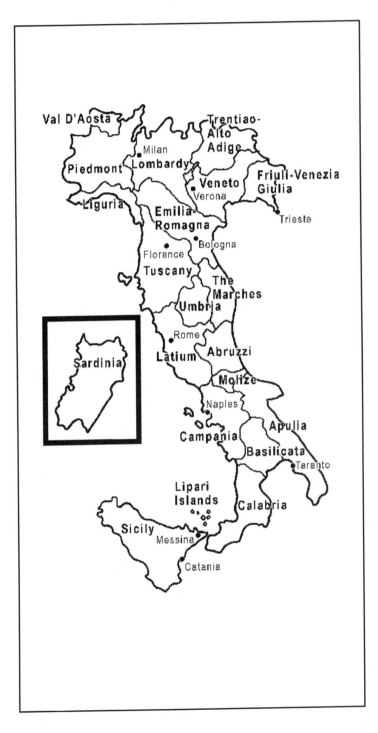

An Idiot's Guide to Additional Resources

By no means comprehensive, the following titles and Web sites are worthy of a glance.

Grammar Plus

Supplement your Italian grammar library with anyone of the following titles:

Colaneri, John and Vincent Luciani. *501 Italian Verbs*. Barron's Educational Series, 1992.

Graziano, Carlos. *Italian Verbs and Essentials of Grammar*. Passport Books, 1986.

Piluso, Robert V. *Italian Fundamentals*. Barron's Educational Series, 1992

Ragusa, Olga. *Essential Italian Grammar*. Dover Publications, 1972.

La Dolce Vita

Some of the many books written that portray one aspect or another of Italian life include:

Barzini, Luigi. *The Italians*. Simon & Schuster Trade, 1996.

Calvino, Italo. *Italian Folktales*. Harcourt Trade Publishers, 1992.

Costantino, Mario, and Lawrence Gambella. *The Italian Way*. NTC Contemporary Publishing Company, 1995.

Grizzuti Harrison, Barbara. *Italian Days*. Grove/Atlantic, 1998.

Hofmann, Paul. *That Fine Italian Hand*. Henry Holt and Company, 1991.

Mayes, Frances. *Under the Tuscan Sun*. Chronicle Books, 1996.

Morante, Elsa. *History: A Novel*. Steerforth Press, 2000.

Spender, Matthew. *Within Tuscany*. Penguin USA, 1992.

The Internet

Use the Internet to supplement your Italian studies. Following are several suggested Web sites:

About Italian Language Subjects

http://www.italian.about.com/mlibrary.htm

Thousands of annotated links arranged by topics including grammar, vocabulary, lessons and exercises, idiomatic expressions, online dictionaries, translation, and children's Italian.

Acquerello Italiano

http://www.acquerello-italiano.com/aihome.php3

Sample audio excerpts from the audiocassette magazine for intermediate and advanced speakers. Includes a transcript of the program with a glossary and study supplement.

Audio Anthology of Italian Literature

http://www.ilnarratore.com/index2.html

Classical and contemporary Italian texts read by narrators, stage actors, and writers available as MP3 audio file downloads.

BBC Italian Language Online For Adults

http://www.bbc.co.uk/education/languages/italian/index.shtml

Transcripts of the popular BBC television program devoted to Italian and supplementary exercises.

Coniugare I Verbi

http://www.virgilio.it/servizi/verbi/

High-performance, automatic verb conjugation and resource for studying a crucial part of the language.

Research Edition of The Divine Comedy

http://www.divinecomedy.org/divine_comedy.html

Three full editions of *The Divine Comedy* online, graphics, maps of the afterlife, and sample manuscript pages from printed versions of Dante. Listen to *The Inferno* as recited by Vittorio Gassman.

Italian Embassy

http://www.italyemb.org

Useful addresses, telephone numbers, directions, travel information, events, and other links.

Il Cinema

The following are some additional movie suggestions. These film classics have entertained millions of people.

1900 (Bertolucci)	*Marcello Mastroianni: I Remember* (Anna Maria Tatò)
The Age of the Medici (Rossellini)	*Miracle in Milan* (De Sica)
Amarcord (Fellini)	*Night of the Shooting Stars* (Paolo and Vittorio Taviani)
Amore (Rossellini)	*Nights of Cabiria* (Fellini)
L'Avventura (Antonioni)	*Open City* (Rossellini)
Ciao Professore! (Wertmuller)	*Paisan* (Rossellini)
City of Women (Fellini)	*Swept Away* (Wertmuller)
La Famiglia (Scola)	*The Spider's Stratagem* (Bertolucci)
The Garden of the Finzi-Continis (De Sica)	*Two Women* (De Sica)
Johnny Stecchino (Benigni)	

Index

A

a (to)
    following verb *andare* (to go), 153
    preposition, infinitive verbs requiring *a*, 200-201
a.c. (*avanti Cristo*), 214
A.D. (*Anno Domini*), 212-213
abbreviations, bilingual dictionaries, 17
absolutes, forming superlatives from adjectives, 338
accents (pronunciation), 26
    acute, 26
    grave, 26
    written, 26
accessories, shopping, 246
action in progress, forming the present progressive tense, 237-238
acute accent, 26
adjectives, 18, 136-148, 335-338
    absolutes, forming superlatives, 336-338
    antonyms, 140
    bello, 143
    buono (good), 144
    cognates, 44
    colors, 140-142
        idiomatic expressions, 142
    communicating with a realtor, 373
    comparisons, 335
        equality, 338
    emotions and characteristics, 138-139
    forming adverbs from, 144
        practicing, 147-148
    modifying, endings, 136-137
    nationalities, 123-124
        practicing, 126
    possessive, 122
    practicing, 138
    quello, practicing, 143
    religions, 125
    weather vocabulary, 208
adverbs, 18, 144-148
    compound tenses, 319
    con plus a noun, 147
    ecco, 126-127
    forming from adjectives, 144
        practicing, 147-148
    irregular adverbs of quantity, 146
    place, 147
    placement, 145-146
    superlatives, 337
    time, 146
advertisements, real estate, 373
affirmative responses to questions, 109
"after the hour" time expressions, 176
agreement, gender, 70
ailments, saints, 347
air travel
    expressions, 152
    verbs, 151
    vocabulary, 149-152
alphabet, spelling your name, 36
amenities/necessities, hotels, 189
anatomy of a verb, present-tense conjugations, 94-95
andare (to go), 152, 229
    followed by *a* (to), 153
    followed by *in* (to), 153
    idiomatic expressions, 65
    practicing, 154
animals, 225-226
Anno Domini (A.D.), 212-213
answering questions, double negatives, 109-110
antonyms, adjectives, 140
apostrophes (indicates the dropping of the final vowel), 27
appetizers (meals), 289
appointments, making a date, 306
–are family, first conjugation verbs, 94-100
    celebrare example, 96
    conjugation
        exceptions, 100-101
        practicing, 101
articles
    definite, 41
        forming plurals, 79
    noun markers, 70
        indefinite articles, 71-72
        singular, definite articles, 70
arts, 307
    cinema/film, 307-308
    music, 309-310

opera, 310
    glossary of terms, 311
    storytelling, 310
    terms, 312
asking questions, 109, 178
    answering, double negatives, 109-110
    c'é and *ci sono*, 116
    practicing, 178
    tags, 109
astrology terms
    atmosphere, 217
    zodiacal signs, 217-218
audiocassettes, listening to Italian, 37
avanti Cristo (a.c.), 214
avere (to have), 117-119, 314-316
    conditional tense, 375
    forming the past, 315
        irregular past participles, 315-316
    future tense, 364
    idiomatic expressions, 66, 118-119
    present perfect tense, transitive verbs, 314
    rules of usage, 118

B

backgrounds (nationalities), 123-124
banking terms, 381
    expressions, 384
    trades/professions, 385
    transactions, 384
bars, 285
    caffè, il (coffee), 286
"be," irregular verb forms, 112
    asking about someone else, 122
    c'é and *ci sono*, 116
        asking questions, 116
        creating negative statements, 116
        practicing translations, 116-117
    essere, 112-116
    stare, 113-116
"before the hour" time expressions, 176
Bellini, 295

bello (adjective), 143
beverages, 270, 295
  Bellini, 295
  wines, 294
bilingual dictionaries, 7, 16
  abbreviations, 17
  grammatical listings, 19
bills, hotels, 192
body parts, 341
  expressions of pain/
    discomfort, 343
  use of *farsi* to express hurt,
    342-343
brain games, vocabulary, 305
buono (good), adjective, 144
buying a home
  adjectives, 373
  verbs, 372

C

c letter combinations, pronunciation, 32
c'é, use with third-person *essere,*
  116
  asking questions, 116
  creating negative statements,
    116
  practicing translations,
    116-117
caffè, il (coffee), 286
calls, telephone operation, 356
camera shop vocabulary, 331
cardinal numbers, 172-174
  using punctuation marks with,
    174
cars, vocabulary, 167
  expressions, 171
  inside the car, 168
  necessary tools, 170
  parts and predicaments,
    169-170
  renting a car, 168
  sample communication, 172
  signs, 171
  types of roads, 169
cartoleria, la (stationery store), 243
centuries, 212
  a.c. (*avanti Cristo*), 214
  A.D. (*Anno Domini*), 212-213
  after year 1000, 213
changing gender depending on
  profession, 77, 120
characteristics of nouns. *See* adjectives
cheeses, 267
ci, denoting place, 339-340
ci sono, use with third-person
  essere, 116

asking questions, 116
  creating negative statements,
    116
  practicing translations,
    116-117
cinema/film, 307-308
clarity, subject pronouns, 87
classical Latin, history of Italian
  language, 12-13
climate, weather vocabulary,
  207-208
clothing, shopping, 245, 251
  conversion table for sizes, 248
coffee (*caffè, il*), 286
cognates, 39
  adjectives, 44
  converting words to Italian by
    changing the endings, 43
  English words used in Italian,
    46
  false, 40-47
  nouns, 45
    feminine, 45-46
    masculine, 45
  places, 41-42
  practicing, 47-51
  time, 41-43
  verbs, 48-49
colloquialisms. *See* idiomatic
  expressions
colors, adjectives, 140-142
  idiomatic expressions, 142
combinations of letters, pronunciation, 31
  letter *c,* 32
  letter *g,* 32-33
  letter *s,* 33-34
commands. *See* imperatives
commas, indicating time, 84
commitment to learning, 8-9
communication by telephone,
  355
  communicating with the oper-
    ator, 358-359
  expressions, 357-358
  types of calls, 356
  vocabulary, 356-357
comparisons, forming from
  adjectives, 335
  equality, 338
compound tenses
  adverbs, 319
  direct object pronouns,
    319-320
  double object pronouns, 321
  future perfect, 367
  indirect object pronouns, 320
con plus a noun, in lieu of an
  adverb, 147

conditional tense, 374
  avere (to have), 375
  essere (to be), 375
  forming, 374
    endings, 374-376
    stem-changing verbs, 377
    verbs, 377
  practicing use, 378
conjugation
  andare (to go), 153
  avere (to have), 117-118
  conoscere (to know someone),
    135
  determining subject pronouns,
    85-86
    clarity, 87
    direct objects, 86
    emphasis, 87
    forms of "you," 88-89
    indirect objects, 86
    politeness, 87
    practicing, 87-88
    versus object pronouns, 87
  dovere (to have to, must),
    97-198
  essere (to be), 112
  fare (to make or do some-
    thing), 182
  future tense, 366-367
  irregular verbs, 202
    andare (to go), 229
    dire (to say/tell), 231
    fare (to do/make), 229
    passare (to pass), 229
    practicing conjugation of,
      230
    rimanere (to remain), 228
    ritornare (to return), 230
    trovare (to find/visit), 229
    uscire (to go out/exit), 227
    venire (to come), 227-228
  piacere (to be pleasing to), 275
  potere (to be able to), 196-197
  practicing, 353-354
  regular verbs, 94
    anatomy of a verb, 94
    first conjugation (*-are* fam-
      ily), 94-101
    present-tense conjugations,
      95
    second-conjugation (*-ere*
      family), 94, 102-105
    third conjugation (*-ire* fam-
      ily), 94, 106-107
  salire (to climb), 182
  sapere (to know something),
    134
  stare (to be), 113
  travel-related verbs, 182
  volere (to want), 195-196

conjunctions, subjunctive mood, 389-390
conoscere (to know someone), 135
consonants
    pronunciation of, 29
    double consonants, 35
continents, 235
contractions
    forming from prepositions, 157-158
    showing possession with *di*, 131
converting English words to Italian, changing the endings, 43
cooking terms, 278
corresponding planets, days of the week, 60
cosmetics store, vocabulary, 349
countries, telling someone where you are from, 234-237
courses (meals), 287
    appetizers and side dishes, 289
    first, 288
    menu, sample, 289
    second, 288

D

dairy products, 267
dates, 212
    centuries, 212
        a.c. (*avanti Cristo*), 214
        A.D. (*Anno Domini*), 212-213
        after year 1000, 213
    holidays, 216-217
    months, 212
    past time, 214
    practicing, 215
    time-related words, 214
days of the week, 58
    corresponding planets, 60
definite articles, 41
    forming plurals, 79
    singular, 70
demonstrative pronouns ("this" and "these"), 135
    introducing family members, 135-136
denoting place, *ci* and *vi*, 339-340
dependent clauses, subjunctive mood, 388-390
describing your needs, 325
    asking others to speak slowly, 326
    camera shop, 331
    dry cleaner's, 329
    electronics store, 332
    grooming vocabulary, 327-328
        stylists' lingo, 328-329

help phrases, 326-327
jeweler's, 331
keeping it simple, 326
missing passport, 332-333
optician's, 330
shoemaker's, 330
writing down questions, 326
descriptive adjectives, 136
    antonyms, 140
    bello, 143
    buono (good), 144
    colors, 140-142
        idiomatic expressions, 142
    emotions and characteristics, 138-139
    modifying, endings, 136-137
    practicing, 138
    quello, 143
desserts/sweets, 295
determining gender, 69
    agreement, 70
    either-gender nouns, 73
    exceptions to the rules, 75
        changing gender depending on profession, 77, 120
        disconcerting genders, 75-76
        fruits, 78
        misbehaving feminine nouns, 77
        misbehaving masculine nouns, 76
    noun markers, 70
        indefinite articles, 71-72
        singular, definite articles, 70
    nouns ending in *e*, 74
    practicing, 78-84
    singular nouns, 72
di
    plus noun, indicating "some of" a larger quantity, 273
    preposition, infinitive verbs requiring *di*, 199-200
dialects, history of Italian language, 13
    Tuscan Italian, 14
dictionaries, bilingual, 7, 16
    abbreviations, 17
    grammatical listings, 19
diminutives, 13
dining out, 281
    bars, 285
        caffè, il (coffee), 286
    courses, 287
        appetizers and side dishes, 289
        first, 288
        second, 288

drinks, 295
    Bellini, 295
    wines, 294
etiquette, 286-287
menu, sample, 289
pizza, 289-290
preparation terms, 291
restaurants, 281-282
    asking for what you want, 282-283
    common phrases, 282
    table-setting vocabulary, 283-284
returning food, phrases to use, 293-294
special needs phrases, 292
spices and seasonings, 291-292
sweets/desserts, 295
dipthongs, pronunciation of, 34-35
dire (to say/tell), 231
direct object pronouns, 253-255
    compound tenses, 319-320
    practicing, 257-258
direct objects, 86
directions, imperatives, 159
    most common commands, 160
    negative commands, 160
    practicing, 161
    regular imperative endings, 159
diretto train, 180
discomfort expressions, 343-345
    idiomatic expressions, 346
    serious medical conditions, 345-347
disconcerting genders, exception to gender determination rules, 75-76
diseases/health conditions, vocabulary, 347-348
disjunctive pronouns, 333
    practicing use, 334
    rules, 334
double
    consonants, pronunciation of, 35
    negatives, responding to questions, 110
    object pronouns, 296
        compound tenses, 321
doubt, expressions of, subjunctive mood, 386
    dependent clauses, 388-390
    imperfect, 392
    irregular forms, 388
    past, 391
    past perfect, 392
    present, 386-388

dovere (to have to, must), 197-198
drawing from other language experiences, 21-22
drinks, 270, 295
  Bellini, 295
  wines, 294
driving cars, vocabulary, 167
  expressions, 171
  inside the car, 168
  necessary tools, 170
  parts and predicaments, 169-170
  renting a car, 168
  sample communication, 172
  signs, 171
  types of roads, 169
drugstore/pharmacy vocabulary, 348
  questions for the pharmacist, 349
dry cleaner's vocabulary, 329

E

ecco, 126-127
Edith Wharton's Italian Gardens, 267
either-gender nouns, determining gender of, 73
electronic messages, 359-360
electronics store vocabulary, 332
emotions (adjectives), 138-139
emphasis, subject pronouns, 87
endings
  conditional tense, 374-376
  forming plurals, 78-79
    always plural nouns, 83
    irregular plural nouns, 82-83
    noun markers, 79
    practicing, 81-83
    rules, 80
    spelling, 81
  future tense, 363
  imperatives, 159
  imperfect tense, 351
    essere (to be) exceptions, 351
    practicing use, 352-353
  modifying descriptive adjectives, 137
  verbs, 50
English words, used in Italian, 46
entertainment, 303
  arts, 307
    cinema/film, 307-308
    music, 309-310
    opera, 310-311
    terms, 312

brain games, 305
making a date, 306
playing field, 305
sports vocabulary, 303-305
equality, forming comparisons from adjectives/adverbs, 338
–ere family, second-conjugation verbs, 94, 102-103
  practicing conjugation, 105
  scrivere example, 102
espresso train, 180
essere (to be), 112
  asking about someone else, 122
  c'é and ci sono, 116
    asking questions, 116
    creating negative statements, 116
    practicing translations, 116-117
  conditional tense, 375
  forming the past, 316
  future tense rules, 364
  rules of usage, 114-116
  use in present perfect tense, intransitive verbs, 314-318
etiquette, dining out, 286-287
etymology (study of words), 15
exceptions
  conjugation, regular *–are* verbs, 100-101
  gender-determination rules, 75
    changing gender depending on profession, 77, 120
    disconcerting genders, 75-76
    fruits, 78
    misbehaving feminine nouns, 77
    misbehaving masculine nouns, 76
exclamations, 57-61
expressions
  air travel, 152
  asking for help, 326-327
  asking for the kind of room you want, 188-189
  asking for what you need, 189-191
  banking, 384
  car travel, 171
  communicating that you don't understand, 161
  food shopping, 273
  food-related, 268
  hotels, 191
    negotiating or paying for a room, 192

how often, 215-216
idiomatic, 61-68
  andare (to go), 65
  colors, 142
  fare (to make or do something), 183
  food-related, 268
  health issues, 346
  opinion phrases, 66
  slang, 62
  time expressions, 64
  travel and transportation, 63
  avere (to have), 118-119
  weather, 206
imperatives, negative commands, 160
introductions, 136
pain/discomfort, 343-345
  idiomatic expressions, 346
  serious medical conditions, 345-347
post-office operations, 361
restaurants, asking for what you want, 282-283
returning food, phrases to use, 293-294
shopping, 247-248
special needs phrases (when dining out), 292
telephone, 357-358
  communicating with the operator, 358-359
time, 175-176
  after the hour, 176
  "before the hour," 176
  practicing, 177
  travel-related, 181
  weather vocabulary, leisure expressions, 210-211

F

fables, using past definite tense (*passato remoto*), 393-394
fabrics, shopping, 250-251
false cognates, 40-47
family members, 129
  introductions, 135
    helpful expressions, 136
fare (to make or do something), 182, 229
  idiomatic expressions, 183
  practicing, 184
farsi, expressing that something hurts, 342-343
fax, using, 359-360

feelings, subjunctive mood, 386
dependent clauses, 388-390
expressions, 118
imperfect, 392
irregular forms, 388
past, 391
past perfect, 392
present, 386-388
feminine gender, 69
agreement, 70
either-gender nouns, 73
exceptions to the rules, 75
changing gender depend-
ing on profession, 77, 120
disconcerting genders,
75-76
fruits, 78
misbehaving feminine
nouns, 77
misbehaving masculine
nouns, 76
noun cognates, 45-46
noun markers, 70
indefinite articles, 71-72
singular, definite articles,
70
nouns ending in *e*, 74
practicing gender determination, 78-84
singular nouns, 72
film/cinema, 307-308
Fine Art of Italian Cooking, The,
267
first conjugation verbs (–are family), 94-100
celebrare example, 96
conjugation exceptions,
100-101
practicing conjugation, 101
first course (meals), 288
fish, 268-269
flashcards, 7
flowers, shopping, 250
food
idiomatic expressions, 268
returning food, phrases to use,
293-294
shopping, 261
dairy products, 267
drinks, 270
expressing quantity,
271-272
fish and seafood, 268-269
food labels, 263
fruits and nuts, 264
idiomatic expressions, 273
indicating "some of" a
larger quantity, 273-274
meats, 265

pasta, 269
practicing putting together
a shopping list, 274
sweets, 271
vegetables, 262-263
verbs, 273
vocabulary, 261
special needs phrases, 292
spices, 291
verbs, 264
forming
adverbs from adjectives,
144-148
conditional tense, 374
avere (to have), 375
endings, 374, 376
essere (to be), 375
stem-changing verbs, 377
verbs, 377
plurals, 78-79
always plural nouns, 83
irregular plural nouns,
82-83
noun markers, 79
practicing, 81-83
rules, 80
spelling, 81
present progressive tense, 238
forms of "you," determining subject pronouns, 88-89
From the Tables of Tuscan Women,
267
fruits, 264
gender determination based
on context, 78
furniture and accessories, vocabulary, 370
future perfect tense, 367
future tense, 363
avere (to have), 364
endings, 363
essere (to be) rules, 364
irregular stems, 365-366
patterns, 365
practicing conjugation,
366-367

G

g letter combinations, pronunciation, 32-33
gender, 69
either-gender nouns, 73
exceptions to the rules, 75
changing gender depend-
ing on profession, 77, 120
disconcerting genders,
75-76
fruits, 78

misbehaving feminine
nouns, 77
misbehaving masculine
nouns, 76
masculine versus feminine, 69
agreement, 70
noun markers, 70
indefinite articles, 71-72
singular, definite articles,
70
nouns ending in *e*, 74
practicing gender determination, 78-84
singular nouns, 72
Giusto? (question tag), 109
Gods, Roman and Greek equivalents, 126
grammar, 17
adjectives, 18, 136
antonyms, 140
bello, 143
buono (good), 144
colors, 140-142
emotions and characteris-
tics, 138-139
forming comparisons,
335-338
forming superlatives,
336-338
modifying, 136-137
nationalities, 123-126
possessive, 122
practicing, 138
quello, 143
religions, 125
adverbs, 18, 144
compound tenses, 319
con plus a noun, 147
ecco, 126-127
forming from adjectives,
144-148
forming superlatives, 337
irregular adverbs of quantity, 146
place, 147
placement, 145-146
time, 146
bilingual dictionary listings,
19
disjunctive pronouns, 333
practicing use, 334
rules, 334
imperatives, 159
most common commands,
160
negative commands, 160
practicing, 161
regular imperative endings,
159
nouns, 17

object pronouns, 253-254
  direct object pronouns, 255-258, 319-320
  double object pronouns, 321
  indirect object pronouns, 255-259, 320
  practicing, 257-259
  rules, 254
objects versus subjects, 21
passive voice, *si* construction, 162
prepositions, 18, 154-156
  forming contractions, 157-158
  rules, 156
pronouns, 18
reflexive pronouns, 297-298
  working with conjugated verbs, 298
reflexive verbs, 299
  changing meaning when made reflexive, 300-301
  practicing use, 301
  reciprocity, 302
  rules, 300
verbs, 18
  conjugated, 18
  infinitives, 18, 50, 198-201
  intransitive, 18
  irregular verbs, 201-202
  modal verbs, 195-198
  piacere (to be pleasing to), 275-278
  transitive, 18
grave accent, 26
Greek Gods, Roman equivalents, 126
greetings, 53
  communications, 57
  important phrases, 55-56
  introductions, 53
    informal phrases, 56
    polite form of address, 54-55
grooming vocabulary, 327-328
  stylists' lingo, 328-329
group I regular –ire verbs, 106-107
group II regular –ire verbs, 107

H

habitual patterns, imperfect tense, 350
  endings, 351-353
Harry's Bar Cookbook, The, 267
have (*avere*), 117-118
  idiomatic expressions, 118-119
  rules of usage, 118

healthcare issues
  body parts vocabulary, 341
  diseases/health conditions, 347-348
  expressions of pain/discomfort, 343-345
  idiomatic expressions, 346
  pharmacy/drugstore vocabulary, 348
    questions for the pharmacist, 349
  serious medical conditions, 345-347
  use of *farsi* to express hurt, 342-343
help phrases, 326-327
helping verbs, 112
historical figures, zodiacal signs, 219
history of Italian language
  classical Latin, 12-13
  dialects, 13
    Tuscan Italian, 14
  etymology, 15
holidays, 216-217
homes, vocabulary, 369
  advertisements, 373
  communicating with a realtor, 371-373
  furniture and accessories, 370
hotels, 187
  amenities/necessities, 189
  asking for the kind of room you want, 188-189
  asking for what you need, 189-191
  invoices, bills, and receipts, 192
  negotiating or paying for a room, 192
  practicing vocabulary and expressions, 192
  tipping, 193
  useful expressions, 191
  vocabulary, 187-188
hour (time), idiomatic expressions, 64
"how about," making a suggestion, 232-233
hypothetical situations, subjunctive mood, 386
  dependent clauses, 388-390
  imperfect, 392
  irregular forms, 388
  past, 391
  past perfect, 392
  present, 386-388

I

idiomatic expressions, 61-68
  andare (to go), 65
  colors, 142
  fare (to make or do something), 183
  food-related, 268
  health issues, 346
  opinion phrases, 66
  slang, 62
  time expressions, 64
  travel and transportation, 63
  avere (to have), 118-119
  weather, 206
il (singular, masculine definite article), 71
immersing yourself in the Italain language, 6
  bilingual dictionaries, 7
  commitment, 8-9
  flashcards, 7
  making tapes of yourself speaking, 8
  multilingual owner's manuals, 7
  radio, 7
  studying with a partner, 7
  watching Italian movies/television, 7
imperatives, 159
  indirect object pronouns, 257
  most common commands, 160
  negative commands, 160
  practicing, 161
  regular imperative endings, 159
imperfect subjunctive mood, 392
imperfect tense, 350
  endings, 351
    essere (to be) exceptions, 351
  practicing use, 352-353
  practicing conjugation, 353-354
impersonal expressions, subjunctive mood, 389-390
important phrases, 55-56
in (to), following verb *andare* (to go), 153
In Nonna's Kitchen, 267
indefinite articles, 71
  feminine, 72
  masculine, 71
indirect object pronouns, 253-256
  compound tenses, 320
  following the imperative (command), 257
  practicing, 258-259

indirect objects, 86
inequality
forming comparisons from
adjectives, 335
forming superlatives from
adjectives, 336
absolutes, 338
forming superlatives from
adverbs, 337
infinitive verbs, 94
anatomy of a verb, 94
present-tense conjugations,
95
practicing, 201
requiring preposition *a*,
200-201
requiring preposition *di*,
199-200
with prepositions, 198-199
without prepositions, 199
infinitives verbs, 18, 50
informal phrases, greetings/
salutations, 56
communicating that you are
studying Italian, 57
information questions, traveling,
177-178
Internet, listening to Italian, 38
interrogative pronouns, *quale*
(which or what), 166
intransitive verbs, 18
use of *essere* (to be) in present
perfect tense, 314-318
introductions, 53
family members, 129-135
demonstrative pronouns,
135-136
helpful expressions, 136
informal phrases, 56
polite form of address, 54-55
invoices, hotels, 192
–*ire* family, third-conjugation
verbs, 94, 106
capire example, 107
dormire example, 106
group I, 106-107
group II, 107
irregular adjectives, comparatives
and superlatives, 336
absolutes, 338
irregular
adverbs
comparatives and superla-
tives, 337
quantity, 146
forms of the subjunctive
mood, 388
past participles, *avere* (to
have), 315-316
plural nouns, 82-83
stems, future tense, 365-366

irregular verbs
andare (to go), 152
followed by *a* (to), 153
followed by *in* (to), 153
practicing, 154
andare (to go), 229
avere (to have), 117-118
idiomatic expressions,
118-119
rules of usage, 118
conjugation
dire (to say/tell), 231
fare (to do/make), 229
passare (to pass), 229
practicing, 230
rimanere (to remain), 228
ritornare (to return), 230
trovare (to find/visit), 229
uscire (to go out/exit), 227
venire (to come), 227-228
essere (to be), 112
asking about someone else,
122
c'é and ci sono, 116-117
rules of usage, 114-116
stare, 113
review, 201-202
Italian regions, 235-236
*Italian Verbs and Essentials of
Grammar*, 17

J–K

jeweler's vocabulary, 331
jewelry, shopping, 244

kitchen items, vocabulary,
284-285

L

l' (singular, masculine or feminine definite article), 71
la (singular, feminine definite
article), 71
labels on food, 263
language CDs, listening to Italian,
38
Latin, classical, history of Italian
language, 12-13
Latium, 12
"let's," making a suggestion, 232
letter combinations, pronunciation, 31
letter *c*, 32
letter *g*, 32-33
letter *s*, 33-34
letter writing, 362

lifestyle, 303
arts, 307
cinema/film, 307-308
music, 309-310
opera, 310-311
terms, 312
brain games, 305
making a date, 306
playing field, 305
sports vocabulary, 303-305
listening to Italian, 37
audiocassettes, 37
Internet audio samples, 38
language CDs, 38
music, 38
literary titles, practicing cognate
translations, 52
lo (singular, masculine definite
article), 71

M

making a suggestion, 231
"how about," 232-233
"let's," 232
non, 233
perche non, 232
responding, 233
volere (to want), 233
masculine gender, 69
agreement, 70
either-gender nouns, 73
exceptions to the rules, 75
changing gender depend-
ing on profession, 77, 120
disconcerting genders,
75-76
fruits, 78
misbehaving feminine
nouns, 77
misbehaving masculine
nouns, 76
noun cognates, 45
noun markers, 70
indefinite articles, 71
singular, definite articles,
70
nouns ending in *e*, 74
practicing gender determination, 78-84
singular nouns, 72
measuring, metric system,
271-272
meats, 265
medical issues
diseases/health conditions,
347-348
expressions of pain/
discomfort/sickness, 344-345

idiomatic expressions, 346
serious medical conditions, 345-347
pharmacy/drugstore vocabulary, 348
questions for the pharmacist, 349
members of the family, 129
introductions, 135
demonstrative pronouns, 135-136
helpful expressions, 136
menu sample, 289
merchandise, stores, 241
accessories, 246
clothing, 245-251
expressions, 247-248
fabrics, 250-251
flowers, 250
jewelry, 244
stationery store (*la cartoleria*), 243
metric system, 271-272
misbehaving nouns (exceptions to gender-determination rules)
feminine, 77
masculine, 76
modal verbs, 195
dovere (to have to, must), 197-198
potere (to be able to), 196-197
practicing, 198
volere (to want), 195-196
modes of shipment, post-office operations, 361
modes of transportation, 165-166
cars, 167
expressions, 171
inside the car, vocabulary, 168
necessary tools, 170
parts and predicaments, 169-170
renting a car, 168
sample communication, 172
signs, 171
types of roads, 169
interrogative pronoun *quale* (which or what), 166
phrases, 181
public transportation, 172
cardinal numbers, 172-174
getting around, 179-180
time expressions, 175-177
trains, 180
verbs, 181
fare (to make or do something), 182-184

practicing conjugation, 182
salire (to climb), 182
modifying adjectives, endings, 136-137
money, banking terms, 381
expressions, 384
trades/professions, 385
transactions, 384
months of the year, 58-59, 212
moods, subjunctive, 386
dependent clauses, 388-390
imperfect, 392
irregular forms, 388
past, 391
past perfect, 392
present, 386-388
motives for learning Italain, 16
music, 309-310
listening to Italian, 38
mythological archetypes, 126

N

nationalities, 123-124
practicing, 126
telling someone where you are from, 236-237
ne partitive pronoun, indicating "some of" a larger quantity, 273-274
needs (describing your needs), 325
asking others to speak slowly, 326
camera shop, 331
dry cleaner's, 329
electronics store, 332
grooming vocabulary, 327-328
stylists' lingo, 328-329
help phrases, 326-327
idiomatic expressions, 118-119
jeweler's, 331
keeping it simple, 326
missing passport, 332-333
optician's, 330
shoemaker's, 330
writing down questions, 326
negative
commands, 160
responses to questions, 109
statements, *non* with *c'é* and *ci sono*, 116
No? (question tag), 109
non, making a suggestion, 233
Nonna's Kitchen, In, 267
noun markers, 70
forming plurals, 79
indefinite articles, 71

feminine, 72
masculine, 71
singular, definite articles, 70
nouns, 17
always plural nouns, 83
cognates, 45
feminine, 45-46
masculine, 45
either-gender nouns, 73
ending in *e*, determining gender, 74
irregular plural nouns, 82-83
singular, determining gender, 72
numbers
cardinal, 172-174
using punctuation marks with, 174
ordinal, 194
rules, 195

O

object pronouns, 127, 253-254
direct object pronouns, 255
practicing, 257-258
double object pronouns, 296
indirect object pronouns, 255-256
following the imperative (command), 257
practicing, 258-259
practicing, 257-259
rules, 254
versus subject pronouns, 87
objects (grammar) versus subjects, 21
opera, 310
glossary of terms, 311
storytelling, 310
operators (telephone), communicating with, 358-359
opinion phrases, idiomatic expressions, 66
optician's vocabulary, 330
ordering in restaurant, ordinal numbers, 194-195
orders, imperatives, 159
most common commands, 160
negative commands, 160
practicing, 161
regular imperative endings, 159
ordinal numbers, 194-195
origin, telling someone where you are from, 236-237

P

pain expressions, 343-345
  farsi, expressing something hurts, 342-343
  idiomatic expressions, 346
  serious medical conditions, 345-347
partitive pronoun *ne*, indicating "some of" a larger quantity, 273-274
partnerships, studying the language with a friend, 7
parts of a car, vocabulary, 169-170
parts of speech (grammar), 17
  adjectives, 18
  adverbs, 18
  nouns, 17
  prepositions, 18
  pronouns, 18
  verbs, 18
    conjugated, 18
    infinitives, 18, 50
    intransitive, 18
    transitive, 18
passare (to pass), 229
passive voice, *si* construction, *si prega* (please), 162
passport, vocabulary to describe missing passport, 332-333
past absolute. *See* past, definite tense
past
  definite tense, 392-393
    fables and stories, use in, 393-394
  participle, construction from present perfect tense, 314
    avere (to have), 315
    essere (to be), 316
    irregular past participles, 315-316
    regular endings, 314
  perfect subjunctive mood, 392
  subjunctive mood, 391
  time, dates, 214
pasta, 269
patterns, future tense endings, 365
pendolino-ETR train, 180
perché non ..., making a suggestion, 232
pharmacy/drugstore vocabulary, 348
  questions for the pharmacist, 349
physical conditions, *avere* (to have), 66

piacere (to be pleasing to), 275-278
pizza, 289-290
placement, adverbs, 145-146
places
  adverbs, 147
  cognates, 41-42
  denoting with *ci* and *vi*, 339-340
  sightseeing, 223
planets, 217
  corresponding to days of the week, 60
playing field, vocabulary, 305
please, to (*si prega*), passive voice, 162
plurals, 78-79
  always plural nouns, 83
  irregular plural nouns, 82-83
  noun markers, 79
  practicing, 81-83
  rules, 80
  spelling, 81
polite form of address, greetings/salutations, 54-55
politeness, subject pronouns, 87
possession, 131
  di contractions, 131
  possessive adjectives, 122, 131-134
post-office operations, 360-361
  expressions, 361
  modes of shipment, 361
potere (to be able to), 196-197
predicaments, cars (vocabulary), 169-170
prendere (to take), 154
preparation terms (meats and vegetables), 291
prepositions, 18, 154-158
  forming contractions, 157-158
  rules, 156
  with infinitive verbs, 198-199
    leaving out the preposition, 199
    practicing, 201
    requiring preposition *a*, 200-201
    requiring preposition *di*, 199-200
present perfect tense, 313
  adverbs, 319
  constructing the past participle, 314
    avere (to have), 315
    essere (to be), 316
    irregular past participles, 315-316
    regular endings, 314

direct object pronouns, 319-320
double object pronouns, 321
indirect object pronouns, 320
practicing conjugation, 353-354
when to use *avere* (to have), transitive verbs, 314
when to use *essere* (to be), intransitive verbs, 314-318
present progressive tense, forming, 237-238
present subjunctive mood, 386-388
present-tense conjugations, regular verbs, 95
professional titles, changing genders, 77, 120
pronouns
  disjunctive. *See* disjunctive pronouns
  subject pronouns. *See* subject pronouns
pronunciation, 25
  accents, 26
    acute, 26
    grave, 26
    written, 26
  consonants, 29
    double consonants, 35
  days of the week, 58
    corresponding planets, 60
  exclamations, 60-61
  idiomatic expressions, 67-68
    andare (to go), 65
    opinion phrases, 66
    time expressions, 64
    travel and transportation, 63-64
  letter combinations, 31
    letter *c*, 32
    letter *g*, 32-33
    letter *s*, 33-34
  months of the year, 58-59
  rolling *R*'s, 28
  stress, 27
  vowels, 28
    dipthongs, 34-35
    practicing, 31
public transportation, 172
  cardinal numbers, 172-174
    using punctuation marks with, 174
  getting around, 179-180
  time expressions, 175-176
    after the hour, 176
    before the hour, 176
    practicing, 177
  trains, 180

Q

quale (which or what), interrogative pronouns, 166
quantity
  expressions, food shopping, 271
    metric system, 271-272
  irregular adverbs of quantity, 146
quello, adjective, 143
questions (asking), 109, 178
  answering, double negatives, 109-110
  c'è and *ci sono*, 116
  tags, 109

R

radio, 7
RAI (Italian television and radio network), 7
rapido train, 180
real estate
  advertisements, 373
  communicating with a realtor, 371-372
    adjectives, 373
    verbs for renting/buying, 372
  home vocabulary (furniture and accessories), 369-370
realtors, communicating needs, 371-372
  adjectives, 373
  verbs for renting/buying, 372
reasons to learn Italian, 4-6
receipts, hotels, 192
reciprocity, reflexive verbs, 302
reflexive pronouns, 297-298
  practicing use, 301
  working with conjugated verbs, 298
reflexive verbs, 299
  changing meaning when made reflexive, 300-301
  practicing use, 301
  reciprocity, 302
  rules, 300
regionale train, 180
regions, Italian, 235-236
regular verbs, 94
  anatomy of a verb, 94
  first conjugation, *–are* family, 94-101
  prendere (to take), 154
  present-tense conjugations, 95

second-conjugation, *–ere* family, 94-105
  third conjugation, *–ire* family, 94, 106-107
religions, 125
renting a car, vocabulary, 168-170
  expressions, 171
  parts and predicaments, 169-170
  signs, 171
renting a home, verbs, 372
Republic of Italy, statistics, 239
responding
  to a suggestion, 233
  to questions, double negatives, 109-110
restaurants (dining out), 281-284
  asking for what you want, 282-283
  common phrases, 282
  returning food, phrases to use, 293-294
  table-setting vocabulary, 283-284
rhotacism, 28
rimanere (to remain), 228
ritornare (to return), 230
rolling *R*'s (pronunciation), 28
Roman Gods, Greek equivalents, 126
Romance languages, rules, 22
rules
  disjunctive pronouns, 334
  forming plurals, 80
  object pronouns, 254
  ordinal numbers, 195
  prepositions, 156
  reflexive verbs, 300
  Romance languages, 22
  use of *avere* (to have), 118
  use of *essere* (to be)
    future tense, 364
    versus *stare* (to be), 114-116

S

s letter combinations, pronunciation, 33-34
saints, invoking in ailments, 347
salire (to climb), 182
salutations, 53
  communications, 57
  important phrases, 55-56
  introductions, 53
    informal phrases, 56
    polite form of address, 54-55
sample menu, 289
sapere (to know something), 134

seafood, 268-269
seasonings, 291-292
seasons, weather vocabulary, 210
second-conjugation verbs
  (*–ere* family), 94-105
  practicing conjugation, 105
  scrivere (to write) example, 102
second course (meals), 288
shoemaker's, vocabulary, 330
shopping
  food, 261
    dairy products, 267
    drinks, 270
    expressing quantity, 271-272
    fish and seafood, 268-269
    food labels, 263
    fruits and nuts, 264
    idiomatic expressions, 268
    indicating "some of" a larger quantity, 273-274
    meats, 265
    pasta, 269
    practicing putting together a shopping list, 274
    sweets, 271
    vegetables, 262-263
    verbs, 264
    verbs and expressions, 273
    vocabulary, 261
  stores, 241
    accessories, 246
    clothing, 245-251
    expressions, 247-248
    fabrics, 250-251
    flowers, 250
    jewelry, 244
    stationery store (*la cartoleria*), 243
showing possession, 131
  di contractions, 131
  possessive adjectives, 131-134
si construction, passive voice, *si prega* (please), 162
sickness
  farsi, expressing that something hurts, 342-343
  pain/discomfort expressions, 343-345
    idiomatic expressions, 346
    serious medical conditions, 345-347
  saints, 347
side dishes (meals), 289
sightseeing
  making a suggestion, 231
    "how about," 232-233
    "let's," 232
    non, 233
    perché non …, 232

responding, 233
volere (to want), 233
verbs, 225
 andare (to go), 229
 fare (to do/make), 229
 passare (to pass), 229
 practicing conjugation, 230
 rimanere (to remain), 228
 ritornare (to return), 230
 trovare (to find/visit), 229
 uscire (to go out/exit), 227
 venire (to come), 227-228
 where to go and what to do, 223
signs, car travel, 171
singular
 definite articles, 70
 nouns, determining gender, 72
sizes (clothing), conversion table for, 248
slang words/phrases, 62
"some of," indicating "some of" a larger quantity
 di + noun, 273
 partitive pronoun *ne*, 273-274
special needs phrases, dining out, 292
spelling
 forming plurals, 81
 names, 36
spices and seasonings, 291-292
sports, vocabulary, 303-305
stare (to be), 112-113
 rules of usage, 114-116
stationery store (*la cartoleria*), 243
statistics, Republic of Italy, 239
stem-changing verbs, conditional tense, 377
stems, infinitive verbs, 94
 present-tense conjugations, 95
stores, 241
 accessories, 246
 clothing, 245-251
 conversion table for sizes, 248
 cosmetics, vocabulary, 349
 expressions, 247-248
 fabrics, 250-251
 flowers, 250
 jewelry, 244
 stationery store (*la cartoleria*), 243
stories (fables), use of past definite tense, 393-394
stressed pronouns. *See* disjunctive pronouns
stress (pronunciation), 27
structure of Italian, basic rules, 22

subject pronouns, 85-86
 clarity, 87
 direct objects, 86
 emphasis, 87
 forms of "you," 88
 indirect objects, 86
 politeness, 87
 practicing, 87-88
 versus object pronouns, 87
subjects (grammar) versus objects, 21
subjunctive mood, 386
 dependent clauses, 388-390
 imperfect, 392
 irregular forms, 388
 past, 391
 past perfect, 392
 present, 386-388
suffixes
 diminutives, 13
 superlatives, 13
suggestions, 231
 "how about," 232-233
 imperatives, 159
 most common commands, 160
 negative commands, 160
 practicing, 161
 regular imperative endings, 159
 "let's," 232
 non, 233
 perché non ..., 232
 responding, 233
 volere (to want), 233
superlatives, 13
 forming from adjectives, 336
 absolutes, 338
 forming from adverbs, 337
sweets/desserts, 271, 295

T

table-settings, vocabulary, 283-284
tags, asking questions, 109
tailor's, vocabulary, 252
tapes, making tapes of yourself speaking Italian, 8
telephone, 355
 communicating with the operator, 358-359
 expressions, 357-358
 types of calls, 356
 vocabulary, 356-357
temperature, weather vocabulary, 209

tenses
 compound tenses, future perfect, 367
 conditional, 374
 avere (to have), 375
 essere (to be), 375
 forming, 374-377
 practicing use, 378
 future, 363
 avere (to have) rules, 364
 endings, 363
 essere (to be) rules, 364
 irregular stems, 365-366
 patterns, 365
 practicing conjugation, 366-367
 imperfect, 350
 endings, 351-353
 practicing conjugation, 353-354
 past definite, 392-393
 fables and stories, 393-394
 present perfect, 313
 constructing the past participle, 314-316
 practicing conjugation, 353-354
 when to use *avere* (to have), 314
 when to use *essere* (to be), 314-318
 present perfect tense
 adverbs, 319
 direct object pronouns, 319-320
 double object pronouns, 321
 indirect object pronouns, 320
 present progressive, forming, 237-238
third-conjugation verbs (*–ire* family), 94, 106
 capire example, 107
 dormire example, 106
 group I, 106-107
 group II, 107
time
 adverbs, 146
 cognates, 41-43
 commas, 84
 expressions, 175-176
 after the hour, 176
 "before the hour," 176
 practicing, 177
 "how often" expressions, 215-216
 idiomatic expressions, 64
time-related words, dates, 214
tipping, hotel services, 193

trades/professions, banking, 385
trains, 180
   diretto, 180
   espresso, 180
   pendolino-ETR, 180
   rapido, 180
   regionale, 180
transactions, banking, 384
transitive verbs, 18
   use of *avere* (to have) in pres-
     ent perfect tense, 314
translation, practicing cognates,
   51
   literary titles, 52
transportation modes, 165-166
   cars, 167
     expressions, 171
     inside the car, vocabulary,
       168
     necessary tools, 170
     parts and predicaments,
       169-170
     renting a car, 168
     sample communication,
       172
     signs, 171
     types of roads, 169
   idiomatic expressions, 63
   interrogative pronoun *quale*
     (which or what), 166
   phrases, 181
   public transportation, 172
     cardinal numbers, 172-174
     getting around, 179-180
     time expressions, 175-177
     trains, 180
   verbs, 181
     fare (to make or do some-
       thing), 182-184
     practicing conjugation, 182
     salire (to climb), 182
travel, 149
   air travel
     expressions, 152
     verbs, 151
     vocabulary, 149-152
   expressing that you don't
     understand, 161
   getting lost, imperatives (direc-
     tions), 159-161
   hotels, 187
     ammenities/necessities, 189
     asking for the kind of room
       you want, 188-189
     asking for what you need,
       189-191
     invoices, bills, and receipts,
       192
     negotiating or paying for a
       room, 192

practicing vocabulary and
     expressions, 192
     tipping, 193
     useful expressions, 191
     vocabulary, 187-188
   idiomatic expressions, 63
   information questions,
     177-178
   modes of transportation,
     165-166
     cars, 167-172
     interrogative pronoun *quale*
       (which or what), 166
     public transportation,
       172-180
   ordinal numbers, rules,
     194-195
   phrases, 181
   verbs, 181
     andare (to go), 152
     fare (to make or do some-
       thing), 182-184
     practicing conjugation, 182
     prendere (to take), 154
     salire (to climb), 182
     trovare (to find/visit), 229
   vocabulary, practicing, 211
Tuscan Italian, 14

U

un (singular, masculine indefinite
   article), 71
un' (singular, feminine indefinite
   article), 72
una (singular, feminine indefinite
   article), 72
uno (singular, masculine indefinite article), 71
uscire (to go out/exit), 227

V

vegetables, 262-263
venire (to come), 227-228
verbs, 18
   air travel, 151
   cognates, 48-49
     practicing, 50
   conditional tense, 377
   conjugated, 18
   conoscere (to know someone),
     135
   endings, 50
   food-oriented, 264
   helping, 112
   infinitives, 18, 50, 198-201

practicing, 201
requiring preposition *a*,
   200-201
requiring preposition *di*,
   199-200
with prepositions, 198-199
without prepositions, 199
intransitive, 18
irregular
   andare (to go), 152-154
   avere (to have), 117-119
   dire (to say/tell), 231
   essere (to be), 112-117, 122
   practicing, 202
   review, 201-202
modal, 195
   dovere (to have to, must),
     197-198
   potere (to be able to),
     196-197
   practicing, 198
   volere (to want), 195-196
piacere (to be pleasing to),
   275-276
   practicing use, 277-278
reflexive, 299
   changing meaning when
     made reflexive, 300-301
   practicing use, 301
   reciprocity, 302
   rules, 300
regular, 94
   anatomy of a verb, 94
   first conjugation (*–are* fam-
     ily), 94-101
   prendere (to take), 154
   present-tense conjugations,
     95
   second-conjugation (*–ere*
     family), 94, 102-105
   third conjugation (*–ire* fam-
     ily), 94, 106-107
renting/buying a home, 372
sapere (to know something),
   134
sightseeing, 225
   andare (to go), 229
   fare (to do/make), 229
   making a suggestion,
     231-233
   passare (to pass), 229
   practicing conjugation, 230
   rimanere (to remain), 228
   ritornare (to return), 230
   trovare (to find/visit), 229
   uscire (to go out/exit), 227
   venire (to come), 227-228
subject pronouns, 85-86
   clarity, 87
   direct objects, 86

emphasis, 87
forms of "you," 88-89
indirect objects, 86
politeness, 87
practicing, 87-88
versus object pronouns, 87
transitive, 18
travel-related, 181
fare (to make or do something), 182-184
practicing conjugation, 182
salire (to climb), 182
Vero? (question tag), 109
vi, denoting place, 339-340
vocabulary
accessories, 246
air travel, 149-152
arts, 307
cinema/film, 307-308
music, 309-310
opera, 310-311
terms, 312
banking, 381
expressions, 384
trades/professions, 385
transactions, 384
body parts, 341
brain games, 305
camera shop, 331
cars, 167
expressions, 171
inside the car, 168
necessary tools, 170
parts and predicaments,
169-170
renting a car, 168
sample communication,
172
signs, 171
types of roads, 169
clothing, 245, 251
cooking terms, 278
cosmetics store, 349
diseases/health conditions,
347-348
dry cleaner's, 329
electronics store, 332
fabrics, 250-251
flowers, 250
food labels, 263
food shopping, 261
dairy products, 267
drinks, 270
expressing quantity,
271-272
fish and seafood, 268-269
fruits and nuts, 264
idiomatic expressions, 268
indicating "some of" a
larger quantity, 273-274

meats, 265
pasta, 269
practicing a shopping list,
274
sweets, 271
vegetables, 262-263
verbs and expressions, 273
food-oriented verbs, 264
grooming terms, 327-328
stylists' lingo, 328-329
homes, 369
advertisements, 373
communicating with a realtor, 371-373
furniture and accessories,
370
hotels, 187-188
ammenities/necessities, 189
asking for the kind of room
you want, 188-189
asking for what you need,
189, 191
invoices, bills, and receipts,
192
negotiating or paying for a
room, 192
practicing, 192
useful expressions, 191
jewelry, 244, 331
kitchen items, 284-285
letter writing, 362
missing passport, 332-333
optician's, 330
pharmacy/drugstore, 348
questions for the pharma-
cist, 349
planning a date, 306
playing field, 305
post-office operations, 360-361
expressions, 361
modes of shipment, 361
public transportation, 172
cardinal numbers, 172-174
getting around, 179-180
time expressions, 175-177
trains, 180
shoemaker's, 330
sightseeing, 223-230
making a suggestion,
231-233
verbs, 225-230
sports, 303, 305
stores, 241
la cartoleria (stationery
store), 243
table-settings, 283-284
tailor's, 252
telephone, 356-357
travel, 211

weather, 206
adjectives, 208
climate, 207-208
expressions of leisure,
210-211
seasons, 210
temperature, 209
volere (to want), 195-196
making suggestion, 233
vowels, pronunciation, 28
dipthongs, 34-35
practicing, 31
vulgarities, 62

W–X

weather, 205-206
idiomatic expressions, 206
vocabulary, 206
adjectives, 208
climate, 207-208
expressions of leisure,
210-211
seasons, 210
temperature, 209
week days, 58
corresponding planets, 60
what (*quale*), 166
which (*quale*), 166
wines, 294
wishes, subjunctive mood, 386
dependent clauses, 388-390
imperfect, 392
irregular forms, 388
past, 391
past perfect, 392
present, 386-388
writing
letters, 362
numbers, 174
written accent, 26

Y–Z

"you" forms, determining subject
pronouns, 88-89

zodiacal signs, historical figures,
218-219

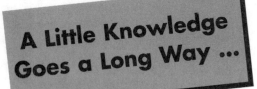
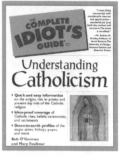

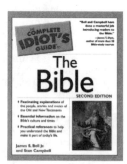

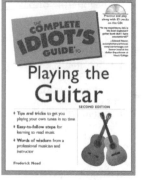

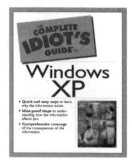